French Oil Sketches and the Academic Tradition

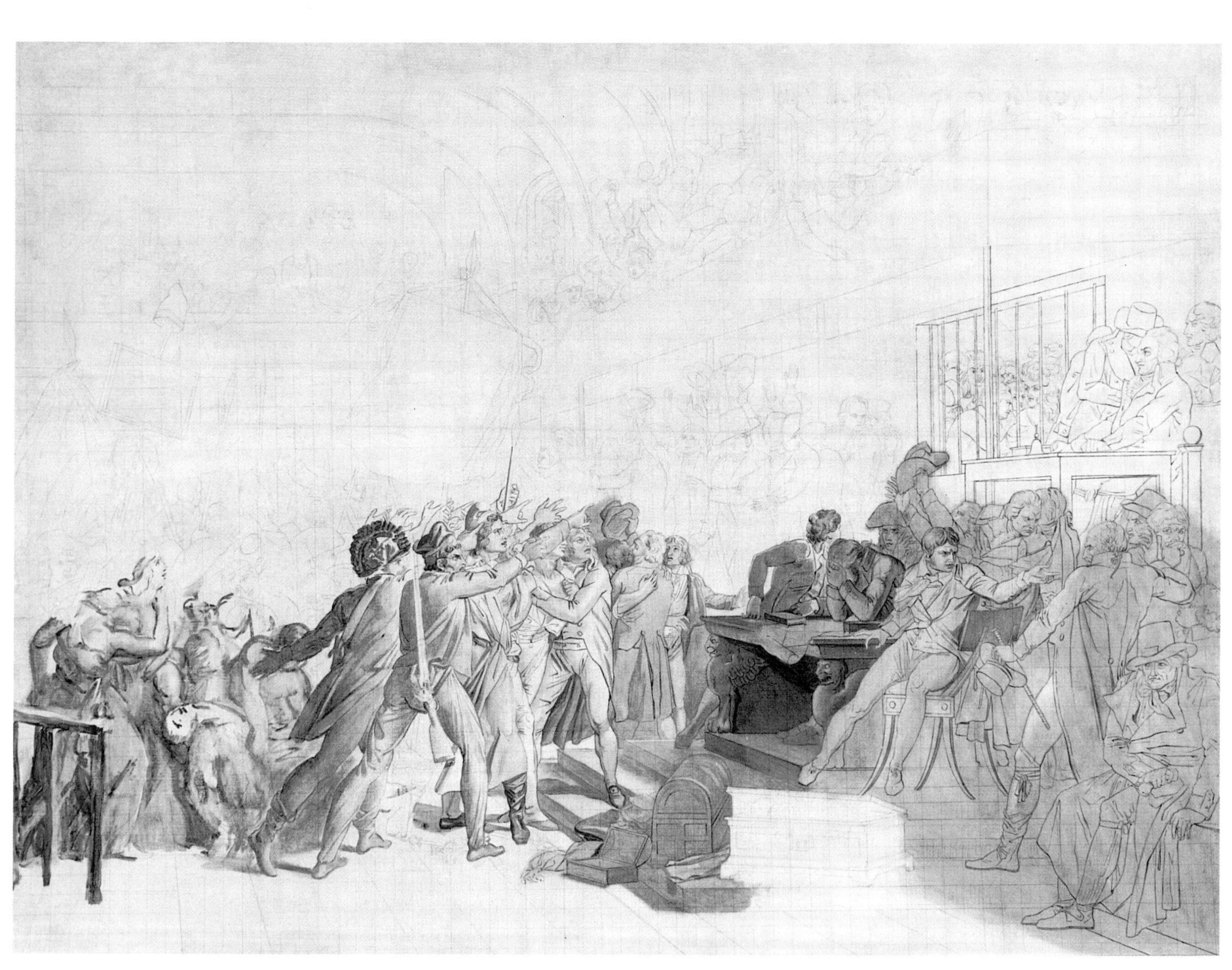

French Oil Sketches and the Academic Tradition

*Selections from a Private Collection
on Loan to the University Art Museum
of the University of New Mexico, Albuquerque*

Introduction
by Peter Walch

Commentaries
*by Joanna R. Barnes and J. Patrice Marandel,
with the assistance of Donna Gustafson,
Alastair Laing, and Alain Latreille*

The American Federation of Arts

in Association with the University of Pennsylvania Press

This catalogue has been published in conjunction with *French Oil Sketches and the Academic Tradition*, an exhibition organized by The American Federation of Arts and the University Art Museum of the University of New Mexico, Albuquerque, with the generous support of the Benefactors Circle of the AFA.

Exhibition tour

Mint Museum of Art
Charlotte, North Carolina
October 14–December 11, 1994

The Society of the Four Arts
Palm Beach, Florida
January 6–February 5, 1995

The Arkansas Arts Center
Little Rock, Arkansas
March 2–June 4, 1995

Michael C. Carlos Museum, Emory University
Atlanta, Georgia
September 22–November 19, 1995

The American Federation of Arts, founded in 1909 to broaden the public's knowledge and appreciation of the visual arts, organizes traveling exhibitions of fine arts and media arts and provides museum members nationwide with specialized services that help reduce operating costs.

Published by The American Federation of Arts
41 East 65th Street, New York, New York 10021
in association with the University of Pennsylvania Press, Blockley Hall, 418 Service Drive, Philadelphia, Pennsylvania 19104

Library of Congress Cataloging-in-Publication Data

French oil sketches and the academic tradition/introduction by Peter Walch: commentaries by Joanna R. Barnes and J. Patrice Marandel with the assistance of Donna Gustafson, Alastair Laing, and Alain Latreille.
  p. cm.
Exhibition tour, Mint Museum of Art, Charlotte, North Carolina, October 14–December 11, 1994 and others.
Includes bibliographical references and index.
ISBN 0-8122-3275-5 (cloth) : $49.95.
ISBN 0-917418-97-2 (paper) : $35.00
1. Painting, French—Exhibitions. 2. Painting, Modern—17th-18th century—France—Exhibitions. 3. Painting, Modern—19th century—France—Exhibitions. 4. Artists' preparatory sketches—France—Exhibitions. I. Barnes, Joanna. II. Marandel, J. Patrice. III. Mint Museum (Charlotte, N.C.)
ND546.F679 1994   759.4'07473—dc20   93-48640   CIP

Cloth edition distributed throughout the world by the University of Pennsylvania Press, Blockley Hall, 418 Service Drive, Philadelphia, Pennsylvania 19104

Publication Coordinator: Michaelyn Mitchell
Design and typography: Steven Schoenfelder
Manuscript Editor: James Leggio

Printed in Hong Kong by South China Printing Co. (1988) Ltd.

Photography of works in the exhibition by Damian Andrus, Albn., except cat. nos. 5, 32, and 87, by Prudence Cuming Associates, London; and cat. nos. 1 and 2, by James Hart.

Front cover: cat. no. 53
Frontispiece: cat. no. 86

Contents

Acknowledgments

The oil sketch, in its several forms, was the means by which painters of the seventeenth, eighteenth, and nineteenth centuries worked out compositions and iconography, studied other works of art, and created detailed examinations of individual motifs. Because it was intimately tied to the learning process, sketching was of paramount importance to the Académie Royale. This publication and the exhibition it accompanies present three centuries of French sketches and in so doing illuminate both the varieties and purposes of this artistic expression and the role the Académie played in the history of European art. We are pleased to present this historically significant and visually arresting group of works to an American audience.

This project reflects the efforts of many individuals. Our warmest thanks go to the owner of the works, who for many years has sought out and collected these sketches. It is through his generosity that we are able to travel this exhibition.

We are most grateful to the curators of the exhibition: Peter Walch, director of the University Art Museum in Albuquerque, and J. Patrice Marandel, curator of European paintings and sculpture at the Los Angeles County Museum of Art. Dr. Walch, Mr. Marandel, and Joanna R. Barnes, a London-based independent art historian, have each contributed substantial research on the collection, published for the first time in this catalogue. Acknowledgments also go to Alastair Laing, advisor on paintings and sculpture at the National Trust, London, and Alain Latreille, independent art historian, who also wrote several entries. Each of the authors has provided research that will continue to be of use to future scholars.

At the University Art Museum in Albuquerque, where this unsurpassed collection is currently on long-term loan, we thank Dr. Walch and Kittu Longstreth-Brown, registrar, for their assistance in this long-distance collaboration. At the AFA, I would like to thank those who contributed most to the realization of this project: Rachel Granholm, curator of education; Donna Gustafson, curator of exhibitions, who also prepared artist biographies; Sarah Higby, exhibitions assistant; Alexandra Mairs, exhibitions/publications assistant; Michaelyn Mitchell, head of publications; and Maria Gabriela Mizes, associate registrar. I want to acknowledge as well the assistance of Sarah Fogel, associate registrar; Evie Klein, scheduler; Thomas Padon, curator of exhibitions; Jillian Slonim, head of public information; and Robert Workman, director of exhibitions.

The authors would also like to acknowledge a number of individuals. Dr. Walch thanks Philippe Grunchec for his professional consultation. Mr. Marandel extends his thanks for help with research and information to Claire Aptel, Jean Aubert, Barbara Bréjon de Lavergnée, Guy Charfnadel, Isabelle Compin, Jean Forneris, Jacques

Foucart, C. Joubert, Eric Moinet, Helen B. Mules, Pierre Rosenberg, and Blandine Salmon. Ms. Barnes would like to thank Charles Jeanneray, Alexander Kader, and Susanna Turner.

We thank Steven Prins & Company and Tres Mowka Designs for the conservation of both paintings and frames; photographers Damian Andrus, Prudence Cuming, and James Hart; Steven Schoenfelder for his handsome catalogue design; and James Leggio for his skillful editing of the manuscript.

It is a pleasure to recognize the participation of the presenting museums: the Mint Museum of Art, Charlotte, North Carolina; the Society of the Four Arts, Palm Beach, Florida; the Arkansas Arts Center, Little Rock; and the Michael C. Carlos Museum, Emory University, Atlanta, Georgia.

Finally, our thanks go to the Benefactors Circle of the AFA, whose contributions helped to make this project possible.

Serena Rattazzi
Director
The American Federation of Arts

Introduction

Peter Walch

This collection of French oil sketches offers a cornucopia of styles and techniques by some of the most adept practitioners of oil painting. With these pictures, we come to comprehend the diverse purposes of the sketch: how it served artistic education, production, and even patronage. Viewed chronologically, these works invite us to examine some three hundred years of European art history, and to appreciate the specifically French variations on a progression of styles from the early Baroque period through the latter part of the nineteenth century. The oil sketch—or, more properly, the controversy over the value of the sketch as opposed to the finished picture—lay at the very heart of the program of the powerful Académie Royale; the changing fortunes of the sketch illuminate important transformations of French art theory and practice over the seventeenth, eighteenth, and nineteenth centuries. Most important of all, in the sketch we are made privy to the innermost workings of artistic intelligence and aspiration. If all art is a window onto other times and places, the sketch allows us to look through that window and witness the artist's process of creation.

Albert Boime, the noted historian of the nineteenth-century French oil sketch, champions the notion that all sketches, from whatever nation or century, tend to look much alike—that there is a single "sketch style," which has evolved little if at all over the years:

> I personally feel that sketching procedures are timeless and a-historical and that save for subject matter (and technological factors like canvas, stretchers and pigment) sketches of different times and places would be difficult to distinguish. Because the sketch is to an eminent degree the product of the primary mental processes, sketches of all times would tend to show a strong resemblance in method—attesting to a kind of "spontaneous universality" of the sketch.[1]

Certainly there is a good deal of truth to Boime's observation, which we can confirm by noting the strong family resemblance between, say, Joseph Parrocel's *Two Scenes from Ancient History* (cat. nos. 7, 8) and Félix Ziem's *Mermaids Under Water* (cat. no. 115). Parrocel, working in the seventeenth century, and Ziem, in the nineteenth, both evidence what Boime calls the "spontaneous universality" of the sketch, through a shared technique of loose, open brushwork and free rhythms of paint. This is, in fact, just exactly the style that most of us associate with the word *sketch.*

But what of the tightly controlled draftsmanship in Laurent de La Hyre's *The Assumption* (cat. no. 4) and Jean-Hippolyte Flandrin's *The Sacrifice of Isaac* (cat. no. 108)? What of the almost porcelain-perfect surface of Jean-Baptiste Regnault's *Achilles Instructed by Chiron* (cat. no. 76)? These sketches, too, come from a wide period of time, from the seventeenth to the nineteenth century. Yet stylistically they seem almost antithetical to

Boime's thesis that all sketches are, by definition, spontaneously painted.

Definition of the sketch is, indeed, part of the problem, and perhaps part of the solution. In the English language, we have in common usage only the single term *sketch* to cover a wide variety of types of paintings that are not finished pictures intended to be sold or placed on public exhibition. But not all sketches were created for the same purpose, and the French have several terms for different types of oil sketches. Exploring some of these terms will help us appreciate the different styles of the pictures in this exhibition.

The generic French word for sketch is *esquisse*; the lengthy discussion of this term in the great eighteenth-century *Encyclopédie* begins:

> This term, which we formed from the Italian word *schizzo*, has for us a meaning more restricted than in its native country: the dictionary of *la Crussa* gives as the meaning of *schizzo: a kind of drawing without shading and unfinished*. It thus appears that the word *sketch*, in Italian, resembles the French word *ébauche*; and it is true that for us *to sketch* can mean *to form strokes that are unfinished and without shading*; but by a peculiarity, *to make a sketch* is *to draw rapidly* the idea for the subject of a picture, to see if it is worth developing further.[2]

So the *esquisse* proper is a preliminary sketch (in oil or another medium) of an entire composition in preparation for a painting. Nicolas Delobel's *Allegory of the Reunion of Lorraine with France* (cat. no. 13) or François-Guillaume Ménageot's *Astyanax Seized from Andromache by Order of Ulysses* (cat. no. 48) both illustrate this usage. What the *Encylopédie* calls an *ébauche* is less familiar to us: it is the drawing and underpainting on the final canvas, which is eventually covered over by the finishing coats of paint. François-Pascal-Simon Gérard's *The 10th of August, 1792* (cat. no. 86) is of great interest in that it was abandoned in this *ébauche* state, allowing us to see how an artist went about laying in both outline drawing and the masses of light and shade during this early stage of making a picture.

Another variety of the sketch is the *étude* (in English, "study"), usually a fairly detailed examination of a single motif—a figure, or sometimes a bit of landscape—made independently of any finished picture, for its own sake. François-André Vincent's *Female Head* (cat. no. 53) and Pierre-Henri de Valenciennes's *Landscape with Ruins* (cat. no. 57) are both *études*. A more fragmentary *étude*, a sort of thumbnail sketch, might also be called a *croquis*.

There is also the *modèle* (from the Italian, *modello*, and frequently the French used the Italian word): this is an oil sketch, usually quite highly finished, made by an artist to show to a patron before undertaking the final, full-scale version. An analogy would be the model that architects often make for presentation to a client. In this exhibition, La Hyre's *The Assumption* (cat. no. 4) is a *modello* for the finished picture now at the Kunsthistorisches Museum in Vienna.

There are no separate French words for other varieties of oil sketches, such as the sketch copy and the *post facto* reduced sketch. The sketch copy, a loosely painted copy of one artist's work by another, was both a popular teaching device and a collectible. Especially in the eighteenth century, many a new or newly expanded residence was furnished with copies of Old Master paintings, and many a young artist made his living creating such copies, either on direct commission from a client or "on spec" for sale through a dealer. Jean-Louis Duhamel's *Saint Francis Returning His Vestments to His Father* (cat. no. 58), done after a painting by the Italian artist Solimena, may—to judge from its prominent signature—have been commissioned by a collector. Regnault's *Achilles Instructed by Chiron* (cat. no. 76) and *Venus and Adonis* (cat. no. 77) can also be classified as sketch copies. They are fully autograph, reduced versions of that same artist's full-scale paintings, executed as keepsakes for Regnault's own delight, and were still in his studio at his death.

• • • • •

This brief discussion of some of the popular types of oil sketches helps account for some of the more striking differences within the exhibition, differences that Boime's assertion of a universal sketch style would not lead us to expect. But beyond the difference between an *esquisse* and an *ébauche*, between an *étude* and a *modello*, these sketches also evidence, through their changing styles, the times in which they were made. Boime's assertion of their a-historicity notwithstanding, there is a definite period flavor to each and every one of these oil sketches. We find in them, hardly less than in finished pictures, the distinctive stylistic imprints of the successive ways most seventeenth-, eighteenth-, and nineteenth-century artists offered up their visions of the world.

In order to understand the variety and vitality of these French oil sketches, therefore, we must also understand the unfolding of the history of Western art from circa 1600 to 1900—three centuries of experimentation and change, which bring us to the threshold of the modern world and modern art. The relevant art-historical styles are, briefly: the Baroque, the dominant artistic mode from about 1600 to 1710; the Rococo, from 1710 to 1770; Neoclassicism, from 1770 to 1810; Romanticism, from 1810 to 1840; and Realism, during the middle decades of the nineteenth century. These style periods provide a convenient chronological framework for discussing large trends.

Seventeenth-century artists never thought of themselves as part of the Baroque. Like many an art-historical term, *Baroque* was first applied retroactively and disparagingly. It was in the later eighteenth century that a number of critics of seventeenth-century art and architecture began to call their predecessors' concoctions *baroque*. This was a way of calling attention to what those critics saw as unorthodox and even unruly aspects of seventeenth-century compositions. The term *baroque* perhaps came from the Arabic *buraq* (pebbly ground) via the Portuguese *barrôco* (rough pearl; we still call an irregular pearl a *baroque*). Another explanation traces the origins of *baroque* to medieval European philosophy, where the term *baroco* described a rather convoluted argument in logic.

By the late eighteenth century, *baroque* was in use by French critics to describe and denounce the extravagances of seventeenth-century art. In our times, much of the denuncitory power of the term has worn away, and *baroque* simply stands for the style (or styles) of the seventeenth century. And yet, for many of us, there remains a tinge of suspicion about the grand ambitions of that century and its artists.

The Baroque is well represented in the exhibition by Simon Vouet's two sketches of angels (cat. nos. 1, 2) done in preparation for a now destroyed fresco at Saint Peter's in Rome. The youthful angels float easily in the golden mists of heaven. Ebullient and optimistic, these paintings celebrate indeterminacy and expansiveness. They soar beyond logic and lift our spirits. They embody the operatic power of the Baroque.

Laurent de La Hyre's *The Assumption* (cat. no. 4) is from a later and more specifically French phase of the Baroque, known as the "Classical Baroque." In the 1630s, a more sober, even grave manner evolved. The palpable weight of the disciples, the cool, clear light, the disciplined outlines of their garments and bodies, all contribute to the mood of reason and control.

In the early decades of the eighteenth century, the Baroque gave way to the Rococo. The term came from the French *rocaille*, meaning a fanciful design derived from the twists and turns of rocks and seashells. Applied originally to the decorative arts, by the late eighteenth century it stood also for the productions of painters, sculptors, and architects—and, like *baroque*, it acquired a distinctly disparaging connotation. Even today, to call someone's speech or writing *rococo* is to imply that it is too elaborate, too ornate, too pretty.

In less loaded terms, how are we to describe the Rococo and, in particular, its distinctiveness when compared with the Baroque? It is private, lighthearted, and intimate, as opposed to the public, serious, and boldly scaled Baroque. The seventeenth century was the century of the absolute monarch and the absolute church—absolute as arbiters of taste and patrons of the arts. Even before the death of Louis XIV in 1715, power in France had begun to slip from the royal palace at Versailles to the drawing rooms (and boudoirs) of Parisian bankers and merchants.

For this newly rising class of patrons there came into being the new style of the Rococo. Jean-Baptiste Deshays's *Scene from "L'Astrée"* (cat. no. 30) stands perfectly for Rococo values. Here, the winged creatures in the sky are not God's angels, but little cupids; they witness not a scene of high religiosity, but rather one of gentle lovemaking. Softly flickering light and elegant pastel colors replace the bold shadows and brilliant palette of the Baroque. Grand opera has been transformed into a delicate minuet.

During the last years of the *ancien régime*, when many people turned against the perceived hedonism and injustice of the monarchy, a new mood of ardent civic virtue arose in France. Philosophers, writers, and artists alike thought their own age to be as corrupt as the late Roman Empire had been. They yearned for the democratic ideals and public morality of the earlier Roman Republic. Thus came into being a new art style: Neoclassicism. For once, we have a term that, if not precisely the one used by the artists of the time, would clearly have been intelligible to them. For it was to the Classical past that a generation of artists, in France, in the rest of Europe, even in America, turned for inspiration.

In painting, Neoclassicism described a shift in subject matter, in style, and in mood. Comparing Guillaume-Guillon Lethière's *The Death of Virginia* (cat. no. 83) with Deshays's *Scene from "L'Astrée"* (cat. no. 30) exemplifies these dramatic distancings from the Rococo. Lethière's subject is an event from about 499 B.C.—that is to say, an event from Roman *history*, rather than from mythology or religion. Virginia has been killed by Virginius, her father, so that she may die rather than be forced into the control of the lustful despot, Appius Claudius. This event incited the citizens and soldiers to revolt and led directly to the founding of the Roman Republic; European audiences in the years around 1800 appreciated the story for its parallels with the French Revolution and with other revolts against corrupt monarchies.

This painting was intended to inform and even to incite its public. Instead of the soft, gentle, elegant manner of painting that characterized the Rococo, we see a hard, wiry draftsmanship. For Neoclassical artists around 1800, stylistic clues were taken from antiquity itself: from Roman statues, and sometimes especially from Greek vases, with their intensely focused outline painting. The great excavations at Herculaneum and Pompeii begun in the middle of the eighteenth century made much more of this material available. Equally important, the Age of Revolutions made antiquity and its art cogently relevant to painters of Lethière's generation.

Romanticism differed from the Baroque, the Rococo, and Neoclassicism in that both term and theory predated the primary manifestations in the visual arts. The first use of the term *Romantic* (which derives from *romance*, a work of literature in French, a Romance language, instead of in Latin) occurs in seventeenth-century England; the first great theoretical writing on Romanticism (still confined to poetry) was published by Friedrich Schlegel in 1798; by 1829, there was already a *history* of Romanticism, written by F. R. de Troeinx—this before many of the key works of the movement were painted, sculpted, composed, or written.

Ary Scheffer's *The Last Communion of Saint Louis* (cat. no. 100) is a landmark of early French Romantic painting. An *esquisse* for a larger canvas Scheffer executed for the Communion Chapel in the Church of Saint-Louis-en-l'Ile, in both subject and style it virtually defines Romanticism. Louis IX, or Saint Louis, King of France, died in 1270 in Tunis while leading the Eighth Crusade. This thirteenth-century story allows us just about everything we want from a Romantic painting: the Middle Ages (knights in armor), the exotic Orient (the two onlookers in turbans), mystery (the flickering candle), and heroic death (the slumped body of Saint Louis glows with supernatural light). Neoclassical painters favored the rigidly geometric, the precisely delineated contour, as we see in Lethière's *The Death of Virginia* (cat. no. 83). By contrast, in Scheffer's *Saint Louis* we find undulating rhythms of pliant bodies and fabrics described in a few swoops of paint; even the setting is within a billowing tent (not the rock-hard, square-cut temples of Roman antiquity, depicted by the Neoclassicists).

Both Romanticism and Neoclassicism continued into the latter part of the nineteenth century. But, beginning in the 1840s, the most vital force in French art and literature was Realism. As a theoretical prescription for the arts, Realism is as old as the ancient Greeks, who delighted in anecdotes about the abilities of their painters to fool animals (and each other) into thinking that works of art were natural objects. However, Realism in the nineteenth-century sense—Realism with a capital *R*—was more than simply an accurate transcription of nature (although it contained that aspect). Realism comprised an empathy for the humble and the everyday—for peasants, landscape, and contemporary garb, as opposed to angels, exotic lands, or the finery of kings. Realism, then, allied itself with the forces of the emerging modern world of towns and industries (with a healthy nostalgia for the countryside). Explicitly or otherwise, it celebrated democracy (and sometimes socialism), and opposed the entrenched hierarchies of monarchies, churches, and academies of art.

Falguière's sketch *Figures Seated Around a Lamp* (cat. no. 119) shows the Realist approach to subject and style. No longer are we transported to a setting distant in time, geography, or even social status from our own. Instead, we see anonymous people of the artist's own time. The value of this painting comes through the concentrated power of observation that it conveys—from the beauty it reveals in this humble, everyday scene, to the beauty and worthiness the artist saw in such scenes. Art has become not a beacon leading to something grand and wonderful beyond quotidian existence, but instead a mirror, reflecting the life of the artist's own time, place, and social station.

One of the most significant accomplishments of Falguière, and the other Realists, was to break with the conventions of subject matter that had defined "important" art in France for centuries. Also significantly, Realism broke with conventions of style. In all previous periods of French art from the seventeenth century onward, artists learned how to paint pictures by looking at and copying what earlier "old master" painters had done. The Realists removed this straightjacket of inherited convention by taking their clues directly from nature, and transposing that nature as directly as possible onto their canvases. We still today accept what we see in Falguière's sketch as "realistic"—not distorted by preconceptions, not altered to conform to notions of ideal beauty.

· · · · ·

Thus, contrary to Boime's assertion that there is a single, universal sketch style, these pictures differ one from another in good measure because they are from different centuries, because they are from the Baroque, or Rococo, or Romantic periods. If artists over the years were not confined to a single sketch style, neither were they restricted to only the style most typical of the period within which they lived and worked. Instead, we see in the sketch—just as in finished paintings from these centuries—that artists frequently adapted their style to the specific subject matter of the project. This may not have been entirely a matter of individual aesthetic choice. In the twentieth century, such a decision is usually considered to belong exclusively to the artist. In earlier times, including all but perhaps the last few decades covered by the paintings in this exhibition, artists often worked very closely with patrons (both individuals and organizations), and the influence of the patrons found immediate expression in oil sketches, as well as in finished pictures.

Consider, for example, the many oil sketches of religious subjects: Léon Cogniet's *Saint Stephen Carrying Alms to a Poor Family* (cat. no. 99), Jean-Baptiste Deshays's *Scene from the Martyrdom of Saint Andrew* (cat. no. 29), Eugène-François-Marie-Joseph Devéria's *Glorification of the Life of Saint Genevieve* (cat. no. 107), Jean-Hippolyte Flandrin's *The Sacrifice of Isaac* (cat. no. 108), Louis Galloche's *Saint Scholastica Obtaining a Storm from Heaven To Prevent Saint Benedict from Leaving, Saint Martin Sharing His Coat with a Beggar*, and *A Scene from the Life of Saint Martin* (cat. nos. 9–11), Laurent de La Hyre's *The Assumption* (cat. no. 4), François-Guillaume Ménageot's *Eleazar Refusing to Eat Pork* (cat. no. 49), Raymond-Auguste Quinsas Monvoisin's *The Holy Family* (cat. no. 102), Joseph Guillaume Roques's *The Birth of the Virgin* (cat. no. 79), Ary Scheffer's *The Last Communion of Saint Louis* (cat. no. 100), Jean Senelle's *The Holy Family* (cat. no. 3), Pierre Subleyras's *Heraclius Carrying the Cross* (cat. no. 15), and Simon Vouet's *Two "Modelli" for Two Groups of Angels* (cat. nos. 1, 2). One is struck by the sheer number of religious paintings, most of them from the supposedly secular eighteenth and nineteenth centuries. At first look, they come in a full range of styles, even including Neoclassicism (Ménageot).

But a closer look at these pictures reveals that they can quite easily be categorized as belonging to one of only two types, both of which go back to the seventeenth century. One group follows the calm, dignified, geometrically ordered tradition of Senelle and La Hyre; Suvée, Roques, and Monvoisin are some of the purer exponents of this school. The other group espouses the more emotional, more physical, more flamboyant tradition of Vouet; Galloche, Deshays, Scheffer, and Devéria are among its later exponents. This pattern makes a great deal of sense. The Church is a very conservative institution; patrons willing to commission church decorations are also, typically, very conservative. Small wonder, then, that artists who undertook religious commissions tended to work in styles that—however much they might be inflected by contemporary stylistic taste—strongly reference time-honored traditions. What is striking is that the stylistic conservatism of the ultimate patron, the Church, finds expression even in the sketch stage of artistic production. Obviously, the sketch was much less private than twentieth-century artistic practice would lead one to think, and the stylistic impact of patronage came much earlier in the artistic process—as early, in some instances, as the *étude* or the *esquisse*—than Boime's notion of "primary mental processes" suggests. The sketch, in this group of religious pictures, shows the stylistic consistency wrought by uniform and relatively unchanging patronage.

Even more consistent is the group of works from this exhibition that have royal subjects: Nicolas Delobel's *Allegory of the Reunion of Lorraine with France* (cat. no. 13), Gabriel-François Doyen's *Nobility Offering the Imperial Russian Children to Minerva* (cat. no. 31), Jacques Sablet's *The Temple of the Liberal Arts, with the City of Bern and Minerva* (cat. no. 56), Charles Meynier's *Allegory of the Birth of Louis XIV* (cat. no. 85), and Merry-Joseph Blondel's *Louis XIV* (cat. no. 93). The Church may be conservative; royals are often downright reactionary, and artists who work for royals tend to be acutely aware of the fact that they should choose a style suitable to their august subjects. The Rococo is too lightweight; Neoclassicism is too republican; Realism is too democratic; even Romanticism is suspect—it calls too much attention to the artist. The proven formula is to go back to the good, old Baroque—lots of spectacle, the easy integration of fact and allegory, and the stylistic reference to the time and taste of Louis XIV (every monarch's idea of what a king should be). And that is exactly the route followed by each of these artists.

Style, in the oil sketch as in the finished painting, can be an artist's response to the special requirements of subject matter and of patronage. Often, it appears from this sampling, such dictates were every bit as important as the specific moment in the history of evolving styles in determining the "look" of a painting. Thus, understanding such requirements goes a long way toward helping us to appreciate these paintings and their makers.

•　•　•　•　•

If the oil sketch is so provocatively redolent of its age and situation, why is it that we today value these sketches perhaps even more than their makers did? In the seventeenth and eighteenth centuries, oil sketches were very much a means to an end. Sometimes they were exhibited (Delobel's *Allegory of the Reunion of Lorraine with France* [cat. no. 13] at the Salon of 1737); a few critical voices were raised in their defense (Roger de Piles in late seventeenth-century France, and Sir Joshua Reynolds in eighteenth-century England); and presumably, for they have survived, a few art patrons collected them. But for most artists, the sketch had nothing anywhere near the importance and worth of the finished picture.

It was the nineteenth century that saw the aesthetics of the oil sketch triumphant. In Impressionism and beyond, the canvas is allowed to show through. The touch of the artist's brush shapes paint three-dimensionally—the sketch *becomes* the finished picture. Even so, not until as late as 1967 was an exhibition devoted entirely to the oil sketch (*Masters of the Loaded Brush: Oil Sketches from Rubens to Tiepolo*, at M. Knoedler &

Company, New York, April 4–29, 1967; the exhibition was organized by the Department of Art History and Archaeology, Columbia University, and the published catalogue, with an introductory essay by Rudolf Wittkower, remains a classic). Since 1967, there have been several other exhibitions; yet the private collection of oil sketches from which the present exhibition is drawn is the only sizeable such collection in existence. Despite all of its abundant charms, the oil sketch remained until recently an orphan of art and art history.

To understand the reasons for this somewhat surprising marginalization of the oil sketch, we must go back to near the beginnings of the history of art covered by this exhibition. We must go back, to be precise, to 1648 and the founding of the Académie Royale de Peinture et de Sculpture (the French Royal Academy of Painting and Sculpture, which hereafter, to avoid confusion and to accommodate several name changes, shall be called simply "the Académie"). We tend, not without reason, to think of any academy as a bastion of conservatism. In the beginning, however, it was quite a different institution.

In the 1640s in France, the real conservatives were the artists in the Mastership, a guild of medieval origin, which exercised a virtual monopoly on the practice and sale of art. Like other guilds (goldsmiths, carpenters, stonemasons, and so on), the Mastership was difficult of access; unless you were the son of a master, you had to go through a long and demanding apprenticeship (or invest a lot of money) to gain admittance.

Equally galling to younger, progressive artists was the fact that the Mastership lumped painters and sculptors together with gilders, housepainters, and the like. It was, in short, a union of artisans. What a blow that was to the self-esteem of those artists, many of whom had trained in Italy, who considered their profession a noble one, allied with the liberal arts of geometry and logic rather than the skilled crafts.

In Italy, things were better. Since the Renaissance, a considerable body of art theory had been produced under the grand slogan (derived from the Roman poet Horace) *Ut pictura poesis* —"painting is like poetry." Painting, in Italy, could be a gentlemanly pursuit; it was nurtured by institutions called academies, which were under the patronage of noble families. The academies accorded recognition to the best sort of art and artists, sponsored lofty discussions of the theory of art, and provided disciplined instruction for aspiring art students.

Younger artists, considering themselves something of an elite, used this Italian model when they founded the Académie Royale in 1648. For their patron, they chose the King, Louis XIV. This was by no means an obvious choice, as Louis XIV was in 1648 only ten years old; real power was held by Cardinal Mazarin, who was very busy fighting off the *Fronde*, a revolt of the Parlement of Paris to limit the authority of the crown. The first few years of the Académie's existence, when it received no effective backing and little financial support from the King, found it more than once close to collapse. Eventually, however, the gamble paid off. Charles Le Brun, one of the founders of the Académie (at age twenty-nine), became the favorite painter of Louis XIV, and that helped a good deal. The Mastership fought a rear-guard action, finally expiring in the eighteenth century.

The Académie, meanwhile, flourished beyond the wildest dreams of its founders. It became the overwhelmingly dominant center for art instruction. In the eighteenth century, the Ecole Royale des Elèves Protégés, sort of an advanced graduate school, was added. The very best students competed for the Prix-de-Rome, which sent them off on full government scholarship to the French Academy in Rome, where they completed their education. After this, the expected career of a successful artist was marked by being first *agréé* (provisionally accepted) and then *reçu* (admitted) by the Académie; a distinguished artist would rise to the rank of professor, perhaps even director. Along the way, he (until after the Revolution, membership was restricted to males) would exhibit at the Académie's Salons—the exhibitions, at first sporadic, then semiannual, then finally annual, held at the Louvre (and named for the Salon d'Apollon, their original venue). These exhibitions were grand events—heavily attended, widely reported on—and served as the only practical way for an artist effectively to put his work before a public audience. The Académie, in short, became what the old Mastership had been: an institution with virtual monopolistic power over anyone who wished a career in the visual arts. Despite many reorganizations and challenges, the Académie's power continued almost to the end of the nineteenth century.

The vast majority of the artists in this exhibition belonged to the Académie; many were among its leadership. Four of the eight directors of the French Academy in Rome during the eighteenth century are in this exhibition; all three of the eighteenth-century directors of the Ecole Royale des Elèves Protégés are also in the exhibition. The Académie and the Salons are frequently cited in the individual catalogue entries, so frequently as to be virtually ubiquitous. To collect the best French art from the seventeenth, eighteenth, and most of the nineteenth centuries is almost by definition to collect the work of artists who were trained by and became members of the Académie.

Beyond that simple fact, the oil sketches in this exhibition are by artists of the Académie because for a long time it was almost exclusively such artists who made oil sketches as part of their creative process. Flower painters, still-life painters, many portrait painters (at least those of modest ambition) could and frequently did exist outside the Académie. They could, and almost always did, create finished pictures without the benefit of preparatory sketches. But to be a history painter—to paint pictures with subjects from the Bible, from great literature, from history, or from classical mythology—and to compete for the most prestigious and lucrative commissions, it was virtually mandatory to subscribe to the tenets of the Académie, go to its school, became a member, and exhibit at the Salons. And it was equally mandatory to make oil sketches as part of the process.

History painters had to make oil sketches because the complicated multifigure compositions demanded of them were difficult to produce without a preparatory sketch. Artists also had to learn to make oil sketches because such sketches served at critical junctures as the device by which the Académie determined a student's suitability for advancement. The contest for the Prix-de-Rome was momentously important for young painters wishing to advance professionally, and was in fact won by perhaps a majority of the artists in this exhibition. Conduct of the competition changed somewhat over the decades, but one phase—the very first—remained quite consistent. All of the contestants, each certified as qualified by a member of the Académie, gathered early in the year (usually in March). In one day, the participants executed a small oil sketch (the format became standardized at 32.5 × 40.5 cm). The subject was dictated by the professor in charge, and the young artists could not leave the work area until the close of the competition. The resulting sketches were then graded by a jury of Academicians, and a select few (usually ten) were asked to execute over the next few weeks a finished picture (again, under closely guarded supervision), upon which basis another jury awarded the coveted scholarship.

At various times, the Académie also ran other competitions based on the oil sketch. In 1760, the Académie instituted an annual contest held in the fall for a *tête d'expression*, a life-size study of a female model's head, rendered so as to depict a specific emotion, and executed over three six-hour sessions. François-André Vincent's *Female Head* (cat. no. 53) reflects the practice of this competition (though it is a bit smaller than the standard size—55 × 46 cm—imposed by the Académie). This expression contest died out before the Revolution. In the nineteenth century, the Académie's school—which had been reformed as the Ecole des Beaux-Arts—held quarterly sketch contests not directly connected with the Prix-de-Rome, during which students executed oil sketches during a twelve-hour day in isolated cubicles. Also during the nineteenth century, the Prix-de-Rome competition grew so large, with as many as one hundred contestants, that a new stage was added. Between the first sketch contest and being allowed to enter the final finished picture phase, students were required to submit to a new competition: the painting of a figure study of a nude, male model posed by the officiating professor.

Sketching in oils was thus an activity sanctioned by the Académie; yet the Académie's attitude toward the oil sketch was tinged with suspicion. For one thing, the Académie Royale (unlike most of its foreign counterparts) did not teach oil sketching in its classes—it did not even teach oil *painting*. At the Académie's school, what the students studied was drawing. They drew first after other drawings and engravings, then after casts of antique statues, and finally after the life model. Some geometry and anatomy were thrown in. Especially at the Ecole Royale des Elèves Protégés, students also took classes in history and literature. Painting instruction came only after a thorough grounding in drawing, and then it took place in the private studios of established artists (often professors)—not, that is, directly in the Académie's own facilities. It was thus in the private studio that the student learned how to sketch in oils, as well as how to produce a finished picture.

Drawing was considered a true intellectual discipline, subject to rules and to reason. Painting—painting of all kinds, but perhaps especially sketching in oil paint—was too intuitive for academic theory or the Académie's practice to be allowed completely within its doors and its curriculum. This attitude went back to the founding decades of the Académie, to the great debates between the Poussinistes (the supporters of Poussin, who stood for geometry, outline, and clarity) and the Rubenistes (the followers of Rubens, who stood for color, intuition, and emotion). This debate raged for centuries: the Neoclassicists were essentially Poussinistes, the Romantics were, by and large, Rubenistes. While over these years a fair share of academicians favored Rubens, the Académie *as an institution* was pretty firmly committed to the ideal of Poussin—which meant to drawing, and not to sketching in oils.

More than just taste or temperament was involved here. In Europe since the Renaissance, the theory of art had based value on the ability to imitate reality. The picture was conceived as a window onto the world; while most artists sought to depict an idealized or improved image of reality, value was thought to accrue as the window was more perfectly transparent, and the painted world more perfectly believable. A sketch, as opposed to a finished picture, clearly fell short on two counts. The "window"—the painted surface—is more obtrusive when the marks on it (the paint, with its palpable traces of the loaded brush) are obvious, as they are in most sketches. We look *through* the smoothly polished surfaces of academic paintings; we look *at* the energized surfaces of most oil sketches (especially most of the *esquisses*), and this comes at the expense of the fictive space behind that surface. Also, the rougher the sketch, the less completely realized are the forms depicted, and the illusion of a world comparable to our own begins to diminish.

Painters of the Académie had another problem with the sketch: it reminded them (and their patrons) of the artisan origins of their discipline. The Académie Royale, as we have seen, came into existence as an alternative to the old guild system, as an organization that could establish painting as a gentlemanly, even noble pursuit. Italy was a model, and beginning in the late fifteenth century, Italian artists and art theoreticians had gone to great lengths to argue the prestige due to the painter. The *paragone*—an oral or written debate about the arts—was one forum for advancing such arguments (this form of discussion was later taken up by the Académie Royale). In one of these, Leonardo da Vinci claimed painting superior to sculpture because the painter is more of a gentleman-scholar, the sculptor more of a manual laborer:

> I do not find any other difference between painting and sculpture than that the sculptor's work entails greater physical effort and the painter's greater mental effort. [The sculptor's] face is pasted and smeared all over with marble powder making him look like a baker, and he is covered with minute chips as if emerging from a snowstorm, and his dwelling is dirty and filled with dust and chips of stone.
>
> How different the painter's lot. He is well dressed and handles a light brush dipped in delightful color. He is arrayed in the garments he fancies, and his home is clean and filled with delightful pictures, and he often enjoys the accompaniment of music or the company of men of letters who read to him from various beautiful works.[3]

In the late twentieth century, this all seems quaint, even faintly ludicrous. We prize—in these oil sketches, and in the art of our own time—evidence of the physical involvement of the artist in the process of creation. The seventeenth and eighteenth centuries were clearly suspicious of the sketch, in part because of its very physicality. The nineteenth century overthrew this prejudice and saw in France the "look" of the oil sketch finally elevated to the status of fully complete, fully satisfying art. Why did this transformation of values take place there and then? Why, somewhat paradoxically, did a rapidly industrializing society in the late nineteenth century come finally to embrace the art of the ostentatiously handmade oil sketch?

A very suggestive answer may be found in Thorstein Veblen's classic book *The Theory of the Leisure Class*, published in 1899. Economist, sociologist, wry observer, and commentator, Veblen looked at the wealthy members of industrial society, and wondered at the inefficiencies he saw. "Conspicious consumption," "conspicious waste," and "conspicious leisure" were Veblen's terms for the characterizing features of this class. Students of working-class origin went to trade schools, where they acquired practical knowledge; the wealthy went to universities, where they spent years learning dead languages and playing sports. For the well-to-do, disutility was a badge of honor, certifying that they had accumulated sufficient wealth to deliberately remove themselves from the necessity to do practical, physical labor.

Leisure-class taste—what mainly concerns us here—was of particular interest to Veblen. At a time when the industrial revolution had put within the economic reach of millions, objects of great precision and utility (mass-produced books, textiles, cutlery), the wealthy turned with avidity to crafts—prizing them for their irregularities and other

signs of hand production, because this showed that they were more expensive than
machine-made goods.

> The appreciation of those evidences of honorific crudeness to which hand-wrought goods owe their superior worth and charm in the eyes of well-bred people is a matter of nice discrimination. It requires training and the formation of right habits of thought with respect to what may be called the physiognomy of goods. Machine-made goods of daily use are often admired and preferred precisely on account of their excessive perfection by the vulgar and underbred who have not given due thought to the punctilios of elegant consumption.
>
> Hence it comes about that the visible imperfections of the hand-wrought goods, being honorific, are accounted marks of superiority in point of beauty, or serviceability, or both. Hence has arisen that exaltation of the defective of which John Ruskin and William Morris were such eager spokesmen in their time; and on that ground their propaganda of crudity and wasted effort has been taken up and carried forward since their time. And hence also the propaganda for a return to handicraft and household industry. So much of the work and speculation of this group would have been impossible at a time when the visibly more perfect goods were not the cheaper.[4]

One can easily extrapolate from Veblen's observations to the situation of the
painting-versus-sketch controversy. In the seventeenth and eighteenth centuries, in
preindustrial France, a tightly, smoothly finished picture gave evidence of costly workmanship—and hence was valued over the rough sketch, which looked too much like folk
art. In the nineteenth century, however, markets of all kinds were flooded with machine-made goods of, in Veblen's term, "excessive perfection." After 1839, the specific market
for representational images began to be flooded by impeccably smooth-surfaced photographs priced within the easy reach of the lower middle classes. Hence, the rise of the
sketch, and of the sketch aesthetic: in a world dominated by the seamless, the polished,
and the completely realized, the spontaneity and open-endedness of the sketch became
rare and treasured virtues.

• • • • •

The diversity and evolution of sketch styles has been one theme of this essay: how different types of sketches served the artistic process, how the sketch was intimately bound up
in the unfolding progression of art history, and how such patrons as the Church or King
could elicit specific stylistic solutions even in the sketch stage. We have also examined
how the sketch created an almost irreconcilable tension between academic theory and
practice: the Académie's notion of an ideal picture was one of timeless, seamless perfection—but to get to that ultimate stage, painters had to go through the sketch process,
mastery of which played a significant role in the Académie's system of education and advancement. This tension was only resolved when, at the end of the nineteenth century,
the sketch triumphed over the finished picture, and the power of the Académie was
largely dissolved.

Veblen offers one explanation for the victory of the sketch at that particular
point in both art and social history: in an industrial world, the patently handcrafted takes
on heightened value. Certainly for late twentieth-century eyes, the freshness, the spontaneity, and the elegance of surface and draftsmanship in these sketches provide an exhilarating relief from everyday banality as they evoke a very contemporary pleasure.

Notes to the Introduction

1. Albert Boime, *The Academy and French Painting in the Nineteenth Century* (2nd ed., New Haven, Conn.: Yale University Press, 1986), p. 205, n. 24.

2. Denis Diderot et al., *Encyclopédie*, vol. 5 (Paris, 1755), p. 981. The entry for *esquisse* was written by the amateur etcher Claude Henri Watelet (and translated by the present author).

3. Leonardo da Vinci, *Paragone*, trans. Irma A. Richter (London: Oxford University Press, 1949), pp. 94 ff.

4. Thorstein Veblen, *The Theory of the Leisure Class* (New York: Random House, 1934), pp. 161 ff.

Suggestions for Further Reading

Books

Boime, Albert. *The Academy and French Painting in the Nineteenth Century*. 2nd ed. New Haven, Conn.: Yale University Press, 1986. First published in 1971, this was the first book-length study to deal with the impact of the sketch on academic theory and practice.

Bryson, Norman. *Word and Image: French Painting of the Ancien Régime*. Cambridge: Cambridge University Press, 1981. On, among other things, the imperative of narration in French painting.

Conisbee, Philip. *Painting in Eighteenth-Century France*. Ithaca, N.Y.: Cornell University Press, 1981. Explores the hierarchy of genres in French art of the eighteenth century.

Hargrove, June (ed.). *The French Academy*. Newark, Delaware: University of Delaware Press, 1990. See especially the article by Antoine Schnapper "The Debut of the Royal Academy of Painting and Sculpture," pp. 27–36, for the motivations and tactics of the Académie founders.

Rosen, Charles, and Henri Zerner. *Romanticism and Realism: The Mythology of Nineteenth-Century Art*. New York: Viking Press, 1984. See especially chapter 8, "The Ideology of the Licked Surface," pp. 203–32, on the nineteenth-century academics' insistence upon finish.

Articles

Herissay, Jacques. "L'Education d'un peintre à la fin du XVIIIe siècle: Germain-Jean Drouais (1763–1788)," *Bulletin de la Societé des Amis des Arts du Département de l'Eure*, 19 (1903), pp. 61–103, and 20 (1904), pp. 61–107. A fine compilation of artistic education on the eve of the Revolution.

Rothstein, Eric. "'Ideal Presence' and the 'Non Finito' in Eighteenth-Century Aesthetics," *Eighteenth Century Studies*, vol. 9, no. 3 (Spring, 1976), pp. 307–32. More about literature and England than the visual arts and France, but provocative and highly useful.

Exhibition Catalogues

Eighteenth-Century French Life-Drawing. Introductory essay by James Henry Rubin. Princeton, N.J.: The Art Museum, Princeton University, 1977. Contains much relevant information on artistic theory and education.

French Eighteenth-Century Oil Sketches from an English Collection. Compiled by Peter Walch. Albuquerque, N.M.: The University of New Mexico Art Museum, 1980. *New Mexico Studies in the Fine Arts*, vol. 5. Catalogues many of the eighteenth-century pictures in the present exhibition.

French Nineteenth Century Oil Sketches: David to Degas. Introductory essay by John Minor Wisdom. Chapel Hill, N.C.: The William Hayes Ackland Memorial Art Center, The University of North Carolina, 1978. A fine discussion of the types of oil sketches.

French Oil Sketches from an English Collection. Compiled by J. Patrice Marandel. Houston: The Museum of Fine Arts, 1975. An earlier catalogue to a good portion of the collection in the present exhibition.

The Grand Prix de Rome: Paintings from the Ecole des Beaux-Arts 1797–1865. Introduction by Jacques Thullier; essay by Philippe Grunchec. New York: International Exhibitions Foundation, 1984. Grunchec painstakingly recreates the education of official artists in post-Revolutionary France.

Masters of the Loaded Brush: Oil Sketches from Rubens to Tiepolo. Introductory essay by Rudolf Wittkower. New York: M. Knoedler & Company, 1967. Remains the standard history of the oil sketch through the eighteenth century.

Notes to the Catalogue

All entries are arranged chronologically by the birthdate of the artist.

Full references for works cited by author may be found in the Bibliography; and to exhibitions, cited by city, in Exhibitions.

Unless otherwise indicated, an artist's biography has been prepared by the writer of the entry or entries it accompanies.

Simon VOUET

(Paris 1590–Paris 1649)

The career of Simon Vouet can be divided in two parts. The first half—which includes his early years in Constantinople, Venice, and Rome, where he arrived in 1614 with a pension from the King—is entirely Italian. The artist not only learned from the great examples Rome provided, but participated fully in the development of the Roman school and the articulation of the Baroque style. To that period belong his great panels for San Lorenzo in Lucina, and the fresco (lost) for Saint Peter's. His return to Paris in 1627, at the request of the King, marks the beginning of his second—French—period. It also marks a significant date in the development of French painting itself. He received major commissions from the Crown, for instance, for the Louvre, Saint-Germain, and Luxembourg palaces. Richelieu and a host of prominent figures of Parisian society were also his patrons. The eloquence of his early compositions eventually gave way to more decorative works, particularly in the late years of his life. Many painters, some of them his former studio assistants, carried on his style for a generation. Vouet is indisputably one of the greatest painters of seventeenth-century France, surpassed only by his rival, Poussin.

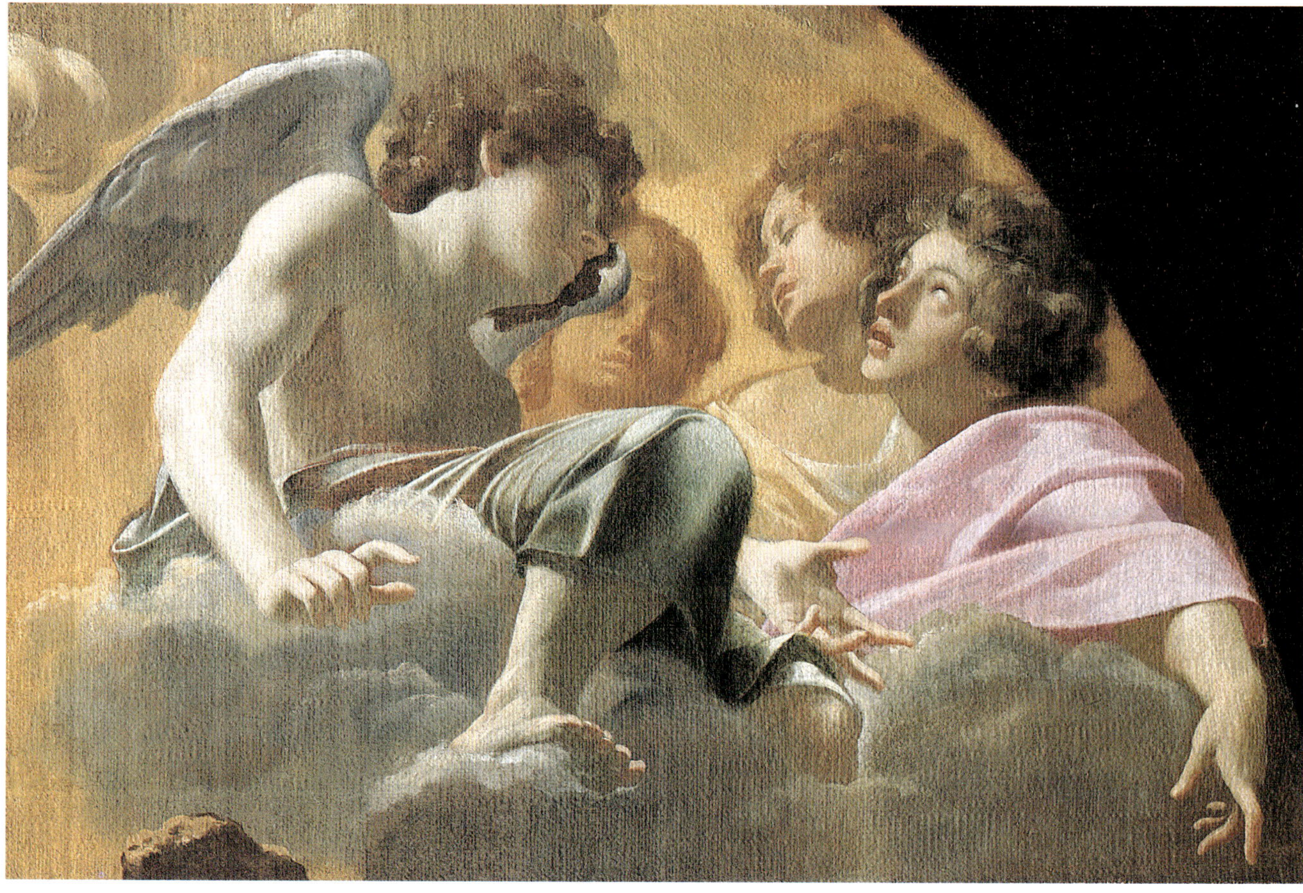

1,2 Simon VOUET
Two "Modelli" for Two Groups of Angels,
1625
Deux *Modelli* pour deux groupes d'anges
Oil on canvas
16 × 24 ¼" (40.6 × 61.6 cm) each

Bibliography: Schleier 1972, pp. 91–92, figs. 43, 44.

Exhibitions: Houston 1973–75, nos. 92, 93.

In 1624, Simon Vouet received the commission to paint an altarpiece for Saint Peter's. It was to be placed in the Coro Novo, or Chancel of the Canons. The history of the commission is well documented (Paris 1990–91, pp. 102–04). The original commission, which was for an altarpiece representing Saint Peter Healing the Sick with His Shadow, was probably never completed. About a year after Vouet received the commission, and after he had executed, by his own account, many drawings for it, it was suddenly decided to transfer Michelangelo's *Pietà* to the Coro Novo. Vouet was still to paint an altarpiece, but it was to illustrate the mysteries of the Passion and was meant as the background for the *Pietà*. This composition, painted in *oglio sul muro*, was apparently in place by early 1626. By 1730, it had been decided to replace it with an altarpiece by Pietro Bianchi (Schleier 1968, pp. 573–74), but Vouet's altarpiece was still in place in 1735, and perhaps even, as argued by Schleier, well into the 1740s.

Destroyed in the eighteenth century, it is known today only through drawings executed after it, and partial *bozzetti* at Hovingham Hall and Besançon (Schleier 1967, pp.
272–75). The two *modelli* presented here offer an important complement to this fragmented reconstitution. In his thorough publication of these *modelli*, Schleier remarks:
"The fact that Vouet elaborated the two groups of angels in the two *modelli*, where the
curved borderline of the arched top is respected, reinforces the hypothesis . . . that
the angels in the upper corners of the [Hovingham Hall] *bozzetto* outside the curved
line were added by the artist afterwards, when he wanted to complete the *bozzetto* to a
rectangular 'quadro' of its own" (Schleier 1972, p. 91).

Schleier has also appropriately stressed the stylistic link that unites these *modelli* to Vouet's own ceiling fresco *The Assumption of the Virgin* in the Alaleona Chapel in
San Lorenzo in Lucina and, in addition, the rich dialogue this period of Vouet's work
establishes with the work of Lanfranco on the eve of his departure for Naples.

J. P. M.

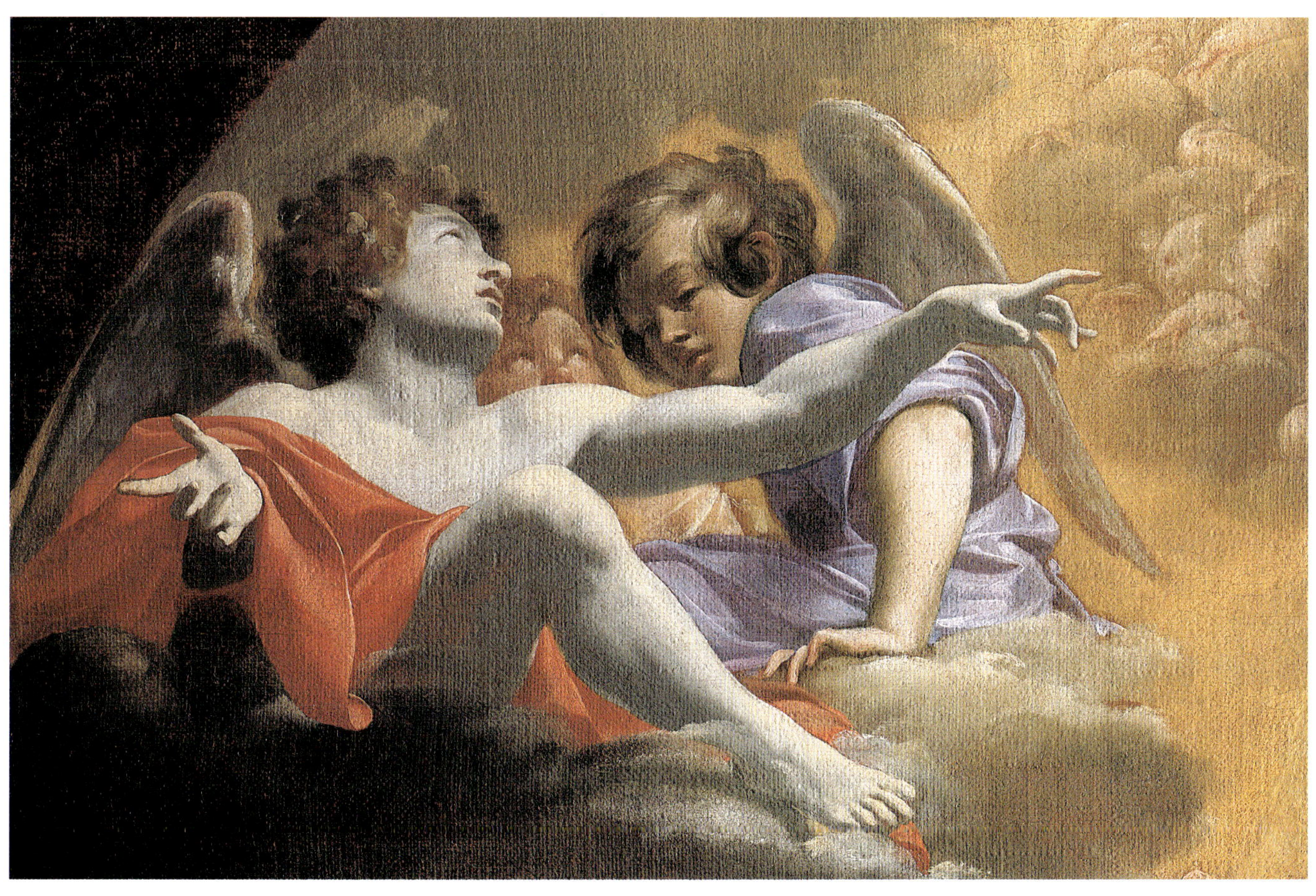

Jean SENELLE

(Meaux 1605?–Paris between 1654 and 1671)

Mysterious and often confused with other artists, Senelle has only recently become the subject of careful study. Born in Meaux, he may have received his first training from Northern artists. In 1640, he was in Paris working under Vignon, but seems to have been more responsive to the works of La Hyre (q.v.), Vouet (q.v.) (both Simon and Aubin), and Lesueur. The importance of the artist on the Parisian art scene of his time remains to be discovered.

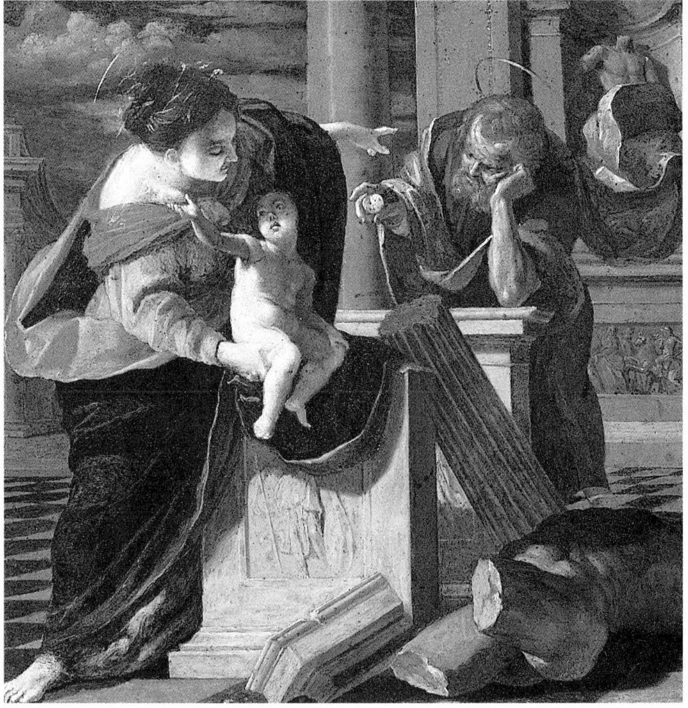

3   Jean SENELLE
The Holy Family, n.d.
La Sainte Famille
Oil on copper
11 ⅜ × 11 ½" (28.9 × 29.2 cm)
On the reverse: The Holy Trinity
(possibly by another hand)

Exhibitions: Houston 1973, no. 55
(attributed to Jean Lemaire).

The attribution of this painting—previously published as a work by Jean Lemaire (1597–1659)—to Jean Senelle, a largely forgotten artist who has been the subject of recent scholarship (Ruiz 1980, 1982; Meaux, 1989), was suggested by Pierre Rosenberg (in conversation with the author). Senelle's early works (such as *The Predication of Saint John the Baptist*, 1629; Meaux, Musée Bossuet) reveal a gifted, if somewhat provincial, artist influenced by Northern Mannerism. After his move to Paris, his paintings reflect instead the rich culture of the capital, and while they show affinities with La Hyre and Vouet, Senelle seems to have responded more favorably to the "naturalism" of Simon Vouet's brother, Aubin (1595–1641), than to the work of Simon Vouet himself.

The painting ought to be compared with the large *Adoration of the Magi* (c. 1644; Meaux, Musée Bossuet), to which it must be close in date. The Meaux altarpiece is considered to be the culmination of the art of Jean Senelle and shows some of the typical features of the artist. The grand theatricality of the *Adoration* is scaled down in this small painting, but the elaborate architectural setting of the large work is nonetheless echoed in the smaller one by an antiquarian's concern for representing columns, Classical reliefs, and fragments. This may seem surprising from an artist who, apparently, never went to Italy, and one whose career has a distinctly Parisian flavor. Senelle's ties with Italy were, however, both intellectual and personal (he had married the sister of the French Caravaggesque painter Valentin de Boullogne). There was no need for a French artist in the seventeenth century to travel to Rome in order to admire and copy antiquities, for these were plentiful in Paris as were images of antiquities in paintings and prints. In addition, revealing similarities—for instance in the somewhat awkward anatomy of the Christ Child repeated in both paintings, and in the elongated hands that are a trademark of the artist—appear in both works.

The Holy Trinity on the reverse is possibly by another hand.

J. P. M.

Laurent de LA HYRE

(Paris 1606–Paris 1656)

aurent de La Hyre was the son of Etienne de La Hyre, a painter recorded as having worked in Poland. Laurent de La Hyre's background is deeply rooted in French painting (he never went to Italy), and his own work is the expression of an urban, Parisian Classicism, opposed in many ways to the Baroque spirit of his contemporary Simon Vouet (q.v.). In 1623, La Hyre was at Fontainebleau, studying Rosso and Primaticcio — the Italian artists who worked there — as well as Dubreuil and Dubois. His training with Georges Lallemant in 1626 is yet another tie with the late Mannerist school. His first works reflect the intellectual nuances and the literary refinement of these French antecedents, but around 1640 La Hyre developed a different style. During this period, his subjects are typically drawn from mythology rather than novels or poetry, and are set in beautifully ordered landscapes enhanced by ruins. La Hyre was also an important painter of religious subjects, from his early *Martyrdom of Saint Bartholomew* (1627; Mâcon, Cathedral of Saint-Vincent) to his late compositions for the Grande-Chartreuse Monastery (1656, *Christ Appearing to the Pilgrims* and *Christ Appearing to Mary Magdalene*), which display restrained but genuine emotion.

4   Laurent de LA HYRE
The Assumption, c. 1653–55
L'Assomption
Oil on canvas
29 ½ × 20 ¾" (74.9 × 52.7 cm)

Exhibitions: Houston 1973–75, no. 50.

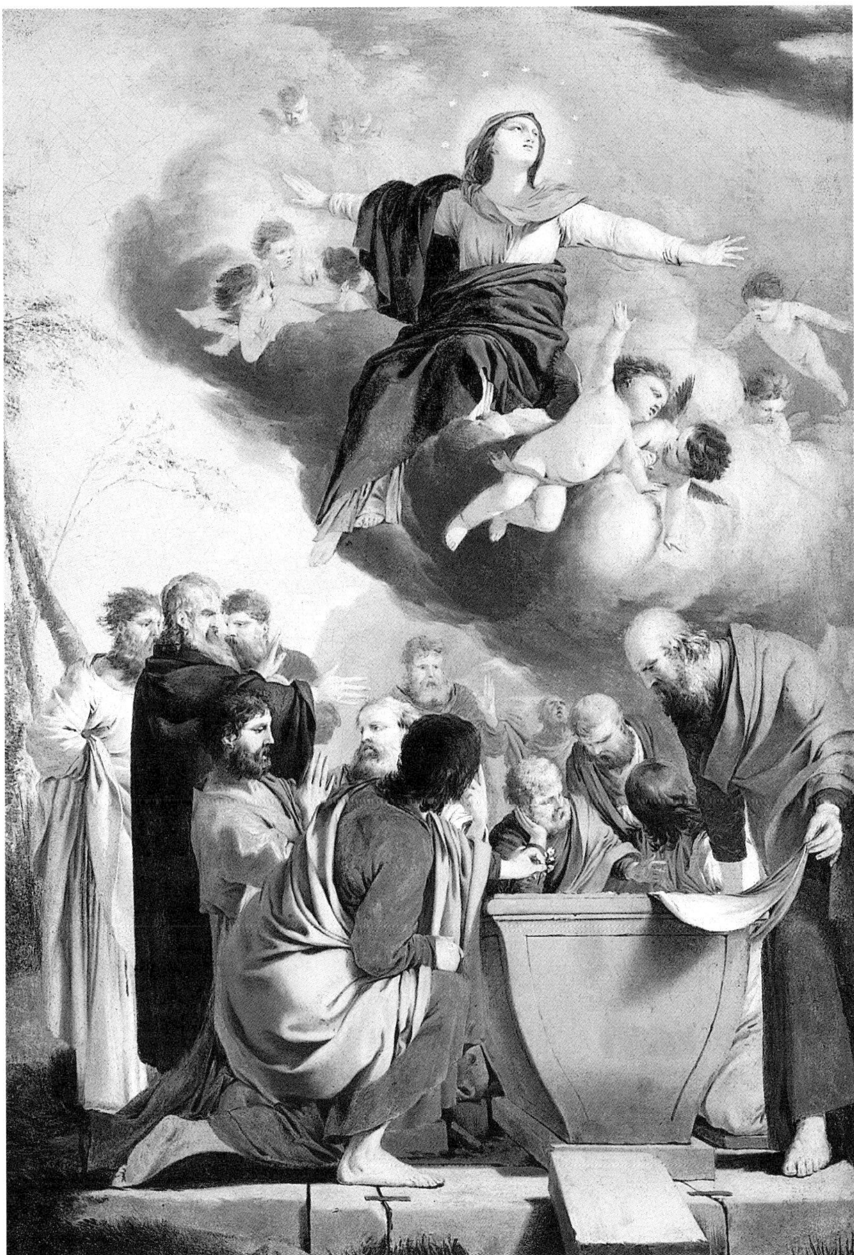

Not mentioned by Rosenberg and Thuillier (Grenoble/Rennes/Bordeaux 1989–90), this highly finished painting belongs to a group of Assumptions by La Hyre, the most famous of which is in the Kunsthistorisches Museum, Vienna. Rosenberg and Thuillier mention, in relation to the Vienna painting, two other identical compositions: one of small dimensions in a private collection, and one on the art market in 1988 (Tokyo 1988). While the high quality of the painting presented here would indicate that it is another original version of the Vienna composition (acquired in 1807), the fact that there are virtually no differences between them excludes the possibility of this work being a study. (La Hyre's sketches typically display differences in composition and detail from the finished paintings.) Rosenberg and Thuillier, while recognizing the quality of the two other versions of the composition, suggest that they may have been executed by artists close to La Hyre, and probably in his studio. Our composition is rectangular, whereas the Vienna picture was originally arched at the top.(The Vienna composition is dated by Rosenberg and Thuillier around 1653–1655.)

La Hyre painted the Assumption on many occasions: a large painting at the Louvre, signed and dated 1635 (Grenoble/Rennes/Bordeaux 1989–90, pp. 188–89), is his earliest known rendition of the subject. There are several mentions of large Assumptions in the literature—as, for instance, a work originally painted for the Célestins of Soissons, later displayed in the cathedral of that city, and now lost. Rosenberg and Thuillier have published two *bozzetti* of the Assumption scene, but have been thus far unsuccessful in relating them to finished paintings: a small and damaged *bozzetto* in a private collection in Paris (ibid., p. 307, no. 270) that already shares some of the characteristics of the Vienna composition, notably in the disposition of the Apostles around the empty tomb of the Virgin; and another *bozzetto*, also in a private Parisian collection (ibid., p. 325, no. 312), of different composition but closer in date to the picture presented here.

J. P. M.

njustly forgotten in the nineteenth century and for much of the twentieth, Jouvenet has been reestablished as one of the major figures of French painting at the turn of the eighteenth century. Born into a family of artists from Rouen, Jouvenet first studied with his father, Laurent, before moving to Paris in 1661 and entering the school of the Académie Royale in 1667. The interest Le Brun showed in him helped establish the younger artist's reputation. In 1673, he received a commission from the guild of the goldsmiths for a large painting for Notre-Dame. Although Jouvenet participated in the decoration of many Parisian hôtels, he was to become the leading religious artist of his time. He received commissions for the decorations of the Church of the Invalides, for the Chapel at Versailles, and for Saint-Martin-des-Champs, among others. From Academician in 1675, he became director (1705) and rector of the Académie in 1707. Jouvenet never went to Italy, but his style betrays a familiarity not only with the Bolognese and Roman traditions but also with the colorism of the Venetian school.

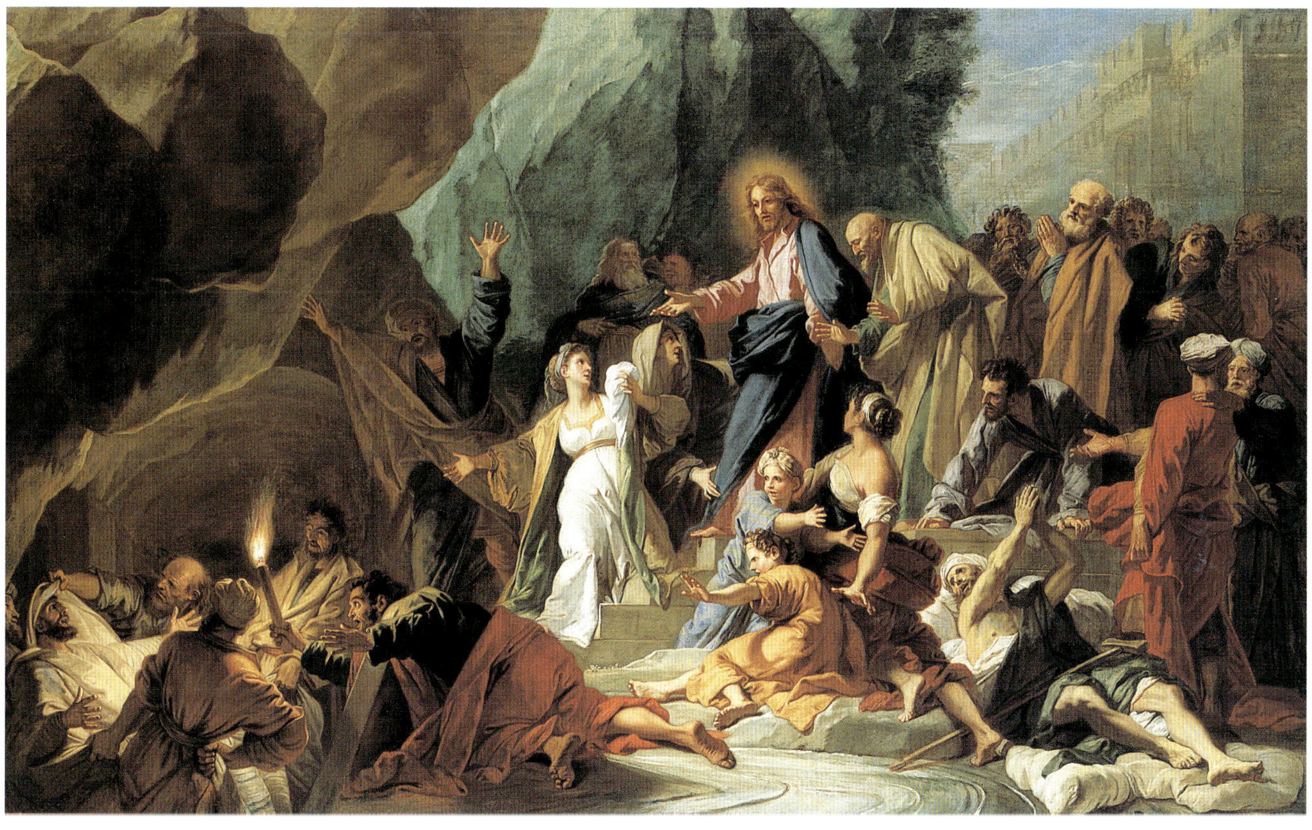

5 Jean JOUVENET
The Raising of Lazarus, c. 1711
La Résurrection de Lazare
Oil on canvas
39 ⅛ × 63 ½ (99.4 × 161.3 cm)

Jouvenet exhibited three large compositions at the 1704 Salon: *Christ in the House of Simon the Pharisee* (Lyon, Musée des Beaux-Arts), *Christ Driving the Merchants from the Temple* (Lyon, Musée des Beaux-Arts), and *The Raising of Lazarus* (Paris, Musée du Louvre). These three compositions, and a fourth one, *The Miraculous Draft of Fishes* (Paris, Musée du Louvre)—not shown at the same Salon— were intended to decorate the nave of the Church of Saint-Martin-des-Champs in Paris. As noted by Schnapper (1974, pp. 133, 211), the four paintings were installed in 1706 (the date they all bear), the delay resulting from the monks inability to pay for them. The abbey was being richly furnished at the time, and in 1703 both Louis de Silvestre and Louis Galloche (q.v.) had been commissioned to execute eleven large paintings illustrating the life of Saint Benedict—a commission that may have exhausted the community's funds. The four paintings remained *in situ* until 1792, when they were confiscated by the Revolutionary government. In 1811, they were given to the two museums. In his Salon of 1763, Diderot (1967, p. 135) praised the composition of Jouvenet's *Lazarus* ("Quelle vie! quels regards! quelle force d'expression!") in order to contrast it with Deshays's rendition of the same subject exhibited that year.

The success of Jouvenet's compositions is confirmed by the fact that in 1712 he delivered to the Gobelins manufactory four cartoons after these paintings (Schnapper 1974, nos. 132, 135, 136). The cartoon for *The Raising of Lazarus* (Lille, Musée des Beaux-Arts), while reproducing the general composition of the Louvre painting, differs in several details. To the right, the walls of a city replace the sky of the first version; under these walls, Jouvenet also added several figures, making his composition more densely populated. He also modified the position of several heads and altered the design of the draperies under the reclining figure on the right.

This recently rediscovered composition, unknown to the literature on the artist and presented in this exhibition for the first time, represents an intermediary stage between the Louvre and the Lille versions. The quality of its execution and the numerous pentimenti throughout the surface of the canvas are sufficient to exclude the possibility of mistaking it for a studio version (several such studio versions or copies after the Louvre picture are listed in Schnapper 1974, no. 119). Here the city walls appear for the first time, but not the additional figures of the Lille version. In small details, Jouvenet made our sketch more readable and successful: thus the right hand of the kneeling woman, to the center right of the composition, which in the Louvre version is somewhat incongruously located over the foot of Christ, is in our version completely omitted. Important changes also affect the figure of the man with outstretched arms to the left: in our sketch, the "second" version, Jouvenet deletes a stone block situated between his legs. More important, the design of his costume is also altered, his cloak no longer disappearing behind his back but falling squarely on the ground. Such a change may lead one to think that the celebrated drawing for that figure (Stockholm, National Museum) is in fact a study for the intermediary version rather than for that of the Louvre.

J. P. M.

Joseph PARROCEL (called des Batailles)

(Brignoles 1646–Paris 1704)

*B*orn into a family of painters, Joseph Parrocel first studied with his brother Louis. Joseph went to Italy around 1667. The work of Salvator Rosa and of the Jesuit battle-painter Jacques Courtois (or Giacomo Cortese) exerted strong influences on him, as did the work of the Venetian painters he studied in Venice. He returned to Paris in 1675 and in 1676 was received into the Académie. Patronized by Louvois, he received commissions for various royal residences (Marly, Versailles). Although Parrocel's fame is based on his military scenes, he was also a painter of religious subjects. For Notre-Dame, he provided a *May* in 1694. His series of etchings on the life of Christ (studies at the Louvre) is justly famous. An original talent open to a variety of influences, Parrocel is one of the most eloquent representatives of the Rubenist movement in France.

6, 7 Joseph PARROCEL
Two Scenes from Ancient History (?), n.d.
Deux Scènes de l'histoire ancienne (?)
Oil on paper on canvas
6 x 11 ⅜" (15.2 × 29.5 cm) each
Signed on back (before relining): *parrocel pinxit*
Inscribed on the period frames: *De monsieur Parroussel* [*sic*]

Exhibitions: Houston 1973–75, nos. 66, 67.

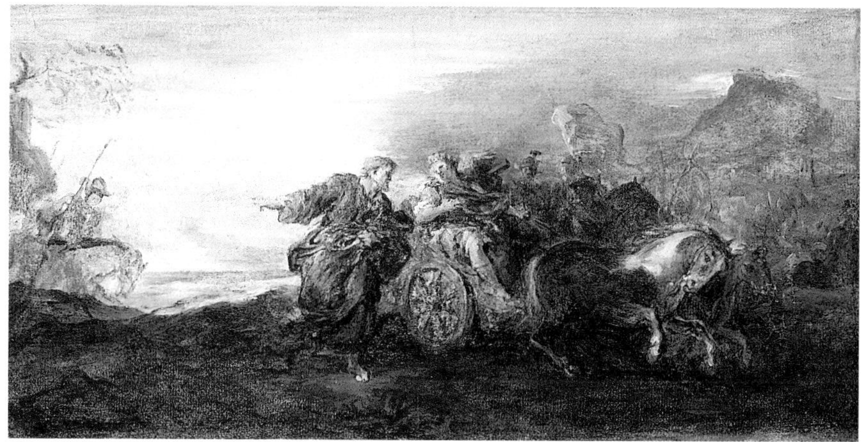

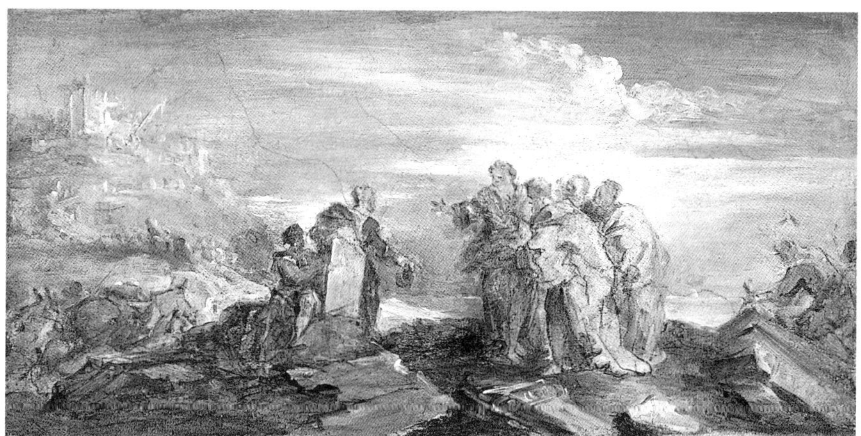

Joseph Parrocel's oeuvre has been reconstructed largely by Antoine Schnapper (1959, 1970). Known essentially as a painter of riders and soldiers in repose, or of battle scenes in the spirit of Salvator Rosa (Schnapper 1985–86), Parrocel also executed religious and genre paintings. One of his major commissions, a series of eleven paintings for the apartments of Louis XIV at Versailles and now partially dispersed in various museums, remains to be fully interpreted. Their current titles, such as *Riders* (Tours, Musée des Beaux-Arts) and *The Halt of Riders* (Lyon, Musée des Beaux-Arts), describe them only superficially. Recently it has been suggested that they may illustrate seldom represented episodes from the *Iliad*. The subjects of the two small paintings in the present exhibition, one of them being the construction of a city, have thus far eluded identification. They too may illustrate a little-known episode from the *Iliad* or the *Aeneid*. Unfortunately, the early accounts of Parrocel's life and work provide no mention of a commission that would describe these paintings.

In spite of the obscurity of their subject and the lack of information regarding their provenance, these two works, which may have been intended as cabinet pictures rather than studies for larger compositions, are important additions to the artist's oeuvre. Their attribution to Joseph Parrocel, confirmed by an inscription—possibly a signature—on the back of one of them (see the photograph in Houston 1973–75, p. 67), is further secured by the many characteristics they share with other works by the artist: spirited drawing, rapid execution, and rich colors, which mark Joseph Parrocel, along with his contemporary La Fosse, as one of the defenders of the Rubenist movement in France. Furthermore, the composition of these small paintings, and in particular the relationship of the figures within the landscape, recalls his *Riders and Prisoners* (Rouen, Musée des Beaux-Arts; Schnapper 1970, fig. 2), which Schnapper puts in the early production of the artist. The paintings presented here justify a later date—definitely after Parrocel settled in Paris in 1675. Comparing these two works with the series of drawings by the artist recently acquired by the Louvre (Paris 1990, pp. 45–66), dated between 1680 and 1700, gives further evidence of a later date.

J. P. M.

Louis GALLOCHE

(Paris 1670–Paris 1761)

ouis Galloche was a pupil of Louis de Boullongne. Winner of the Prix-de-Rome competition in 1695, Galloche remained in Italy only two years, from 1697 to 1699, because of financial problems that obliged him to subsidize his own stay. Received at the Académie in 1711, he had a brilliant official career. He took part in both the 1727 and 1747 Concours. Galloche worked essentially for the Church, without, however, neglecting secular genres. A modest and studious artist, according to his early biographer, the Abbé Gougenot, Galloche is best remembered for the quality of his pupils (including Lemoyne and Natoire) and for the lectures he delivered late in life to the Académie, in which he encouraged not only the study of nature, but also of a variety of artists ranging from Raphael to Van Dyck.

8   Louis GALLOCHE
Saint Scholastica Obtaining a Storm from Heaven to Prevent Saint Benedict from Leaving, 1703
Sainte Scholastique obtenant du ciel une pluie accompagnée de tonnerre pour empêcher Saint Benoit de partir et de la quitter
Oil on canvas
8 ⅜ × 17 ⅝" (21.3 × 44.8 cm)

Provenance: Bernard Chesnais, Paris; Galerie Joseph Hahn, Paris.

Exhibitions: Paris 1972, no. 9; Houston 1973–75, no. 22.

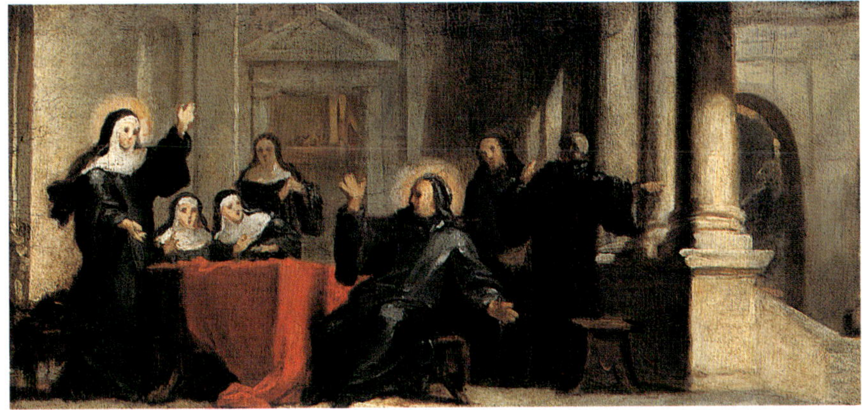

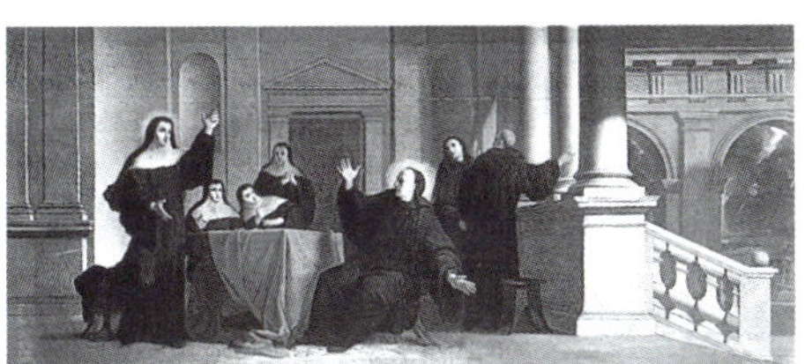

Fig. 1. Louis GALLOCHE. *Saint Benedict at the House of His Sister, Saint Scholastica* (Saint Benoît chez sa soeur Scholastique), 1703. Oil on canvas. Musées royaux des Beaux-Arts de Belgique, Brussels. Photo: Copyright A.C.L.—Brussels.

This painting is a study for a large work, now in the Musées royaux des Beaux-Arts de Belgique, Brussels (fig. 1), which was originally part of a series of eleven paintings devoted to the Life of Saint Benedict in the Refectorium of the Abbey of Saint-Martin-des-Champs in Paris. Galloche painted two episodes of the saint's life for that series: the above-mentioned subject and *The Miracle of Saint Benedict and the Axe* (whereabouts unknown). Louis Silvestre painted the nine remaining episodes, of which only six are known today. (One of them is in the museum at Beziers, one in Perpignan, one in the Louvre, and three in Brussels; see Weigert 1932, pp. 420–21. For the correct identification of the paintings and the history of the cycle, see Montgolfier 1962.) P. Marcel (1904, p. 96), who first attempted an identification of the Saint-Martin-des-Champs paintings, points out—following Dussieux and Soulié's publication (1854–56, vol. 2, p. 91) of Louis Gougenot's *Vie de Galloche*—that Galloche was *agréé* at the Académie on March 3, 1703, upon presentation of these two paintings. In creating these works, a particular challenge faced the painter. According to Gougenot, Galloche's father had remarked to his son that the habits of the Benedictine monks and nuns were not "black enough." Thereupon Galloche copied two compositions by Van Dyck, remarkable in particular for the deep black of the sitters' costumes, an exercise that enabled him to treat with dexterity the subtle modulations of the black vestments of his monks ("He brilliantly manipulated the chiaroscuro offered by the dark robes of the monks").

It is not known how the majority of the works in the series found their way to Brussels, where they were purchased by the museum in 1830, although the ensemble is known to have been dismantled at the time of the French Revolution (Montgolfier 1962, p. 291).

A drawing for the whole composition is in a private collection in Paris.

J. P. M.

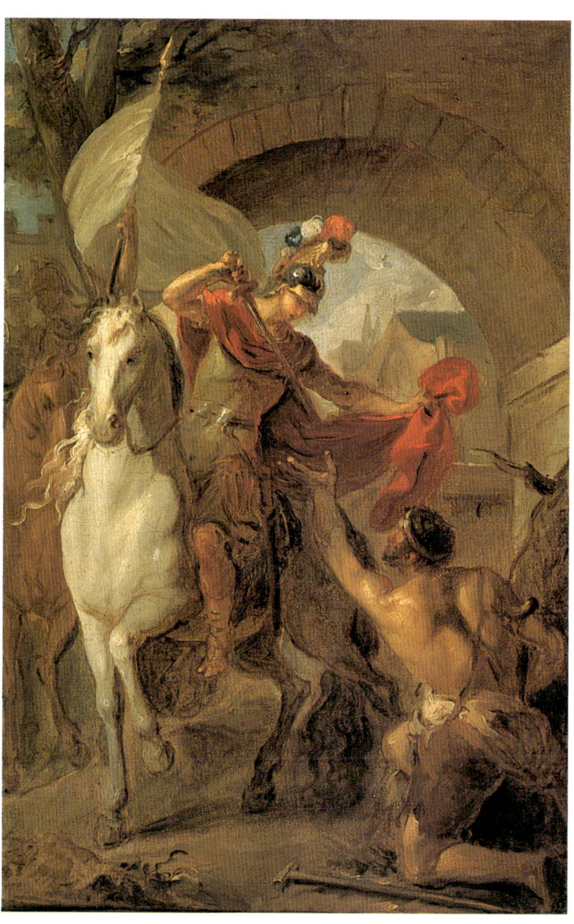

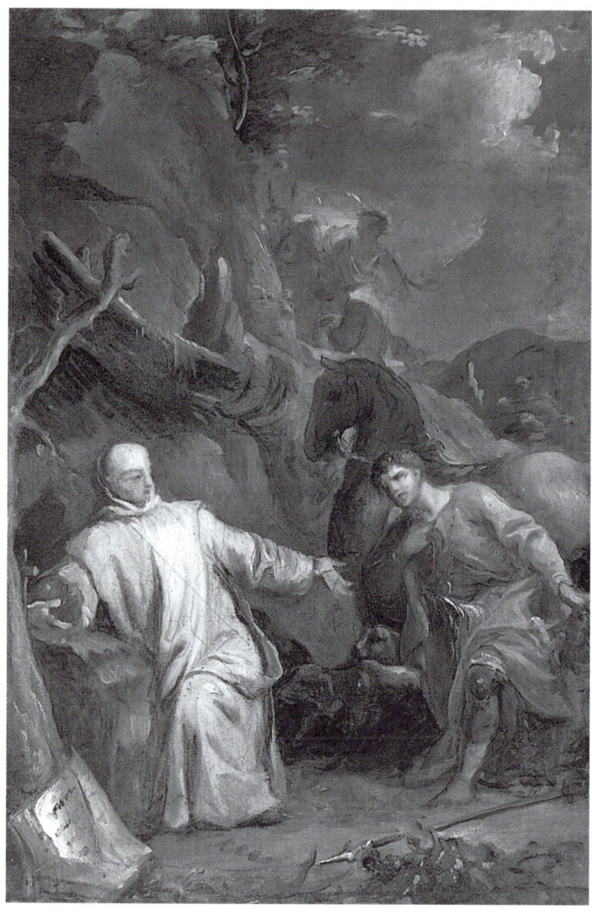

9   Louis GALLOCHE
    Saint Martin Sharing His Coat with a Beggar, n.d.
    Saint Martin partageant son manteau avec un mendiant
    Oil on canvas
    15 ⅝ × 10 ⅜" (39.7 × 26.4 cm)

10   Louis GALLOCHE
    A Scene from the Life of Saint Martin (?), n.d.
    Un Épisode de la vie de Saint Martin (?)
    Oil on canvas
    15 ⅝ × 10 ⅜" (39.7 × 26.4 cm)

Provenance: Galerie Joseph Hahn, Paris.

Exhibitions: Paris 1972, nos. 10, 11; Houston 1973–75, nos. 23, 24.

The attribution of these oil sketches to Louis Galloche is confirmed by the existence of three drawings by him, related to the scene of Saint Martin Sharing His Coat, at the Musée du Louvre (inv. nos. 26668, 26669, 26670). The identification of the subject of the second sketch, however, is not entirely satisfactory. Exhibited since 1972 as *Saint Hubert Visiting Saint Lambert*, it cannot represent this scene. Saint Hubert apparently met Saint Lambert when the latter was already a bishop—and not a monk as depicted here. Furthermore, the kneeling Hubert does not carry any of the attributes that would allow us to identify him as that saint. Finally, the pairing of a scene from the life of Saint Martin with one from the life of Saint Hubert would seem unmotivated by any symmetry between the two saints' lives. We would like to suggest instead that the subject of this painting may be a seldom-represented episode from the life of Saint Martin. It is known that Martin of Tours—when a soldier in the Roman army—objected to serving the Emperor, on the grounds of his Christian belief. Imprisoned and discharged—and after performing the famous deed of sharing his coat with a beggar, near Amiens (an episode often represented)—he resumed his civilian life, became a disciple of Saint Hilary (c. 300–367) at Poitiers, then traveled to his native Pannonia (Hungary) and Italy before returning to Poitiers. There he again met Hilary—himself just back from exile—and became an eremitic monk at Ligugé (Farmer 1978, p. 265). Perhaps Galloche's composition shows Martin, having exchanged his military uniform for civilian clothing, asking to be admitted as a monk. His humble gesture and the broad and welcoming gesture of the monk—an eremite himself, as indicated by the hut under which he sits—seem to reinforce that interpretation.

Given the relationship between the artist and the Parisian monastery of Saint-Martin-des-Champs, it is tempting to see in these sketches a project for that institution, but this can remain only conjectural, as no document proves that Galloche's contribution to the abbey went beyond the commission described in the preceding entry. Furthermore, the style of these sketches, with their bright and golden colors, acknowledging the art of Rubens and Van Dyck, suggests a date closer to his *Dido and Aeneas* (Paris, Musée du Louvre), executed in 1737, than to the 1703 commission.

J. P. M.

Jean-François DE TROY

(Paris 1679–Rome 1752)

Jean-François de Troy was the son and pupil of the portraitist François de Troy. Though his father tried to dissuade him from a career as a painter, Jean-François de Troy persisted and was accepted as a pensioner at the French Academy in Rome. In Italy from 1699 to 1706, he traveled from Rome to Florence, where he found a wealthy patron, and then to Pisa. He returned to Paris in 1708, the year he exhibited his reception piece, *Niobe and Her Children*, at the Salon. De Troy became professor at the Académie in 1719 and by 1725 was acknowledged as one of the leading painters in France. A prolific artist well known for his large mythological and religious scenes, de Troy also produced portraits, landscapes, and genre scenes. Director of the French Academy in Rome from 1738 until his death, he continued to exhibit regularly at the Salons in Paris. D.G.

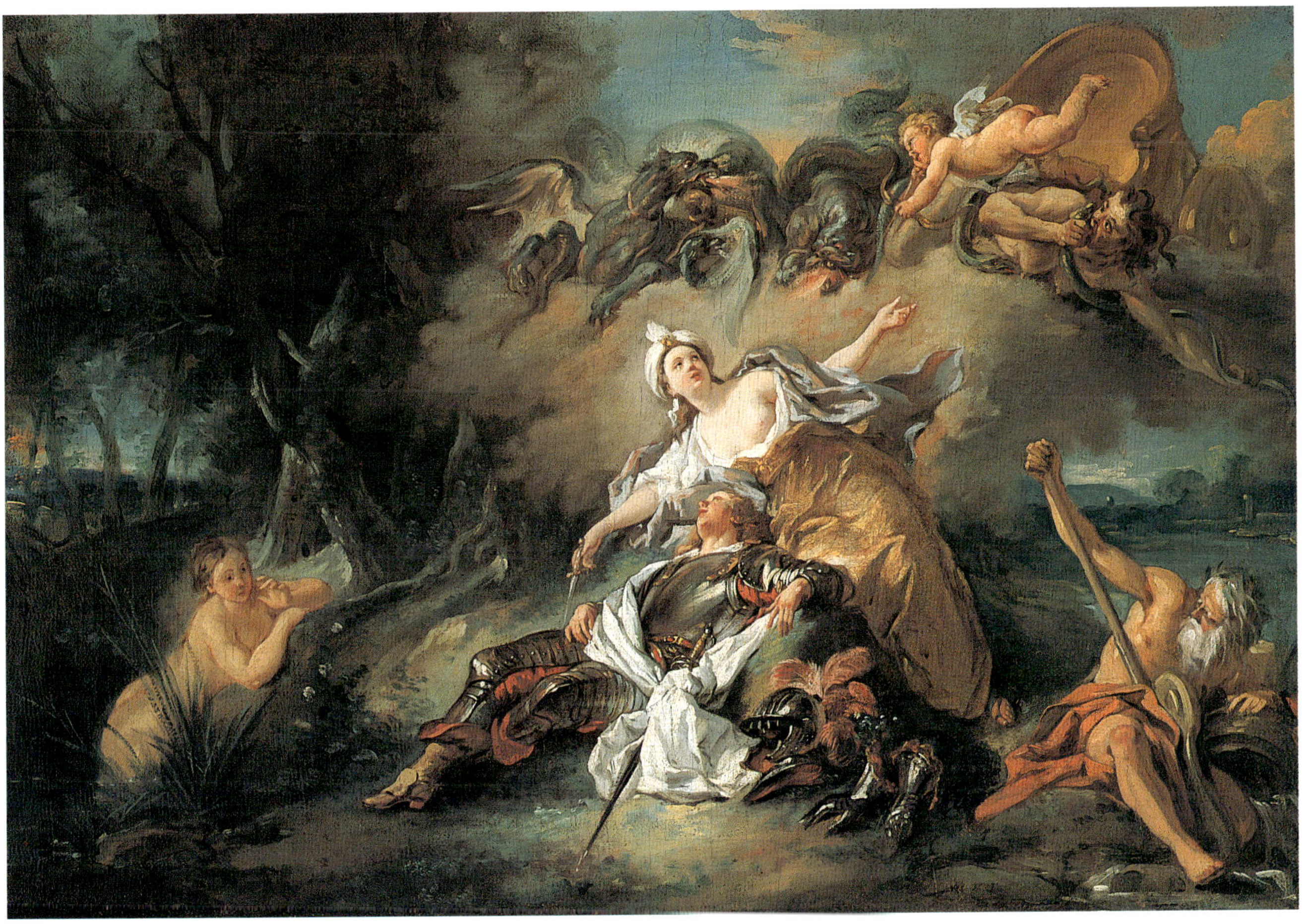

11 By or after Jean-François DE TROY
Armida Prevented by Love from Assassinating the Sleeping Rinaldo, c. 1725
Armide defendue par l'Amour d'assassiner Renaud endormi
Oil on canvas
20 ½ × 30 ¼ × (52.1 × 76.8 cm)
Verso: indecipherable red wax seal, with apparently Germanic coat of arms

Exhibitions: Albuquerque 1980, no. 63.

Jean-François de Troy's finished painting (whereabouts unknown), to which this sketch is related, measured no less than four feet high by six feet across, and was exhibited twice in 1725. The subject derives from the great Christian epic by Torquato Tasso, *Gerusalemme liberata* (1580/81, Canto XIV, stanzas 65–67). Coincidentally, the year before the painting was exhibited, a new French translation by J.-P. Mirabaud of Tasso's epic had been published. But the subject's popularity in eighteenth-century France and the specific scene represented here owe more to Quinault and Lully's opera *Armide* (1686).

Another version of the present sketch was identified by Jacques Vilain when it appeared in Paris in 1970, and was then acquired for the Musée des Beaux-Arts in Lille (see Vilain 1971, no. 6, pp. 353–56; Oursel 1971, no. 1; Dunkerque/Lille/Valenciennes 1980, no. 71; and London 1993, no. 46). Now that the initial excitement of its discovery has died down, it is clear that the Lille sketch is not by de Troy.

It is extremely difficult to determine the authorship of an autograph oil sketch, and even more difficult to determine the author of a copy sketch because many of the connoisseur's clues, often personal mannerisms indicative of a particular artist, are hidden or unclear in a copy sketch. However, in the Lille picture a slightly coarse character and even a carelessness in the handling and an over-assertive palette suggest the hand of Jean-Baptiste Deshays. Deshays's master was Boucher and, as revealed by a previously unpublished description of the posthumous sale of Jean-Claude Gaspard de Sireaul (December 3, 1781), Boucher was for a time a student of de Troy's. This same document also reveals the existence of a copy sketch by Boucher after the very de Troy reproduced here, but of virtually identical dimensions to the sketch in Lille. We may suppose that Boucher had made a copy sketch of de Troy's (postdating his student years), and that this was available for his own pupil, Deshays, to copy (later selling it, or passing it on to Sireaul, like so many of his drawings).

The question remains: is our sketch the original by de Troy that Boucher had copied, or is it a copy sketch by another pupil of Boucher's? While the handling is not like the London sketches by de Troy, this may be a reflection of the fact that if this sketch is by de Troy himself, it antedates any of his other known sketches by a decade. Ultimately, there seems only one way of resolving the matter, and that is by juxtaposing the Lille sketch and this one with some of de Troy's other sketches of similar scenes in order to closely compare the stylistic affinities between works known to be by de Troy and works without documentation.

A. Laing

Jean RESTOUT

(Rouen 1692–Paris 1768)

Nephew and pupil of Jean Jouvenet (q.v.), Restout took the place left vacant by his uncle's death in 1717 as the leading painter of religious subjects. Academician in 1720 with *Alpheus and Arethusa* (Rouen, Musée des Beaux-Arts), proving that the artist was comfortable with mythological subjects too, Restout elaborated on the style established by Jouvenet, conferring on his figures the grace and elegance that are his distinctive trademarks. His greatest religious commissions (among them, *The Death of Saint Scholastica*; Tours, Musée des Beaux-Arts) are imbued as well with a poignant austerity that sets them apart from the production of his contemporaries. His secular projects are also abundant and include works for the Gobelins tapestry manufactory, Versailles, the Hôtel de Soubise, and for Frederick II at the Neues Palais, Potsdam.

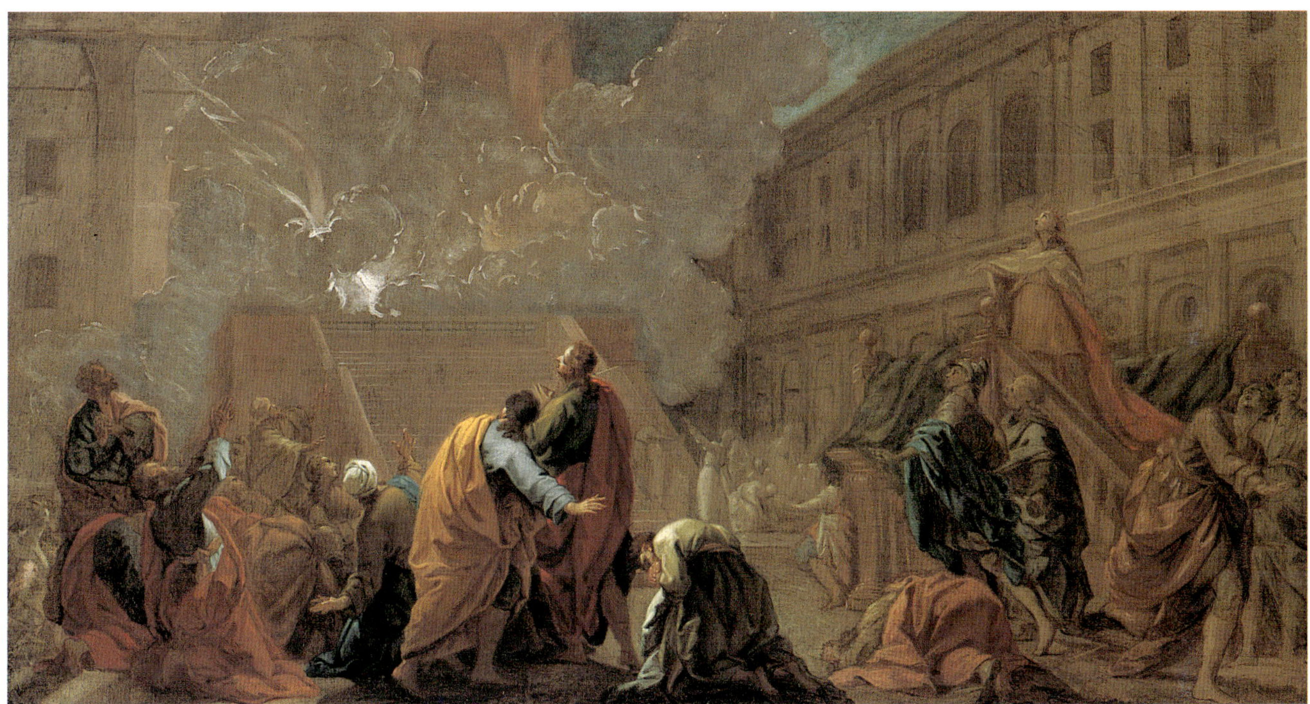

12   Jean RESTOUT
The Dedication of the Temple of Solomon,
1743
La Consécration du Temple de Salomon
Oil on canvas
19 ¼ × 35 ⅜" (48.9 × 89.9 cm)

Exhibitions: Albuquerque 1980, no. 54.

Restout's only entry at the 1743 Salon was an immense painting (4.37 × 8.10 m) representing the rare subject of the Dedication of the Temple of Solomon (Paris, Musée du Louvre; see Rouen 1970, no. 55; the painting is now in need of conservation). The subject, taken from Kings (8: 10–11), shows the temple filled with a cloud: "It came to pass, when the priests were come out of the holy place, that the cloud filled the house of the Lord. So that the priests could not stand to minister because of the cloud: for the glory of the Lord had filled the house of the Lord."

Besides this sketch, Restout executed at least two preparatory drawings. One, at the Musée des Beaux-Arts, Rouen (Rouen 1970, no. 24), is probably Restout's earliest thought for *The Dedication*. Collaged pieces demonstrate the artist's revisions and his search for a suitable composition. The other drawing, at the Musée des Beaux-Arts, Orléans (Rouen 1970, no. 25), squared for transfer, is closer to our sketch and represents a further step toward the solution finally adopted.

J.P.M.

Nicolas DELOBEL

(Paris 1695–Paris 1765)

P.J. Mariette gives scant and slightly erroneous information on the painter, whom he held in low esteem. Pupil of Boullongne, Delobel befriended Bouchardon in Rome. He was received into the Académie in 1732 (not 1737, as stated by Mariette). The same author preferred to his history paintings ("il pretendoit aux grandes machines") views of Rome the artist had allegedly executed "sur le lieu." Delobel's work is not yet well enough known to confirm or deny Mariette's judgment.

13 Nicolas DELOBEL
Allegory of the Reunion of Lorraine with France, 1737
Allégorie de la réunion de la Lorraine à la France
Oil on canvas
12 ⅜ × 10 ⅜" (31.4 × 26.4 cm)

Exhibitions: Salon of 1737; Albuquerque 1980, no. 14.

Bibliography: Engerand 1901, p. 139, no. 2; Adhémar 1957, p. 175.

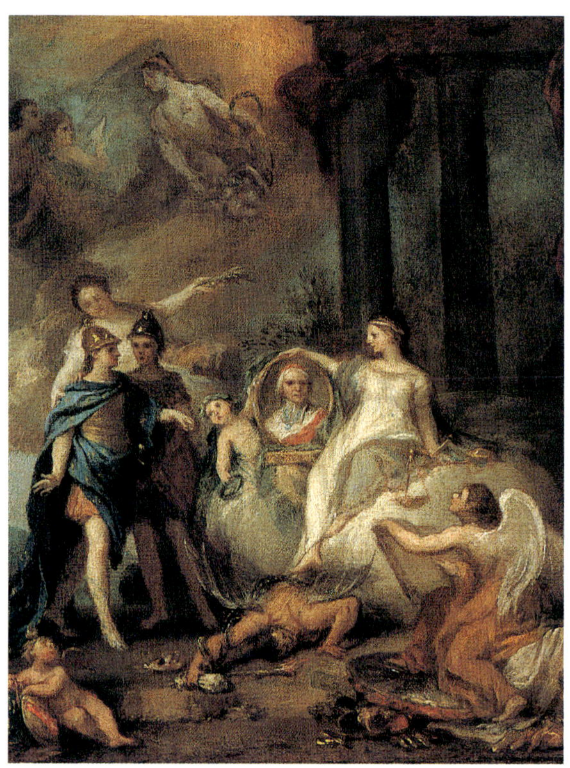

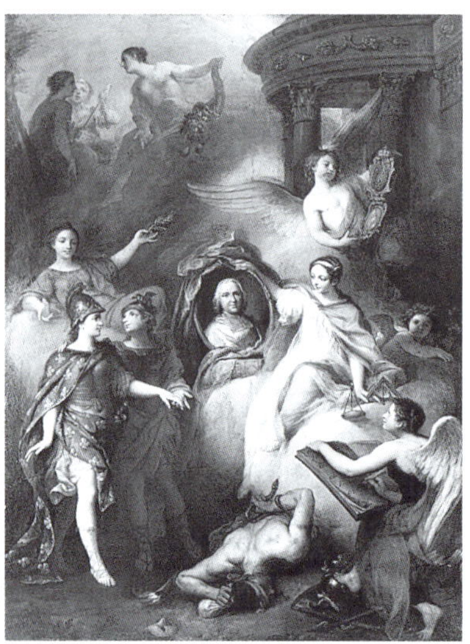

Fig. 2. Nicolas DELOBEL. *Allegory of the Reunion of Lorraine with France* (Allégorie de la réunion de la Lorraine à la France), 1737. Oil on canvas. Musée Historique Lorrain, Nancy. Photo: © Gilbert Mangin.

Mariette judged the artist severely: "C'étoit un génie froid, il n'avait aucune couleur. Il prétendoit pourtant aux grandes machines" (Mariette 1853–54, vol. 2, p. 85). Perhaps justified, this judgment helped eclipse the fame of an artist who enjoyed a solid reputation during his lifetime. Among his compositions, only one has retained the occasional attention of later critics (Adhémar 1957): the large painting commemorating the reunion of Lorraine with France, executed in 1738 and exhibited at the Salon that year. Its sketch, presented here, had been shown at the Salon of 1737 ("une Pensée allégorique en esquisse, sur la Réunion de la Lorraine à la France, sous le Ministère de Monseigneur le Cal. de Fleury, par M. Delobel, Académicien"; see Adhémar 1957, pp. 175–77). The elaborate iconographic program of the painting, fully explained in the 1738 Salon *livret*, is in fact easily decipherable: Lorraine and France, two helmeted and united figures are led by Peace (holding an olive branch) toward a medallion portrait of Cardinal de Fleury, the Minister who had been instrumental in the conclusion of the treaty between the two countries. The medallion is held by Equity, while History (holding a tablet) records the event, and Abundance, overhead, personifies the wealth that should derive from such a union. The terms of the treaty called for the unification of Lorraine with France upon the death of Stanislas Leczinski, whose daughter Marie was Louis XV's queen. The finished painting is at the Musée Historique Lorrain, Nancy (fig. 2). It follows the general composition of the sketch, with the addition of a winged figure holding the arms of France and Lorraine above the figure of Equity: a burning flame atop her head designates her as zeal and love of Fatherland. Purchased for 1500 livres, the painting was engraved by C. N. Cochin *père* in 1738 and placed in 1739 in the King's Cabinet.

J. P. M.

ubleyras studied with Antoine Rivalz in Toulouse from 1717 to 1719. He remained in Toulouse until 1726, when he moved to Paris, where he won the Prix-de-Rome in 1727. In 1728, he left for Rome, never to return to Paris. He lived at the Palazzo Mancini, the seat of the French Academy, until his marriage in 1739 to Felice Maria Tebaldi. His brief career belongs to the Roman school, although he never severed his ties with France (he executed paintings for the cathedrals of Grasse and Toulon, 1741) and is somewhat marginal in the Roman milieu. He worked for the Church, notably for Saint Peter's, and for an illustrious clientele that included the Duke of Saint-Aignan. Subleyras was also an incisive portrait painter, and did not neglect genre painting.

14 Pierre SUBLEYRAS
Seven Angels Adoring the Christ Child, c. 1730–40
Sept Anges en adoration de l'Enfant-Jésus
Oil on canvas
11 ¾ × 8 ⅞" (29.8 × 22.5 cm)

Provenance: Costantino Bartolomei (?) + 1767; M. de Bèze; his sale, April 1, 1775, no. 95; Prince de Conti; his sale, April 8, 1777, no. 705; anonymous sale, January 19, 1778, no. 97; Anthony M. Clark; his sale, London, Christie's, July 6, 1978, no. 58.

Exhibitions: Albuquerque 1980, no. 57.

Bibliography: Paris/Rome 1987, p. 221, under no. 50, fig. 1.

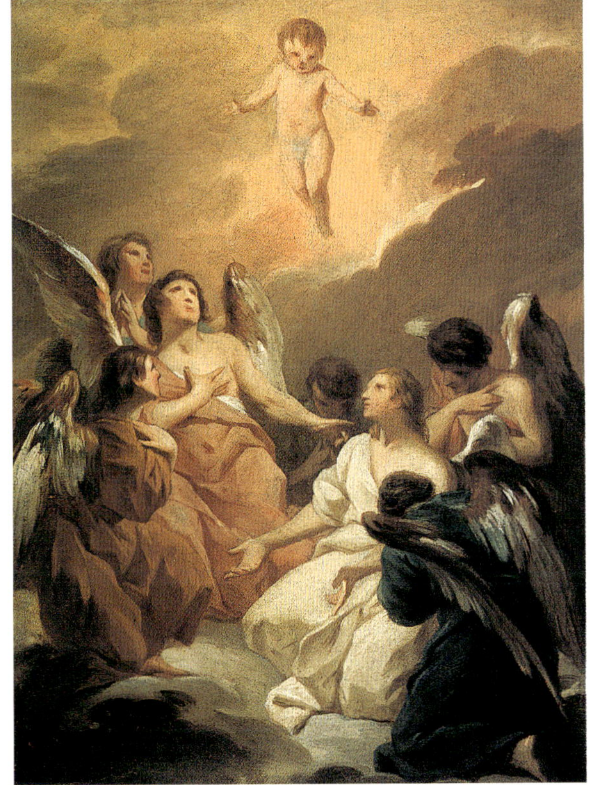

In his entry devoted to the preparatory drawing (Paris, Musée du Louvre, Cabinet des Arts Graphiques, inv. 32934) for this little painting, Pierre Rosenberg (Paris/Rome 1987, p. 221, no. 50) established the provenance of this work and confirmed the date of 1730–40 given to the painting by Anthony Clark. There are some differences between the painting and the preparatory drawing, for instance, in the attitude of the angel to the extreme right, and the design of the wings of the kneeling one in front of him. The most important change, the attitude of the Child—ascending in the drawing, descending in the painting—does not affect the rare iconography of this representation. In his own copy of the composition, executed presumably at the time he was apprenticed under Subleyras in Rome (1744–47), Joseph-Siffred Duplessis also altered the iconography and replaced the Christ Child with the Lamb (Carpentras, Musée des Beaux-Arts).

J. P. M.

15   Pierre SUBLEYRAS
Heraclius Carrying the Cross, n.d.
Héraclius portant la croix
Oil on canvas
16 ⅛ × 12 ½" (41.0 × 31.8 cm)

Provenance: Serra, Duca di Cardinale,
Naples.

Exhibitions: Houston 1773–75, no. 76 (as
representing Saint Ambrose and the
Emperor Theodosius).

Bibliography: Paris/Rome 1987, pp. 151,
298–99, fig. 8.

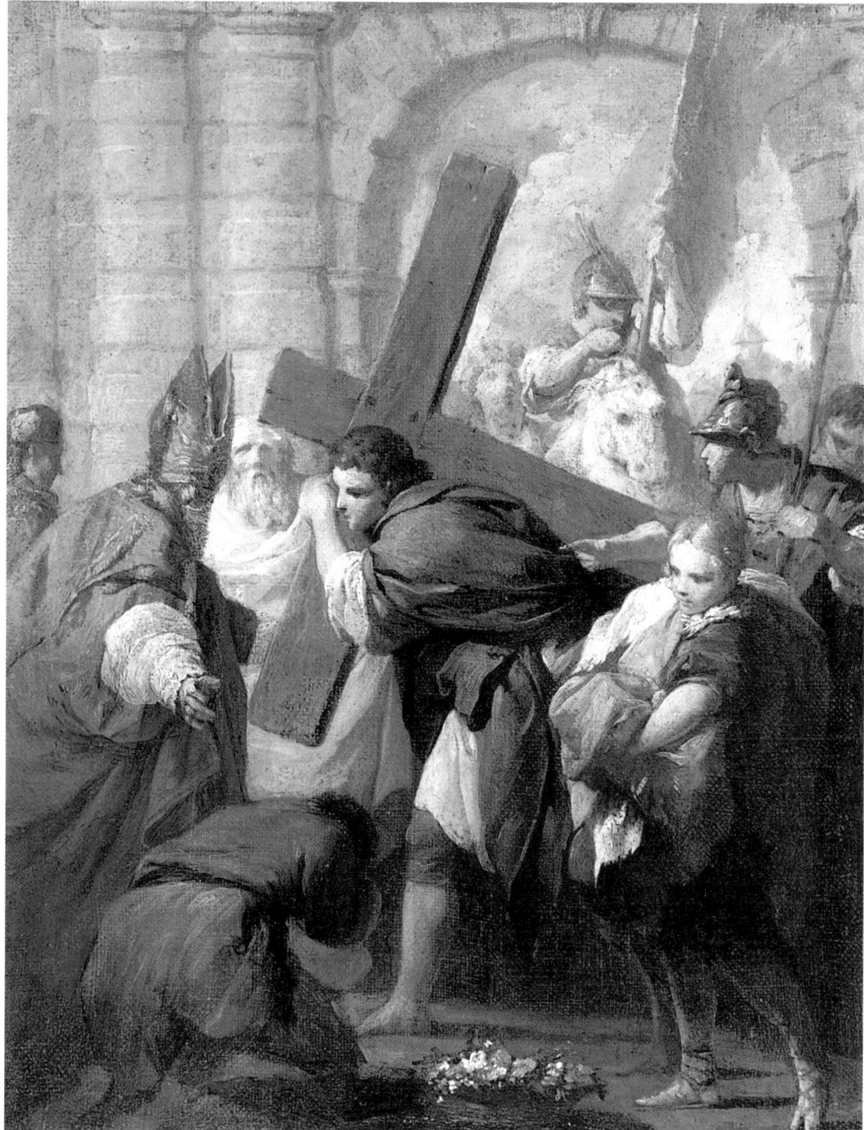

The correct identification of the subject of this small painting was first proposed by
Alastair Laing. The picture was reproduced under its rightful title in the catalogue of
the exhibition devoted to Subleyras in 1787. The Emperor Heraclius (c. 575–642) is
credited with bringing the True Cross to Constantinople as part of the spoils taken
during his campaigns on the eastern front of the Empire (in 627–628; see Macler 1904).
Because the sketch bears the same message as Subleyras's *Saint Ambrosius Giving
Absolution to Emperor Theodosius* (Perugia, Galleria Nazionale dell'Umbria)—the submission of the secular to the spiritual—it is tempting to associate the two paintings,
especially as the dimensions of our sketch correspond to those of Subleyras's small
painting of Saint Ambrosius giving absolution, from the Accademia di Belle Arti of
Perugia (on loan to the Galleria Nazionale; see Paris/Rome 1987, p. 298, fig. 6). But
is that painting a *bozzetto*, a *ricordo*, or a reduction of the large work? Unfortunately,
there exists no document that allows us to associate the two paintings. Pierre Rosenberg (Paris/Rome 1987) has suggested that our sketch could be related to a painting
of the same subject commissioned for the Church of Saint-Vincent at Carcassonne by
Pierre de Poulhariez, a patron of the artist before, and perhaps even after, his departure for Rome in 1728. The painting's present whereabouts are unknown.

J.P.M.

François BOUCHER

(Paris 1705–Paris 1770)

Boucher, perhaps more than any other painter of the mid-eighteenth century, represents the era of Louis XV. He was the student of François Lemoine between 1721 and 1723 and also worked in the studio of J. L. Cars, where he was employed making engravings after the work of Watteau. Boucher won the Prix-de-Rome in 1723, but did not travel to Italy until the spring of 1728, when he accompanied Carle Vanloo. He returned to Paris in 1731 and exhibited his reception piece, *Rinaldo and Armida*, in 1734. Professor in the Académie from 1737, in 1765 he was named director and Peintre du Roi. Boucher played an influential role in the dissemination of French Rococo taste throughout Europe; his drawings and easel paintings were circulated through engravings and copies. During his long career he was continuously busy on decorative and other commissions in Paris and in the royal residences outside the capital; he also produced stage sets for the opera and tapestry designs for the Beauvais and Gobelins workshops, where he was inspector from 1755 to 1765. Toward the end of his life his popularity waned under the censure of critics like Denis Diderot and others. Boucher's many students included Jean-Honoré Fragonard, Ménageot, and Gabriel-Jacques de Saint Aubin.

D.G.

16   François BOUCHER
Monument to Mignard, c. 1735
Le Monument à Mignard
Oil on canvas
28 ½ × 22 ⅝" (72.4 × 57.5 cm)

Exhibitions: Houston 1973–75, no. 3;
Tokyo/Osaka/Hokkaido/Yokohama 1990,
no. 15, reprod. p. 48.

Provenance: Posthumous sale of
Pierre-Hippolyte Lemoyne, Hôtel Bul-
lion, Paris (Duchesne Aîné), May 18 ff.,
1828, lot 95, under "Divers Maîtres":
"Tombeau de Mignard, peint en grisaille,
d'après la sculpture de J-B. Lemoyne,
telle qu'elle était dans l'église de Jacobins de la rue St. Honoré. Hauteur 27
pouces. Largeur 21 pouces." [Sold for
6 francs 10 sous].

This sketch in *en camaïeu* (a pinkish-brown monochrome) may, as Marandel suggested in 1975, record a maquette for the monument completed by Jean-Baptiste Lemoyne
le jeune (1704–1778) in 1744; but one has to ask with what end in view? And why
should Lemoyne have owned it? Instead, we believe that it is a rather late testimony
to Boucher's friendship with the sculptor Lemoyne.

The monument in the Church of the Jacobins (rue Saint-Honoré, Paris; demolished 1795), unveiled in 1744, was broken up during the Revolution, and only the bust of Mignard and the supplicant figure of his legitimized daughter, Catherine, Comtesse de Feuquières, survive, in a simplified arrangement in the nearby Church of Saint-Roche.

Lemoyne, whose forte was portraiture rather than works of the imagination, may have turned to Boucher to devise a design for the monument. The specific impulse to do so may have derived from the fact that the design of the tomb required the incorporation of preexisting elements. Mignard's daughter, Catherine, had contracted with the sculptor Jean Dedieu (1646–1727) soon after her father's death in 1695 for a monument to Mignard in colored marbles. This was to have had an allegorical figure of Painting reclining on a sarcophagus, accompanied by a child holding an escutcheon; in addition there was to be a pedestal supporting a bust of the painter, which was to be provided by his daughter, and a ten-foot-high obelisk bearing the coat of arms of the deceased.

Although the monument often carries the attribution "Inventé & exécuté par *le Moine*," this is doubtful, except for the bust of Mignard. Certain elements, notably the sarcophagus and obelisk, may already have been prepared for Dedieu's monument. Boucher may have been given the challenge of weaving these and the bust into a convincing ensemble—something that required the pictorial eye of the painter as much as Lemoyne's gifts as a sculptor.

Boucher's employment of a monochrome oil sketch (particularly when the actual monument must have contained colored marbles and bronze), rather than a drawing, to work out the design may seem curious. But it may have been used partly because Boucher was apparently happier working out complicated allegories with the brush rather than the pencil. The handling of the sketch—and even more so, the character of the two *putti*—suggests a date closer to that of the commission for the monument, around 1735, than to that of its completion.

A. Laing

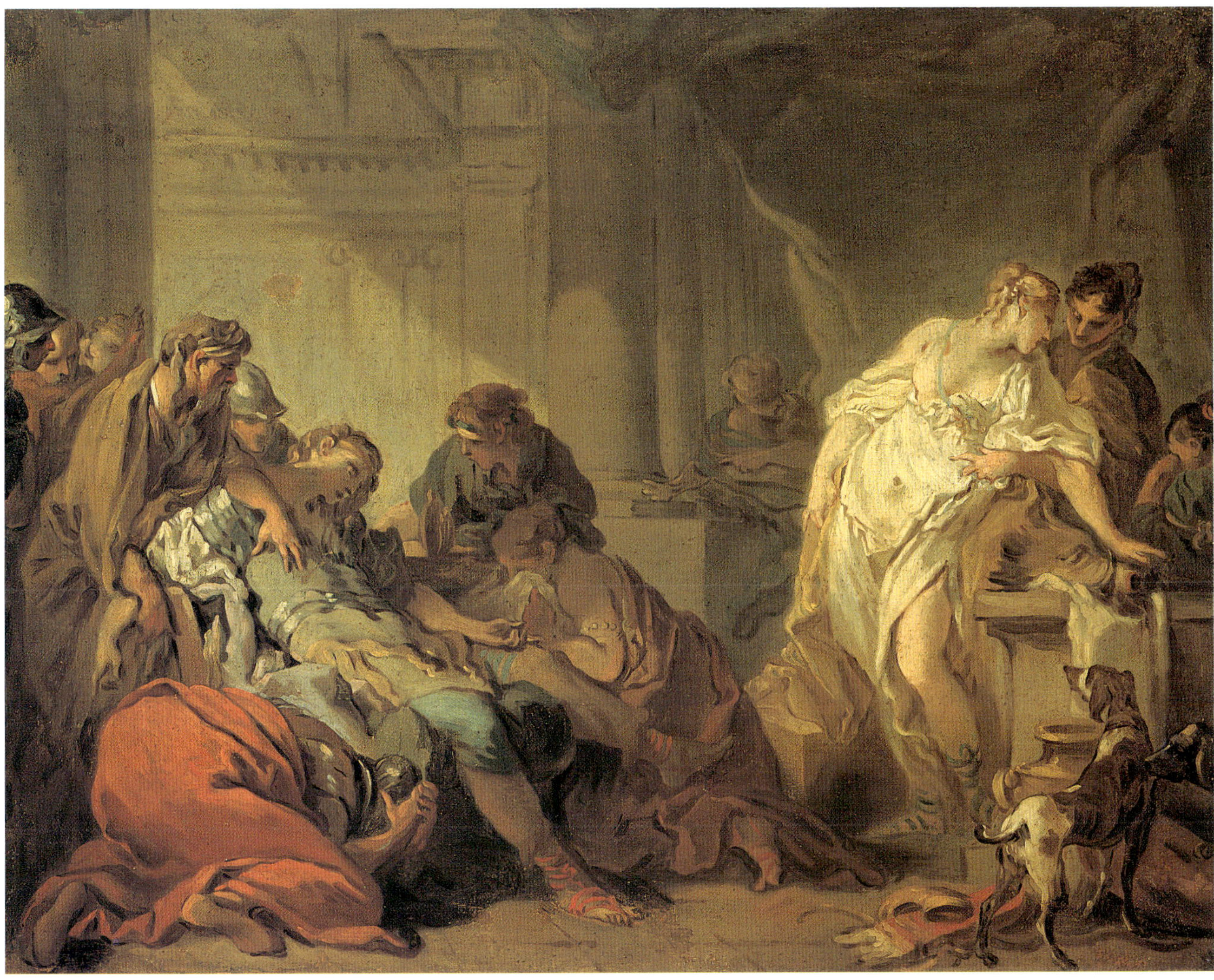

17 François BOUCHER
Death of Meleager, c. 1727
La Mort de Méléagre
Oil on canvas
20 ⅛ × 26 ¼" (51.1 × 66.7 cm)

Exhibitions: Albuquerque 1980, no. 12 (attributed to Dandré-Bardon); Tokyo/ Osaka/Hokkaido/Yokohama 1990, no. 3, reprod. p. 37.

Bibliography: New York/Detroit/Paris 1986–87, p. 107, fig. 81.

In his *Metamorphoses*, Ovid tells the story of the death of Meleager (the heroic hunter of the Calydonian boar), which was caused inadvertently by his mother, Althea, who burned a log whose life span was equal to that of her son. Here the hero is seen surrounded by followers trying to revive him or deploring his imminent death. The seldom represented episode is surprising for Boucher, an artist who often preferred more generic depictions of the gods and heroes of antiquity.

Several versions of this work are mentioned in the literature or are known today. A sketch of this subject, paired with *Birth of Meleager*, figured in the posthumous sale of the painter Dandré-Bardon (June 23 ff., 1783, lot 5). Perhaps for that reason, our *Death of Meleager* has occasionally been attributed to that artist (as is the case, for instance, with a pair identified as *Birth of Oedipus* and *Death of Meleager* at the Musée Bargoin, Clermont-Ferrand). The freedom of its execution has led some to venture an attribution to Fragonard (New York/Detroit/Paris 1986–87, p. 107). However, this sketch can be firmly attributed to Boucher on stylistic grounds. The sinuous shapes of the figures, the blending of their faces into their elongated and graceful bodies recall those found in a group of early drawings executed as projects for engraved illustrations in Father Gabriel Daniel's *Histoire de France* (Ruch 1964; New York/Detroit/Paris 1986–87, pp. 42–43, figs. 2–9). A. Laing has proven that these illustrations appeared first in 1729 and were begun probably around 1727, on the eve of Boucher's departure for Italy. A similar date should be proposed for our sketch.

It is not known if this small work was developed into a larger composition. Yet the fact that several versions exist—apparently all autograph—is indicative of its success and of the growing fame of the artist prior to his stay in Italy.

J. P. M.

Carle VANLOO

(Nice 1705–Paris 1765)

orn into a family of painters, Carle Vanloo was first trained under his brother Jean-Baptiste, and while with him in Rome, under Benedetto Luti and Pierre Legros. In Paris by 1720, Vanloo obtained the Prix-de-Rome in 1724, but reached Rome only in 1728. He spent three years there executing a number of works, among them, the ceiling fresco for the Church of San Isidoro. He subsequently settled in Turin, working at Stupinigi and for the Royal Palace. Back in Paris in 1734, he became an Academician in 1735 and obtained important commissions from the Church (seven paintings for the choir of Notre-Dame-des-Victoires, 1746–55). He was made governor of the Ecole des Elèves Protégés in 1749, rector of the Académie in 1754, Premier Peintre du Roi in 1762, and director of the Académie in 1763. Vanloo enjoyed enormous success throughout the continent. Grimm called him "the first painter of Europe." Although sometimes critical of his compositions (see cat no. 19), Madame de Pompadour and the French court lavished their patronage upon the artist.

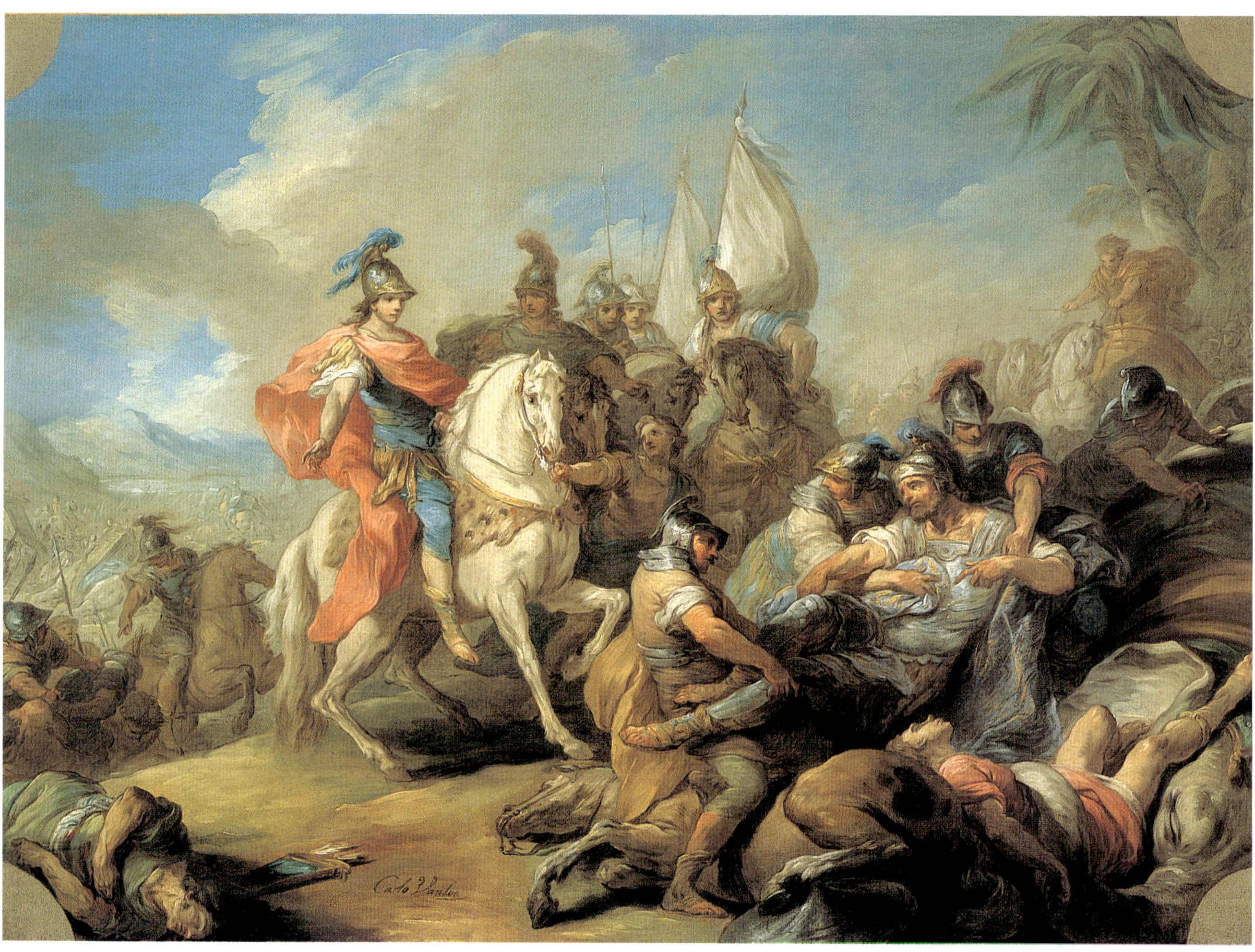

18   Carle VANLOO
The Victory of Alexander over Porus,
c. 1738
Alexandre vainqueur de Porus
Oil on canvas
25 ⅞ × 36" (65.7 × 91.4 cm)
Signed lower left: *Carlo Vanloo*

Provenance: H. D. Molesworth, London.

Exhibitions: London 1968, no. 447;
Albuquerque 1980, no. 65.

Bibliography: Rosenberg 1969, p. 99;
Nice/Clermont/Ferrand/Nancy 1977, no.
64; New York/New Orleans/Columbus
1986–87, p. 139, no. 126.

The legend of Alexander the Great's victory over Porus, the Indian king who resisted Alexander's invasion of the Punjab, illustrates the magnanimity of the Macedonian monarch. Impressed by his adversary's courage, Alexander chose him as ruler of the region and deputy to the Greek government. Such a heroic tale was particularly fitting for a royal commission. The story was suggested to François Lemoyne in 1736 by the agents of Philip V of Spain as a subject suitable for the decoration of the throne room at La Granja. After Lemoyne's suicide in 1737, the commission was given to Carle Vanloo, considered by the Marquis de la Miña, Spanish Ambassador to France, to be the best history painter at the time. The painting was to be part of a group of eight subjects illustrating the life of Alexander. Vanloo was the only French artist of the group, which included Conca, Creti, Masucci, Parodi, Pittoni, Solimena, and Trevisani. The work he produced for this commission suffered a fate not unique in the history of Vanloo's work (see the next entry): it was destroyed by the artist, after its exhibition at the Salon of 1738. A second version, begun immediately thereafter, was exhibited at the Salon of 1739 and dispatched to Spain in 1741. It is now at San Lorenzo, in the Escorial.

That second version shows considerable differences with the large study presented here, which might be closer to the earlier version. The entire right part of the composition has been altered, and in the final version, the figures are larger and closer to the picture plane, intensifying the dramatic encounter between the two main protagonists of the story.

The choice by La Miña of Vanloo seems justified in the wake of Lemoyne's death, however, another strong contender could have been Charles-Joseph Natoire, whose heroic cycle devoted to the Life of Clovis, painted between 1735 and 1738 for Philibert Orry's Château of La Chapelle-Godefroy, predates Vanloo's work for La Granja. One of Natoire's paintings for that cycle, *The Battle of Tolbiac* (1735; Tours, Musée des Beaux-Arts), seems to have influenced not only Vanloo's composition of this subject, but also its light and clear colors.

J. P. M.

19 Carle VANLOO
The Three Graces, c. 1763
Les Trois Graces
Oil on canvas
23 × 18 ⅛" (58.4 × 46.0 cm)

Provenance: Chevalier Damery; his sale, Paris, 26–27 Brumaire, An XII (November 18–19, 1803), no. 22; Marquis de Salamanca (a seal bearing the arms of that family is on the stretcher).

Exhibitions: Houston 1973–75, no. 84.

Bibliography: L. Réau 1938, p. 91, no. 22 (engraving); Lastic 1974, pp. 194, 195–96, 197, reprod. p. 197, fig. 1; Nice/Clermont/Ferrand/Nancy 1977, no. 177; Paris 1984–85, p. 376, under no. 111; New York/New Orleans/Columbus 1986–87, p. 139, no. 125.

Engravings: (A) In reverse by J. J. Pasquier (1718–1785). The engraving is dedicated to Prince Charles de Salm-Salm, and bears the indication that it is "Tiré du Cabinet de M. de Damery." (B) In the same direction as the painting but with the addition of a garland of flowers at the top, by Françoise-Héléonore Hemery, 1772.

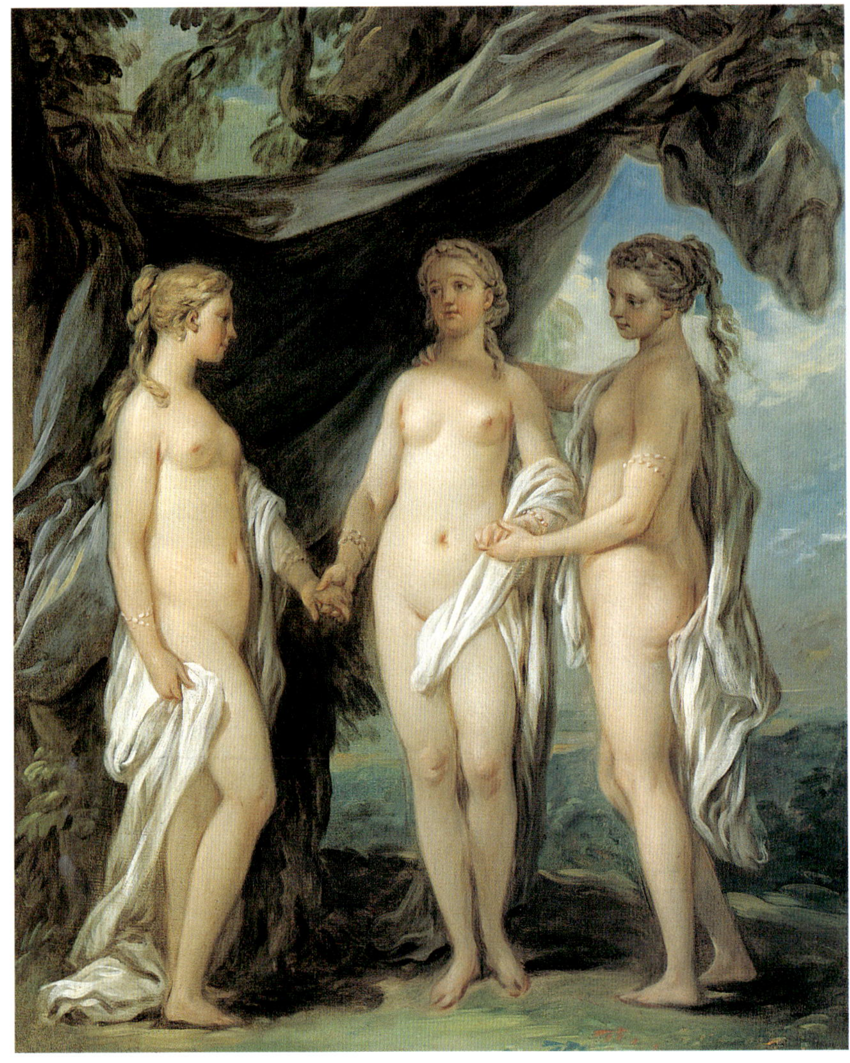

The subject of *The Three Graces* was suggested to Vanloo in 1761 by Pierre-Michel Hennin, a French diplomat in Warsaw (Chennevières 1886, pp. 101–05, 122–25). The tragic fate of that composition is well known. In spite of its success with the amateurs, the work failed to impress Madame de Pompadour, according to Bachaumont (1763). The Marquise, in fact, ridiculed Vanloo's work by saying, "ça des Grâces, ça des Grâces" (You call those Graces!). Mortified, the artist tore up his canvas at the closing of the exhibition. The composition shown at the 1763 Salon is therefore known today only through the descriptions written at the time—notably by Diderot. He described the figures thus: "The one to the right of the viewer is seen from the back, the one in the middle faces him, the third is seen in profile. A *putto* on the tip of his toe, set between the two last mentioned and turning his back to the viewer, winds a garland that goes over the buttocks of the one seen from the back and hides the natural parts of the one seen frontally. . . [These Graces] are heavy, oh so heavy." The description does not fit the composition of the painting presented here, and the arrangement of the figures is closer in fact to the second version of the subject, which Vanloo exhibited at the Salon of 1765. (This later painting, executed to fulfill the wish of the original commissioner of the first version—the Countess Mnizsech, daughter of Count Bruehl—to own a painting of the subject, is now in the Château of Chenonceaux.) However, the heavy features of the Graces and the green tonality of the painting—also disliked by Diderot—clearly relate this painting to the first version of Vanloo's *Three Graces*.

G. de Lastic (1974) suggested cautiously that this painting preceded all other versions of the subject. Known through its engravings, it achieved a fame of its own. A Sèvres vase attributed to Ch.-N. Dodin in the Huntington Collection (San Marino, California; see Wark 1962, p. 100, reprod. p. 57, no. 106) and a cup, also by Dodin (Paris, private collection), mentioned by G. de Lastic, reproduce its composition exactly.

J. P. M.

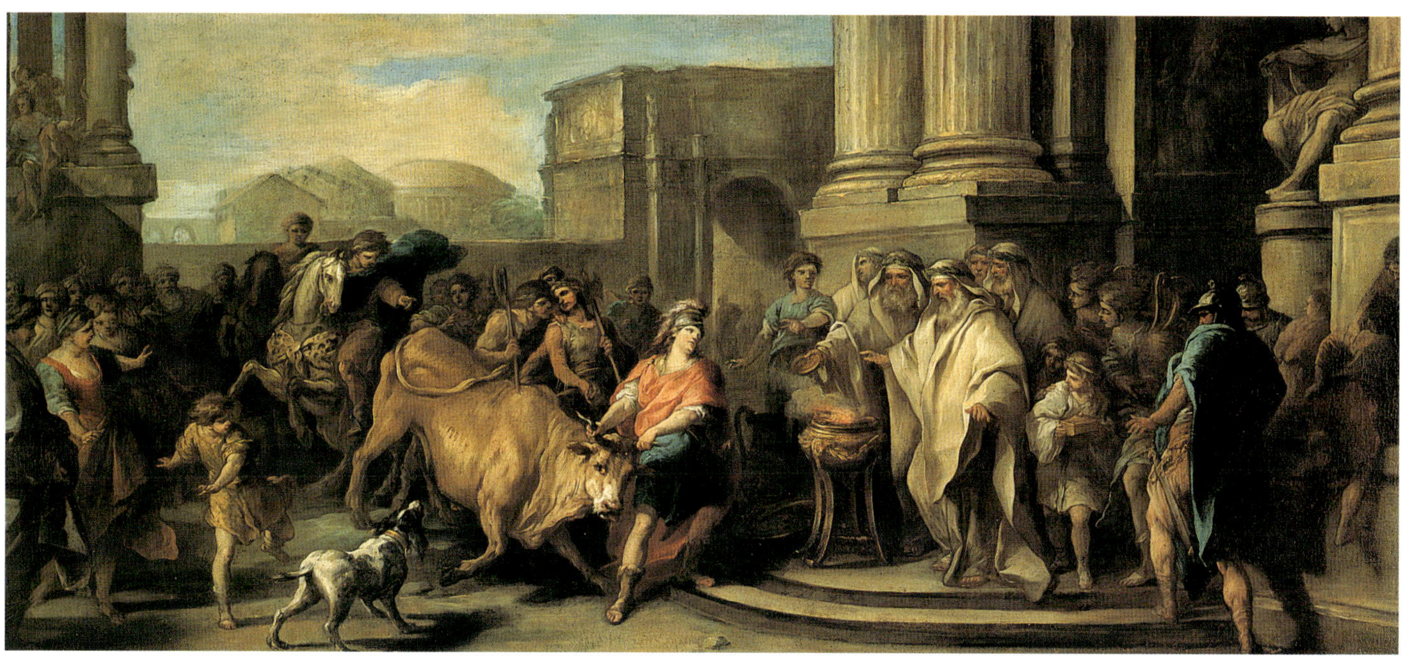

20   Carle VANLOO
Theseus Taming the Bull of Marathon,
n.d.
Thésée domptant le taureau de Marathon
Oil on canvas
26 × 58" (66.0 × 147.3 cm)

Exhibitions: Houston 1973–75, no. 83.

Bibliography: Nice/Clermont/Ferrand/
Nancy 1977, no. 33; New York/New Or-
leans/Columbus 1986–87, p. 139, no. 127.

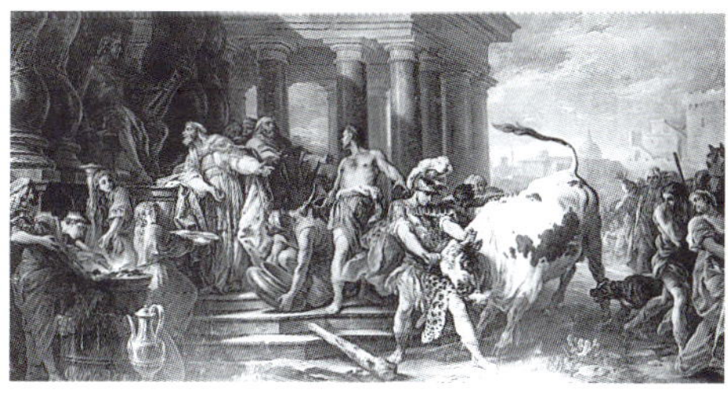

Fig. 3. Carle VANLOO. *Theseus Taming
the Bull of Marathon* (Thésée domptant
le taureau de Marathon), c. 1731–34. Oil
on canvas. Musée des Beaux-Arts, Nice

Marie-Catherine Sahut lists five versions of this seldom represented episode of the
life of Theseus (Plutarch, I, 14). The five compositions adopt the same elongated format, but show considerable differences in the repartition of figures, their movements,
and dispositions.

In his *Life of Theseus*, Plutarch compares the hero to his relative, Hercules. Both
are avengers: "He set forth with a design to do injury to nobody, but to repel and to
revenge himself on all those that should offer any." Having set Theseus's character,
Plutarch lists his deeds: "Longing to be in action, and desirous to make himself popular, [he] left Athens to fight with the bull of Marathon, which did no small mischief to
the inhabitants of Tetrapolis." Vanloo represented the following episode: "Having over-
come [the bull], he brought it alive in triumph to the city, and afterward sacrificed it
to the Delphinian Apollo" (Plutarch, pp. 6, 9).

A large painting (113 x 222 cm) of the same subject in the Musée des Beaux-
Arts, Besançon, figured in 1787 in the Bandeville sale; in the catalogue it is described
as having been painted in Turin for Lorenzo (or Laurent) Somis, brother-in-law of
the painter. This would put the painting between 1731 and 1734, when the painter is
known to have been in that city. The same sale catalogue mentions that the painter
was called to Paris around 1744 "pour peindre le grand Tableau qui a été exposé au
Sallon du Louvre." This is the gigantic canvas (3.50 x 7.04 m, and somewhat reduced!)
in the Musée des Beaux-Arts in Nice (fig. 3), which served as a cartoon for a Gobelins tapestry first woven between 1746 and 1749 (Tours, Musée des Beaux-Arts), and
later between 1773 and 1779 (Stockholm, Royal Castle), and 1779 and 1787 (Paris,
Mobilier National). In 1744, Vanloo had received a commission for seven cartoons
illustrating the life of Theseus, but only this composition was delivered and woven.

While it is easy to recognize the smaller oblong version of the Nice composition
in the Pushkin Museum, Moscow (formerly Yossoupof collection), as its reduction
(rather than its sketch), it is harder to situate our painting and another sketch (Brussels, private collection; Nice/Clermont/Ferrand/Nancy 1977, no. 34) in the creative
process of the artist. Sahut argues that both sketches are stylistically early and could
have been preparatory to the Besançon picture.

J. P. M.

Louis-Michel VANLOO

(Toulon 1707–Paris 1771)

Louis-Michel Vanloo studied with his father, Jean-Baptiste, in Turin, Rome, and Paris. He won the Prix-de-Rome in 1725 and was in Rome with his brother, François, and his uncle, Carle, from 1727 until 1732. He was elected to the Académie in 1733 and became associate professor in 1735. His career in France was cut short by his appointment as court painter to Philip V of Spain. In 1751, he co-founded the Academia de San Fernando. Returning to France in 1753, he obtained royal commissions. In 1765, he succeeded his uncle as director of the Ecole des Elèves Protégés.

21   Louis-Michel VANLOO
Portrait of Louis XV, n.d.
Portrait de Louis XV
Oil on canvas
10 ⅛ × 7 ½" (25.7 × 19.1 cm)

Exhibitions: Albuquerque 1980, no. 69.

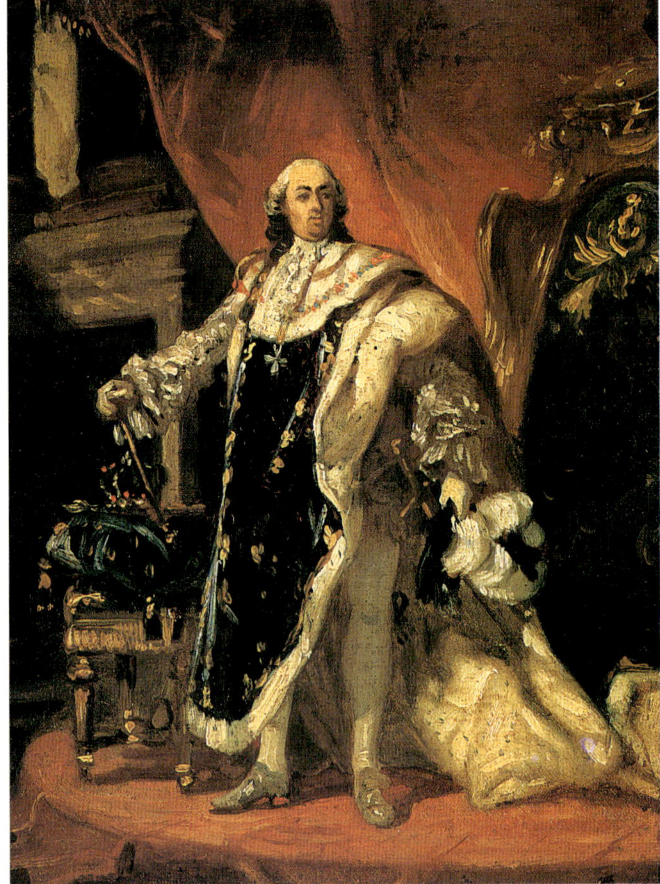

A large version of Louis-Michel Vanloo's portrait of Louis XV was exhibited at the 1761 Salon. Saint-Aubin drew it in his copy of the Salon *livret*, and Diderot commented that it was "beau, bien peint," but he criticized the ermine around the neck and the type of costume, which he found more suited to a "president de parlement," a high dignitary, than to the King himself (Diderot 1967, p. 31). The criticism is hardly valid, as Louis XV is shown wearing the official *manteau du sacre*, or coronation cape, the appearance of which neither the King nor the painter could alter. Vanloo's finished painting (London, Wallace Collection) was repeated in several versions (probably with the help of studio assistants).

The composition is traditional and shows little change from Hyacinthe Rigaud's portrait of Louis XIV at the Louvre, a work that had established once and for all the style for royal French portraiture. Only slightly humanized (the King is holding his hat), Vanloo's portrait provided in turn a model for the portraits of later monarchs: it was adapted by Antoine-François Callet for his portraits of Louis XVI, and was the prototype David returned to in 1807 for an official portrait of Napoleon after the Emperor had rejected a bolder composition intended for Genoa (see Paris 1989–90, pp. 433–36).

J. P. M.

(Paris 1711–Paris 1781)

*B*orn into a family of painters, Noël Hallé —who was also the brother-in-law of Restout (q.v.) —was tutored by his relatives. Winner of the Prix-de-Rome in 1736, he left for Rome in 1737 and remained there for seven years. Hallé became Academician in 1748 and produced numerous decorative works for the Crown. His particular relationship with the art of tapestry (he remained in Rome three years beyond the usual time in order to execute cartoons after Raphael's works in the Stanze) led him not only to create original cartoons for the Gobelins, but also to become the overseer of the manufactory in 1771. His taste for large, even gigantic, compositions did not prevent him from painting smaller genre pieces and portraits. His activity as a religious painter should also be taken into consideration to fully account for the breadth of his talent.

22 Noël HALLE
Saint Anne Revealing to the Virgin the Prophecy of Isaiah, c. 1749
Sainte Anne révélant à la Vierge la prophétie d'Isaïe
Oil on canvas
24 ⅝ × 16 ¼" (62.5 × 41.3 cm)

Exhibitions: Albuquerque 1980, no. 32; Rochester/New Brunswick/Atlanta 1987–88, no. 27.

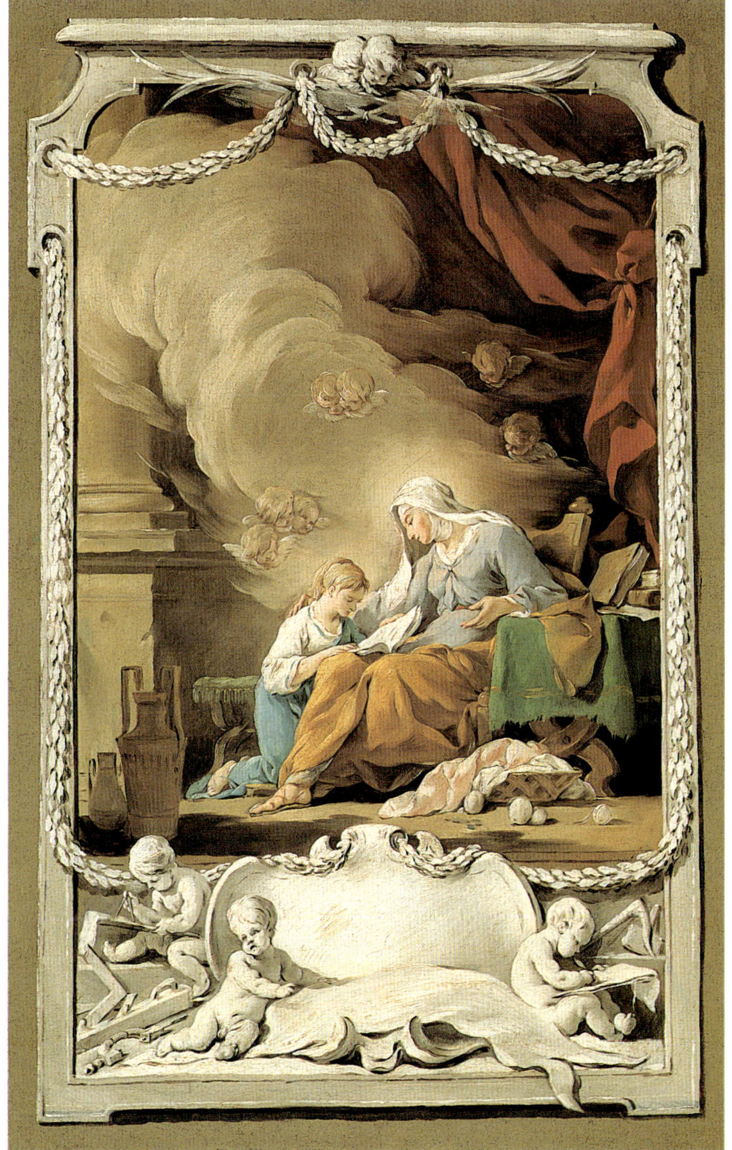

This ornate sketch, with its reserved cartouche and elaborate painted frame surrounding the central image, is clearly a highly finished study for an engraving. The iconography of the lower tier, representing *putti* holding set-squares and other carpentry tools, is surprising only if one believes this image to represent the traditional Education of the Virgin, a theme common in Christian iconography, and which Fragonard, among other artists in the eighteenth century, treated with particular success

(Cuzin 1988, nos. 273–75). It is, however, easily understood by virtue of the fact that the composition was commissioned by the Guild of Master Carpenters of Paris and its Surroundings, the seat of which was in the Church of the Carmelite Fathers of the Billettes. The Guild's devotion to Saint Anne can be explained. Saint Anne, the mother of the Virgin, not only taught Mary the virtues and charity, but also how to read in the Holy Scriptures the prophecy of her own destiny as the Mother of God. Thus, the Virgin being the first "living" tabernacle, it was natural for the carpenters, who counted among their functions the making of wooden tabernacles, to select as an appropriate image of devotion this revelation to the Virgin Mary. Hallé's composition, bearing in the garlands the names of the guild members, was first engraved by Etienne Fessard in 1749 (see Gaston 1909, p. 10, no. 28; Paris 1991–92, pp. 172–73, no. 116). His plate was reissued, still under the auspices of the Guild, in 1760 (Paris 1991–92, p. 174, no. 117) and again in 1766 (ibid., no. 118).

J. P. M.

Unknown Artist

23   Unknown artist
Scene from Roman History, n.d.
Scène de l'histoire romaine
Oil on canvas
24 ⅞ × 18 3/4" (63.2 × 47.6)

Exhibitions: Houston 1973 75
(attributed to Dumont le Romain).

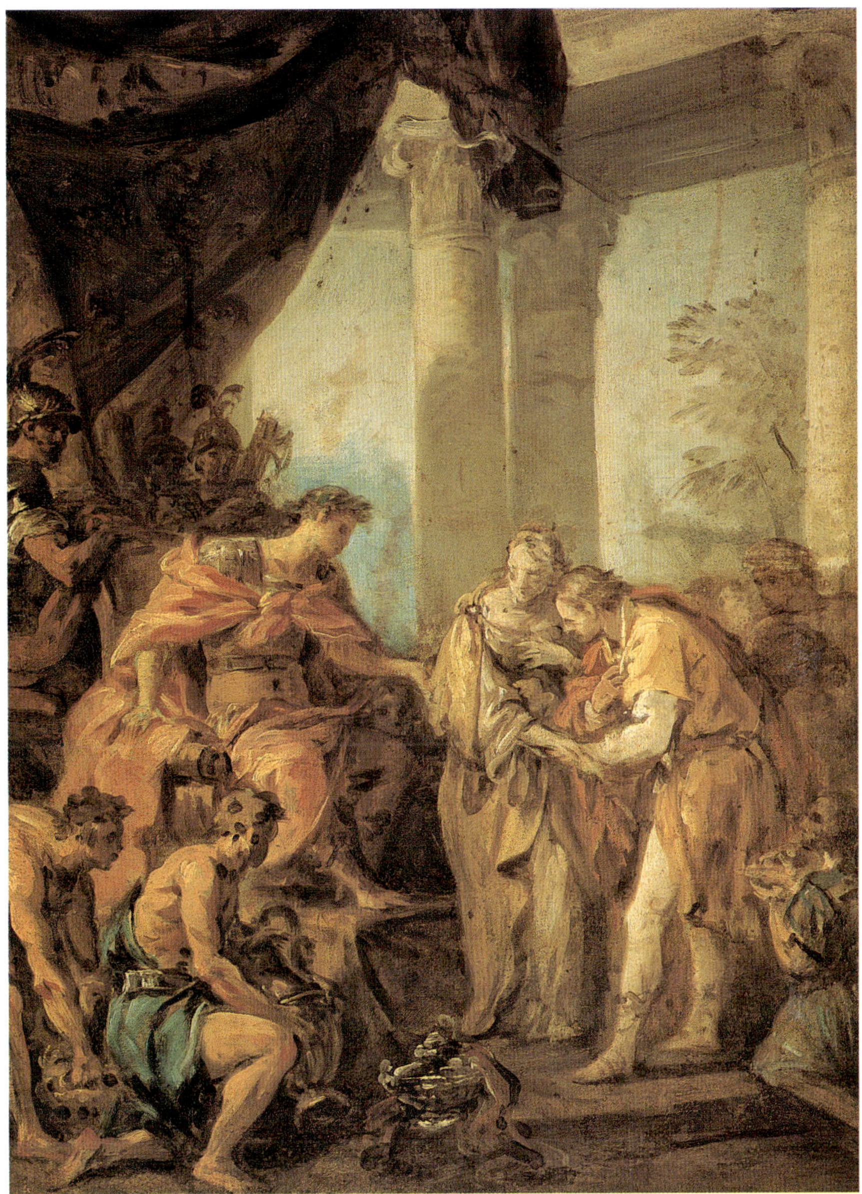

The attribution to Dumont le Romain suggested in 1973 cannot be maintained.
Unfortunately, however, it is impossible to put forward another name for this lightly
executed sketch. As has been noted before, the subtle coloring of the work suggests
an artist aware of Venetian models.

J. P. M..

24 Unknown artist
Funerary Allegory, n.d.
Allégorie funeraire
Oil on canvas
23 ⅛ × 16 ⅞" (58.7 × 42.9 cm)

Exhibitions: Houston 1973–75,
no. 68 (attributed to Jean-
François Parrocel).

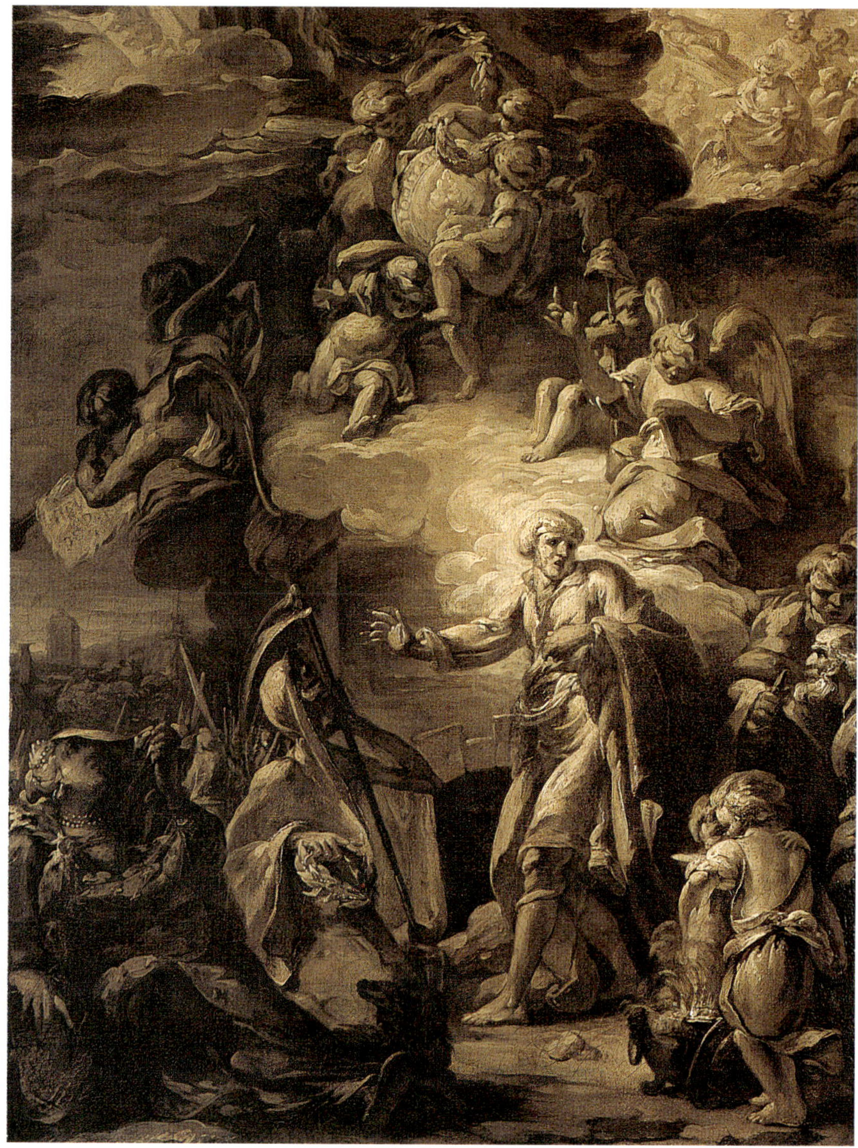

Probably a study for an engraving, this monochrome sketch has not yet been convincingly attributed (nor has the meaning of the allegory—which seems to include an
element of caricature—been properly deciphered). Some details, such as the children
in the right foreground, recall Noël Hallé; others, such as the old man seen in profile
to the right, recall Doyen. The figure on the left covering her head suggests Gamelin.
It is, however, more likely that the author of this work was a provincial artist, perhaps from the south of France.

J.P.M.

<h1 style="text-align:center">Jean-Baptiste-Marie PIERRE</h1>

(Paris 1714–Paris 1789)

A pupil of Charles-Joseph Natoire, Pierre obtained the Prix-de-Rome in 1734. From 1735 until 1740, he studied in Rome, drawing lessons from Raphael, the Bolognese, and also from the Bamboccianti. Upon his return to France, he produced small genre works that betrayed these influences. It was, however, in the more official history painting that Pierre was to distinguish himself. Academician in 1742, Pierre led a brilliant official career. In 1748, he was made professor at the Académie. Enjoying at first the protection of the Duke of Orléans, Pierre became in 1752 his Premier Peintre before becoming in 1770 — upon Boucher's death — Premier Peintre du Roi and director of the Académie, a position he held in perpetuity from 1778. In spite of the criticism of Diderot, who may have disliked the man even more than the works, Pierre remains one of the greatest figures of his generation.

25 Jean-Baptiste-Marie PIERRE
Scene from Ancient History (?), n.d.
Scène de l'histoire ancienne (?)
Oil on canvas
11 ⅛ × 9 ⅝" (28.3 × 24.4 cm)

Exhibitions: Houston 1973–75, no. 70.

Bibliography: New York/New Orleans/Columbus 1986–87, p. 141, no. 146.

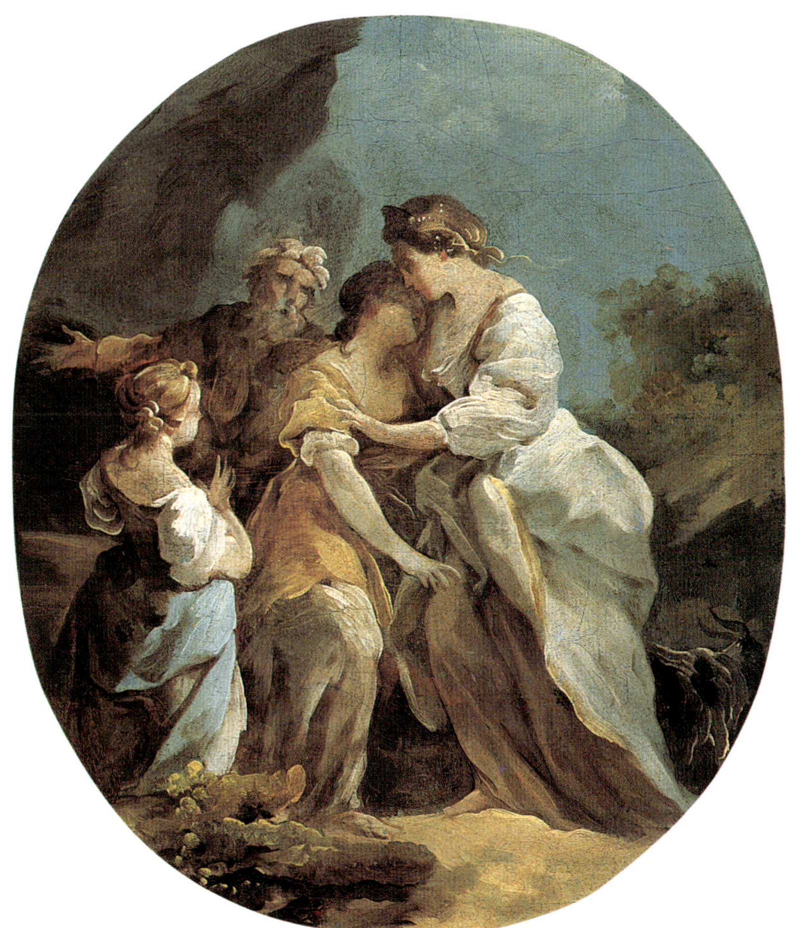

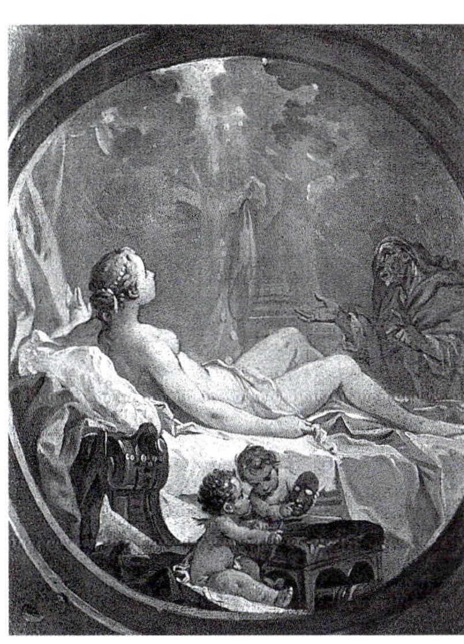

Fig. 4. Jean-Baptiste-Marie PIERRE. ***Danae*** (Danaë), n.d. Oil on canvas. The Museum of Foreign Art Sinebrychoff, Helsinki. Photo: Giraudon.

The fine features of the figures, with their pointed noses and elongated fingertips, are sufficient to designate this small painting as a typical work of Jean-Baptiste-Marie Pierre. It is impossible for this author to decipher whether its subject is ancient or biblical history, mythology, or, as has been suggested recently by Peter Walch, a scene from a contemporary novel. Arguments can be brought forward for each of these genres.

The oval format, although not rare, is less frequent in Pierre's oeuvre than in that of his rival, Boucher. A painting representing Danae, traditionally attributed to Boucher but definitely by Pierre (fig. 4), can be compared to our sketch not only because of its oval format, but also because of such details as the face of Danae, close to that of the young girl to the left in our composition.

J.P.M.

Nicolas-Blaise LESUEUR

(Paris 1716–Berlin 1785)

Son of the woodcut engraver Nicolas-Lesueur and pupil of Jean-Baptiste Vanloo, Nicolas-Blaise Lesueur twice won the second-place Prix-de-Rome, but never went to Italy on a scholarship. His entire career transpired in Berlin. In 1751, he became professor at the Berlin Academy, of which he was the director from 1756 until his death. He participated in the decoration of projects such as the Chinese Pavilion at Potsdam and provided cartoons for the Berlin Tapestry Manufactory.

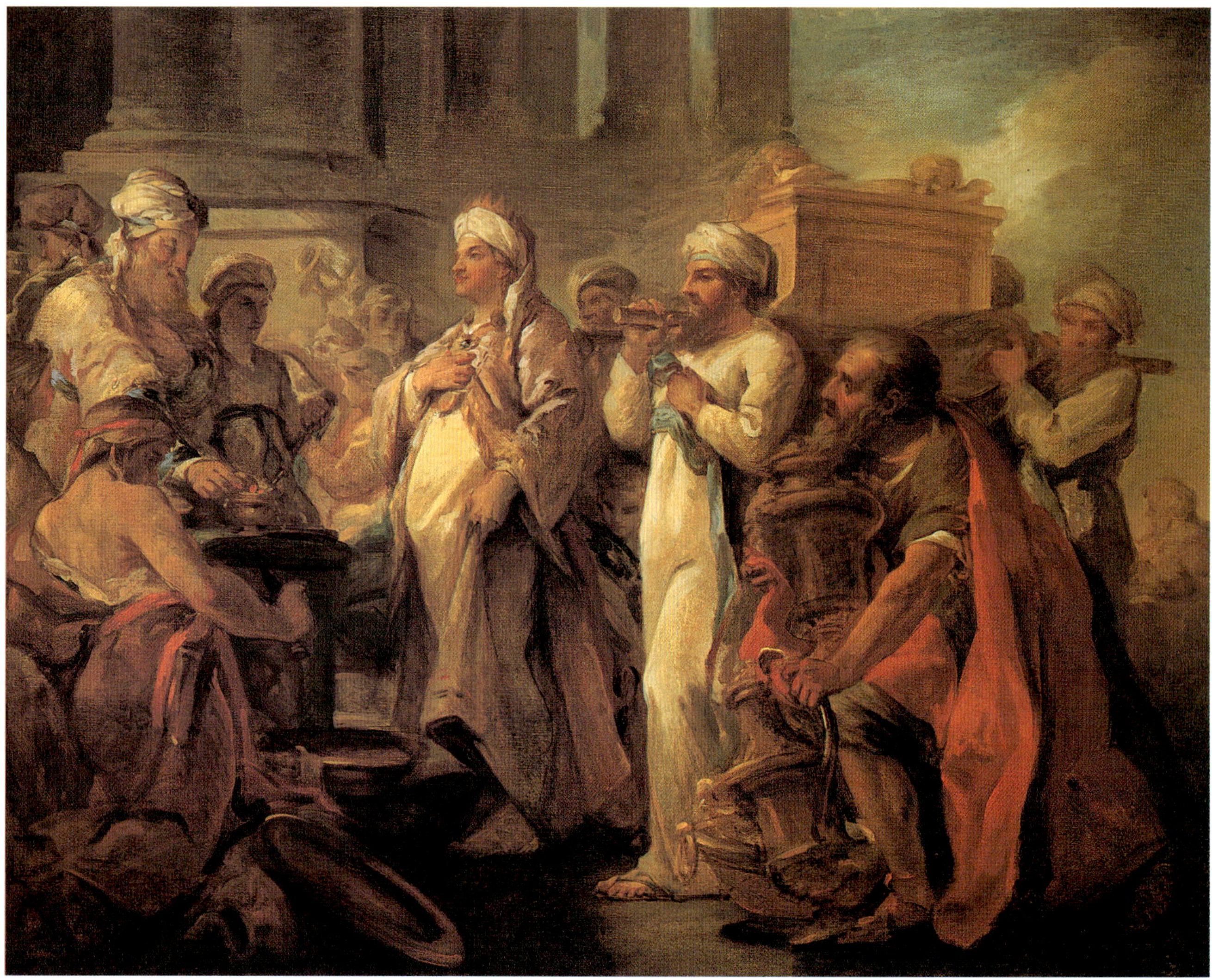

26 Nicolas-Blaise LESUEUR
Solomon Ushering the Ark into the Temple, n.d.
Salomon portant l'Arche à l'intérieur du temple
Oil on canvas
28 ¾ × 36" (73.0 × 91.4 cm)

Perhaps because of his failure to win the Prix-de-Rome itself, which would have allowed him to complete his studies in Italy and embark on the regular curriculum of French artists, Nicolas-Blaise Lesueur left France in 1748. He left in the company of Amédée Vanloo and settled in Berlin, where he successively taught and became director of the Academy. The low esteem in which the painter was held is reflected in the cruel judgment of Mariette, who wrote that in Berlin "he did much better for himself than he would have in Paris." His production in Germany seems to have included a large amount of decorative work, stage designs, and cartoons for tapestries (*Story of Psyche*; Potsdam, Neues Palais). His painting oeuvre remains, however, to be reconstructed. Only his two entries for the Prix-de-Rome competitions are known: that of 1739, *King Hezekiah Commanding the Brazen Serpent to Be Destroyed*, shown in 1977 at the Heim Gallery, London (London 1977, no. 18); and the 1745 entry, now at the Musée des Beaux-Arts, Caen, for which this is a study without significant differences.

J.P.M.

Joseph-Marie VIEN

(Montpellier 1716–Paris 1809)

Following his early apprenticeship with local artists in his hometown, Vien settled in Paris in 1740. He studied with Charles-Joseph Natoire, and in 1743 won the Prix-de-Rome. From 1744 until 1750, he studied at the French Academy in Rome (directed at the time by Jean-François de Troy). In Rome, Vien adopted a powerful style marked by his interest in the Baroque tradition. Upon his return to France in 1750, he was received at the Académie in 1754. In Paris, and particularly after his famous *Love's Seller* (1763), Vien became the principal exponent of the "Neo-Greek" style. Madame du Barry preferred him to Fragonard for the decoration of her residence at Louveciennes. Vien influenced French art through his teachings at the Académie, and later at the French Academy in Rome, which he directed from 1775 until 1781. The most influential artist of his time, Vien was made a member of the Senate by Napoleon in 1799. His reputation was such that he was buried at the Panthéon.

27 Joseph-Marie VIEN
Venus Emerging from the Sea,
c. 1754–1755
Venus sortant de la mer
Oil on canvas
12 ¾ × 16 ¼" (32.4 × 41.3 cm)
Inscribed on the back: *Esquisse de M. Vien faite à Rome*

Provenance: The artist; his sale, Paris, 1809, no. 93; Sotheby's, London, July 16, 1980, no. 228.

Bibliography: Paillet 1809, p. 19, no. 93; Gaethgens/Lugand 1988, p. 155, no. 112 (reprod.).

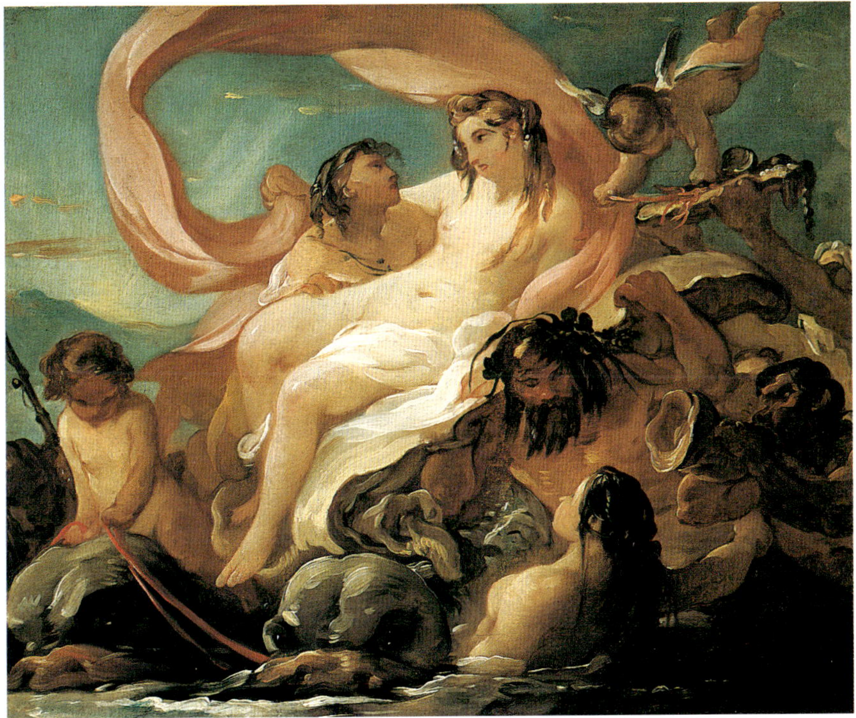

This painting has been related by Gaethgens and Lugand to the large composition executed by Vien, probably on commission from the Tsarina Elizabeth, for Tsarskoye-Selo. That painting, which was damaged during World War II and substantially restored, had been exhibited without much success at the 1755 Salon. The composition of this sketch shows considerable differences from the final work (also known by a drawing at the Albertina, Vienna; Gaethgens/Lugand D.65) and reflects more closely a composition by Pierre (Caen, Musée des Beaux-Arts; inv. 73.1.1), sometimes associated with the painting of this subject that Pierre exhibited at the 1746 Salon (*Revue du Louvre*, 1976, nos. 5–6; reprod. p. 360).

    Gaethgens and Lugand list another sketch of the same subject (p. 111), now lost, which also figured in the sale of the artist's studio in 1809.

    The inscription on the back of the painting, with its misleading information (Vien lived in Rome from 1744 until 1750, and from 1775 until 1781), is a later addition.

J. P. M.

Jacques-Antoine BEAUFORT

(Paris 1721–Rueil 1784)

erhaps because of his lack of success at the Salons, where he exhibited regularly from 1767 until 1783, very little is known of Beaufort's life. He became *agréé* in 1766 and an Academician in 1771. He participated in the decoration of the chapel of the Ecole Militaire in Paris. His most famous composition—due to its influence on J.-L. David—is the one included in this exhibition.

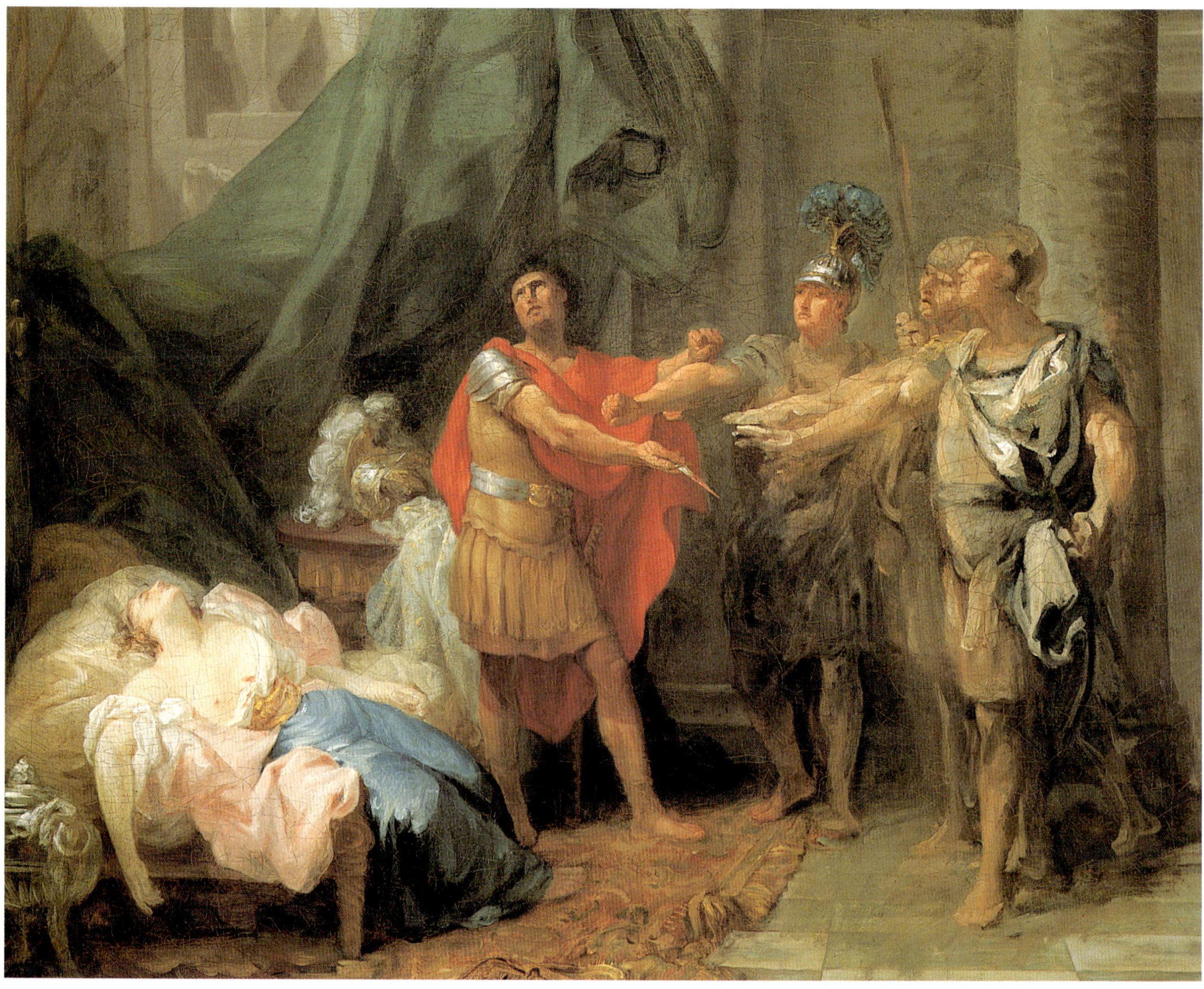

28   Jacques-Antoine BEAUFORT
The Oath of Brutus, c. 1771
Le Serment de Brutus
Oil on canvas
25 ⅞ × 31 ⅝" (65.7 × 80.3 cm)

Provenance: Barnett Hollander, London.

Exhibitions: Toledo/Chicago/Ottawa
1975–76, no. 5; Albuquerque 1980, no. 2;
Rochester/New Brunswick/Atlanta 1987–
88, no. 1.

Bibliography: Dupont de Nemours
(1779; cited in Seznec/Diderot 1967, p.
146); Rosenblum 1961, p. 12 (attributed
to an unknown artist); Seznec/Diderot
1967, pp. 145–46, 203-04, fig. 83 (attributed to Beaufort); Lee 1969, pp. 360 ff.;
Rosenblum 1970, pp. 269–75 (attributed
to an unknown artist); London 1972,
under no. 20; Rosenberg/Schnapper 1970,
p. 760; Brookner 1980, p. 77, fig. 38 (as
possibly by J.-L. David).

It reveals something about the history of taste for official eighteenth-century French painting that this sketch achieved notoriety before the rediscovery of the finished composition Beaufort exhibited at the Salon of 1771. Already in 1779, Dupont de Nemours wrote in his commentary of that year's Salon, "We should not forget that we have from his hand a very good sketch representing the Deliberation of Brutus and Collatinus following Lucretia's death" (cited in Seznec/Diderot 1967, p. 146). However, the author may have been referring to a more finished sketch, published by Rosenberg and Schnapper in 1970 and at that time in the collection of André Marie in Rouen.

In any case, both sketches and the Salon painting fell into oblivion, emerging only recently. The correct attribution to Beaufort of the sketch in this exhibition was made by Seznec, who recognized it from the descriptions of the 1771 Salon picture. The latter, in the Musée Muncipal, Nevers, was published by Rosenblum in 1970. That author, finding the discrepancies between the Salon picture and the sketch too great, believed the sketch to be by another artist working after Beaufort. Further doubts were expressed by Anita Brookner (1980, p. 77), who suggested that it might be by David himself. Rosenberg and Schnapper again correctly reattributed our sketch to Beaufort on the basis of their discovery of the more finished sketch in Rouen. In that sketch, as in the Nevers picture, Brutus brandishes, rather than extends at arm length, the knife Lucretia had used to kill herself, a detail suggesting that the Rouen sketch is closer in date to the Nevers picture. In his entry on the painting (Albuquerque 1980, no. 2), Walch notes that a third sketch for the same composition had appeared on the London art market in 1979 (London 1979, no. 5). Its whereabouts today are unknown.

The importance of this composition, both in terms of its antecedents and its influence, has been well established. Beaufort derived his composition from Gavin Hamilton's painting of the same subject, known to him probably through its engraving by Domenico Cunego published in 1768. In turn, David, well aware of Beaufort's composition, remembered it not only for his own *Oath of the Horatii* (1784) but also in studies intended for *The Tennis Court Oath* (Paris 1989–90, p. 248).

J. P. M.

Jean-Baptiste DESHAYS

(Rouen 1721–Paris 1765)

The son of a painter, Deshays studied under a succession of artists, but Jean Restout and François Boucher were his most influential teachers. Deshays won the Prix-de-Rome in 1751 and traveled to Italy in 1754, where he studied the work of the Caracci, Rubens, and other masters of the Baroque. In or around 1758, he returned to Paris and married the daughter of Boucher. Deshays was *agréé* at the Académie in 1759, and made a highly successful debut at the Salon of that year exhibiting *The Martyrdom of Saint Andrew* (Rouen). He was named associate professor at the Académie in 1760 and exhibited to great acclaim at the Salons of 1761 and 1763. Esteemed by Diderot for his dramatic treatments of religious subjects, Deshays died at the age of thirty-five, abruptly ending a promising career.

D.G.

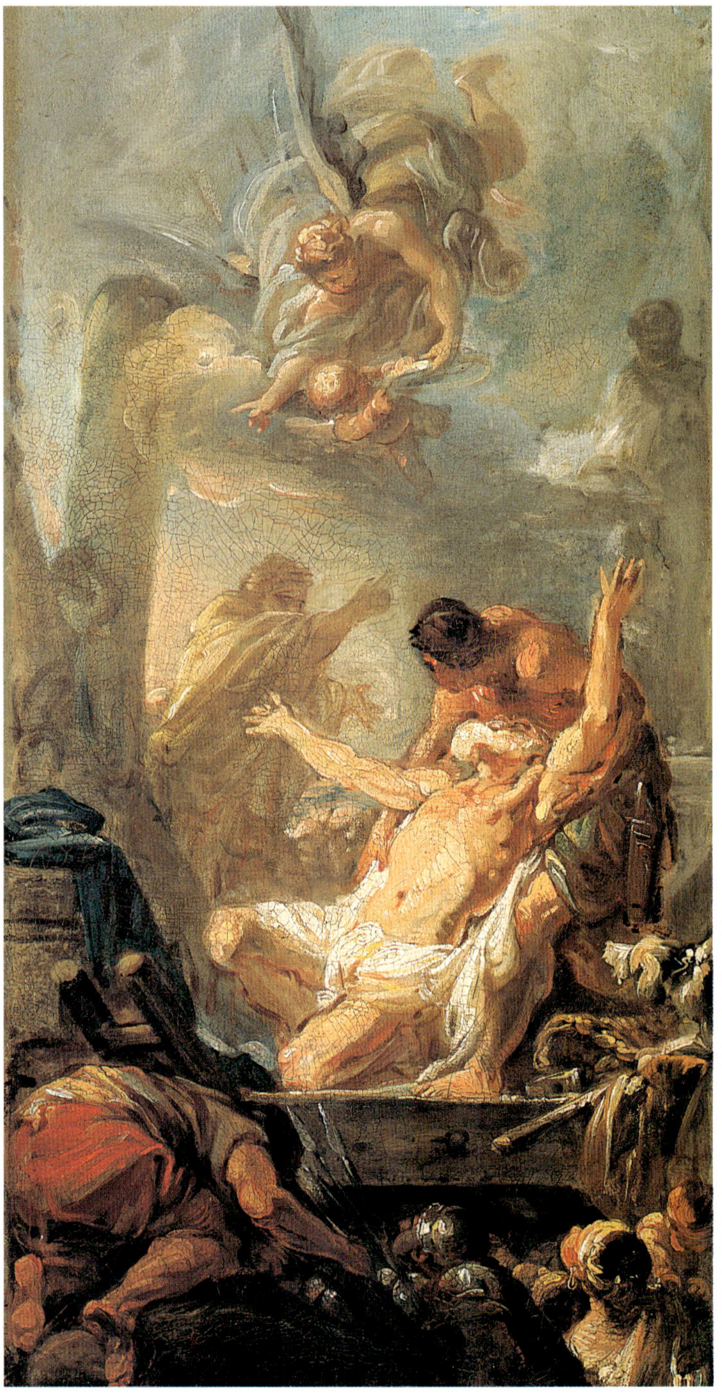

29 Jean-Baptiste DESHAYS
Scene from the Martyrdom of Saint Andrew, 1758
Scène du Martyre de Saint André
Oil on canvas
21 ⅜ × 11 ¾" (54.3 × 29.8 cm)

Exhibitions: Houston 1973–75, no. 10.

Among the several compositions based on the life of Saint Andrew executed by Deshays for the Church of Saint-André in Rouen (and now in the Musée des Beaux-Arts, Rouen), the one for which this is a preliminary study is particularly important. Executed immediately upon the artist's return from Italy, the work's monumental vigor betrays the influences Deshays had assimilated during his stay in Italy, the most obvious being Domenichino's and Mattia Preti's decorations based on the life of Saint Andrew, at S. Andrea della Valle. Deshays used the composition as his *morceau d'agrément* at the Académie. It was also exhibited at the 1759 Salon, where most critics praised its composition and colors. Only Diderot remarked laconically that he could not comment on a picture that was placed too high.

The oil sketch differs considerably from the large painting. In the latter, while the position of the saint is similar, he is being forcibly asked to worship the statue of a pagan god. In the study, however, while a Roman magistrate points to a statue of an idol, the saint kneels in front of the cross to which he is about to be affixed. It is this version that was engraved by Philippe Parizeau in 1759.

Marc Sandoz published another, slightly different, sketch for the same composition (1951, [1960]), which he identified as lot 105 in Deshays's posthumous sale (and part of the Trouard sale in 1779). It is impossible to establish to which of the two studies that provenance belongs.

J. P. M.

30 Jean-Baptiste DESHAYS
Scene from "L'Astrée," c. 1763
Scène tirèe de *L'Astrée*
Oil on paper on canvas
12 ⅜ × 9 ¾" (31.4 × 24.8 cm)

Exhibitions: Houston 1973–75, no. 90
(attributed to Vincent).

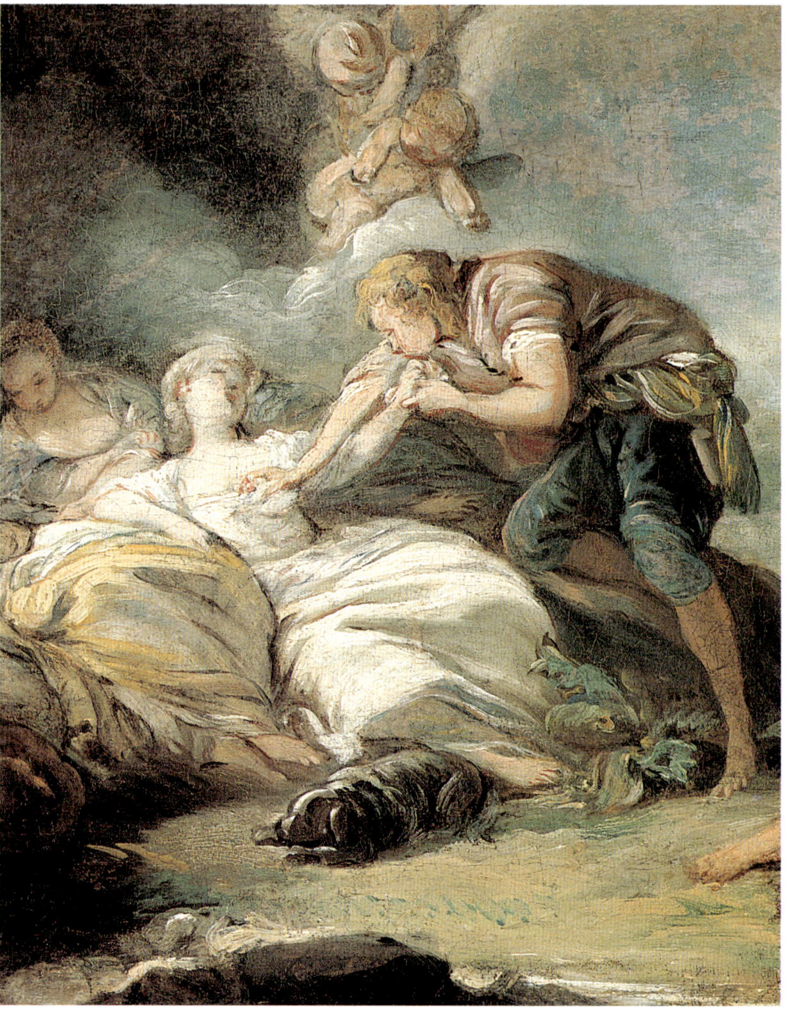

Tentatively attributed to Vincent at the time of its only previous exhibition, this spirited sketch is instead a partial study for *Diana and Astrée Asleep by the Fountain of Love*,
a large composition executed by Deshays as a cartoon for a Beauvais tapestry. The
subject of the tapestry is drawn from Honoré d'Ufré's *L'Astrée*, a novel first published
in 1610 and still widely read throughout the eighteenth century.

Deshays's contributions to the tapestry manufactory at Beauvais remain largely
unknown, although fairly well documented (Sandoz [Deshays] 1979, pp. 89, 131–36,
138–39). His main work there, a "suite" with subjects from Homer's *Iliad*, was woven
three times, in 1761, 1765, and 1771. Another project, based on *L'Astrée*, was intended
to include six pieces. The six cartoons may indeed have been delivered, but only three
were considered for manufacture, the remaining three having been judged "très mau-
vais" by André Charlemagne Charron, Oudry's successor at the head of the manufactory. Beside the cartoon already mentioned, the other two accepted subjects represented Celadon Emerging from the Waters and The Fountain of True Love.

It is known that two weavings were ordered, including the first one in 1763 for
the King. Sandoz mentions that the cartoons still existed in 1820, and that one oil
sketch representing an episode in the adventures of Celadon (*Celadon Giving a Letter
to Astrée, His Mistress*), possibly related to the series, was part of the posthumous
Deshays sale (lot 114).

The correct attribution of the present sketch is particularly important since Deshays's tapestry work has often been erroneously attributed to Boucher. Thus Juliette
Niclausse (1948), misidentifying somewhat the scene to which our sketch belongs as
"Les bergères endormies," gave its authorship to Boucher, a mistake often repeated
(see *L'Estampille*, no. 139, June 1986). Indeed while the translation into the tapestry
medium blurs the differences between Boucher and his gifted son-in-law, making the
confusion of authorship understandable, the style of this study belongs clearly to
Deshays.

J. P. M.

Gabriel-François DOYEN

(Paris 1726–Saint Petersburg 1806)

Doyen was the pupil of Carle Vanloo. He received the second-place Prix-de-Rome in 1748 and left for Rome in 1750, remaining there until 1756. He became an Academician in 1758. One of his better-known compositions was a Death of Virginia, executed for Parma, a court where he had sojourned on his way back to France from Italy. Greater success awaited him with his *Miracle des Ardents* (1767), a painting still *in situ* in the Church of Saint-Roch in Paris. Yet his brilliant style, influenced above all by Rubens, did not survive the changes of aesthetics promoted by D'Angiviller. No longer a recipient of great commissions, Doyen reluctantly left for Russia in 1792, and never returned to France.

31 Gabriel-François DOYEN
Nobility Offering the Imperial Russian Children to Minerva, n.d.
La Noblesse offrant les enfants russes à Minerve
Oil on canvas
37 ⅜ × 28" (94.9 × 71.1 cm)

Provenance: Delaroff collection (seal on stretcher).

Exhibitions: Houston 1973–75, no. 13.

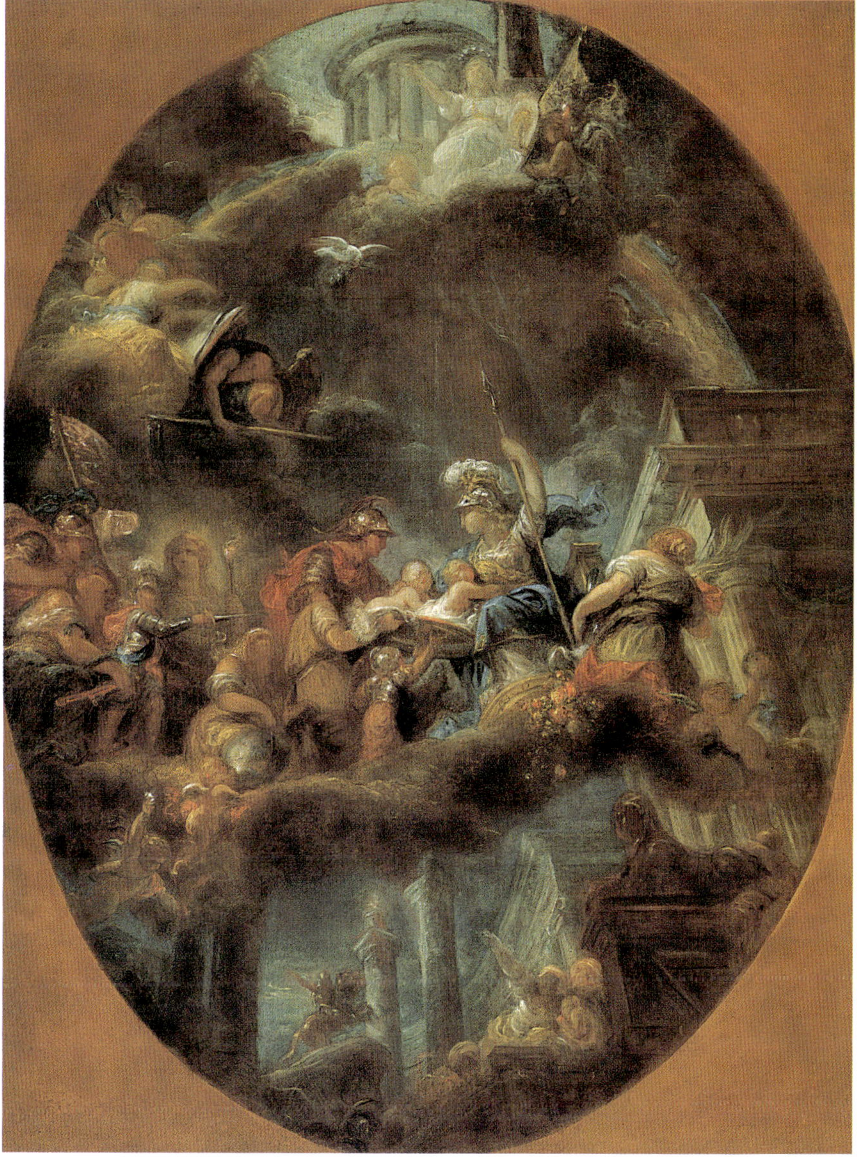

This large and important sketch is a study for a commission from the Grand Duke Paul for a ceiling painting intended to be placed in the Cabinet of the Empress Mother (Catherine II) at Saint Michael's Castle. According to Marc Sandoz (1975), who did not know this sketch, the commission was given to Doyen before 1796. Following the assassination of Paul I in 1801, the ceiling was transferred to the Hermitage. Since 1850, it has been displayed in the so-called Escalier du Conseil, now the main staircase of the museum. According to Reimers (1807), the painting was left unfinished by Doyen. In his description of the Hermitage, Souslov (1928) identified the subject as "the Russian nobility personified by a warrior presenting on a shield its children to Minerva (possibly an allusion to the grandsons of Catherine II: Alexander and Constantine); Abundance, personifying the wealth of the State, is at the children's feet; in the background one sees a fully armed heroic figure surrounded by History and Time, writing the annals of the State, and Renown announcing them to the world."

Doyen, who had left Paris for Russia in 1792—not without dutifully asking Louis XVI for his permission (one of the last such documents signed by the King)—in order to become First Painter to the Empress and associate director of the Imperial Academy for a period of three years, remained in Russia until his death fourteen years later, having been forced into permanent exile by the Revolutionary events in France. His warm reception in Russia, first by Catherine herself, and later by her son Paul I, who showed particular kindness to the aging French artist, must have compensated him for the flagging interest and harsh criticisms his works had received in France. His compositions had been judged by many to be confused and indecipherable, and his colors artificial. Indeed by the late 1770s, Parisian taste found Doyen's Rubenism —the last expression of that trend before the Romantic period—insufferable. In Russia, however, his style was still largely acceptable and was in fact particularly appropriate to Paul I's conservative taste.

Sandoz has tentatively proposed to recognize in a drawing at the Hermitage— an allegory of Catherine II—a first idea for this commission (1975, pp. 89, and 93, pl. 284-I), but no solid evidence corroborates this assertion.

J. P. M.

32 Gabriel-François DOYEN
Head of an Old Man, c. 1770
Tête de vieillard
Oil on paper on canvas
21 ⅝ × 16" (54.9 × 40.6 cm)
On the reverse (removed during lining):
Study of a nude man

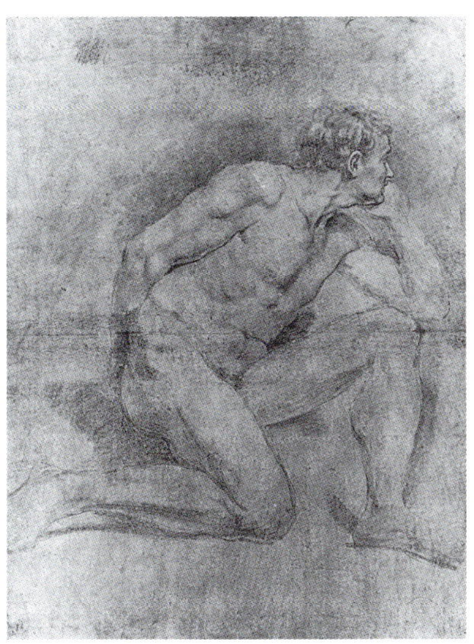

Fig. 5. Gabriel-François DOYEN. ***Nude Study*** (Etude académique), c. 1770. Oil on paper on canvas. Private collection, Paris. Photo: Prudence Cuming Associates.

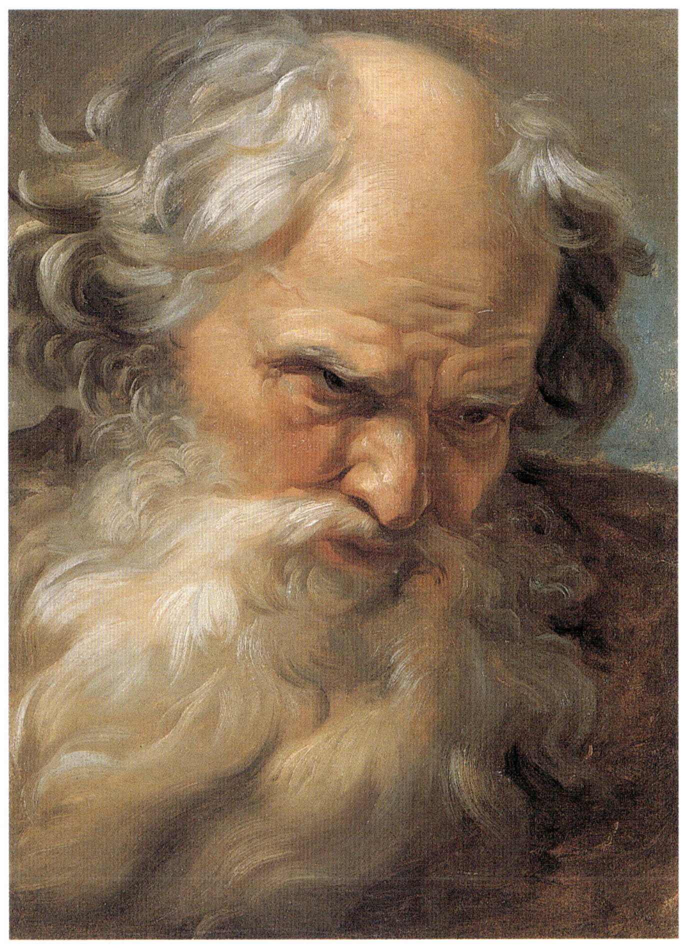

In its effervescence, this powerful head of an old man is reminiscent of the paintings of identical subjects executed by Fragonard from 1767 onwards (Cuzin 1988, pp. 131–34). However, the application of paint in long sweeping strokes is different from Fragonard's nervous and fragmented use of the medium. Nor does this study bear the influence of Rembrandt evident in Fragonard's treatments of the subject. It is nevertheless appropriate to look among Fragonard's contemporaries for the author of this painting. Although his personality and career could not be more different from Fragonard's, it is known that Gabriel-François Doyen, the artist to whom we attribute this spirited sketch, responded favorably to some aspects of Fragonard's work. At the Salon of 1761, for instance, Doyen exhibited *Young Girl Busy Reading a Booklet with Her Dog on Her Lap* (Cuzin 1988, p. 253, n. 18), a lost painting whose subject may reflect the influence of Fragonard's *Figures de fantaisie*. In 1767, one of Fragonard's two painting entries in the Salon, *Head of a Bearded Man Seen in Profile* (Cuzin 1988, p. 94, cat. no. 145 or 146), may also have triggered Doyen's interest in such *têtes d'expression*. (This was the last time that Fragonard showed at the Salon, whereas Doyen's own *Miracle des ardents* for the Church of Saint-Roch, in the same exhibition, established his reputation.)

Our attribution to Doyen is strengthened by a comparison of our sketch with an engraving by Gilles Demarteau after a now lost drawing by the artist. The engraving was exhibited at the Salon of 1771 (Sandoz 1975, p. 153, fig. 12). Although the engraving is not precisely of this head, there are sufficient similarities between the two works to confirm the attribution. Furthermore, the academic study on the verso of this oil study (fig. 5) can be compared to a red chalk drawing by Doyen published by Sandoz (Paris, Ecole Nationale des Beaux-Arts; Sandoz 1975, fig. 13). The Paris drawing, which seems to be of the same model, is inscribed "Life Class of Monday, January 14, 1771. M. Doyen." According to Sandoz, the drawing is a "teacher's model" executed by Doyen, who had been an assistant professor at the Académie since 1767. The date of 1771 is particularly relevant in light of the Demarteau engraving exhibited at the Salon of that year.

J. P. M.

63

(Fecamp 1726–Paris 1759)

e Mettay obtained the Prix-de-Rome in 1748. *Agréé* by the Académie upon his return from Italy, where he received the encouragement of Natoire, Le Mettay never became Academician. He executed some large religious compositions during a stay in Turin, and worked in the same manner in Lyon, but devoted himself increasingly to landscape painting.

33 Pierre-Charles LE METTAY
Jacob Taking Leave of Laban, c. 1743–48
La Séparation de Jacob et de Laban
Oil on canvas
14 ¾ × 20 ½" (37.5 × 52.1 cm)

Exhibitions: Houston 1973–75, no. 56.

Bibliography: Chomer 1981, pp. 83, 88, fig. 4.

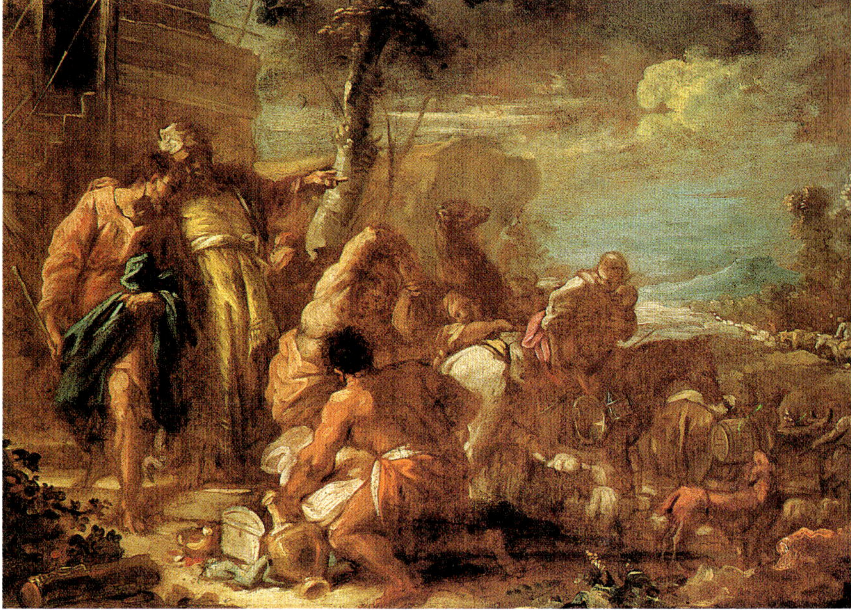

First established in the Houston catalogue on the strength of a comparison with a drawing at the Louvre (inv. 30969), the attribution of this oil sketch to Le Mettay has been confirmed by Gilles Chomer in his important contribution to the rediscovery of this little-known master (1981, p. 83). Chomer, however, rectified the misidentification of the subject as the Departure of the Prodigal Son, identifying it instead as a seldom represented episode from Genesis 31-32 in which Laban and Jacob, once reconciled, take leave of one another. The subject places Le Mettay's composition more pointedly within the circle of his teacher, François Boucher, who had treated the same subject in a painting now lost, but known through a drawing, an engraving, and a copy (Ananoff 1976, vol. 1, pp. 172–73, n. 35; the copy figured under an attribution to Jeaurat in Paris 1972, no. 16). Le Mettay's composition may owe something to Boucher's but ignores the iconographic tradition that includes two witnesses to the scene, Leah and Rachel, Jacob's wives.

The reconstruction of Le Mettay's oeuvre is too incomplete to advance an exact date for this sketch, although its relationship to Boucher's composition implies a fairly early date. Le Mettay entered Boucher's studio around 1742–43 and left for Rome after having won the Concours in 1748. It is probably during those five years that the sketch was executed. Chomer has noted furthermore the kinship, especially in terms of its proportions and its subject drawn from the Old Testament, between this sketch and the type of paintings executed for the Prix-de-Rome between 1745 and 1747 (no candidate was considered skilled enough to win the competition until Le Mettay's success in 1748). Though youthful, this sketch displays characteristics one finds later in some of Le Mettay's more mature history paintings: firm modeling of the figures, a tendency to outline them, and rich, golden colors that suggest the influence of Jean-François de Troy even more than Boucher (Chomer 1981, pp. 9–12, 89–90).

J. P. M.

François-Joseph CASANOVA

(London 1727–Brühl 1802)

*B*orn in London of Venetian parents, François-Joseph Casanova was the brother of the celebrated author of the *Memoirs*. Pupil of Guardi in Venice, the vagaries of his subsequent life led him to Dresden, Paris, and Vienna. He was received into the Académie in 1763 and given many important commissions. His patrons included the Prince de Condé, Catherine II, and Madame du Barry. His panels for the latter's residence at Louveciennes are now in the museum in Rennes.

34 François-Joseph CASANOVA
Riders, n.d.
Cavaliers
Oil on canvas
21 ½ × 26 ½" (54.6 × 67.3 cm)

Exhibitions: Houston 1973–75, no. 7.

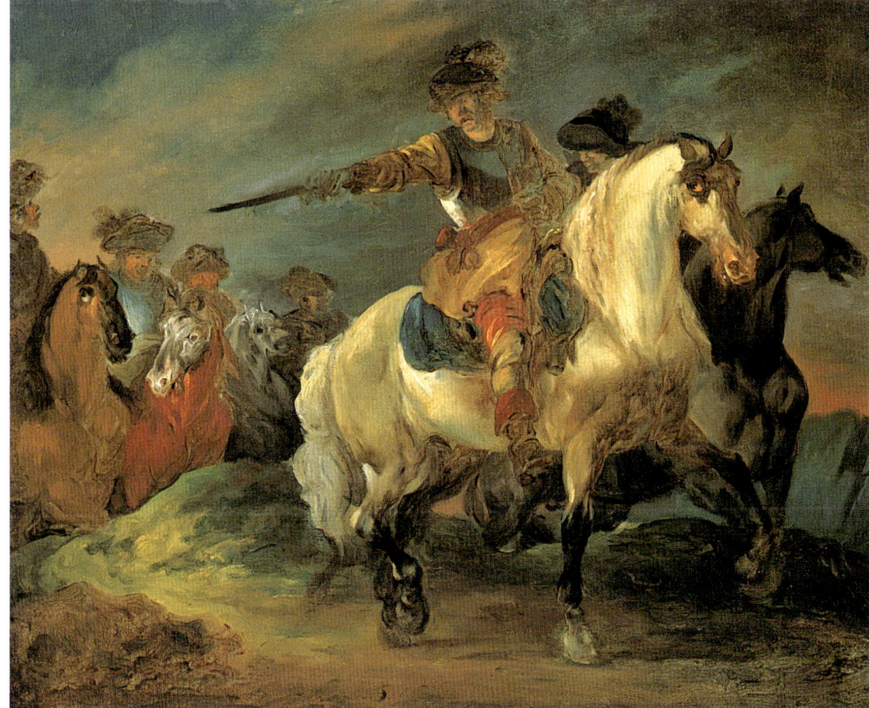

It is fitting that François-Joseph (also called Francesco) Casanova, a truly international painter who worked in Paris, Dresden, and Vienna, specialized in painting cavalry battles: this genre, well-established since the seventeenth century, had been the domain of Dutch artists (Philips Wouwermans, 1619–1668), French painters (Jacques Courtois, 1621–1676; Joseph, 1646–1704; and Charles Parrocel, 1688–1752), and Casanova's own master, the Venetian Francesco Simonini (1686–1755). Treating identical subjects in an often related style, individual works by these artists, which appealed to a German or Eastern European clientele (Simonini worked for the Schulenburgs, Casanova for the Prince of Kaunitz), are frequently confused. The genre demanded an exacting skill at rendering the anatomy of animals, as well as an ability to convey in paint the physical and emotional power of battle. Typically, these artists chose not to represent specific military events (although Casanova was eventually commissioned by Catherine II to paint the attack on the fortress at Oczackow and the victory of Potemkin), but instead translated actual scenes into a type of generic battle. This transformation of historical subjects into a genre motif is best exemplified in the commission Casanova received from the Beauvais tapestry manufactory in 1763 for furniture upholstery. There may be a link between this painting, where the riders are not represented in action, and the individual figures and small groups he created for Beauvais. Unknown to Jean A. Axelette (whose unpublished thesis, written in 1929, is to date the only attempt at cataloguing the large opus of the artist), this painting can best be compared to the two presented, respectively, in 1970 and 1972 at the Galerie Sanct Lucas, Vienna, and also to *Bulgarian Rider* at the Dunkerque Museum (Dunkerque/Valenciennes/Lille 1980, no. 46). While the authorship of the work seems beyond doubt, it is almost impossible to propose a date for it, as the artist's production changed very little throughout his career.

J. P. M.

Nicolas Guy BRENET

(Paris 1728–Paris 1792)

Pupil of Charles Coypel and François Boucher (q.v.), Brenet also studied at the Ecole des Elèves Protégés with Carle Vanloo (q.v.) and Dandré-Bardon. Brenet went to Rome in 1756 and first exhibited at the Salon in 1763. His fame began with his 1769 reception piece to the Académie. Admired by Diderot, Brenet received important commissions from the Church as well as the State. His ability to treat history painting with dignity and eloquence secured him a strong position in the development of French painting at a time of change and renewal.

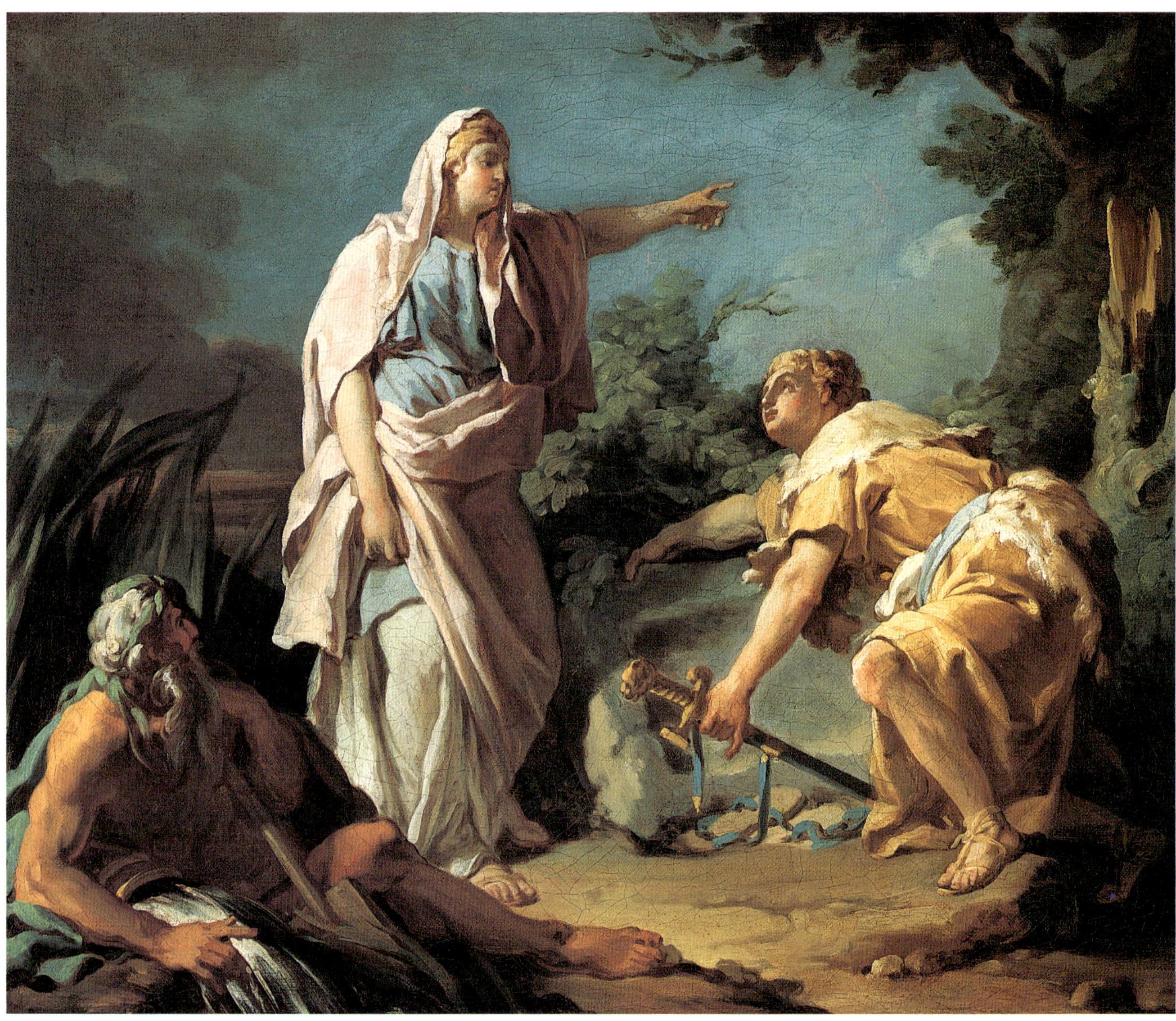

35   Nicolas Guy BRENET
Aethra Showing her Son Theseus the Place Where His Father Had Hidden His Arms, 1768
Aethra montrant à son fils Thésée l'emplacement où son père avait caché ses armes
Oil on canvas
19 ¾ × 23 ½" (50.2 × 59.7 cm)

Exhibitions: Houston 1973–75, no. 4.

Bibliography: Montaiglon 1875–92, vol. 7, p. 377; Sandoz 1979, p. 93; Paris 1984–85, p. 144.

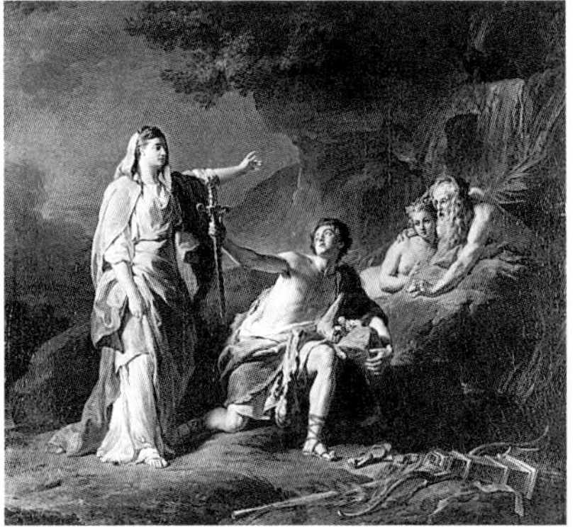

Fig. 6. Nicolas Guy BRENET. ***The Young Theseus Retrieving the Arms of His Father*** (Le Jeune Thésée retrouvant les âmes de son père), 1769. Oil on canvas. Ecole nationale supérieure des Beaux-Arts, Paris

This episode from Plutarch's *Life of Theseus* (I,3,6) had been treated by at least two great French painters of the seventeenth century—Nicolas Poussin (Chantilly, Musée Condé) and Laurent de La Hyre (Budapest, Museum of Fine Arts)—before Brenet painted his own version of the subject in 1768.

Aethra, daughter of Pittheus, bore a child to Aegeus, who "being desirous of children, and consulting the oracle of Delphi, received the celebrated answer which forbade him the company of any woman before his return to Athens." Having related the obscure oracle to Pittheus, the governor of Troezen, the latter "prevailed upon him . . . whether by persuasion or deceit, to lie with his daughter Aethra." Aegeus, suspecting Aethra to be with child, "left a sword and a pair of shoes, hiding them under a great stone that has a hollow in it exactly fitting them," and commanded Aethra that "if she brought forth a son who, when he came to man's estate, should be able to lift up the stone and take away what he had left there, she should send him to him with these things with all secrecy." Brenet has represented the next scene in which "Aethra, conducting him to the stone, and informing him who was his true father, commanded him to take from thence the tokens that Aegeus had left" (Plutarch, pp. 4–5).

Painted as his reception piece to the Académie, it was well received at the Salon of 1769, even by the exacting Diderot, who found the composition "suavement fait, harmonieux" in spite of a lack of correctness he noticed in the drawing of the figure of Theseus, and the position of the arms of the hero's mother, which he found uninspired.

Brenet had presented the sketch for the large painting, now at the Ecole nationale supérieure des Beaux-Arts, Paris, to the members of the Académie in 1768 (fig. 6). Having had his project approved, Brenet nevertheless brought substantial changes to the composition. The shift from an oblong to an almost square format led him to give his Theseus a more central position, emphasizing the importance of the hero and making the narration more explicit. The somewhat unresolved and unfortunate position of Theseus in the sketch—crouching in an unconvincing effort to lift the rock under which his father's sword is hidden—is transformed in the final painting, through the artifice of an effective, if theatrical, gesturing of the hero. Theseus in the final work is a figure of greater elegance, providing a perfect counterpoint to the rigid, formal stance of Aethra. The substitution of an embracing nymph and river god for the conventional river god of the sketch (more a "filler" than a protagonist in the story) is also a welcome change that carries the representation into the realm of bucolic poetry. In making this alteration Brenet was possibly influenced by such groupings as found in Boucher's mythological paintings or the example of Venetian artists, particularly Tiepolo, whose nymphs seem the prototype of Brenet's.

J. P. M.

Antoine RENOU

(Paris 1731–Paris 1806)

Pupil of Pierre (q.v.) and Vien (q.v.), Renou obtained the second-place Prix-de-Rome in 1758. From 1760 until 1766 he worked at the court of the Polish King Stanislas Leczynski, then traveled to Rome in 1766. That same year he was *agréé*. In 1781 he was received into the Académie. Renou also wrote plays and poems, as well as a French translation, "L'Art de peindre," of the Latin poem by C.-A. Duquesnoy (published in 1789).

36   Antoine RENOU
Laban Searching for His Idols, 1753
Laban cherchant ses dieux
Oil on paper on canvas
11 ⅞ × 13 ⅞" (30.2 × 35.2 cm)

Exhibitions: Houston 1973–75, no. 5
(attributed to Brenet).

Bibliography: Rolle/Montaiglon 1875–92,
vol. 6 (1745–1755), p. 366; Sandoz 1979,
pp. 48, 77, no. 4B (attributed to Brenet).

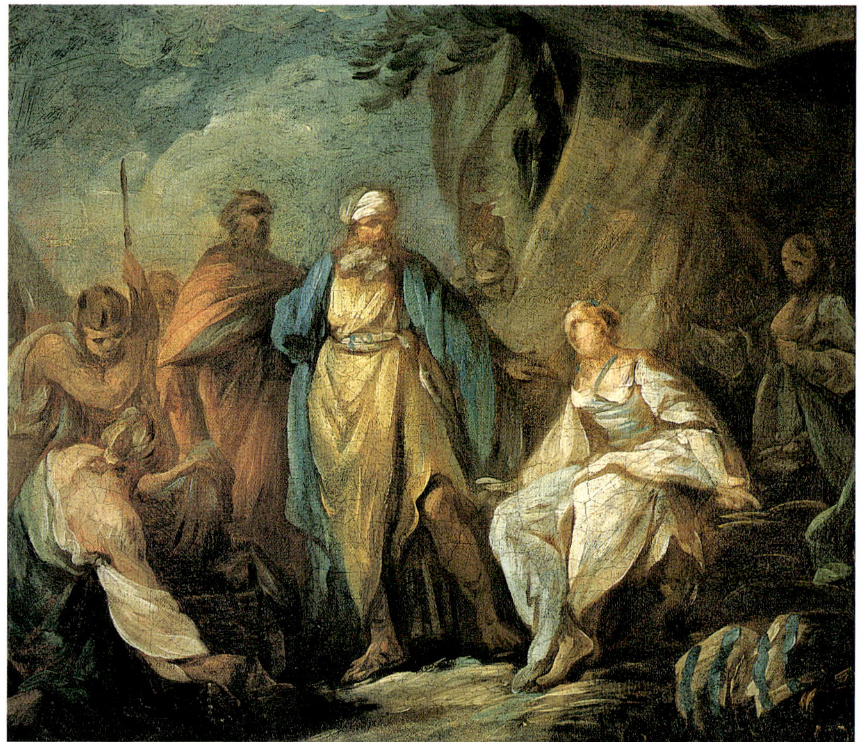

Although largely forgotten today, Antoine Renou was a regular exhibitor at the Paris Salons from the 1760s until the time of the French Revolution. His career is usually considered to have begun with the second-place Prix-de-Rome he received in 1758 for *Abraham Leading Isaac to His Sacrifice*. The rediscovery and proper attribution of our sketch add therefore an important and early element to the oeuvre of the artist.

Called in 1753 to work for the Crown, Philippe-Benoit de La Rue (1718–1780) left vacant a place at the Ecole Royale des Elèves Protégés. Three candidates presented sketches to the Académie to be allowed to compete for the position: Gabriel de Saint-Aubin (1724–1780), Nicolas-Guy Brenet (q.v.), and Antoine Renou. The subject treated by the three artists was Laban Searching for His Idols. Saint-Aubin's sketch is now at the Cleveland Museum of Art, while Brenet's lost entry is known through a description of its engraving (the engraving , known to Prosper de Baudicourt [1859–61, vol. 2, p. 159], cannot be located). The description has led to the confusion of this sketch with Brenet's composition. Indeed both Brenet's and Renou's entries must have shared similarities dictated by the iconography of the subject. Brenet's composition, however, showed Rachel "putting her hand on the young Joseph" and featured "a large palm tree in front of a tent." These elements are absent from the present composition, but appear in what may be a repetition of the subject by Brenet himself, but at a later date (Perez 1973, p. 201). Neither Renou's nor Saint-Aubin's spirited sketch won the competition. Brenet obtained the position at the Ecole Royale.

J.P.M.

$\mathscr{P}$upil of J.-B.-M. Pierre (q.v.), Jollain was received into the Académie in 1773. He worked for several royal residences (Bellevue, Petit Trianon, Fontainebleau), but seems to have been particularly successful in painting history subjects on a small scale. His work is largely unknown today.

37   Nicolas-René JOLLAIN *le jeune*
The Refuge, 1769
Le Refuge
Oil on canvas
21 ¾ × 12 ⅝" (55.2 × 32.1 cm)

Exhibitions: Albuquerque 1980, no. 33.

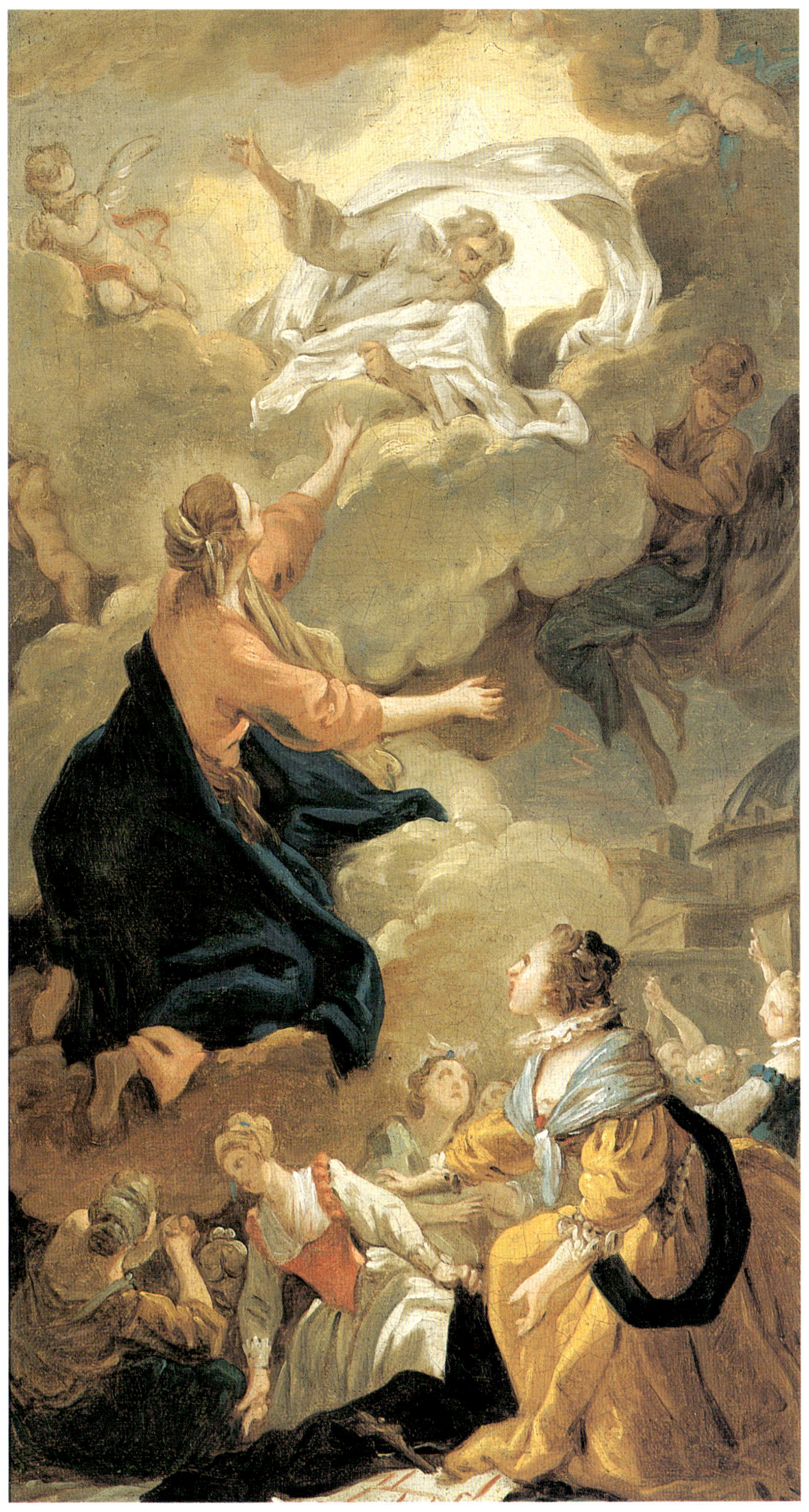

A regular exhibitor at the Paris Salons between 1767 and 1791, Nicolas-René Jollain presented six compositions in 1769. Five of them depicted mythological subjects, while the largest of all, *The Refuge*, was a religious composition featuring secular elements. Drawn by Saint-Aubin in his *livret* (Dacier 1909) with the annotation "pour Besansson," the picture was commissioned for the Chapel of the Convent of Our Lady of Refuge in Besançon. The building itself, built between 1735 and 1749, appears in the background of the painting. The Refuge was a convent whose mission was to protect virgins and rehabilitate "fallen" women. In the picture, its founder, Madame de Ransin (d. 1639), is shown imploring the intercession of the Virgin. God, in a gesture of clemency, prevents the Exterminating Angel from punishing the sinners.

Diderot (Seznec/Diderot 1967, p. 109), describing the subject with a touch of irreverence, admired nevertheless the "effect" produced by the painting, praising in particular its colors and general harmony. In contrast, the critic found the five mythological subjects so poor that he could not believe the same artist had painted them.

Walch (Albuquerque 1980, p. 22) has already discussed the similarities between this composition and Gabriel-François Doyen's *Miracle des ardents* (1767; Paris, Church of Saint-Roch). In both paintings the artists had to face the challenge of subjects in which representations of the terrestrial and celestial realms had to be combined. They succeeded in doing so through the artifice of an elegant, spiraling composition. Diderot, who had commented on Doyen's *Miracle* in his 1767 Salon (Seznec/Diderot, 1963, pp. 178-91), must have also noticed the dependence of Jollain's composition on Doyen's. Typically, he concludes his comment on Jollain's *Refuge* by saying that only Vien could have done better, thus referring to Vien's large *Predication of Saint Denis*—also shown at the 1767 Salon, and the pendant of Doyen's *Miracle* at the Church of Saint-Roch—a work that in his comments Diderot had subtly contrasted with Doyen's, and to which he had given his preference.

J. P. M.

Jean-Bernard RESTOUT

(Paris 1752–Paris 1797)

Son and pupil of Jean Restout, Jean-Bernard Restout was *agréé* in 1765 and received into the Académie in 1769. Although his paintings betray the influence of his father, his work can be easily differentiated. Unlike his father he did not treat religious subjects but devoted most of his production to mythological compositions that already display a Neoclassical gravity. Restout *fils* received commissions for royal residences, among them, Grand Trianon. During the Revolution, he played a political role as president of the Commission for the Arts (1793).

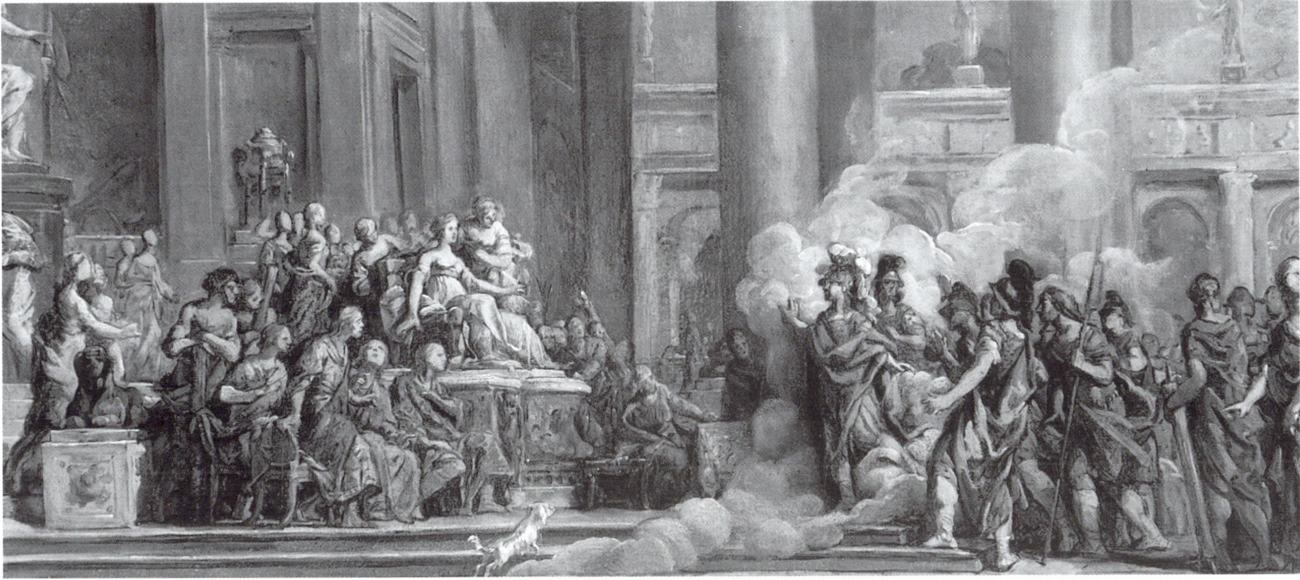

Jean-Bernard RESTOUT

38   *The Arrival of Aeneas in Carthage*, c. 1772–74
L'Arrivée d'Enée à Carthage
Oil on paper on canvas
12 ¼ × 27 ¾" (31.1 × 70.5 cm)

39   *The Departure of Dido and Aeneas for the Hunt*, c. 1772–74
Le Départ de Didon et Enée pour la chasse
Oil on paper on canvas
12 ⅝ × 15 ¾" (32.1 × 40.0 cm)

Exhibitions: (38) Houston 1973–75, no. 86 (attributed to J.-M. Vien); (39) Albuquerque 1980, no. 55 (attributed to Jean Restout).

Bibliography: (38) New York/New Orleans/Columbus 1986–87, p. 142, no. 154 (attributed to J.-M. Vien).

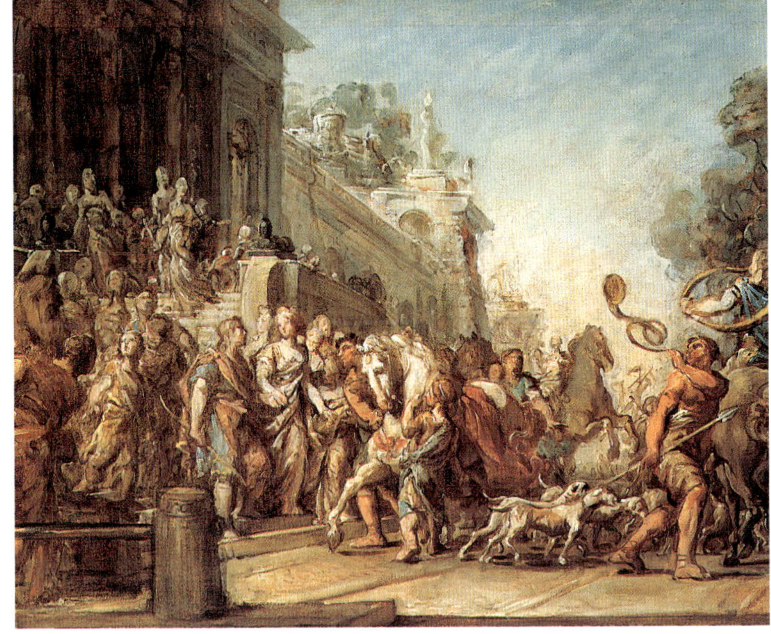

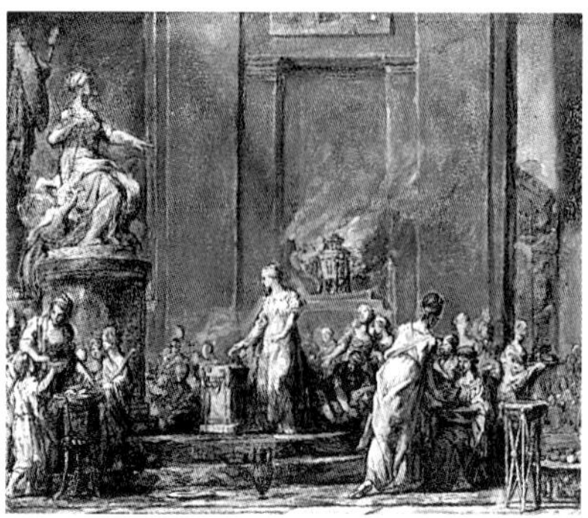

Fig. 7. Jean-Bernard RESTOUT. *The Sacrifice of Dido* (Le Sacrifice de Didon), n.d. The Metropolitan Museum of Art, Van Day Truex Fund, 1983 (1983.429)

These two small paintings, purchased at different times and from different sources, represent a substantial addition to the little-known oeuvre of Jean-Bernard Restout, the son and pupil of the more famous Jean Restout. *The Arrival of Aeneas in Carthage*, formerly attributed to Vien, was correctly attributed to its author when an old label affixed to the back of *The Departure of Dido and Aeneas for the Hunt* revealed that both paintings belonged to a series of projects commissioned from J.-B. Restout by the Marquis de Marigny to be executed in tapestry at the Gobelins. A letter from J.-B.-M. Pierre to the Marquis de Marigny written in March 1772 indicates the list of subjects and that "one could entrust M. Restout with the execution of these tapestries' cartoons." Engerand (1901, p. 426, n. 3) also notes this project and its mention in a list of commissions (Etat des ouvrages ordonnés), dated 1774, but referring to a commission given in 1772 (Paris, Archives Nationales, o 1 1933). The same document states, "les esquisses sont faites." The tapestries were apparently never executed, nor were their cartoons, which in addition to these two subjects were to represent the Tempest Ordered by Juno, the Refuge Sought by Dido and Aeneas in a Grotto, the Sacrifice of Dido, and finally the Death of Dido.

In the first episode, Restout scrupulously followed the requirements of the commission, which stipulated that the artist set his scene "in a reception hall, the configuration of which should allow one to see through the architecture the beautification of that burgeoning city."

The correct attribution of these two sketches to Restout *le jeune* has allowed us to identify a sketch for the fourth scene, *The Sacrifice of Dido* (fig. 7). Purchased in 1983 as a work of Vien by the Metropolitan Museum of Art, New York (Bean 1986, no. 308), it is painted in the same distinctive manner and with the same palette as the two sketches presented here. Its dimensions, equal to those of *The Departure*, give the composition an almost square format, slightly unusual for a painting but appropriate for a tapestry project.

J. P. M.

*L*a Vallée was trained as a history painter, under Jean-Baptiste Descamps, an artist from Rouen, and later under Pierre (q.v.). He won the Prix-de-Rome in 1759, spent three years at the Ecole des Elèves Protégés, and went to Rome from 1762 until 1777. Famous for his landscapes in the manner of Poussin, he added the seventeenth-century artist's surname to his. He became a member of the Académie only in 1789. By then Lavallée-Poussin had practically relinquished history painting in favor of decorative compositions that featured antique motifs.

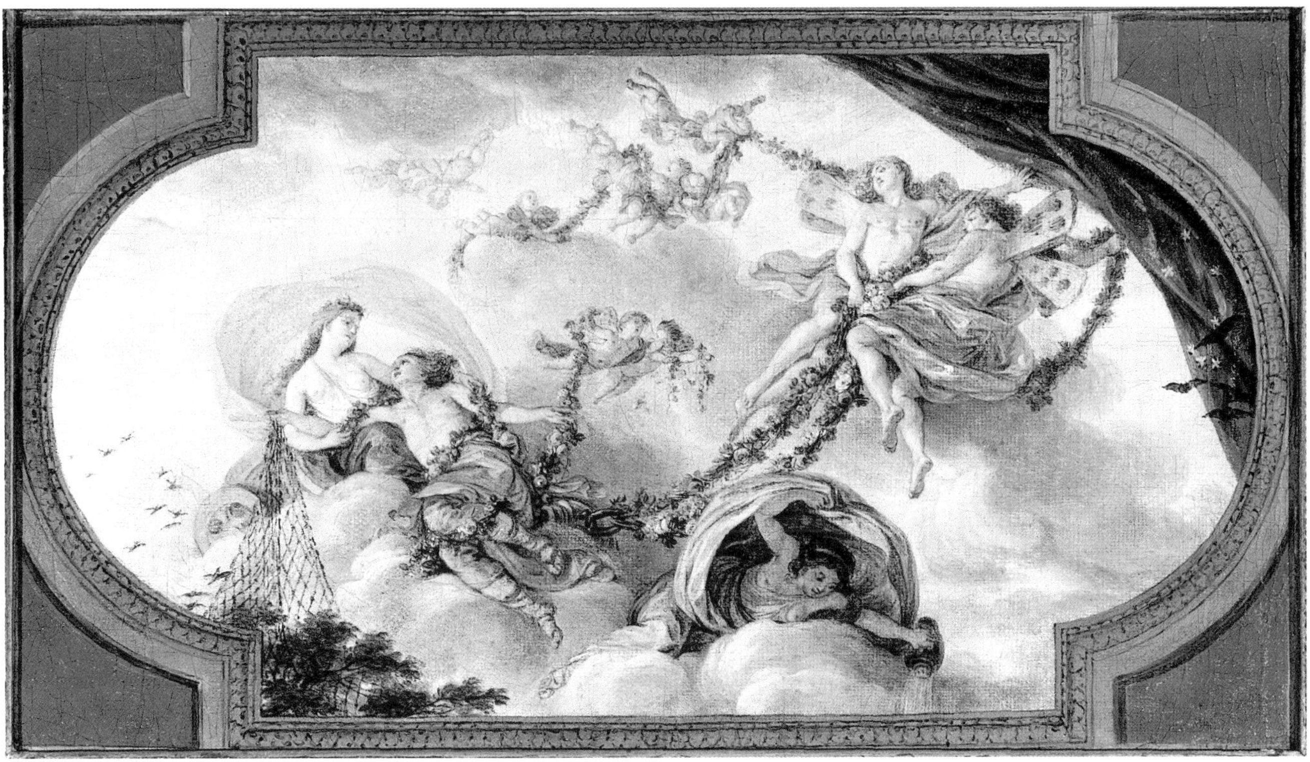

40 Etienne de LA VALLEE, later known as
LAVALLEE-POUSSIN
***Design for an Allegorical Ceiling
Decoration***, c. 1779
Projet de décoration de plafond
Oil on canvas
9 × 15 ¾" (22.9 × 40.0 cm)
Inscribed on the reverse: *La Vallee*

Exhibitions: Albuquerque 1980, no. 36.

The subject of this allegory was interpreted by Peter Walch (Albuquerque 1980) as the passage of time: "Two winged Zephyrs push back the curtain of night, whose closing dominion is also indicated by a group of bats. In the middle, a personification of rain (or morning dew) showers water on the world below . . . Pulled in a chariot attached by a garland of flowers to the Zephyrs, two figures . . . may be identified as Aurora (the Goddess of Dawn) and Apollo (the God of Day)."

It is tempting to establish a link between this composition and Lavallée-Poussin's ceiling for the salon of the Hôtel Grimod de La Reynière, built around 1778–79. This elegant house, by the lesser-known architect Nicolas Barre, was located at the corner of the Place de La Concorde and Avenue des Champs-Elyseés. It was demolished in the early twentieth century and replaced by the present United States Embassy. Its plan and elevation, as well as its interior decoration by J. L. Clérisseau (1721–1820), were documented in a series of watercolors executed by the Polish architect J. C. Kamsetzer (1753–1795), who visited Paris in 1782. Among these watercolors, which are kept in the University Library, Warsaw (Batowski 1935; Réau 1937, pp. 7–17; Batowski/Kwiatwowski 1978, pp. 77–81; for a fuller account of the project, see McCormick 1990, pp. 164–78), is a rendition of the ceiling representing "the hours of the day," which Lavallée-Poussin had executed in the salon of the Hôtel. While the copy by Kamsetzer is not a full view of the ceiling project, it shows a group that could be identified as Aurora and Apollo. Although it differs from the sketch presented here—and is probably truthful to the ceiling *in situ* when Kamsetzer visited the place—the relatively infrequent appearance of the subject, as well as the paucity of ceiling decorations in Lavallée-Poussin's oeuvre, leads us to believe that it may well be another design for the same commission.

J.P.M.

Jean-Baptiste LEPRINCE

(Metz 1734–Saint-Denis-du-Port, near Lagny 1781)

Genre painter and a typical eighteenth-century *petit maître*, Leprince studied with Boucher (q.v), whose minor compositions he often imitated. These works would not have been sufficient to establish his reputation, but Leprince distinguished himself in the representation of Russian genre scenes that captivated the public with their fresh exoticism and their fastidious technique learned from the Dutch masters. He traveled extensively in Russia and in 1764–65 published several series of etchings of Russian costumes and genre subjects. His famous *Russian Baptism* was his reception piece at the Académie in 1765. Later in life, when Leprince was criticized by the likes of Diderot for the repetitiousness of his Russian subjects, the artist devoted himself to landscape painting.

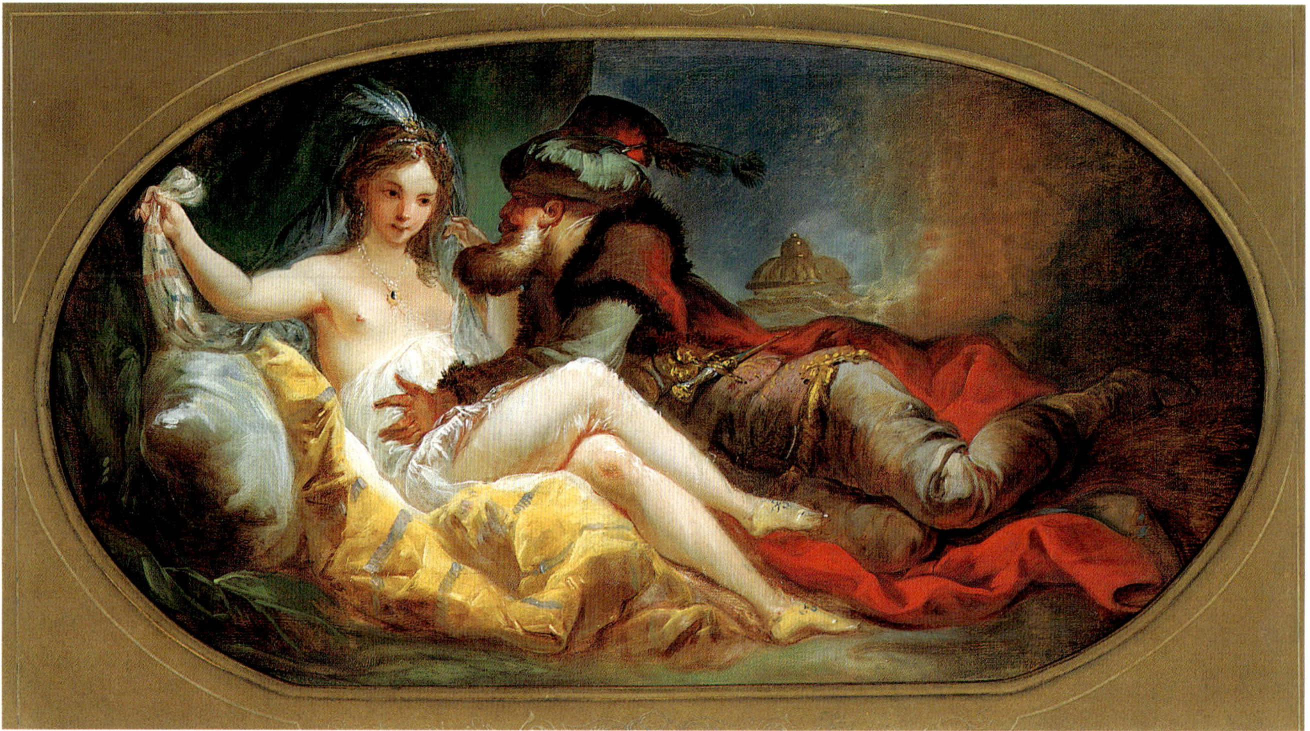

41   Jean-Baptiste LEPRINCE
Harem Scene, n.d.
Scène de harem
Oil on canvas
17 ¾ × 28 ¾" (45.1 × 73.0 cm)

Exhibitions: Houston 1973-75, no. 61

Leprince's extensive travels through Russia allowed him to produce an impressive body of work that introduced a note of truth into the fashion in the eighteenth-century for exotic genre painting. Yet, though his Russian or Turkish peasants typically wear the right costumes, in all but a few full-fledged genre scenes they are depicted either in the attitudes of the protagonists of a *fête champêtre*, or in dignified situations suitable for Roman or mythological heroes.

This oval painting, probably intended originally as an overdoor, shows another and lesser-known aspect of Leprince's talent. Here the artist participates in the well-established genre of imaginary Oriental subjects. The innocent eroticism of the scene—a mere pretext to paint the nude—is deeply rooted in the Western tradition. The contrast between the very young woman and her mature suitor is reminiscent of such subjects as Susanna and the Elders or Pan and Syrinx.

This painting has been related (Houston 1973–75, no. 61) to another work of the same shape and size by Leprince at the Musée Cognacq-Jay in Paris (Burollet 1980, no. 70). Entitled *La Sultane*, it also represents a nude young woman in the company of a suitor dressed in Oriental costume, in this case a Chinese-inspired robe. It has unfortunately been impossible to trace the provenance of the Cognacq-Jay painting beyond its first appearance in the Beurnonville sale in 1881 or to establish with certainty that both paintings were once pendants, although their identical size and comparable subjects, treated respectively in the related genres of *turquerie* and *chinoiserie*, certainly point in that direction.

J. P. M.

Nicolas-Bernard LEPICIE

(Paris 1735–Paris 1784)

L épicié's impeccable academic course of study exemplifies the career of a gifted and admired artist in eighteenth-century France. Pupil of Carle Vanloo, he was *agréé* at the Académie in 1764, received as Academician in 1769, and made professor in 1777. He exhibited regularly at the Salon, but his career was cut short by his early death at the age of forty-nine. He produced history and religious paintings, toward which the critics were severe, and a larger production of genre paintings, which established his lasting reputation.

42 Nicolas-Bernard LEPICIE
The Visitation, 1769
La Visitation
Oil on canvas
23 ¾ × 13 ⅜" (60.3 × 34 cm)

Provenance: Possibly Lépicié sale, Paris, Basan, 1785, no. 25.

Exhibitions: Possibly Salon 1769, no. 28; Albuquerque 1980, no. 40; Rochester/New Brunswick/Atlanta 1987–88, no. 34.

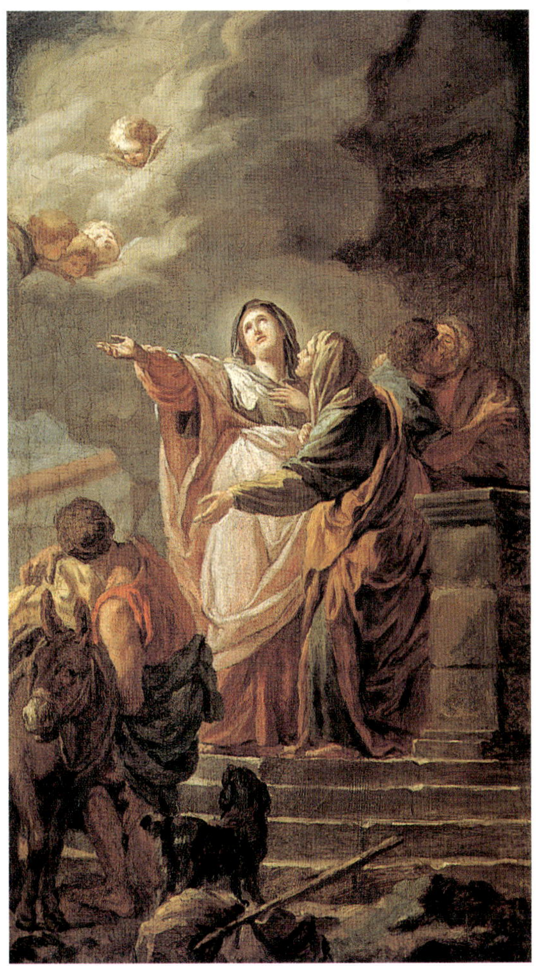

This painting, related to a large composition (whereabouts unknown) executed by Lépicié for the Cathedral in Bayonne in 1768, may be the small version exhibited at the 1769 Salon, although, as noted by Walch (Albuquerque 1980, p. 25), another version of slightly different dimensions, signed and dated 1769 (Gaston-Dreyfus 1923, p. 31, no. 12), may be a stronger contender. (That other version, according to Rosenthal [Rochester/New Brunswick/Atlanta 1987–88, p. 121, n. 1], may have been in a New York private collection at the time of the Rochester exhibition.)

In spite of having remarked in his own copy of the Salon *livret* that this *Visitation* was an "excellente esquisse," Diderot began his comments on Lépicié's substantial group of works on view at the Salon that year (nos. 123–30) by writing: "Of Lépicié I remembered nothing" (Seznec/Diderot 1967, p. 101). Diderot's attention at the Salon of that year was directed mostly toward Greuze's production, including his controversial *Septimus-Severus*. Although he was able to appreciate the quality of Lépicié's composition, its somewhat antiquated style, alluding to Jouvenet, did little to arouse the interest of so astute a critic as Diderot. Later in his brief career, Lépicié relinquished religious and history painting to devote his talent to genre painting, creating some of his most memorable works.

J. P. M.

Jacques GAMELIN

(Carcassonne 1738–Carcassonne 1803)

*G*amelin's career, in spite of a brief stay in Paris, took place almost entirely in the south of France. He enjoyed the protection of a powerful patron, the Baron de Puymaurin, who sponsored his studies under Rivalz in Toulouse and then in Paris. Puymaurin also sent him to Rome, where he spent ten years and acquired a certain notoriety. In 1775, he returned to France and published his famous—although unsuccessful at the time—*Nouveau Recueil d'Ostéologie*. Active in Montpellier, Narbonne, and Carcassonne, Gamelin also participated in the French Revolution (about which he left some lively descriptions). Anatole France borrowed his name and some of his traits for the hero of his novel *Les Dieux ont soif*.

43   Jacques GAMELIN
The Fountain of Love, c. 1790s
La Fontaine d'Amour
Oil on canvas
7 ¾ × 10 ⅛" (19.7 × 25.7 cm)

Exhibitions: Houston 1973–75, no. 25.

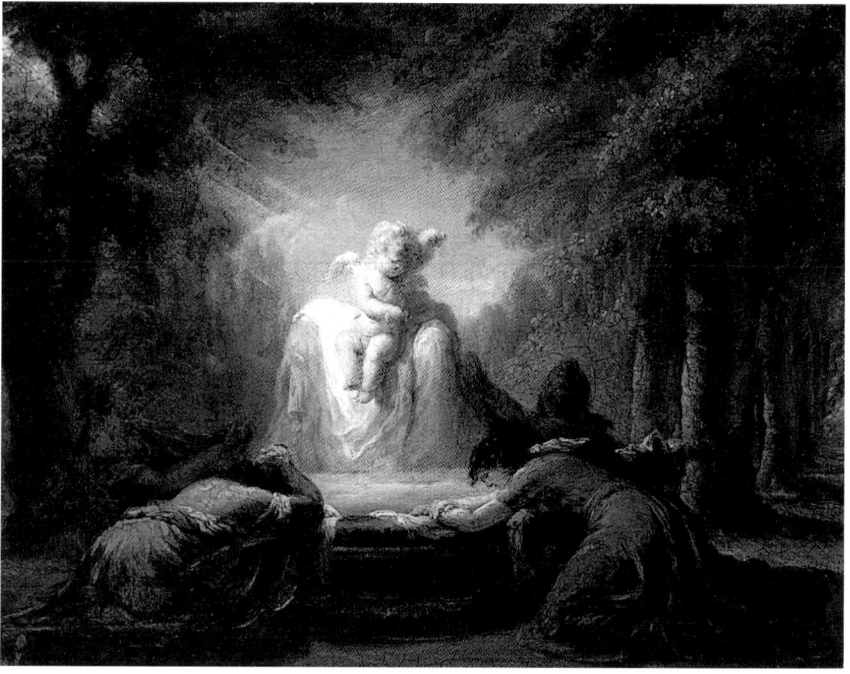

Gamelin's work is diverse. He treated all subjects, from battle scenes in the tradition of Parrocel (q.v.) and Casanova (q.v.) to religious and historical compositions to genre scenes. As a member of the cosmopolitan group of artists active in late eighteenth-century Rome, Gamelin had firsthand knowledge of the early Neoclassicism formulated at the time. The abbreviated, unorthodox drawing of his compositions and his violent colors seem to reflect occasionally the fantasy and eccentricity of such contemporaries as Fuseli, Goya, and Sergel. Some of these qualities appear in this small painting.

Invocations to Love are common images in late eighteenth-century French painting, from Boucher and Fragonard (*The Fountain of Love*, 1785; London, Wallace Collection) to Vien and Greuze, not to mention more minor masters such as J.-F. Schall (to whom the present painting was once attributed). Yet this one displays neither an erotic frenzy nor a stilted dignity, but instead, an almost humorous mood, perhaps poking fun at the group of women, some despairing, some supplicant, kneeling around the monument in positions reminiscent of Hubert Robert's washerwomen. Such a desire to make the representation more "real" or direct is not inconsistent with Gamelin's nonclassical treatment of historical subjects.

The execution of the painting itself, notably the schematic faces and brilliant colors, strongly suggests an attribution to Gamelin. The same qualities can be found for instance in the small painting *Generosity of the Roman Ladies* (1795, private collection; see Paris 1979, no. 16, reprod.). A date in the 1790s seems appropriate for this painting as well.

J. P. M.

Jean-Jacques-François LE BARBIER

(Rouen 1758–Paris 1826)

Le Barbier won at the age of seventeen the first prize for drawing at the Rouen Académie. He then entered the studio of Pierre (q.v.) in Paris. After a stay in Rome at his own expense, he was sent to Switzerland in 1776 to sketch the sights of that country. Academician in 1785, he participated regularly in the Salon from 1781 until 1814, most often exhibiting paintings based on antique subjects.

44 Jean-Jacques-François LE BARBIER
Children at Play with a Satyr, n.d.
Enfants jouant avec un satyre
Oil on panel
10 ⅝ × 8 ⅜" (27.0 × 21.3 cm)
Inscribed on stone base: *L.B.*

Exhibitions: Salon of 1781, no. 205 (?);
Albuquerque 1980, no. 37.

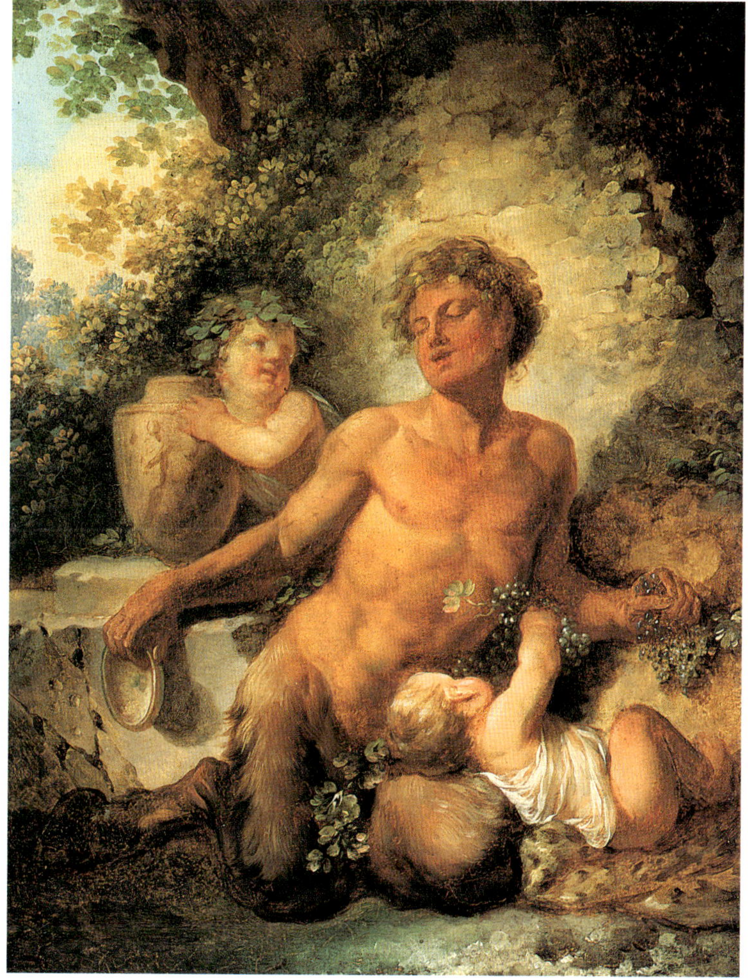

A pupil of Pierre, Le Barbier became a regular exhibitor at the Paris Salon from 1781 onwards. Known primarily for his renditions of Classical subjects, Le Barbier also executed small cabinet pictures in a manner often close to his teachers. While official taste and patronage in the later part of the eighteenth century may have turned many artists away from light mythological compositions, there was still sufficient public demand for some painters to continue to produce these works.

In this picture, Le Barbier shows his commitment to a taste for a somewhat old-fashioned style. His painting recalls both Pierre's and Noël Hallé's versions of related subjects (*The Dangers of Wine*, 1759; Musée des Arts de Cholet), and the works of Jacques-Philippe Caresme (1734–1796), a contemporary of Le Barbier's who specialized in bacchanalian scenes.

It is possible that this painting corresponds to one of Le Barbier's entries in the 1781 Salon (no. 205): "A child playing with grapes." A signed drawing of a satyr by Le Barbier (whereabouts unknown; photograph in the Service d'Etude et de Documentation, Musée du Louvre, Paris), close to the spirit of this painting, is dated 1781.

J.P.M..

*S*uvée received his first training in his native city, which at the time was part of the Austrian Lowlands. In 1763, he was in Bachelier's studio in Paris and in 1771 won the Académie's first prize. In Rome in 1772, he was influenced, like many painters of his generation, by the renewed interest in antiquities and executed many red chalk drawings of Rome, of the Campagna, and of ruins. Back in Paris in 1778, he participated in the Salons from 1779 until 1796, becoming an Academician in 1780. In 1792, he was made director of the French academy in Rome, but the position was immediately abolished (on the recommendation of David). Only in 1801 —after the Revolutionary turmoil that caused Suvée to be jailed for a time subsided—could he assume his functions in Rome. He transferred the French Academy to its present location, the Villa Medici. Suvée's oeuvre includes official commissions from the Crown, cartoons for tapestries, an important religious production, and some fine portraits.

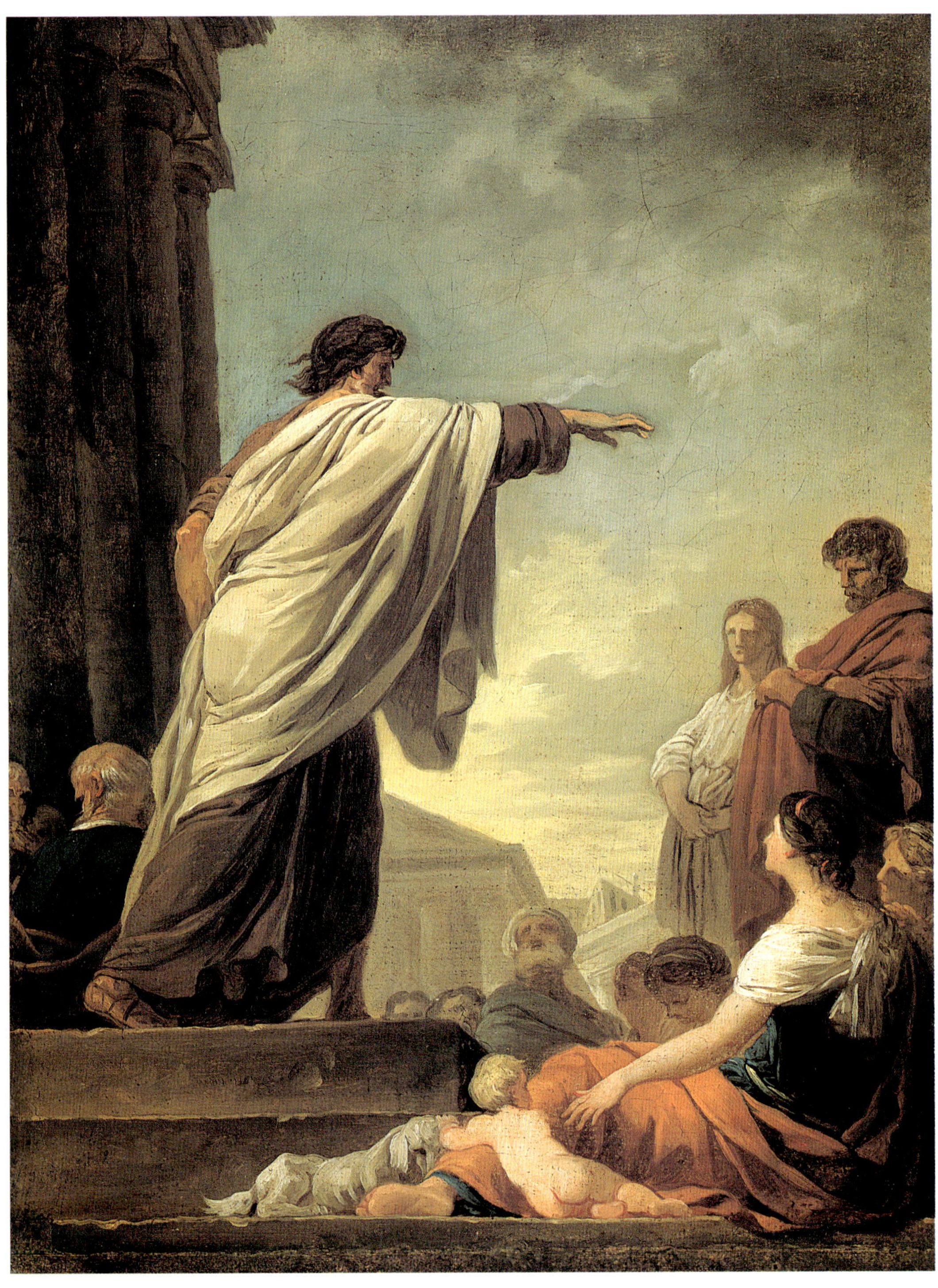

45 Joseph-Benoit SUVEE
The Predication of Saint Paul, n.d.
La Prédication de Saint Paul
Oil on canvas
19 ¾ × 15 ¼" (50.2 × 38.7 cm)

Provenance: Galerie Joseph Hahn, Paris.

Exhibitions: Salon of 1779, no. 191; Paris 1972, no. 28; Houston 1973-75, no. 77.

Bibliography: Bellier/Auvray 1885, vol. 2, p. 535; Dupont de Nemours 1908, p. 85, n. 187.

In spite of his foreign birth, Suvée competed for and won the Prix-de-Rome in 1771 with his *Fight of Mars and Minerva* (Lille, Musée des Beaux-Arts). Upon his return from Rome, the artist made a strong debut at the Paris Salon. Some of the ten works he exhibited there in 1779 were of considerable dimensions, notably his *Birth of the Virgin* (Paris, Church of the Assumption; *modello* at Montpellier, Musée Fabre), the most commented-upon painting among those he sent. The *livret* of the Salon includes two *esquisses*—our *Predication of Saint Paul* and a *Death of Cleopatra*—but does not indicate the final destination of these compositions. It must be assumed that Suvée submitted the sketches only to illustrate the breadth of his talent, and that they do not relate to any precise commission (the indication in the *livret* that these sketches are 10 *pieds* high is evidently erroneous).

It is unknown whether Suvée executed this painting in Rome or immediately upon his return, in time for exhibition at the Salon. In spite of the simplicity of its composition, dominated by the powerful figure of the predicating saint, Suvée's painting is not particularly forward-looking, nor is it entirely original. It reflects the influence of Vien—the director of the French Academy in Rome during the second half of Suvée's first sojourn in Italy—and, specifically, Vien's composition *Saint Denis Preaching to the Gauls* (1767; Paris, Church of Saint-Roch). Suvée's somewhat timid approach to the subject offers a mirror image of Vien's composition: all elements present in Vien's 1767 painting—colonnade, steps, figures of listeners, even the gesturing of the saint—are repeated here in reverse. Compared to the innovations of David, his contemporary, Suvée's art seems hesitant. It is, however, his respect for tradition, even for modern tradition, that accounted for Suvée's success and that led him to become director of the French Academy in Rome.

J.P.M.

François-Guillaume MENAGEOT

(London 1744–Paris 1816)

Son of the art dealer and landscape painter Augustin Ménageot, François-Guillaume was taken to Paris as a child. He studied painting at the Académie Royale first under Jean-Baptiste Deshays and then François Boucher. In 1766, Ménageot won the Prix-de-Rome with *Tomyris Ordering the Head of Cyrus Plunged into a Bowl of Blood* and spent three years at the Ecole des Elèves Protégés before going to Rome, where he attended the French Academy. He returned to Paris in 1774 and in 1777 was *agréé* by the Académie, his reception piece being a large historical painting entitled *Learning Holding Back Time*. He exhibited at the Salon for the first time in the same year and won praise for his vast painting *The Leave-taking of Polyxena and Hecuba*. Ménageot received numerous commissions for religious and historical subjects, the most outstanding of these was *The Death of Leonardo da Vinci*, which was exhibited at the 1781 Salon. Following this, Ménageot reverted, in the main, to Classical and allegorical subjects. In 1787, he was appointed director of the French Academy in Rome, and, following his resignation in 1792 (as a result of his inability to deal with the revolutionary fervor of the students), he retired to Vicenza. In 1797, he was appointed professor at the Academy of Florence, and in 1801 returned to France to become professor at the Ecole Nationale de Peinture et Sculpture. Ménageot's subject matter varies between small, slightly erotic mythological scenes and larger historical works.

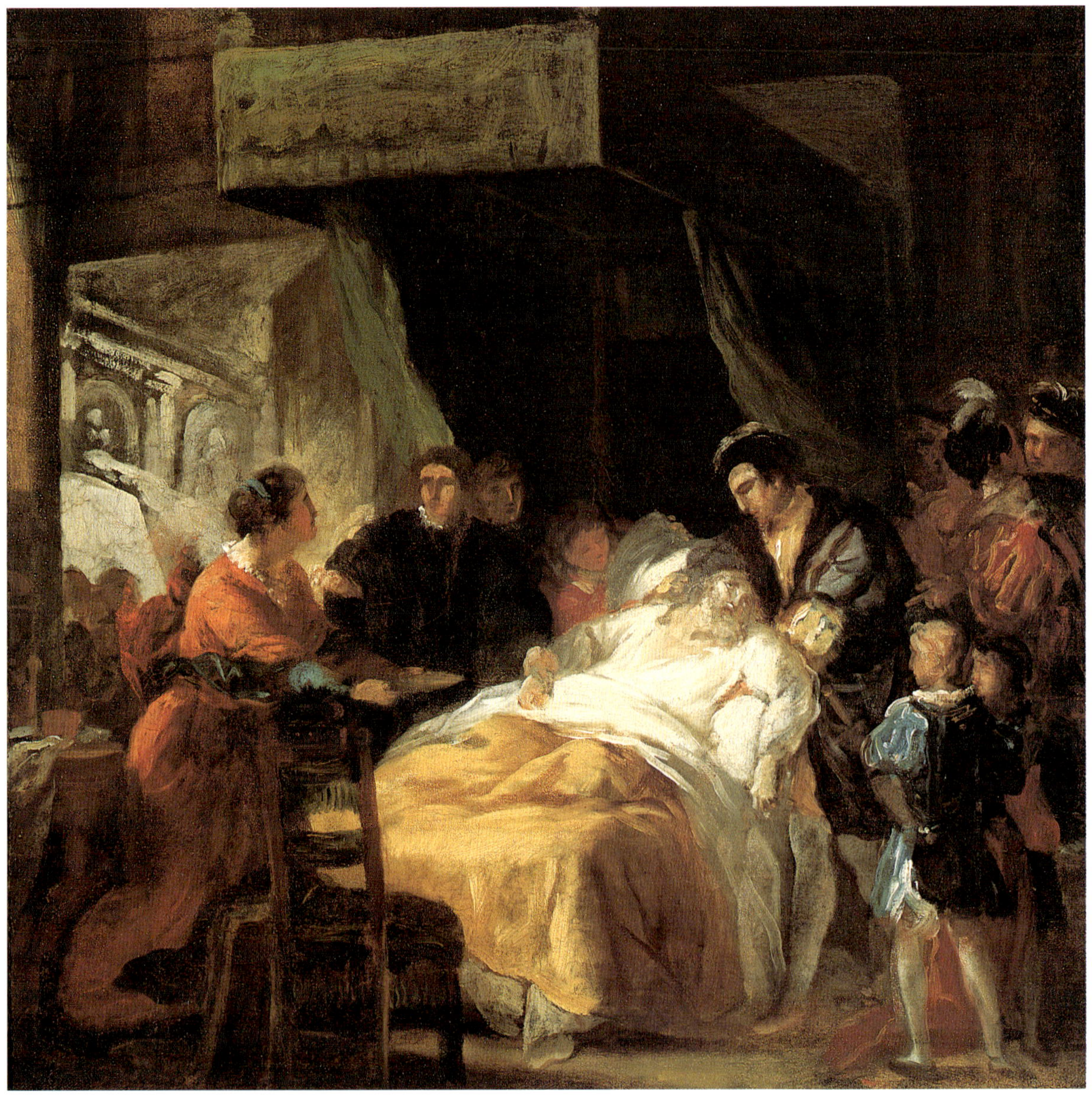

46 François-Guillaume MENAGEOT
***The Death of Leonardo da Vinci in the
Arms of François I***, c. 1781
Léonardo da Vinci mourant dans les bras
de François I
Oil on canvas
21 ⅜ × 21 ⅝" (54.3 × 54.9 cm)

Provenance: Comtesse de Provence (?);
Girodet-Troison, sold Paris April 11–25,
1825, no. 414; Walferdin, sold Paris April
12–16, 1880, no. 146; Henri Haro, sold
Paris March 18–20, 1912, no. 195; Louis
Mairet collection; private collection,
Geneva; M. J. Tully, London; Christie's,
New York, January 15, 1986, no. 81
(reprod.).

Exhibitions: Rochester/New
Brunswick/Atlanta 1987, no. 39.

Bibliography: Antal 1935, p. 162, pl. IIB;
Florisoone 1948, p. 113, pl. 155;
Seznec/Diderot 1967, p. 330 illus.; Lossky,
1967, p. 50, illus.; Willk-Brocard 1978, p.
67, cat. no. 12, fig. 23; Paris 1984–85, p.
330.

The Death of Leonardo was commissioned by the Bâtiments du Roi in 1780 to serve as
a model for a series of Gobelins tapestries illustrating the *History of France*. The final
painting, signed and dated 1781, was exhibited in the Salon of that year and went
directly into the collection of Louis XVI. This vivid preliminary sketch for the painting that brought Ménageot his greatest critical acclaim is thought to have belonged
to the Comtesse de Provence, sister-in-law of Louis XVI, because the engraving of
the composition by F.-P.-F. Garreau, executed in 1781, bears her coat of arms.

In 1810, the final painting entered the collection of the Musée Napoléon and
from there was moved to Fontainebleau. In 1842, when the painting was moved to
the staircase at Versailles, its original square format, as attested by this preliminary
sketch, was altered. Cropped at the top to reduce its height and widened by the addition of a section of canvas on the left painted by Pierre Franque, the work became
rectangular. Finally it was transferred to the Musée de l'Hôtel de Ville at Amboise,
the town where the deathbed scene had taken place.

The subject of the painting is recounted in Vasari's *Lives of the Artists*. The elder-
ly Leonardo struggled to greet François I from his sickbed, but being too weak, fell
back and expired in the King's arms. In its anecdotal historicism, depicting the death
of the Italian Renaissance genius and the sympathetic humanity displayed by
François I, the work is a clear precursor of the nineteenth-century *troubadour* style of
painting. There were, however, precedents for the treatment of the subject. Angelica
Kauffmann had exhibited a painting titled *Leonardo da Vinci Expiring in the Arms of
Francis I* at the Royal Academy, London, in 1778 (no. 174), and there is also an
undated drawing of Leonardo's death by Richard Cosway (Truro County Museum
and Art Gallery), which may also predate Ménageot's work.

The traditional composition of the work is typical of Ménageot's other designs
and reflects the influence of seventeenth-century Bolognese painting. The skillful use
of color, chiaroscuro, and brushwork are as evident in the present sketch as in the
final canvas. Ménageot painted a number of similar histories and allegories, including
Allegory of the Birth of the Dauphin (1782; Paris, Musée du Louvre), *Dagobert I Ordering
the Construction of the Church of Saint-Denis* (Douai, Church of Saint-Pierre), and *The
Marriage of Prince Eugène Beauharnais* (Versailles).

J. P. M.

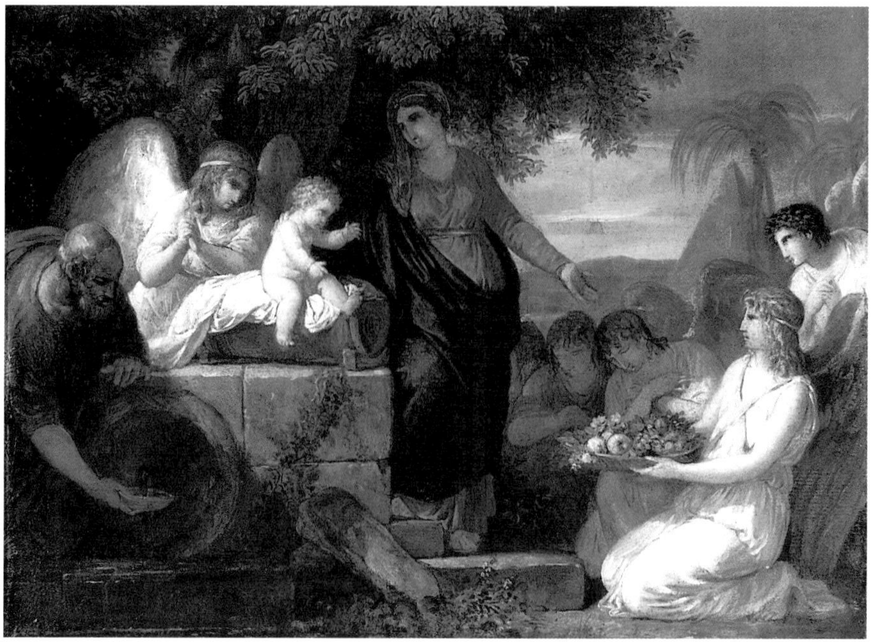

47 François-Guillaume MENAGEOT
The Rest on the Flight into Egypt, 1796
Le Repos durant la fuite en Egypte
Oil on paper on canvas
9 ⅞ × 13 ⅝" (25.1 × 34.6 cm)
Inscribed on the back of the original
frame: *Vente Clermont-Tonnerre 1802.*

Provenance: December 10–13, 1900,
Clermont-Tonnerre sale, Hôtel Drouot,
Paris, no. 20, bought Michel; Marquis de
Lastic Collection, Paris.

Exhibitions: Houston 1973–75, no. 62.

Bibliography: Willk-Brocard, 1978, p. 76,
cat. no. 28, fig. 49.

Nicole Willk-Brocard has identified this sketch as *The Holy Family Served by Angels* recorded as no. 20 in the catalogue of the Clermont-Tonnerre sale held in Paris in 1900. The inscription on the back of the original frame is therefore erroneous, since there was no Clermont-Tonnerre sale in 1802, but a work of this description by Ménageot is listed in the sale of 1900.

This sketch is related to an altarpiece in the sanctuary of Monte-Berico in Vicenza. The format of the final composition is entirely different from the horizontal emphasis of the sketch, being vertical with a rounded top (see Willk-Brocard 1978, p. 76, cat. no. 28, fig. 49). The subject derives from the *Apocrypha* and illustrates the Virgin resting on the flight into Egypt.

Willk-Brocard regards this religious composition as vital in an assessment of Ménageot's oeuvre. An importance is placed on the landscape, the static grouping of the people, and the use of light. There is a serenity and a slightly archaizing quality in both the sketch and the final painting, which seem to reflect a very personal vision. It may indicate the inner calmness that Ménageot felt as a result of residing in Vicenza, away from the political turbulence. The Republic of Venice had preserved its neutrality between France and Austria, which made it an attractive location for émigrés, and Ménageot had settled there after leaving Rome in January 1793. This painting, presumably designed to Ménageot's own personal taste and satisfaction, differs considerably from the officially commissioned history paintings (see cat. nos. 46 and 48). Ménageot painted the altarpiece in gratitude for the warm welcome he had received from the inhabitants of Vicenza. The painting was accepted by a decree on July 18, 1796, and on January 14, 1797, was placed on the altar of the Holy Virgin in the Church of the Madonna del Monte. A month later, when French troops entered, Ménageot left Vicenza.

Willk-Brocard has remarked that this sketch is very characteristic of Ménageot's preliminary studies. In his search for the most satisfactory composition, he has not only changed the distribution of the figures, but has also reversed them all, apart from the Virgin, a procedure that can be noted in the preparation of the composition of *Astyanax Seized from Andromache by Order of Ulysses* (cat. no. 48). Another feature typical of Ménageot's studies is the mask-like faces, which have very little definition.

There is a further painting, slightly wider in format, (private collection; Willk-Brocard 1978, p. 77, cat. no. 29, fig. 50), which relates to the composition. It may also be a preparatory sketch for the altarpiece, but could equally be a study for an easel painting.

J.R.B.

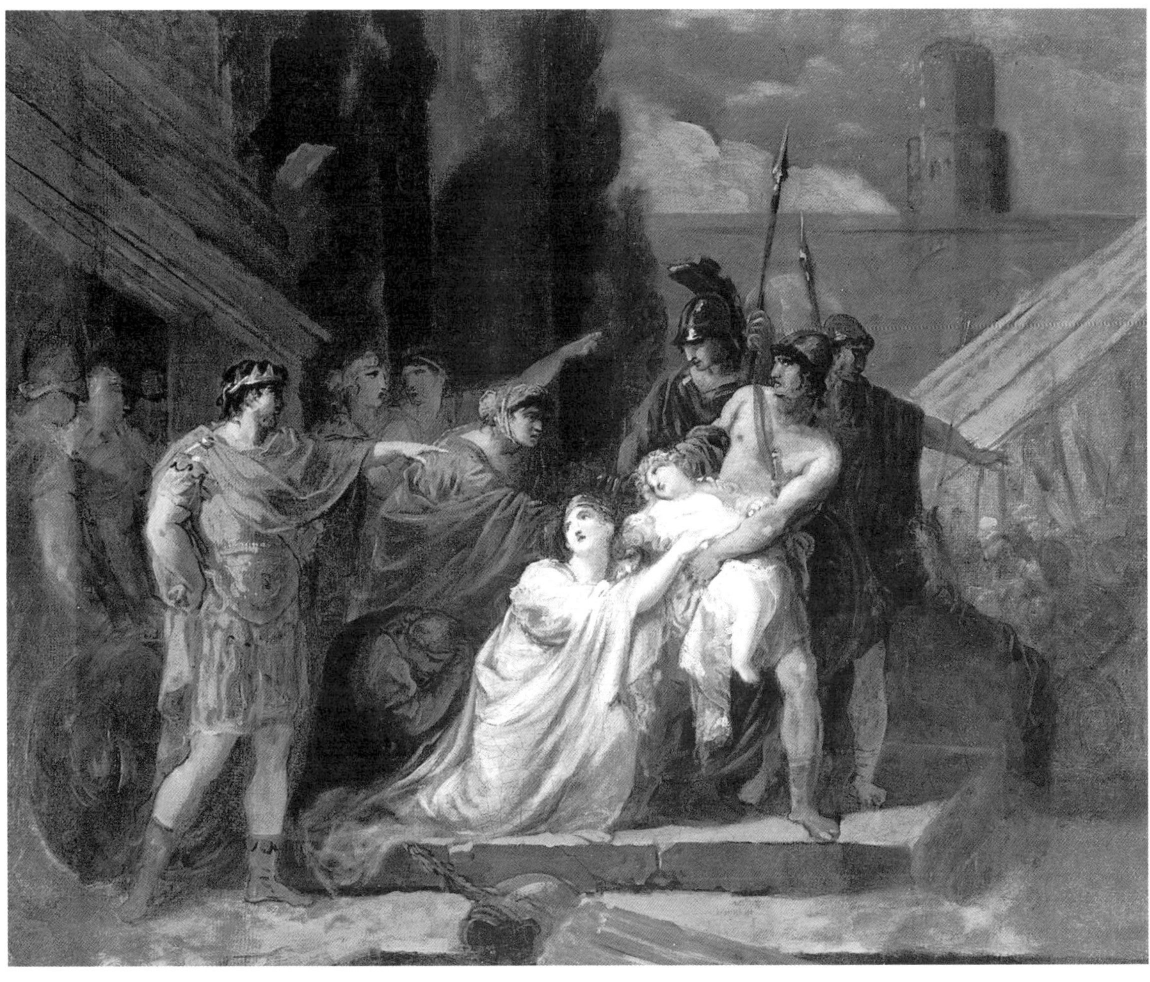

48 François-Guillaume MENAGEOT
Astyanax Seized from Andromache by Order of Ulysses, 1783
Astyanax arraché des bras d'Andromaque
par ordre d'Ulysse
Oil on canvas
21 ¼ × 25 ⅞" (54.0 × 65.7 cm)

Exhibitions: Houston 1973–75, no. 64.

Bibliography: Willk-Brocard 1978, p. 71,
cat. no. 19, fig. 35.

This is the preparatory sketch for the large painting commissioned in 1783 by the Bâtiments du Roi, which is now in the Musée des Beaux-Arts, Angers (inv. 131; Willk-Brocard 1978, p. 70, cat. no. 18, fig. 34). The final painting was exhibited in the Salon of 1783 and entered the collections of Louis XVI that September. The Jury des Arts rejected the subject as a model for the Gobelins tapestry series.

The 1783 Salon contained about thirty history paintings, and the subject of Andromache featured three times, in works by Jacques-Louis David, Joseph-Marie Vien, and Ménageot. While David's *Andromache Mourning Hector* (Paris, Ecole Nationale des Beaux-Arts) was highly successful, by comparison the critics were rather severe on Ménageot's interpretation of the subject and his composition.

Astyanax Seized from Andromache by Order of Ulysses marks a distinct movement in Ménageot's style toward Neoclassicism. The figures are given monumentality and stand before the perspective of a background of Classical architecture. The subject comes from Greek legend and is recounted by Euripides in *The Trojan Women*. Astyanax was the small son of Andromache and Hector. During the Trojan War, Hector was killed by Achilles, and after the capture of the city, Astyanax was seized from his mother and hurled from the battlements, to prevent possible future revenge for his father's death. In the seventeenth century, Racine had made Andromache the subject of one of his most successful tragedies.

The present sketch is particularly interesting, since it reveals how in the final composition Ménageot completely reversed his first thoughts and added the kneeling female figure in the left foreground. This working procedure is closely echoed in his other preparatory sketches (see cat. no. 47).

There are two further preparatory works for the final composition. The inventory drawn up on the death of J. B. P. Lebrun in 1813 recorded a small painting on paper in square format, which subsequently appeared in the Lebrun sale, May 26, 1814, no. 102. A drawing for the composition is also known (Dupan sale, March 26, 1840, no. 1465).

J. R.B.

83

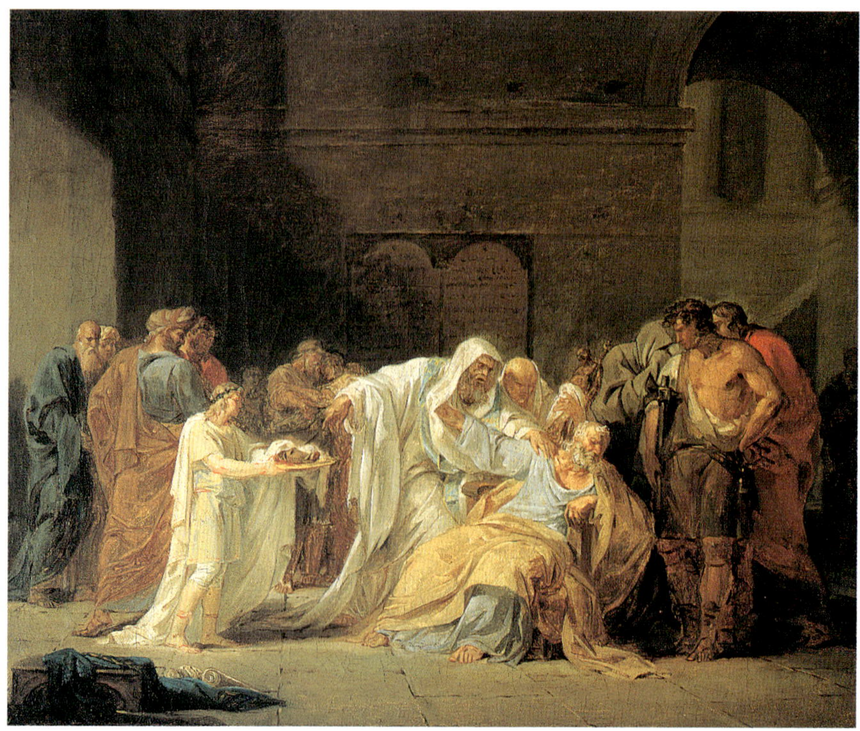

49 Attributed to François-Guillaume
MENAGEOT
Eleazar Refusing to Eat Pork, c. late
1780s
Eléazar refusant de manger la viande
de porc
Oil on canvas
16 ¾ × 20 ⅜" (42.5 × 51.8 cm)

Exhibitions: Houston 1973–75, no. 63.

The subject of *Eleazar Refusing to Eat Pork* is taken from an episode in the second book of Maccabees (6: 18–31) in the *Apocrypha* of the Old Testament. The scene depicts Eleazar, Aaron's son and the chief priest of the tribe of the Levites, being forced to eat pork by Antiochus IV Epiphanes, the Greek king of Syria. This event formed part of the King's fierce suppression of the Jews, in his attempt to Hellenize Judea. Eleazar took a noble stand against his oppressor, preferring death "rather than a life of pollution." He had been present at the time when the food laws were given to Moses (see Leviticus 8) and was responsible for passing them on to future generations: "It becometh not our years to dissemble, said he, that through this, many of the young should suppose that Eleazar, the man of fourscore years and ten, had gone over unto an alien religion."

Robert Rosenblum (1967, p. 64) has pointed out that the subject provided a religious, as well as an exotic, *exemplum virtutis*. It was treated several times by artists toward the end of the eighteenth century. Berthélémy exhibited a painting of the subject at the 1789 Salon (Musée d'Angers), and in 1792 it was the selected subject for the Prix-de-Rome, which was won by Charles-Paul Landon.

This sketch is not included in Willk-Brocard's monograph on Ménageot (1978), probably since she is of the opinion that the frieze-like composition is not typical of his style (see Houston 1973–75, no. 63). There are, however, convincing stylistic parallels in Ménageot's work, even, to an extent, in terms of the composition. His painting *The Supplication of Meleager by His Family* (Paris, Musée du Louvre; Willk-Brocard 1978, fig. 44), for example, which was executed in 1788–89 and exhibited at the 1791 Salon, has a similar frieze-like grouping of the figures.

It is significant that Jacques-Louis David exhibited his powerful Neoclassical painting *The Death of Socrates* (New York, The Metropolitan Museum of Art) at the 1787 Salon, and that it was heralded by his contemporaries as a masterpiece of composition. In this work, David heightened the drama of the scene by placing the characters, in frieze-like manner, on the same picture plane. It seems likely, therefore, that both Ménageot's composition of *The Supplication of Meleager by His Family* and that of the present sketch were inspired by the Davidian precedent.

J. Patrice Marandel has further pointed out the strong stylistic similarity between the features of the semi-clad figure of Antiochus IV Epiphanes on the right of the present sketch and the head of Cupid in Ménageot's pen-and-ink drawing *Cupid and Psyche* of 1784 (Paris, Musée du Louvre; Willk-Brocard, fig. 141). The stylistic affinities between this sketch and the above works suggest that it is datable to the last years of the 1780s.

J.R.B.

Piat SAUVAGE

(Tournai 1744–Paris 1818)

Sauvage first studied at the Academy of Tournai before settling in Paris in 1774. After being received into several provincial academies and the Académie de Saint-Luc in 1781, he finally became a member of the Académie Royale in 1783. Sauvage painted mostly *trompe l'oeil*, which he exhibited regularly at the Paris Salons between 1781 and 1804. By 1780 he had become official painter to the Prince de Condé. He also worked at Versailles, Fontainebleau, Compiègne, Rambouillet, and Saint-Cloud, providing, in particular, overdoors intended to resemble marble, bronze, or cameo. He retired to his native country, Belgium, and was active at the end of his life in Brussels and Tournai.

50 Piat SAUVAGE
Grisaille of Putti, n.d.
Putti (grisaille)
Oil on canvas
11 ¾ × 8 ¾" (29.8 × 22.2 cm)

Exhibitions: Albuquerque 1980, no. 56.

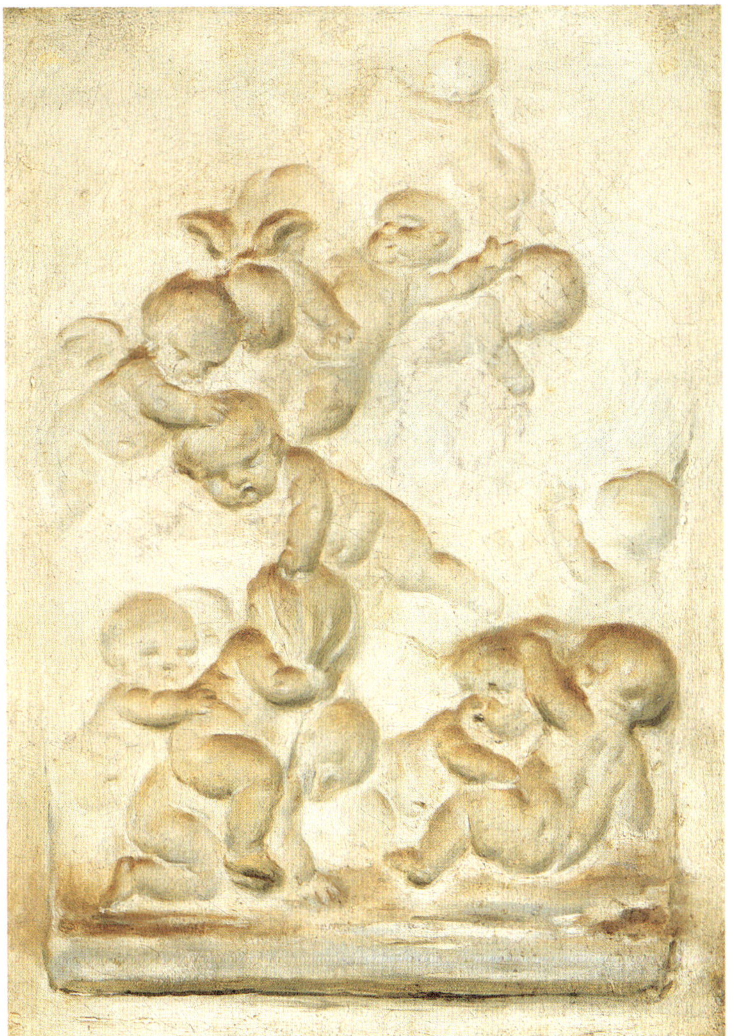

The tradition of simulating sculptures in *trompe l'oeil* paintings was well-established, particularly in Northern Europe, where Jacob de Wit (1695–1754) had distinguished himself in that technique. Piat Sauvage continued the tradition and produced countless such *trompe l'oeil*, which were often intended as overdoors in boiserie panels. This type of decorative panel was particularly popular in late eighteenth-century France. Even Chardin presented three monochrome *trompe l'oeil* at the Salons of 1769 and 1771 (see Paris/Cleveland/Boston 1979, nos. 131–33).

This small painting, executed more vigorously than Sauvage's more finished works, creates a double visual pun in being not just a painting simulating a sculpture, but a painting of a sculpture (indicated by the ledge at the bottom of what appears to be a freestanding relief).

J. P. M.

François-André VINCENT

(Paris 1746–Paris 1816)

Pupil of Vien (q.v.), Vincent obtained the Prix-de-Rome in 1768. He was in Rome from 1771 until 1775. His debut at the Paris Salon of 1777 was highly acclaimed. In 1778, his *Arrest of President Molé* (Paris, Palais-Bourbon) revealed his predilection for scenes from modern history, thus anticipating the *troubadour* current of the nineteenth century. Vincent is a varied artist. His work has often been confused with Fragonard's, with which it shares, particularly in the drawings, an ebullient exuberance. Vincent can also be calm and measured, particularly in his representations of antique subjects. His originality is proof of the complexity of French painting during the late eighteenth and early nineteenth centuries.

51 François-André VINCENT
Boreas and Oreithya, n.d.
Borée et Orithye
Oil on canvas
12 ¼ × 9 ⅝" (31.1 × 24.4 cm)

Provenance: Alfred Saucède, sold Paris, Hôtel Drouot, February 14, 1879, no. 63 (attributed to J.-B. Lemoyne); Léon-Michel Lévy, sold Paris, Hôtel Drouot, June 17–18, 1925, no. 145 (attributed to J.-B. Lemoyne).

Exhibitions: Albuquerque 1980, no. 6 (attributed to F. Boucher).

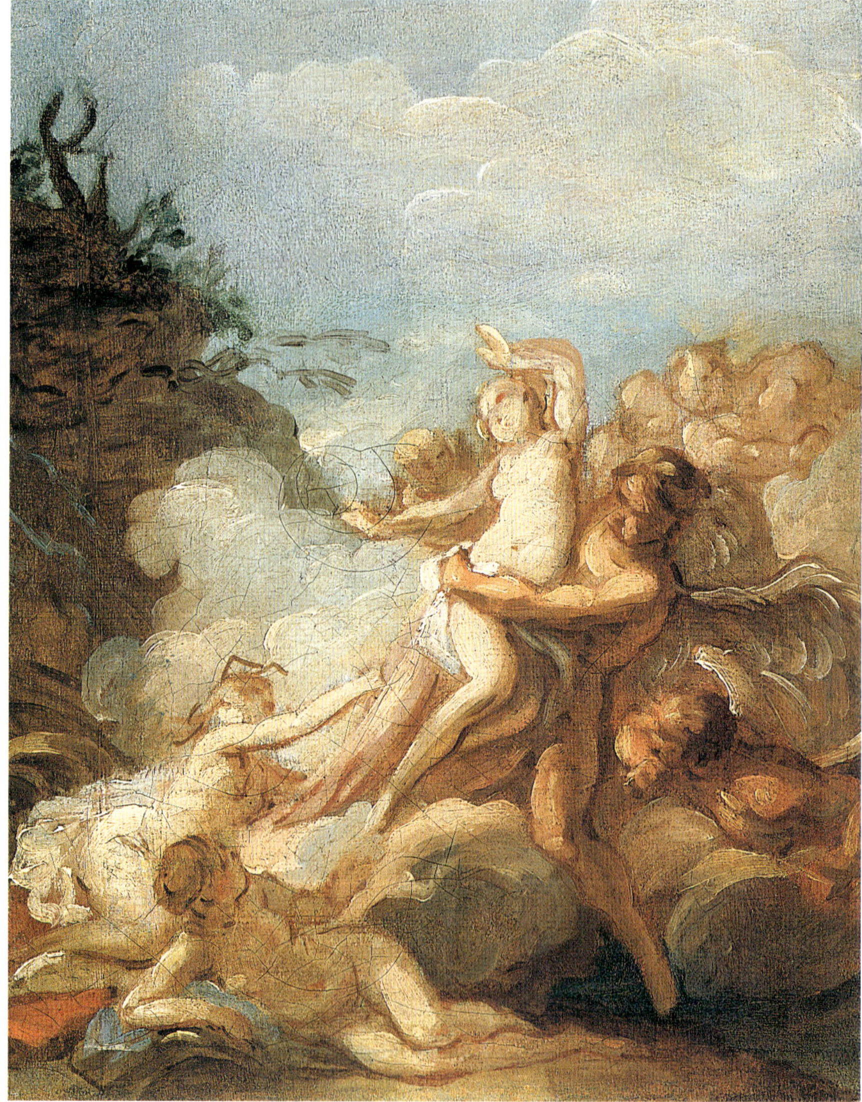

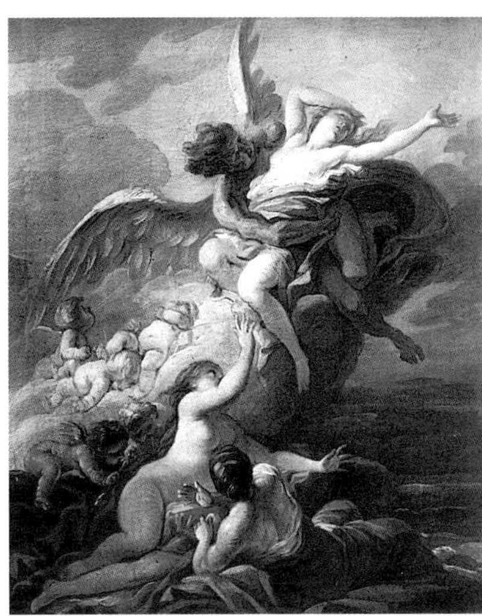

Fig. 8. François-André VINCENT. *The Abduction of Oreithya* (L'Enlèvement d'Orithye), c. 1770–71. Oil on canvas. Musée des Beaux-Arts de Rennes

Previously attributed to J.-B. Lemoyne and to Boucher, this sketch is related to a painting in the Musée des Beaux-Arts de Rennes (fig. 8) once cautiously attributed to Lagrenée, and now convincingly attributed to Vincent (Cuzin 1980, pp. 80, 82).

Although the composition of this sketch differs from that of the Rennes picture —in which the position of the Boreas and Oreithya group is reversed—many details, such as the attitude of the water nymph reaching for Oreithya, indicate the dependence of one composition on the other.

The subject, taken from Ovid's *Metamorphoses* (6, 692–721), represents Boreas, the personification of the North Wind, abducting his future wife Oreithya, daughter of Erechteus, King of Athens. An oft-represented story in French and Italian painting of the seventeenth and eighteenth centuries (Pigler 1974, vol. 2, pp. 54–55), it had been depicted twice by Boucher: in 1750, as a cartoon for the Beauvais tapestry manufactory (Ananoff 1976, vol. 2, p. 48, no. 349), and in 1769 in one of the four large mythological paintings now at the Kimbell Art Museum, Fort Worth (ibid., pp. 301–04, no. 677). It is conceivable that Boucher's late picture, or perhaps a drawing connected to it by Ananoff (ibid., p. 302, fig. 1764), provided Vincent with a model for his own. Indeed the delicate brushwork and light flesh tones of this sketch are more characteristic of the vigorous sketch style of Boucher than of Vincent. The dependence on Boucher justifies the early date of 1770–71 advanced by Cuzin for the Rennes composition. When Vincent returned to the subject in 1781 and 1782 with two paintings exhibited at the 1783 Salon (reproduced in Cuzin 1980, p. 82, figs. 2, 3; the 1782 version, now at the Prefecture, Chambéry, became the artist's reception piece into the Académie), he dramatically altered the composition by eliminating the Boucher-like water nymphs seen here and replacing them with a more dynamic, standing nymph attempting to hold back Oreithya. The oil sketch (Tours, Musée des Beaux-Arts), closely related to the 1781 version, is executed in an energetic style that shows the direction the artist took in the decade that separates it from our sketch.

J. P. M.

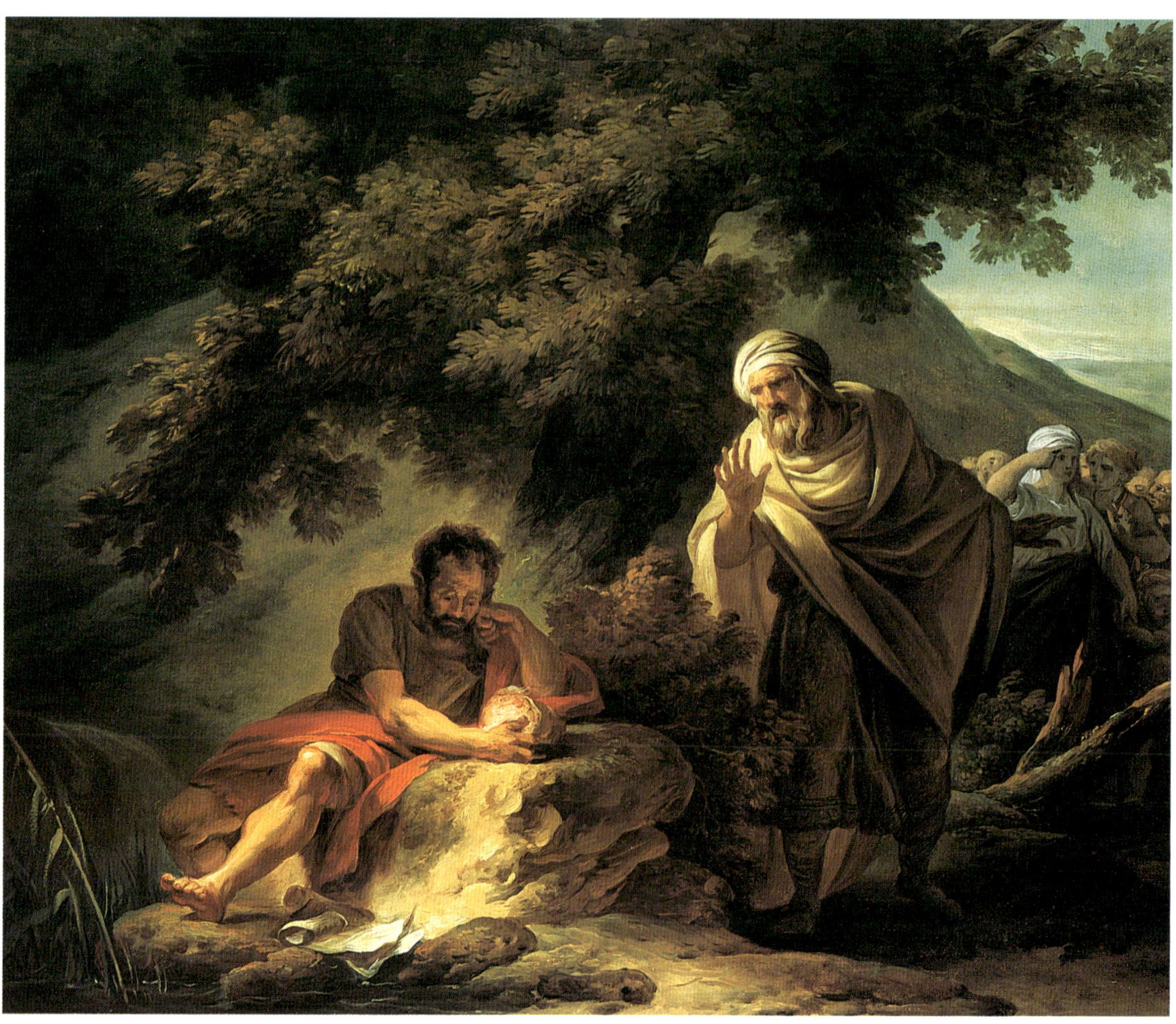

52 François-André VINCENT
Democritus Among the Abderitans, n.d.
Démocrite chez les Abderitains
Oil on canvas
18 × 21 ¾" (45.7 × 55.2 cm)

Provenance: Jacques Petit-Hory, Paris.

Exhibitions: Salon of 1791, no. 348;
Houston 1973–75, no. 89; Rochester/New
Brunswick/Atlanta 1987–88, no. 60.

Bibliography: Dézallier d'Argenville
1791, p. 42.

In spite of its relatively small size, this painting is in all likelihood the one exhibited at the 1791 Salon with five other works by Vincent, including his large *Pyrrhus at the Court of Glaucias, King of Illyria* (see the following entry). Uniformity of size was not a goal of the exhibitors, who preferred to show the variety of their talents and, as in this case, their ability to treat a typical subject of the *grande peinture* on the scale of a cabinet picture. There is no known larger version of the subject by Vincent.

Democritus of Abdera was a Greek materialist philosopher who, according to an antique tradition related by, among others, Cicero, in his letters *Ad Atticum*, was shunned by his countrymen. Here Vincent has represented him in the traditional contemplative attitude of the wiseman reflecting on human destiny by looking at a skull. His fellow Abderitans, richly dressed, poke fun at him—one of them points to his own forehead to signify the madness of the philosopher, another holds back his companions, as if to test this for himself. While extolling the virtues of the individual, the subject differs slightly from other examples of civic virtue that were common in late eighteenth-century French art. By contrasting the solitary genius with the unappreciative crowd, it prefigures paintings from the Romantic era, such as Delacroix's poignant *Torquato Tasso in the Hospital for the Insane*, the first version of which was painted in 1824.

Dézallier d'Argenville's comment that the work was executed with a "thick and heavy brush" (*un pinceau gras et pâteux*) is surprising considering the smooth finish of the painting's surface.

J. P. M.

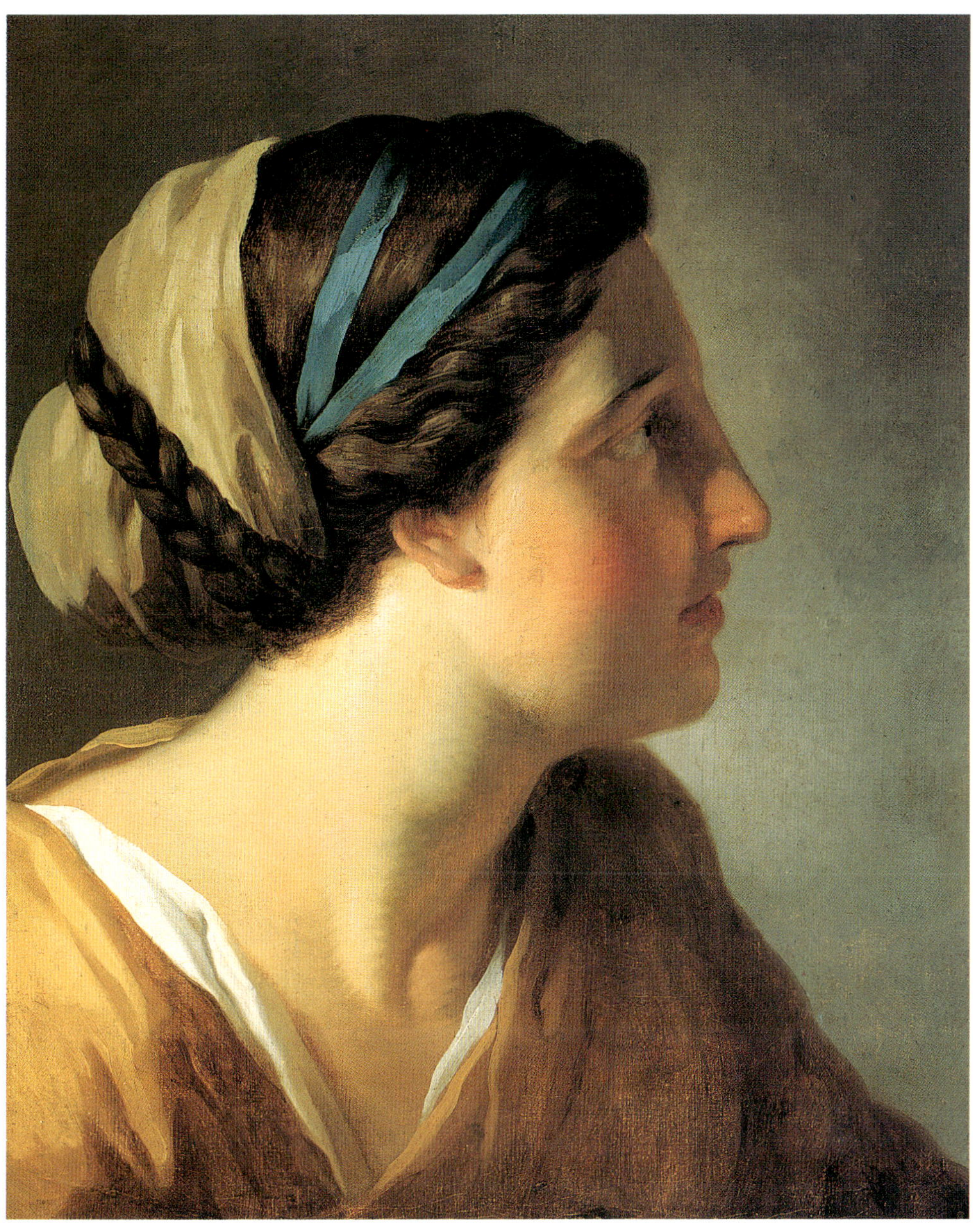

53   François-André VINCENT
      Female Head, c. 1787-90
      Tête de femme
      Oil on canvas
      18 × 14 ⅞" (45.7 × 37.8 cm)

      Exhibitions: Albuquerque 1980, no. 70.

It is difficult to establish the relationship of such a finished study to a given painting. Rather it belongs to the well-established tradition of the *tête d'expression*, an exercise to which students at the Académie had to submit. Yet there is a strong resemblance between this idealized head and individual figures in some paintings by Vincent. This sketch invites a particular comparison with, for instance, the heads of several female attendants in the two paintings executed by Vincent for the Residenz at Koblenz and now at the castle in Zidlochovice, Czech Republic: *Augustus and Cinna*, 1787, and *Pyrrhus at the Court of Glaucias, King of Illyria*, 1791 (see Seelig 1990). Further comparison can be made with a sheet of studies in a French-private collection, published by Cuzin (1986), which also features a similar head. The sureness of this sketch's execution leads us to advance a date close to the Koblenz pictures (1787–90).

J. P. M..

Adelaïde LABILLE-GUIARD

(Paris 1749–Paris 1803)

*S*uccessively pupil of the miniature-painter François-Elie Vincent and of his son François-André (q.v.), whom she eventually married in 1800, Adelaïde Labille-Guiard also studied for a brief time with Georges de La Tour. She first exhibited a pastel at the Académie de Saint-Luc in 1774. In 1783, she was received at the Académie (along with Vigée-Lebrun) and subsequently became the official painter of the King's aunts (Peintre de Mesdames). Perhaps she shared some of the ideals of the French Revolution, as she remained in France for its entire duration, exhibiting for the last time in 1800.

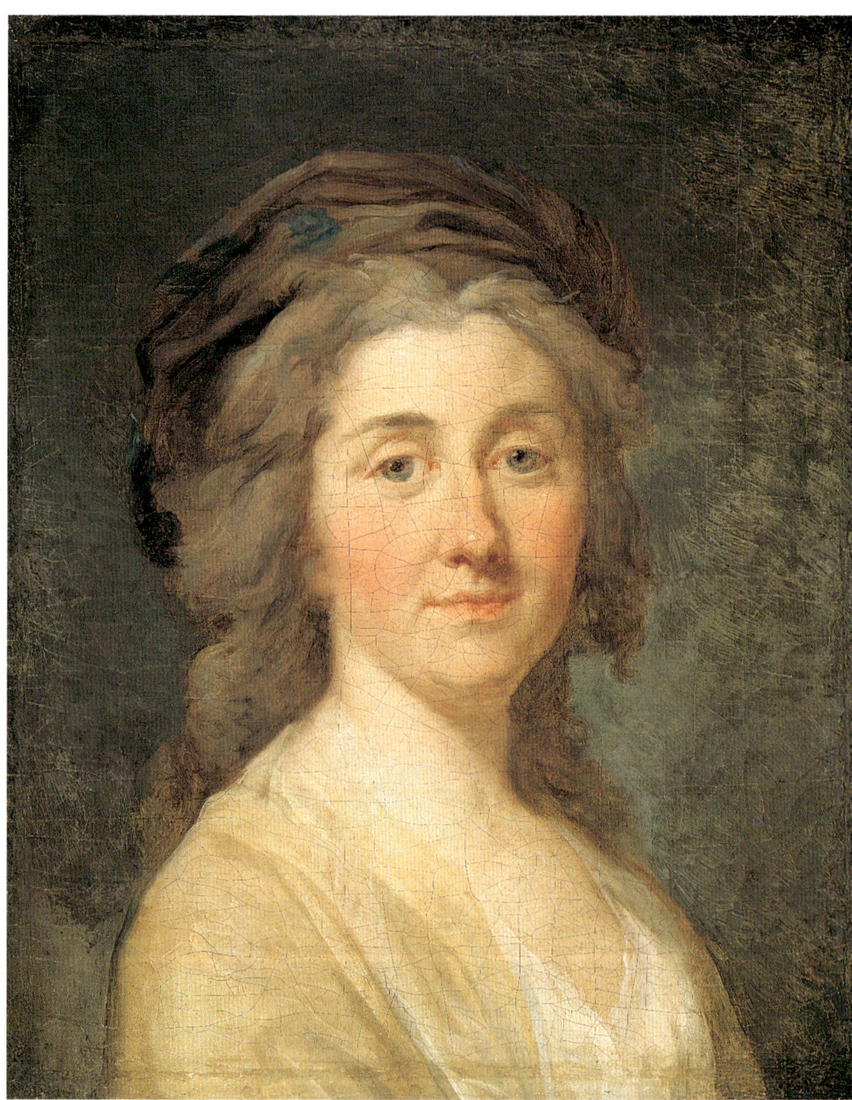

54   Adelaïde LABILLE-GUIARD
Portrait of a Woman (Self-Portrait?),
n.d.
Portrait de femme (Autoportrait?)
Oil on canvas
20 × 16" (50.8 × 40.6 cm)

Provenance: Marquis de Saint-Lève d'Aguerre (stamp on stretcher, and second stamp on stretcher).

Exhibitions: Houston 1973–75, no. 47.

This portrait can be attributed to Labille-Guiard on stylistic grounds. The direct, unpretentious, presentation of the sitter suggests a portrait of the Revolutionary period, during which Labille-Guiard (who did not emigrate like her rival, Vigée-Lebrun) modified the courtly style that had earned her the position of Peintre de Mesdames to fit current taste. Here the lightly sketched background echoes in many respects David's amazing portraits of the late eighteenth century. The portrait's immediacy also implies that it is either a very close friend or possibly a self-portrait. As always, Labille-Guiard is able to convey emotion and a certain sweetness without falling into sentimentality. In 1785, judges of her *Self-portrait with Two Pupils*, presented that year at the Salon, had admired the artist's "simple and true manner."

J.P.M.

Jacques SABLET

(Morges, Switzerland 1749–Paris 1803)

First apprenticed to his father, Jacques Sablet entered the studio of Vien (q.v.) in 1775 and followed his master to Rome. Sablet would probably have remained in Rome, had his career there not been interrupted by the Revolutionary events of 1793 (see the biography of Fabre, cat. no. 84). Sablet returned to Switzerland and then settled in Paris, where he exhibited at the Salons from 1793 until his death. The last years of his life were marked by the patronage of Lucien Bonaparte, Napoleon's brother, whom he accompanied to Spain in 1800–01. In Spain with Lethière (q.v.), he bought works of art for the collections of Lucien Bonaparte. Napoleon's uncle, Cardinal Fesch, an insatiable collector, owned at least fifteen works by Sablet. His oeuvre includes mythological paintings and allegories, but his early ambitions in this grand manner were thwarted; his clientele preferred his portraits and Italian genre scenes.

55 Jacques SABLET
Helen Saved by Venus from the Wrath of Aeneas, 1779
Enée poursuivant Hélène
Oil on paper on canvas
9 ½ × 13 ½" (24.1 × 34.3 cm)

Exhibitions: Houston 1973–75, no. 14.

Bibliography: Nantes/Lausanne/Rome 1985, p. 47, under no. 6.

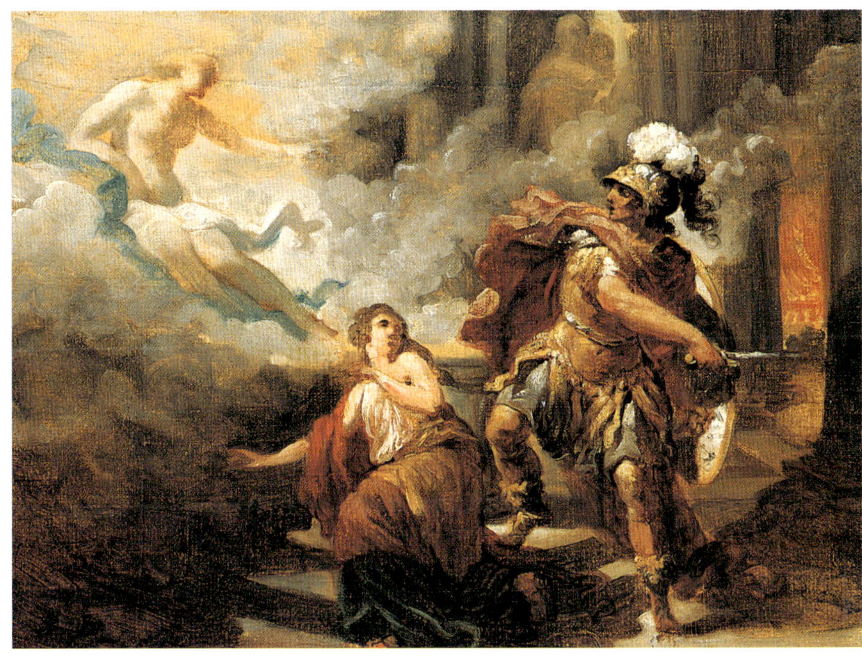

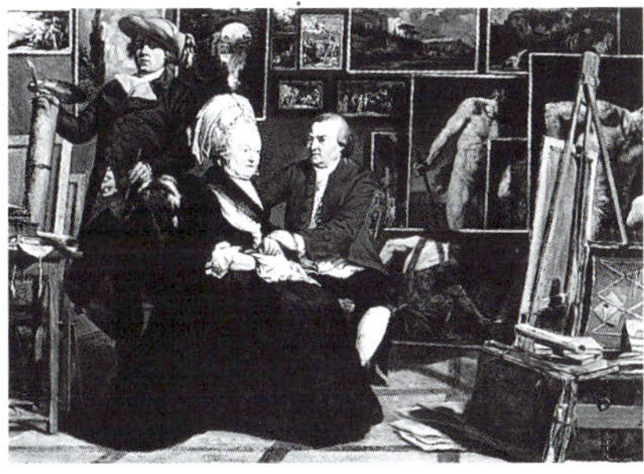

Fig. 9. Jacques SABLET. *The Painter in His Studio with His Parents* (Le Peintre dans son atelier avec ses parents), 1781. Oil on canvas. Musée Cantonal des Beaux-Arts, Lausanne. Photo: JC Ducret, MCBA.

Once tentatively attributed to Doyen (Houston 1973–75, no. 14), this sketch is instead an important document in the career of Jacques Sablet. Its attribution is confirmed beyond doubt by the fact that it figures in the upper left corner of the artist's studio in the painting executed in 1781 representing the artist at the easel with his parents sitting in his atelier (fig. 9).

The location of the finished painting, wrongly attributed by Nagler (1845, vol. 14, pp. 127–28) to "Franz" (François, the artist's brother and himself a genre painter), is unknown today. In 1779, Sablet had sent the finished work, along with a sketch for *The Temple of the Liberal Arts* (see the following entry), from Rome to Lausanne to be exhibited at the studio of his father, Jacob Sablet (see Archives Cantonales Vaudoises, Mémorial J. H. Polier de Vernand, CXLI). The subject of that painting and this sketch is taken from Virgil (*Aeneid*, II, 590–600) and was meant as an expression of gratitude on the part of Sablet for the support he had received for his studies in Rome.

These works were executed by Sablet at a moment of great hope in his early career. In 1777, he had won a second prize at the Accademia di San Lucca and been admitted in 1779 into the Accademia di Parma upon presentation of his *Death of Pallas* (Piacenza, Museo Civico). In spite of these successes, the history paintings he sent to Switzerland, *Struggle between Mars and Minerva* (whereabouts unknown) and this episode from the Aeneid—deemed "two of his most beautiful paintings"—won him no critical acclaim. Sablet devoted the rest of his life to genre painting.

J. P. M.

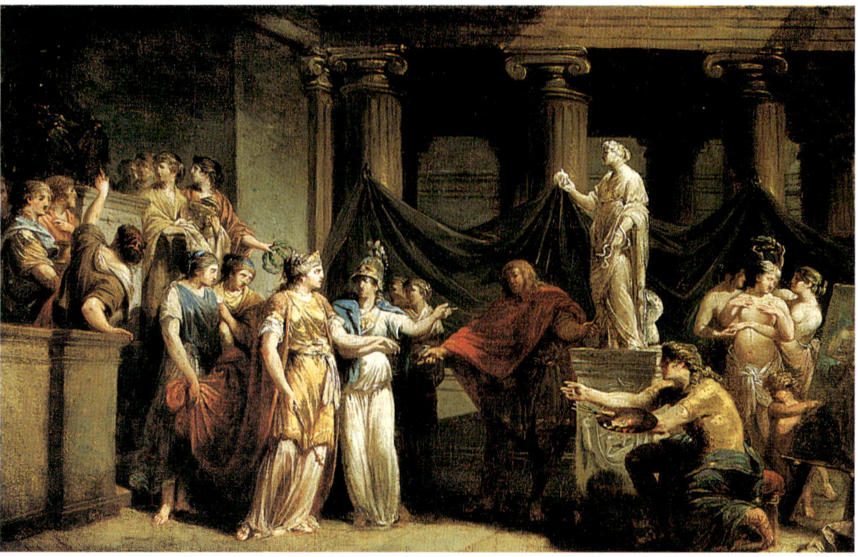

56 Jacques SABLET
The Temple of the Liberal Arts, with the City of Bern and Minerva, 1779
Le Temple des arts libéraux, avec la ville de Berne et la déesse Minerve
Oil on canvas
13 ¼ × 21" (33.7 × 53.3 cm)

Exhibitions: September 21, 1779, at Jacob Sablet's (the artist's father) in Lausanne; Houston 1973–75, no. 105 (as anonymous).

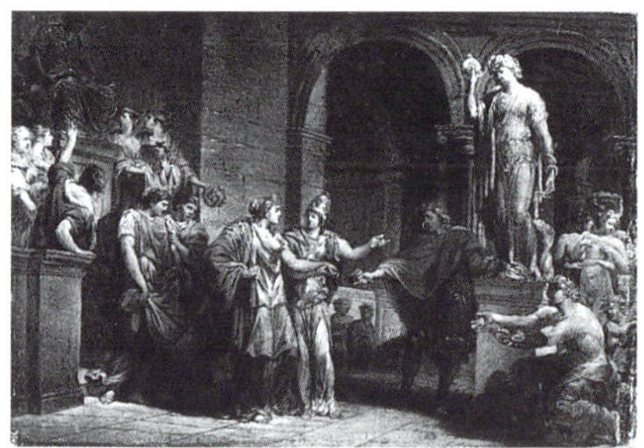

Fig. 10. Jacques SABLET. *The Temple of the Liberal Arts, with the City of Bern and Minerva* (Le Temple des arts libéraux, avec la ville de Berne et la déesse Minerve), 1779. Oil on canvas. Musée Cantonal des Beaux-Arts, Lausanne. Photo: JC Ducret, MCBA.

The literature on the artist (see Nantes/Lausanne/Rome 1985, no. 5) has accepted the sketch of the same subject in the Musée Cantonal des Beaux-Arts, Lausanne (fig. 10), as the one sent by Sablet from Rome to Lausanne in 1779 and exhibited at the studio of his father, Jacob Sablet. It is clear, however, that the sketch represented by the artist on the wall of his studio (fig. 9), is the one sent to his father and presented in this exhibition. Small differences include the size and shape of the architectural element to the left of the composition; the right arm of the sculpture, close to the head of the goddess in the Lausanne sketch and more generously extended in our sketch; and the background architecture. In the Lausanne sketch, the architecture features an arcade, while in both the present sketch and its representation in the painting of the artist's studio, we find a series of Ionic columns partially hidden by a tapestry.

In 1778, Sablet, then in Rome, first approached the government of the Republic of Bern with the hope of obtaining a commission. In 1779, he sent to Lausanne a painting intended to thank the authorities for material support, as well as this sketch of a composition intended to glorify the role of Bern in the patronage of the arts. In spite of the obvious flattery, the sketch was rejected. Nevertheless, Sablet painted the final composition, a large canvas (2.26 × 1.78 m; Bern, Kunstmuseum, inv. 816; see Nantes/Lausanne/Rome 1985, no. 6) dated 1781, which was accepted and paid for by the senate of the city.

Both the final composition and its sketch display a more austere style than his *Helen and Aeneas* of the same year; even so his art remains far less rigorous than that of his master, Vien.

J. P. M.

Pierre-Henri de VALENCIENNES

(Toulouse 1750–Paris 1819)

Valenciennes is one of the foremost landscapists of the early nineteenth century, not only because of his paintings, but because of his activities as a teacher and theoretician of Classical landscapes. His ambition was to raise the Académie's esteem of landscape painting to equal that of history painting. Author of *Eléments de perspective practique à l'usage des artistes: Suivis de réflexions et conseils à un élève sur la peinture et particulièrement sur le genre du paysage* (1799/1800, and 1820), Valenciennes was responsible for the creation of the Prix-de-Rome du Paysage Historique in 1816. Student of Despax at the Royal Academy of Toulouse and of the miniaturist Bouton, he visited Italy for the first time in 1769 and then entered the atelier of Doyen (1771). Living in Italy from 1777 to 1784–85, he traveled to Sicily in 1779 and to France for a short visit during which he met Joseph Vernet—who gave him a single lesson in perspective and its application to painting, described in his book on perspective. He was made a member of the Académie in 1787 with his reception piece *Cicero Discovers the Tomb of Archimedes at Syracuse* (Toulouse, Musée des Beaux-Arts). In 1812, Valenciennes succeeded Dandrillon as professor of perspective at the Ecole Imperiale des Beaux-Arts and occupied that position until his death. His influence was widespread; among his many students were Achille Michallon (the first winner of the landscape prize), Jean Victor Bertin, Jean-Baptiste Deperthes, and Sarazin de Belmont.

D.G.

57 Pierre-Henri de VALENCIENNES
Landscape with Ruins, n.d.
Paysage avec ruines
Oil on paper on canvas
13 × 19" (33.0 × 48.3 cm)

Provenance: Galerie de Bayser, Paris.

Exhibitions: Paris 1973–74;
Albuquerque, no. 64.

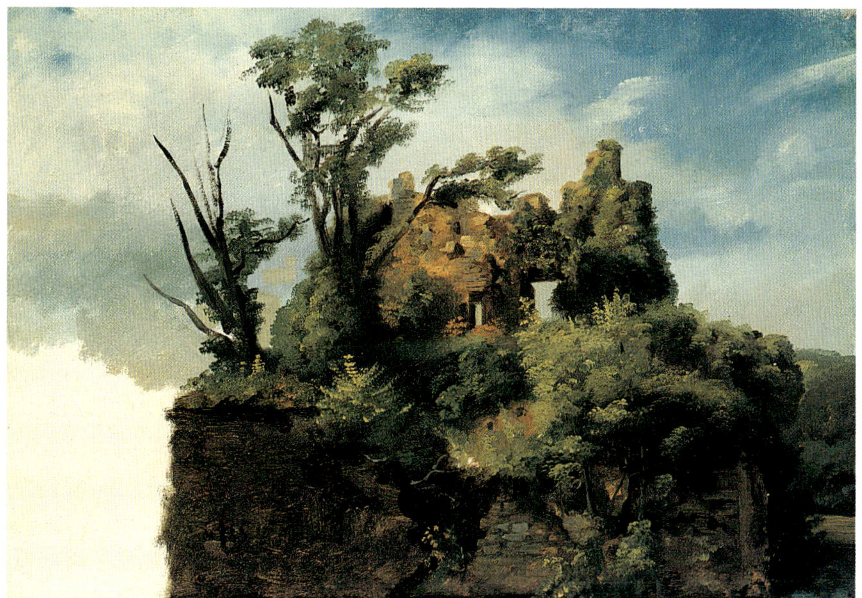

This attractive study almost certainly depicts an Italian site. The exact location has not been identified, although, as Peter Walch has pointed out (see Albuquerque, cat. 64), there are similarities with the Roman ruins at the Villa Farnese, which were painted by Valenciennes on several occasions, as for example, two sketches from the Donation de Croy in the Louvre (see *Peintures: Ecole francaise XIX siècle*, 1961, nos. 1842, 1846, reprod.).

This study is characteristic of the artist's Italian sketches painted between 1782 and 1785, and its naturalism displays the influence of Joseph Vernet. The artist has created a feeling of transience by his subtle treatment of the sky and clouds and by the effect of light.

Valenciennes's sketchbooks contain a number of drawings, with color notes, that can be directly related to his oils, indicating that it was sometimes his practice to execute sketches in the studio from preparatory drawings. The immediacy and freshness of handling in the present sketch, however, suggest that like most of Valenciennes's oils painted on paper and laid down on canvas, it was executed directly from nature.

J.R.B.

(active in Paris in the latter part of the 18th century)

*N*othing is known of this painter other than the mention of his acceptance into the Académie de Saint-Luc.

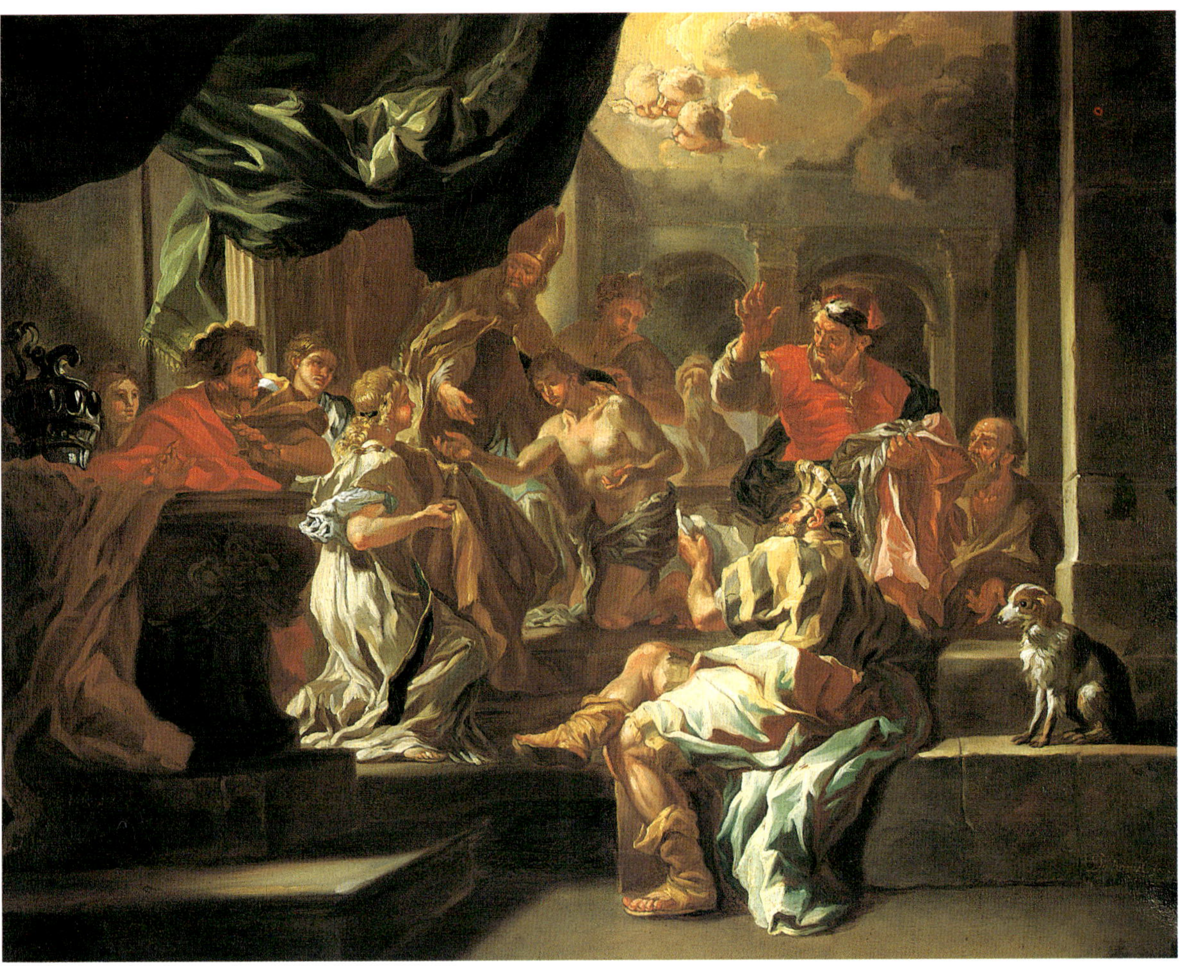

58   Jean-Louis (?) DUHAMEL
Saint Francis Returning His Vestments to His Father (after Solimena), n.d.
Saint François rendant ses vêtements à son père
Oil on canvas
28 ½ × 36" (72.4 × 91.4 cm)
Signed lower right: *J* [?] *Duhamel*

Exhibitions: Houston 1973–75, no. 16.

The illegibility of the first initials of the signature renders the authorship of this painting problematic. There were several artists named Duhamel active during the eighteenth century, but their works are unknown today. Furthermore, the fact that this painting is a faithful copy after Solimena's fresco in the Church of Santa Maria Donnaregina in Naples (1683) makes any attempt at isolating the artist's personal style even more conjectural. We would like to suggest cautiously that this work may be by Jean-Louis Duhamel, a painter active in Paris, who had been received into the Académie de Saint-Luc in 1771.

It was only in the second half of the eighteenth century that it became customary for pupils at the French Academy in Rome to travel to Naples. Beginning in 1750, they were able to apply for a month's residency in that city. In 1787, traveling to Naples to study became an obligation. Although Duhamel is not recorded as a pupil of the French Academy, he may have followed fellow artists there. Although the painting is a copy after a Solimena in Naples, it is not clear that Duhamel traveled to Naples: copies—some autograph, such as the one today in the Musée des Beaux-Arts, Châlon-sur-Saône—were circulating throughout Europe. In any case, this copy shows the increasing variety of sources and models made available to French artists who, during the eighteenth century, were no longer confined to the strictly orthodox examples of the Classical masters.

J. P. M.

Jean-Pierre SAINT-OURS

(Geneva 1752–Geneva 1809)

Pupil of Vien (q.v.), Saint-Ours won the Prix-de-Rome in 1780 and left immediately for Rome, where he stayed until 1792. He spent the rest of his life in Geneva, where he executed portraits, Italianate landscapes, and illustrations for books, among them, Rousseau's *Le Lévite d'Ephraïm*, 1795–1809.

59 Jean-Pierre SAINT-OURS
Cupid and Psyche, c. 1789-90
L'Amour et Psyché
Oil on panel
13 ⅞ × 15 ¾" (35.2 × 40.0 cm)
Old stamp on the reverse: Altieri (?)

Exhibitions: Albuquerque 1980, no. 22 (attributed to Gagneraux).

Bibliography: Rome/Dijon 1983, p. 129, under no. 50 and n. 4.

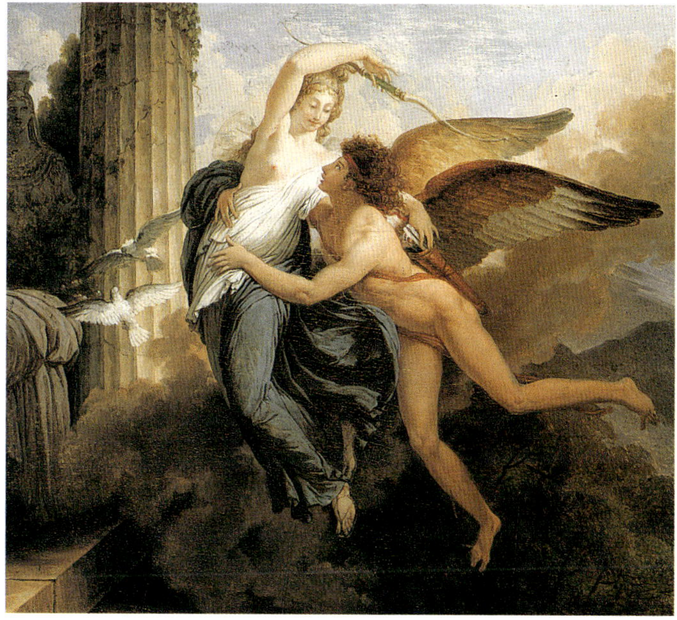

Previously attributed to Gagneraux, this finished study was identified by Sylvain Laveissière (Rome/Dijon 1983, p. 129) and published under its true authorship in 1983. The decoration of the so-called Pompeian Room at the Palazzo Altieri represents one of the major decorative programs of the last years of the eighteenth century in Rome. In conjunction with the marriage of Prince Paluzzo Altieri to Marianna Lepri di Sassonia, the decoration was ordered by the groom's father, Prince Emilio Altieri, in 1789. The program of the room—established with the help of Vito Maria Giovinezzi (1727–1823)—was based on the theme of Psyche, an appropriate subject to celebrate a wedding. Several artists participated in the decoration, including Félice Giani, Bénigne Gagneraux, and Jean-Pierre Saint-Ours. The latter, according to the historian of the palace, Armando Schiavo (1962, pp. 141–42), accepted the commission in a letter of August 3, 1789, and in 1792 was paid 130 *scudi* for an overdoor representing the Reunion of Cupid with Psyche. The painting was apparently delivered, but either never installed or else removed at a later date to be replaced by a painting of Diana scolding Cupid, which does not fit the iconographic program of the room. According to Laveissière, quoting from D. Daud-Bovy and F. Boissonnas (1903), the painting was at the time of the latter publication in the collection of a Dr. H. Goudet in Geneva. A drawing of the same composition—bearing an inscription stating that the dimensions of the painting were "4 pieds 6 pouces sur 3 pieds 7 pouces" (115 × 145 cm), is in the Musée d'Art et d'Histoire in Geneva (inv. 1915–94). Furthermore, Birgitta Sandström (quoted in Rome/Dijon 1983, p. 129) has pointed out the existence of a drawing by Félice Giani (New York, Cooper-Hewitt Museum, Smithsonian Institution) that shows the disposition of the room with the intended placement of the painting by Saint-Ours. This drawing may, however, be a project for the room rather than a representation of the room itself and is therefore not sufficient proof to establish that the painting was ever installed. In his autobiography, quoted by Laveissière, (Rome/Dijon 1983, p. 129, n. 3), the artist states ambiguously: "I delivered in January 1792 the painting to Prince Alfiery [*sic*], who was so pleased with it that he had it placed in the bedroom until the apartment was ready, and he paid me on the spot."

J. P. M.

Henri-Pierre DANLOUX

(Paris 1755–Paris 1809)

A pupil of Lépicié, Danloux first exhibited at the Exposition de la Jeunesse in 1771. From 1775 until 1780, he was in Rome, having followed Vien (q.v.) there. Between 1780 and 1791, Danloux lived in Lyon, Paris, and Italy. In 1791, he emigrated to England, where he became a successful portrait painter —not only for French society in exile but also for an appreciative English clientele. Danloux returned to France in 1800 but achieved little success. His oeuvre offers an interesting and rare link between French and English painting.

60 Henri-Pierre DANLOUX
Portrait of a Man, n.d.
Portrait d'homme
Oil on canvas
16 ½ × 13" (41.9 × 33.0 cm)

Exhibitions: Houston 1973–75, no. 9.

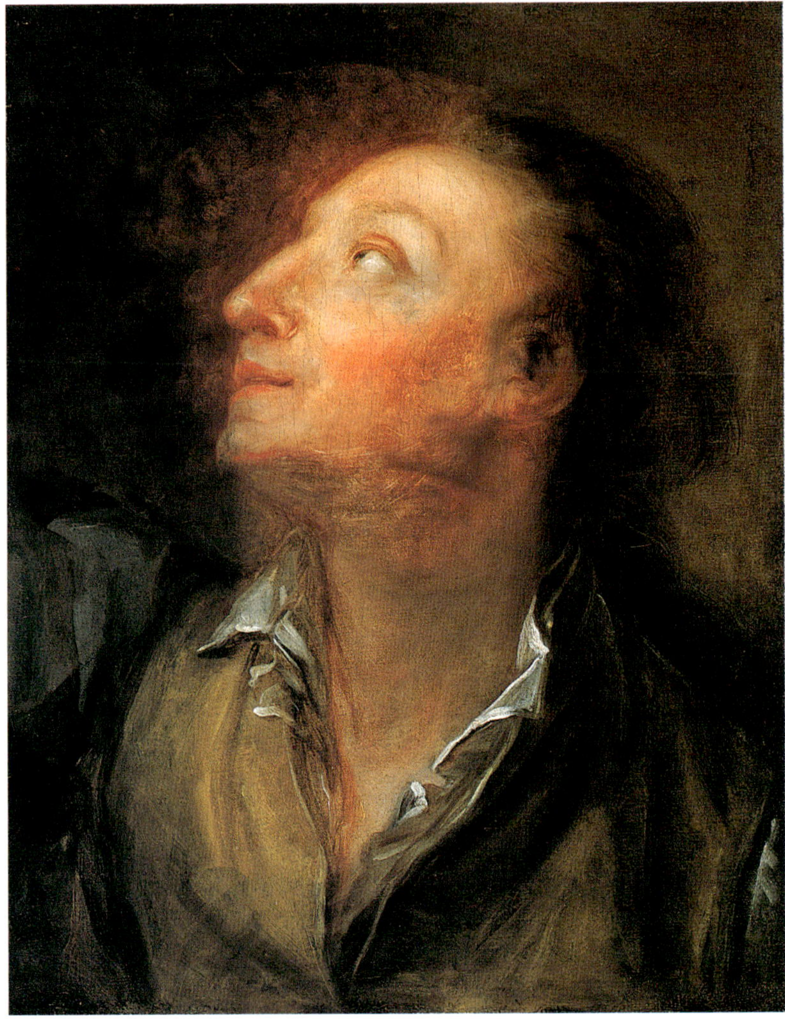

Unknown to Portalis (1910), this spirited portrait can be attributed, on the basis of comparison with other works, to Henri-Pierre Danloux. Better known for his formal portraits executed in the English style, Danloux was equally capable of creating light-hearted and spontaneous works. Because of the casual dress of the sitter and the upward tilt of his head—a typical expression on the eighteenth-century stage—it is possible to identify the model as an actor. In the eighteenth century, actors were often represented wearing informal attire, and striking such histrionic poses.

Actors were a favorite subject for Danloux. Upon his return from Rome to Paris in 1785, Danloux executed portraits of two celebrated actors, Dugazon (Paris, Musée de la Comédie-Française; Portalis 1910, reprod. facing p. 20) and Caillot (whereabouts unknown; Portalis 1910, reprod. p. 19). It may be possible to associate this portrait with one of the several actors' portraits the artist exhibited at the Exposition de la Jeunesse, held on the Place Dauphine, Paris, in 1773 (Portalis 1910, pp. 8–9). A date early in the career of the artist seems appropriate.

J.P.M.

Jean-Baptiste HILAIRE

(Audun-le-Tiche 1753–Paris after 1822)

Like his mentor, Leprince (q.v.), Hilaire traveled extensively. In the company of the Comte de Choiseul-Gauffier, he visited the Ottoman Empire and illustrated the Comte's *Voyage pittoresque de la Grèce*. Hilaire exhibited at the Salon de la Jeunesse and at the Salon de la Correspondance in 1780. In his work, the fascination for exotic scenes is matched by a genuine ethnographic interest.

61–72 Jean-Baptiste HILAIRE
Twelve Costumes of the Ottoman Empire, n.d.
Douze costumes de l'Empire othoman
Gouache on paper, mounted on panel
approximately 7 ½ × 4 ⅝" (19.1 × 11.7 cm) each

Provenance: Private collection, Venice.

Exhibitions: Houston 1973–75, nos. 35–46.

Bibliography: Boppe 1989, p. 281, no. 8.

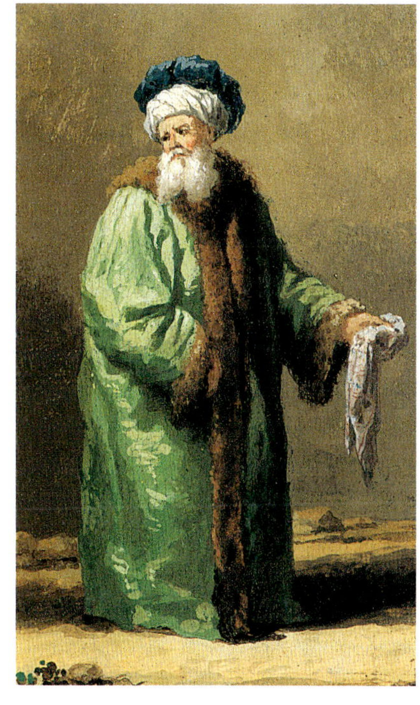
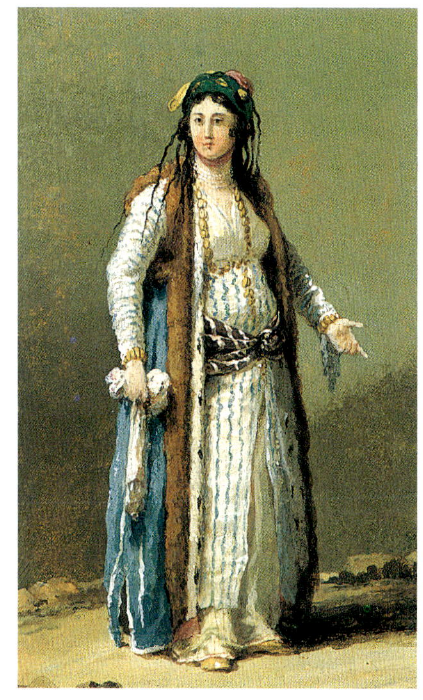
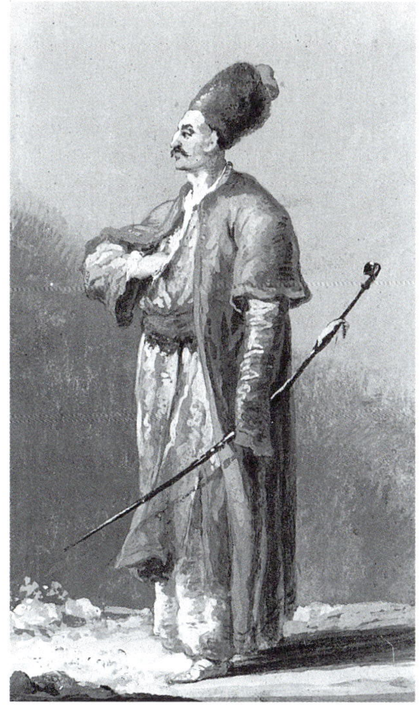
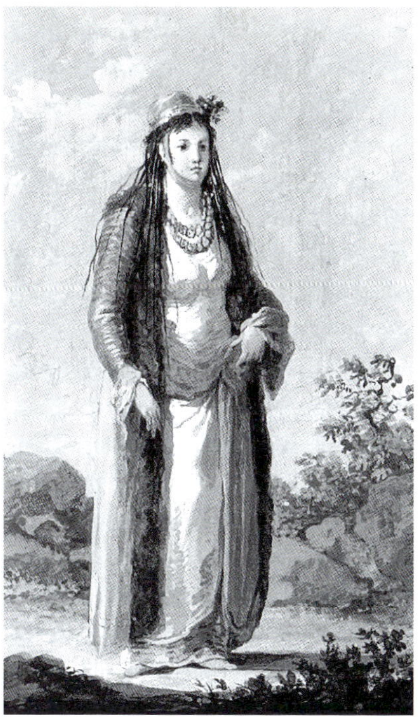

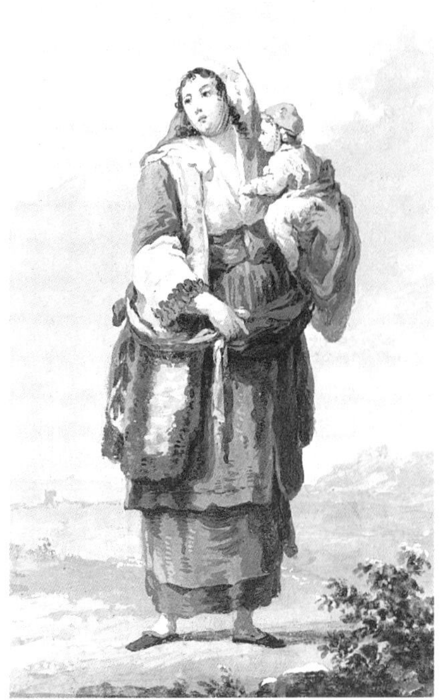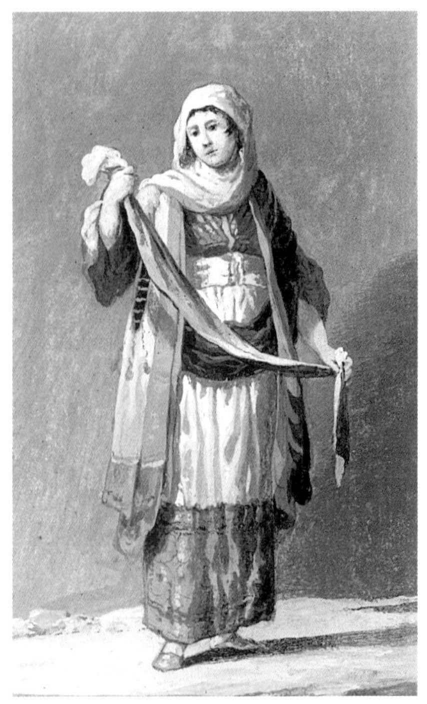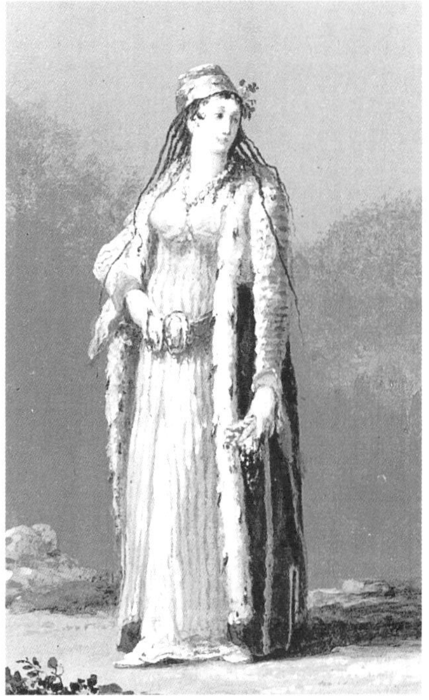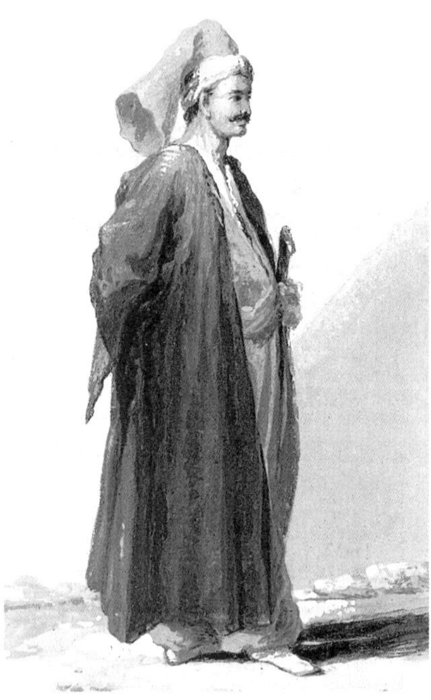

While many painters continued to represent an imagined Orient, a new pictorial exoticism developed in the late eighteenth century, more accurate in its rendition of places, costumes, and situations. Artists traveled then with greater ease, going to distant countries in order to gather information to illustrate publications. Many of Hilaire's drawings were engraved and used as illustrations in Choiseul-Gauffier's *Voyage pittoresque de la Grèce* (the publication of which began in 1782) and Mouradgea d'Ohsson's *Tableau général de l'Empire othoman* (1787).

This series of twelve individual figures represents, with meticulous care in the rendition of the costumes, various types from the Ottoman Empire. All of the women wear costumes that identify them as Greek or Frankish (Christian), whereas the men wear official court costumes. The series was apparently not engraved and may have been created simply for its decorative appeal: individual figures and their costumes from

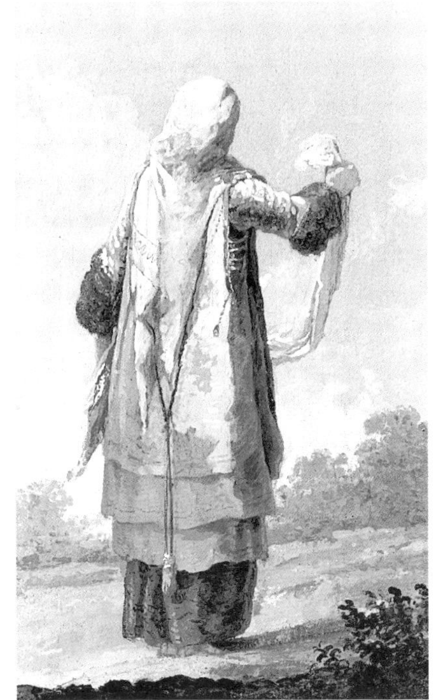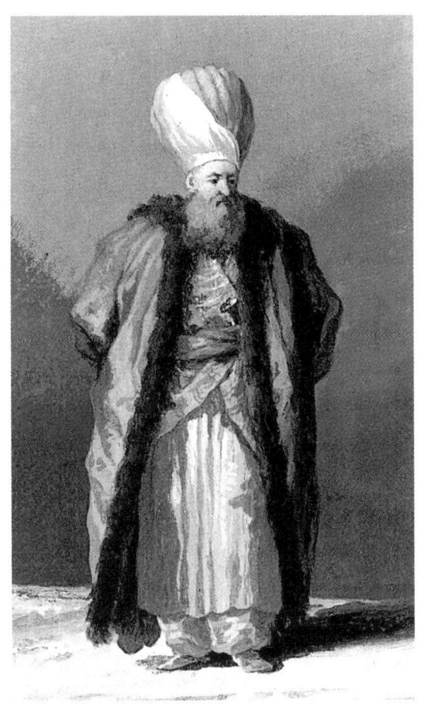

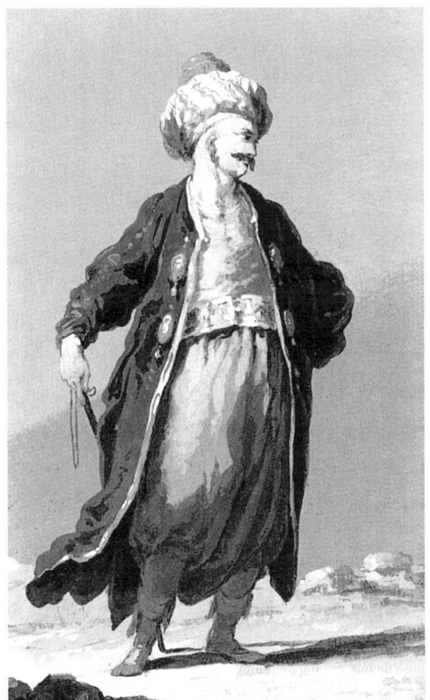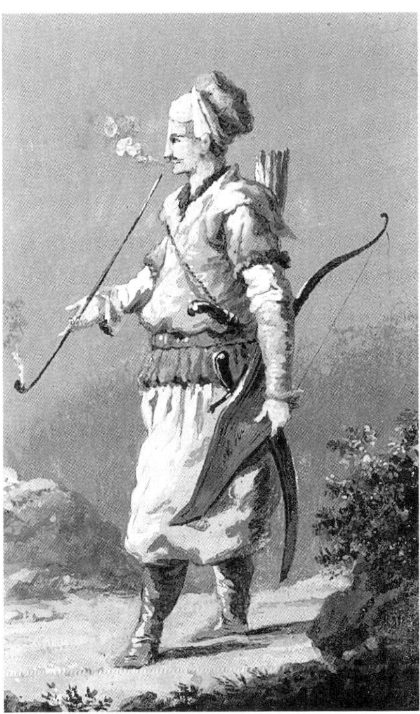

the Ottoman Empire constitute a category sui generis among the representations of the Orient. Louis-Francois Fauvel (1753–1838), vice-consul in Athens and an amateur artist, executed a series of watercolors, dated 1794, which are close enough to Hilaire's to suggest a direct influence (see Boppe 1989, p. 229). Our series should also be compared to the celebrated plates by Manzoni (active 1795–1813) for his *Costumes orientaux inédits dessinés d'après nature en 1796, 1797, 1798* (Paris, 1813; see Boppe 1989, p. 265).

J. P. M.

99

Charles-Nicaise PERRIN

(Paris 1754–Paris 1851)

Perrin, with Regnault (q.v.), won the second-place Prix-de-Rome in 1775. In Rome from 1780 until 1784, he became Academician in 1787, exhibiting regularly at the Salon between 1787 and 1822. Perrin's production includes seldom-represented mythological or historical subjects and portraits, as well as some religious paintings.

73 Charles-Nicaise PERRIN
The Death of Seneca, 1788
La Mort de Sénèque
Oil on canvas
15 × 16 ¾" (38.1 × 42.5 cm)

Exhibitions: Albuquerque 1980, no. 44.

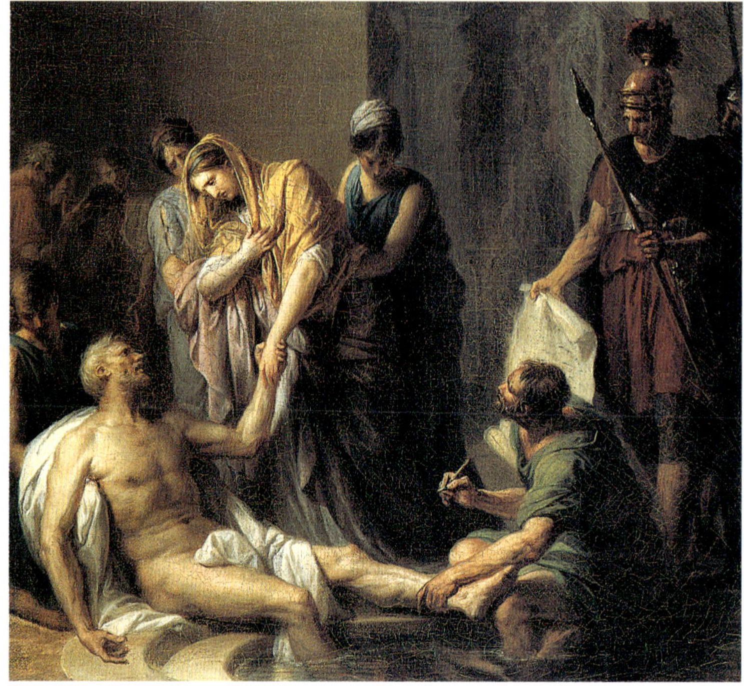

In *Annales* (XV, 63), Tacitus recounts the history of Emperor Nero's teacher, the philosopher Seneca. Fallen out of favor and accused of participating in the conspiracy of Piso, Seneca was ordered by his former pupil to commit suicide. Tacitus's description of Seneca's death, as unsparing as it is exacting, describes the philosopher not only opening his veins, but also drinking poison to ensure his end. The stoic courage of Seneca became a favorite subject for French painters in the second half of the eighteenth century and was treated by Noël Hallé (Salon of 1750), Perrin (Salon of 1789), Lefebvre (Salon of 1791), and Bougault (Salon of 1795), among others. Most artists treating this subject at the end of the eighteenth century could not escape the influence of David's composition of 1787 on a related theme, *The Death of Socrates* (New York, The Metropolitan Museum of Art). Yet in the painting Perrin submitted to the jury of the 1789 Salon (Dijon, Musée des Beaux-Arts), the artist may have been closer to the kind of pathos present in an earlier composition by David, *The Grief of Andromache* (1783, Paris; Ecole Nationale Supérieure des Beaux-Arts). In David's composition—as in Perrin's—as much attention is devoted to the emotion of Andromache in one case, Pauline in the other, as to the brutal description of the naked and dead or dying hero.

The composition of the study presented here is quite different from the final painting in Dijon; yet there is little doubt that both paintings were executed at about the same time, and that this one may be an earlier thought for the 1789 project. A drawing of the same subject was part of the sale after the artist's death (Paris 1991, p. 42). Although its composition is somewhat closer to that of the painting in Dijon, it is still different, and may also represent another step toward the composition retained by the artist for his 1789 painting.

Stylistically, the painting is particularly close to Perrin's contemporary works, such as his *Spartan Women Aiding Their Husbands*, exhibited at the 1787 Salon (see Montargis 1989, no. 26).

J. P. M.

Baron Jean-Baptiste REGNAULT

(Paris 1754–Paris 1829)

A precocious talent, the young Regnault led an adventurous life. At an early age he followed his father to America and spent five years working as a ship-boy. His first training was with the painter Jean Bardin, with whom he went for the first time to Italy. In 1775, he obtained the second-place prize of the Académie, which allowed him to return to Rome, where even as a student his works were admired. In 1783, he became an Academician with his famous *Achilles Instructed by Chiron* (cat. no. 76). A regular exhibitor at the Salon, Regnault left an immense oeuvre including some very large paintings commissioned in honor of Napoleon. Regnault's real vocation was, however, to treat mythological subjects, which he did in a style that evidences the influence of Bolognese artists, as well as his passion for antiquity and his delicately refined sensuality.

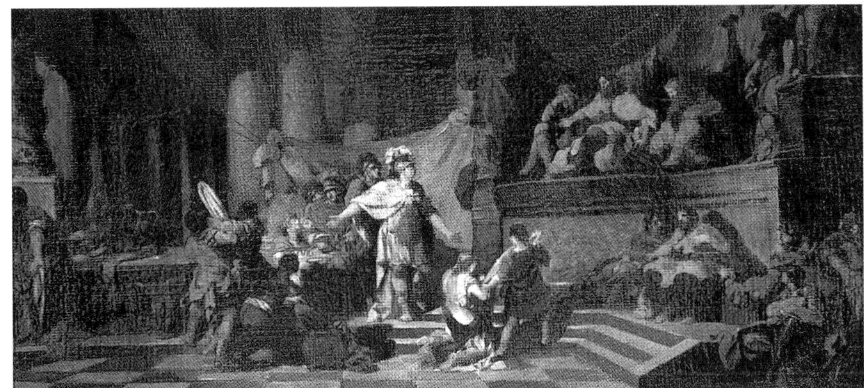

74   Baron Jean-Baptiste REGNAULT
Aeneas Offering Presents to King Latinus and Asking Him for the Hand of His Daughter, 1778
Enée offre des présents à Latinus et lui demande sa fille en mariage
Oil on canvas
9 ¼ × 19 ¼" (23.5 × 48.9 cm)
Inscribed: *Renaud f 1778*

Exhibitions: Salon of 1783, no. 169; Albuquerque 1980, no. 3 (attributed to Jean-Baptiste Benard).

Formerly identified as *King Cyrus Directing Sheshbazzar to Restore the Sacred Vessels to the Temple* and wrongly attributed to Jean-Baptiste Benard, this painting is in fact signed "Renaud," which was the artist's patronym until 1785, when he changed it to Regnault. Rather than the episode from the book of Ezra formerly suggested, we recognize in this painting an episode equally rare in painting from the legend of Aeneas. It is told by Cato in a fragment of his *Origines* (I, 11), and again by Virgil in the *Aeneid* (VII, 58–106). The painting represents Aeneas offering gifts to King Latinus and asking for the hand of his daughter, Lavinia. A painting of this subject is mentioned in the 1783 Salon *livret* among the works exhibited by Jean-Baptiste Renaud, with the indication that it was an *esquisse*.

One may wonder why a work executed in 1778 was not shown until the Salon of 1783. In 1776, Regnault, winner of the Grand Prix, had gone to Rome. Shortly upon his return, he was *agréé* in 1782. The Salon took place between his receiving that distinction and his reception into the Académie on October 25, 1783. Regnault exhibited for the first time at that Salon and was represented by more than thirty works, essentially history paintings, a field in which he was to distinguish himself. Regnault was eager to demonstrate how much he had achieved during his sojourn in Rome, and therefore included in his submissions to the jury works, such as this sketch, which had been painted while a pensioner.

Regnault's development as an artist paralleled David's, an artist who, in spite of Regnault's originality and considerable success, overshadowed him throughout his career. This sketch, ambitious in both composition and narrative intention, was executed the same year that David exhibited in Rome his *Funeral of Patroclus* (Dublin, National Gallery of Ireland; the painting, conceived around 1777, was shown at the 1781 Paris Salon, also as an *esquisse*). Common to the two paintings are the elongated format, similarities between the figures of Aeneas and Achilles, and powerful highlights that both David and Regnault used to endow individuals or small groupings of figures with a particularly dramatic prominence.

J. P. M.

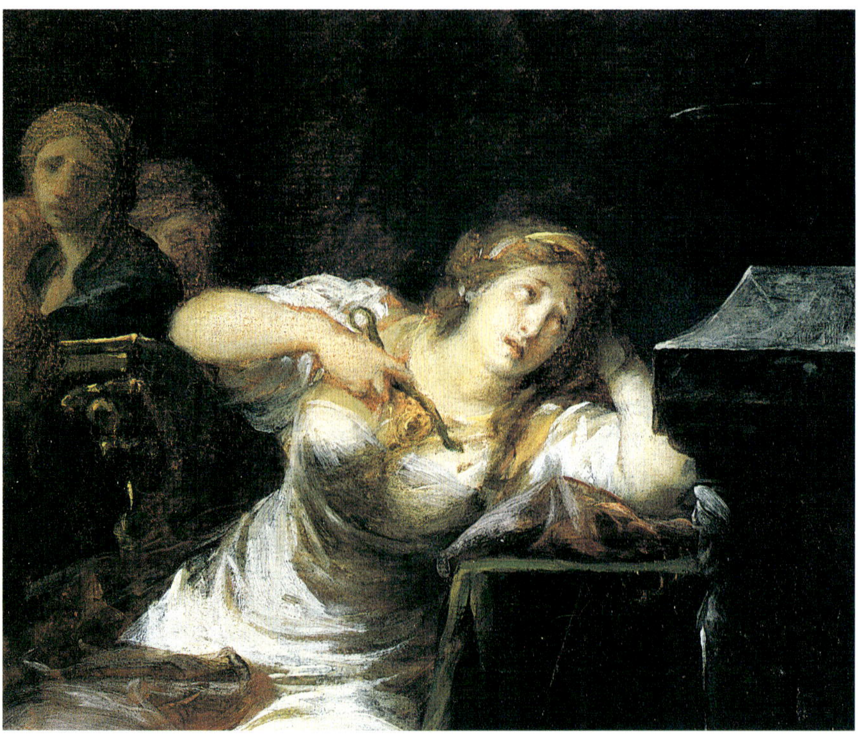

75   Baron Jean-Baptiste REGNAULT
Cleopatra, n.d.
Cléopatre
Oil on paper on panel
6 ¼ × 7 ¼" (15.9 × 18.4 cm)
Inscribed on the back: *1830*

Provenance: the artist; his sale, Paris, March 1–3, 1830, no. 4; Paris, Hôtel Drouot, March 20, 1972 (Salle 11), no. 5.

Exhibitions: Houston 1973–75, no. 72.

Regnault painted the subject of Cleopatra several times. His most famous version is a painting (now in the Kunstmuseum, Düsseldorf) shown in a private exhibition at the Louvre in 1799. Another composition of the subject was sold at Sotheby's, Monte Carlo, on June 18, 1988 (no. 911). Neither painting resembles this small sketch, which was owned by the artist at the time of his death.

Any attempt to establish a chronology of Regnault's undocumented or undated works is made particularly difficult by the fact that his style changed little throughout his long career. Here, for instance, the debt he acknowledges to the Bolognese tradition may not necessarily mean that it is a youthful work, done in the enthusiasm of the artist's sojourn in Italy. Based on the coarse brushstroke comparable to those in a sketch of *Venus and Adonis* in the Louvre, dated around 1814, Christopher Sells has, in fact, cautiously suggested that it may have been executed after 1800, but cannot establish a firmer date for it.

J. P. M.

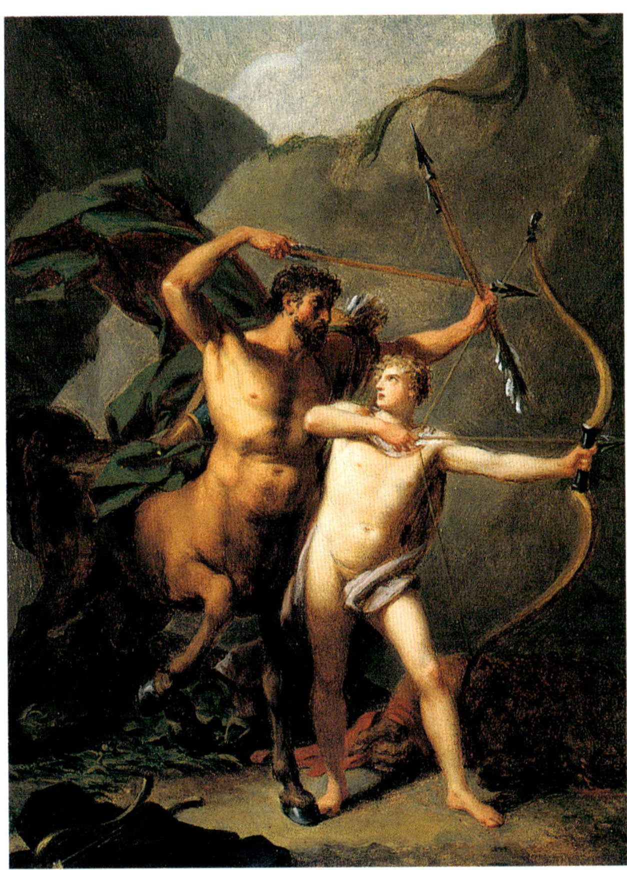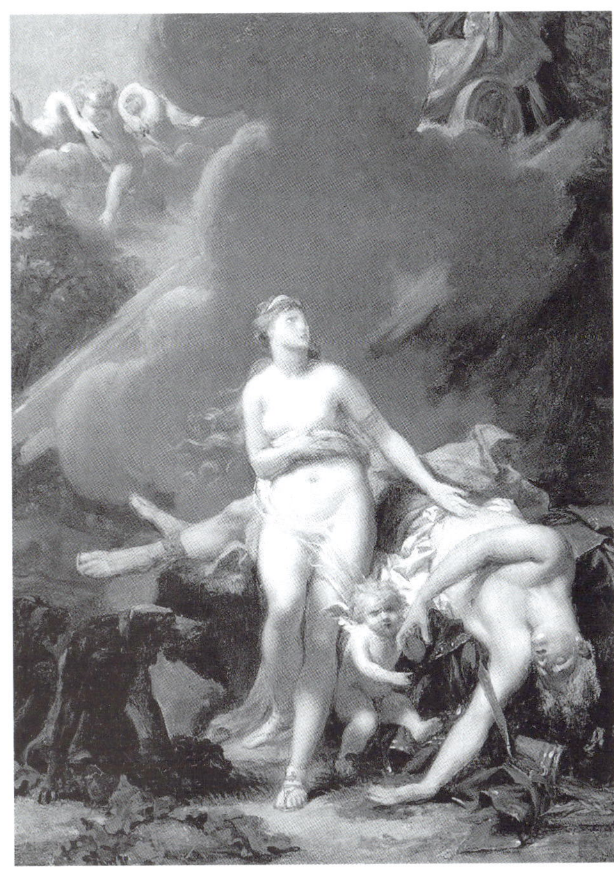

76 Baron Jean-Baptiste REGNAULT
Achilles Instructed by Chiron, n.d.
L'Education d'Achille
Oil on panel
8 ¾ × 6 ¾" (22.2 × 17.1 cm)

Exhibitions: Albuquerque 1980, no. 51.

77 Baron Jean-Baptiste REGNAULT
Venus and Adonis, n.d.
Vénus et Adonis
Oil on panel
8 ½ × 6 ⅝" (21.6 × 16.2 cm)

Exhibitions: Albuquerque 1980, no. 52.

Regnault often repeated his compositions, and by the end of his life had assembled a collection of twenty-four small paintings that were autograph repetitions of some of his most famous works (Lenoir 1830, p. 31). *Achilles Instructed by Chiron* (Paris, Musée du Louvre) had been Regnault's reception piece at the Académie in 1783, while *Venus and Adonis*, painted in 1812, but untraceable since 1913, is known today only through a preparatory oil sketch at the Louvre (Sells 1974, pp. 405–07, fig. 1) and the reduction presented here.

Christopher Sells has pointed out that these two small paintings are numbers 50 and 65 in the sale of Regnault's studio in 1830 (Sale, Paris, March 1–3, 1830) and that they belong to the above-mentioned series of reductions ("petites esquisses terminées, sujets tirés des Métamorphoses d'Ovide"). Other known works from the same series include four paintings, of roughly identical dimensions to the ones presented here, at the Mobilier National, Paris (Sells 1974, figs. 2–5); and two others mentioned in the literature and last seen when sold at the Hôtel Drouot, Paris, on June 3 1935 (nos. 141, 142; Sells 1974, p. 408, n. 13).

These paintings differ from Regnault's preparatory sketches in several ways. First, they are all painted on panel, whereas Regnault favored a technique of oil on paper laid down on canvas for his sketches. (Such is the case for the *Venus and Adonis* from the Louvre, and for the sketch for *Achilles Instructed by Chiron* in the Detroit Institute of Arts). Second, both sketches show small differences from the finished paintings, whereas these two reductions follow them precisely. Finally, the brushstroke in our sketches is uniform and indicates that these paintings, reproducing works created twenty-nine years apart, were executed at about the same date and, very likely, late in the artist's career.

J.P.M.

*P*upil successively of Lépicié (q.v.), Brenet (q.v.), and Casanova (q.v.), Taunay reputedly worked outdoors with other young painters such as Demarne and Bidauld. He exhibited landscapes at the Salon de la Jeunesse in *1777* and *1779*, and at the Salon de la Correspondance in *1782*. In spite of not having won the first prize, he went to Rome on the recommendation of Vien (q.v.) and Pierre (q.v.). *Agréé* at the Académie in *1784*, he never became a full-fledged Academician. During Napoleon's reign, he enjoyed the protection of Empress Josephine. After the collapse of the Empire, Taunay left with a group of French artists invited to establish a fine arts academy in Rio de Janeiro, where he stayed for five years. Taunay exhibited at the Paris Salon from *1787* until *1827*. A genre painter above all, Taunay also executed historical compositions—notably battle scenes during the Empire—as well as other subjects.

78 Nicolas-Antoine TAUNAY
Elegiac Portrait of a Man Seated near a Tombstone and Holding a Miniature Portrait, n.d.
Portrait élégiaque d'un homme assis auprès d'un tombeau et tenant en main une miniature
Oil on paper on canvas
6 ¼ × 4 ⅜" (15.9 × 11.1 cm)
Inscribed on the stretcher: *Taunay* [old handwriting]

Exhibitions: Houston 1973–75, no. 79.

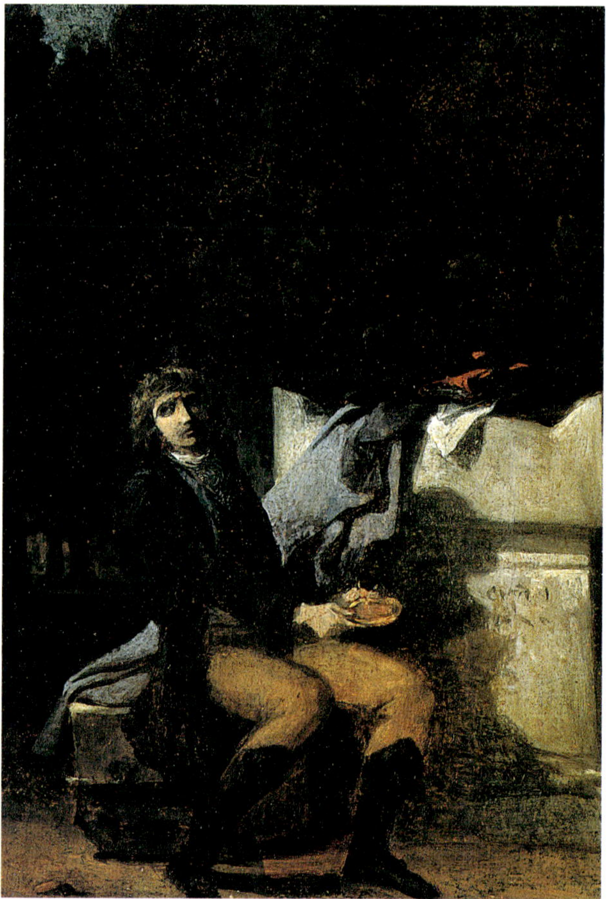

This elegiac portrait combines two well-established iconographic traditions—the presentation by a mourning figure of the image of a departed person depicted in a miniature (Praz 1971, pp. 218–21) and the representation of a single figure meditating near a funerary monument (occasionally surmounted by a bust) or a tombstone. The motif of the mourner, which enjoyed immense popularity among painters and writers during the Neoclassical and early Romantic periods, was used both for allegories (Vincent, *Melancholy*, 1801; Château de Malmaison) and for representations of specific individuals, as is the case here.

The attribution to Taunay is based on an old inscription on the stretcher. While there is no reason to doubt the attribution, this work does represent an unusual foray for the artist, closer to a tradition illustrated in the paintings of Jacques Sablet (q.v.). Taunay is better known for his many lighthearted genre scenes, typically set in parks or gardens, executed in an impeccable technique enhanced by porcelain-like surfaces.

J. P. M.

Born in Toulouse, Roques studied locally with Rivalz and Despose. He began to exhibit his paintings as early as 1772. Roques won the Prix-de-Rome in 1778 and subsequently sojourned in Rome. He conducted his career entirely in the south of France, mostly in Montpellier, where he taught, and his native Toulouse. During the Revolutionary period, he executed several compositions illustrating contemporary events (*Celebration of the Federation*, 1790, and *Death of Marat*, 1793; Toulouse, Musée des Augustins). The cycle of paintings for the Church of Notre-Dame-de-la-Daurade is among his most celebrated compositions. Roques is remembered as the revered master of Ingres.

79   Joseph Guillaume ROQUES
The Birth of the Virgin, 1810
La Naissance de la Vierge
Oil on canvas
58 × 29" (147.3 × 73.7 cm)

Exhibitions: Peoria 1980, no. 46;
New York 1980, no. 1.

Bibliography: Toulouse 1989–90,
under no. 147.

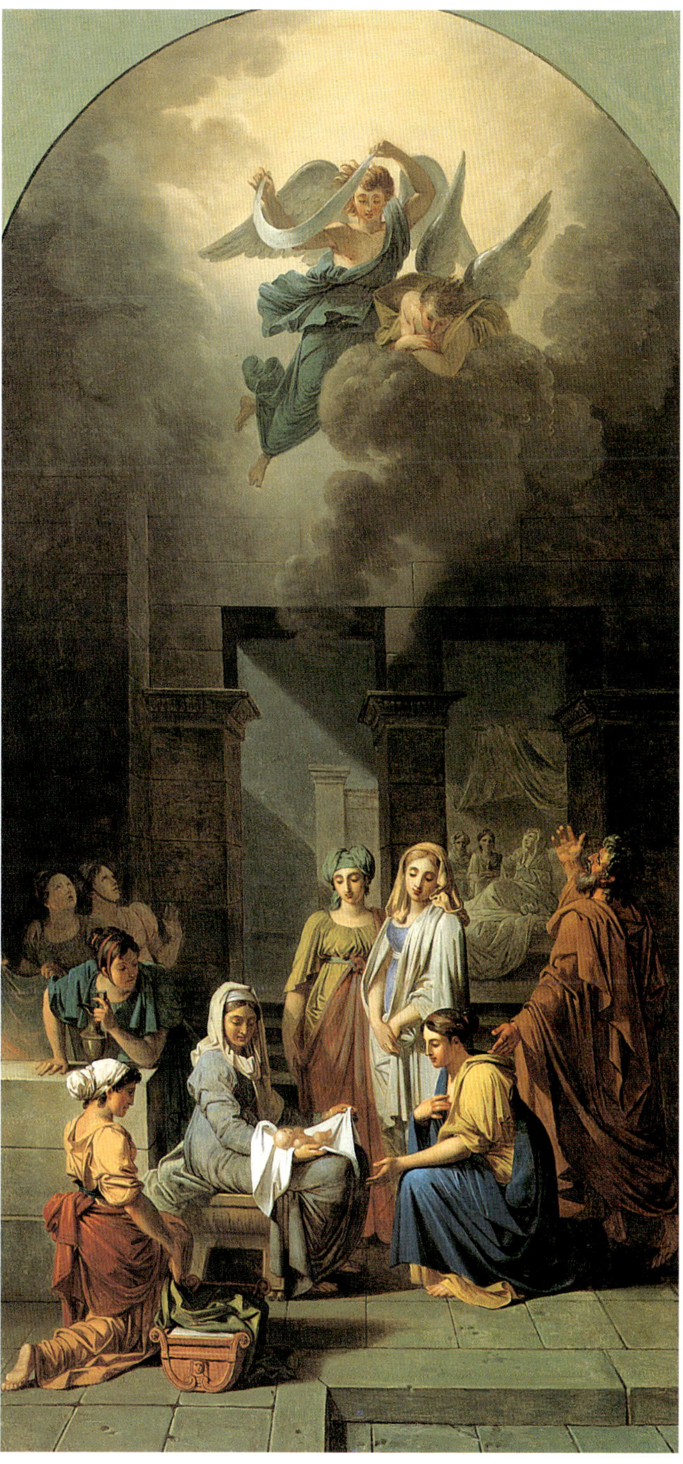

Executed between 1810 and 1821, the seven paintings illustrating the life of the Virgin for the choir of the Church of Notre-Dame-de-la-Daurade in Toulouse confirmed Roques as the prime exponent of a full-fledged Neoclassical style in southwestern France. Roques—who lived and worked in Toulouse and Montpellier—is far from being a provincial artist. His sophisticated style betrays the influence of Vien, whom he knew while a pensioner at the French Academy in Rome, as well as an awareness of the latest manifestations of modern taste, exemplified in the most advanced paintings submitted at the Paris Salons.

The seven paintings of the Daurade are particularly significant for reintroducing in the early nineteenth century, after years of neglect, the rhetoric and majesty of sacred painting, and combining these elements with the new narrative clarity associated with David and his followers (contacts between David and Roques appear to have taken place in Rome). The seven paintings were not executed at the same time, and bear dates from 1810 to 1823. The earliest of the series is in fact *The Birth of the Virgin*, which recalls to a certain extent Suvée's rendition of the same subject (1779; Paris, Church of the Assumption, *modello* at Montpellier, Musée Fabre). The treatment of individual figures and their groupings suggest the rhythm of Poussin's mature compositions, for example, *Moses Rescued from the Bullrushes* (1647; Paris, Musée du Louvre) and *Eliezer and Rebecca* (1648; Paris, Musée du Louvre).

In 1988, the Musée des Augustins in Toulouse purchased seven *modelli* for the Daurade paintings, including one on this subject (Toulouse 1989–90, no. 147). Different in details from the sketch shown here, it represents an earlier thought for the large painting. The finished surface of our sketch may indicate that it is a *ricordo* of, rather than a *modello* for, the Daurade composition. Jean Penent, in the entry of the above-mentioned catalogue, also lists a smaller replica in the Church of Loubens-Lauragais and a copy in the Church of Saint-Félix-Lauragais, thus showing the popularity of this composition.

J. P. M.

Louis-Léopold BOILLY

(La Bassée 1761–Paris 1845)

Arnould-Polycarpe Boilly, a sculptor, was the only teacher of his young son, Louis, until 1775. At that time Louis left his father's care to stay with the Augustinian prior at Douai, where he was given the opportunity to develop his talents. As early as 1779, Boilly was in Arras, where he painted more than three hundred portraits. He arrived in Paris in 1784. The *scènes galantes* that he produced in these years were popularized by engravings and enthusiastically collected. During the Terror, he and his work were denounced by a member of the Société Républicaine des arts, probably as a result of his great success, but he was able to convince the Société of his revolutionary fervor and avoid the guillotine. The 1791 decree that opened the Salon of the Louvre to all artists gave Boilly the opportunity to exhibit with his peers. He sent *The Swoon* to the Salon, and two years later he exhibited five works. In 1804, he won a first-class medal for his painting *The Arrival of the Stagecoach in La Cour des Messageries*. He was married twice and had six children by his first wife; his son, Simon, was the father of the painter Eugène Boilly. In 1833, at age seventy-one, he was awarded the Legion of Honor by Louis-Philippe.　　D.G.

80　Louis-Léopold BOILLY
View of a Lake, 1797
Vue d'un lac
Oil on canvas
9 × 12" (22.9 × 30.5 cm)
Signed: *L. Boilly 1797*

Provenance: John Tillotson; sold Christie's, London, 17 December 1985, lot 26.

Exhibitions: London 1981, no. 41.

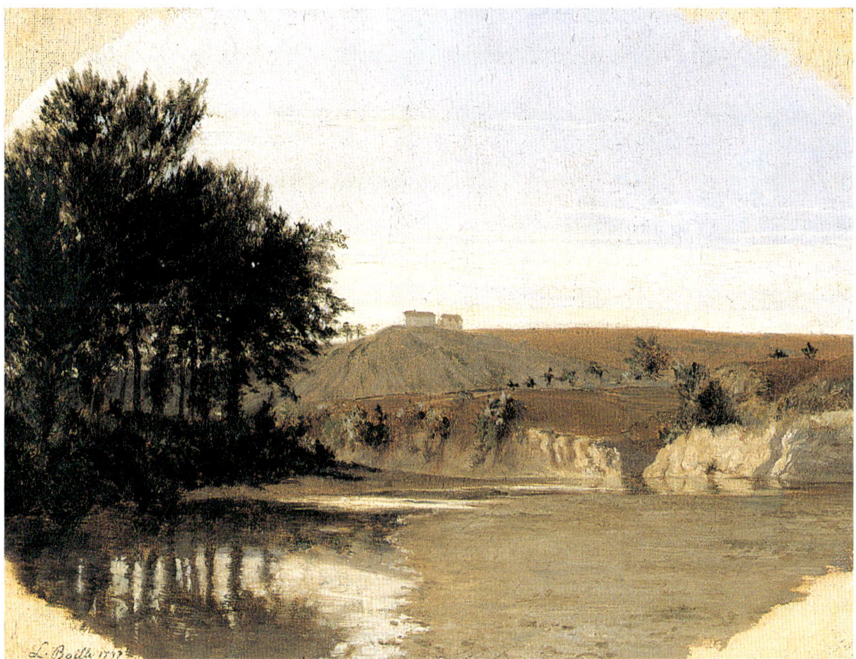

Boilly's oeuvre is comprised virtually exclusively of portraits and genre scenes. This sketch, dated 1797, is his only known landscape painting. It is, however, evident that he continued to work in this genre, since twenty years later the Salon *livret* records that he exhibited two landscapes that year; *Landscape with Figures and Animals* and *Landscape with Italianate Buildings*. From early in his artistic career, Boilly favored portraits in outdoor settings, sometimes giving the landscape a Romantic atmosphere that reflected the sitter's state of mind. Boilly executed several such portraits under the Directoire and Consulat. One fine example is the *Portrait of a Man*, paired with a female portrait, probably of his wife, in the Musée des Beaux-Arts in Lille, of 1800 (Lille 1988–89, no. 35). The gentleman is depicted mending a wooden bridge, against a wooded and rolling landscape, and comparison may be made with the present landscape in the feathery treatment of the foliage and the subtle play of light and shade. The present sketch, however, has a far more impressionistic quality. The use of a clean, lucid palette and the play of light creating reflections in the water give a delightful freshness to the sketch and make it particularly attractive. It was almost certainly painted *plein-air* by the artist for his own pleasure, probably with the intention of later working it up in the studio either into a finished landscape or into the background of one of his portraits.

It is interesting to note that this sketch formerly belonged to the collector John Tillotson, who had a love of landscape painting, particularly *plein-air* works.

J.R.B.

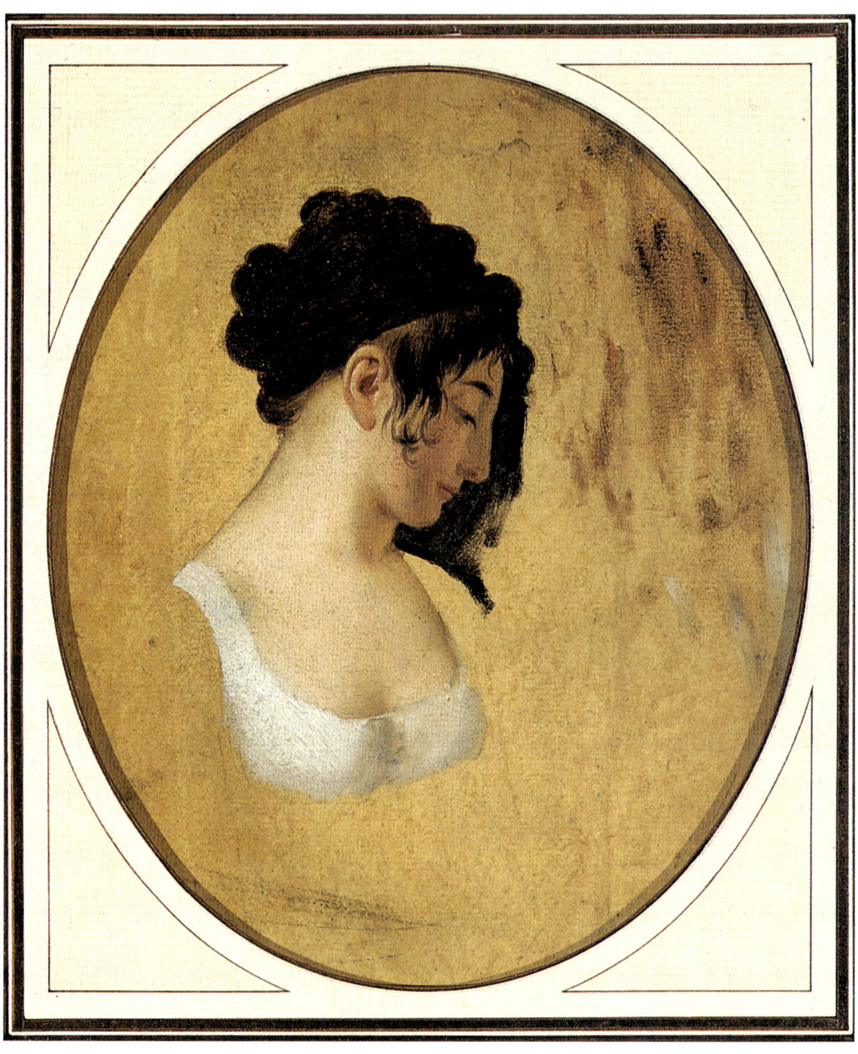

81   Louis-Léopold BOILLY
Profile of a Young Woman's Head, c. 1794
Profil de tête de jeune femme
Oil on paper on canvas
10 ⅛" 8 ¾" (25.7 × 22.2 cm)

Exhibitions: Houston 1973–75, no. 2.

Bibliography: Lille 1988–89, p. 118
(reprod.).

This is a preliminary oil sketch for the profile of the young mother in Boilly's painting *Fête de famille* (Boulogne-sur-Mer, Musée du Château), which is datable to around 1803. The informal and spontaneous quality of the sketch suggests that the painter was well-acquainted with his model, and it is likely she was a member of his family. This profile certainly comes close to portraits of his first wife, the *arrageoise* Marie-Madeleine-Josephe Desligne (1764–1794), and can be compared with a chalk portrait drawing by Boilly in the Musée du Château, Boulogne-sur-Mer (see Lille 1988–89, no. 11). Family scenes of mothers and children appealed to Boilly, and it seems entirely appropriate that he used his own wife as his model and that he continued to make reference to this preliminary sketch even after her death. Indeed, this profile recurs in several other compositions, namely, *Young Savoyard Boys with Their Pet Marmot* (1807) and *Entrance to the Turkish Garden* (1812).

     Boilly frequently made incomplete preliminary sketches in the medium of oil on paper, and similar compositions exist for some of his other important works, notably *The Exhibition of David's "Coronation of Napoleon"* (Musée de Quimper), *The Connoisseur of Prints* (Paris, Musée du Louvre), and the studies for the series in *A Gathering of Artists in Isabey's Studio* (Lille, Musée des Beaux-Arts). A telling comparison can be made with a sketch in the same medium (Lille, Musée des Beaux-Arts; Lille 1988–89, no. 16), which was formerly identified by Paul Marmottan (1913, p. 208) as Boilly's son, Julien-Léopold, but is in fact more likely to represent his half brother, Félix (b. 1790), the son of Marie-Madeleine-Josephe Desligne (see Lille 1988–89, p. 48). The similarity of these two oil sketches suggests that they were executed *en famille* around 1794.

J. R. B.

*P*upil of Doyen (q.v.), Lethière obtained the second-place Prix-de-Rome in 1784. In Rome from 1786 until 1790 and later from 1807 until 1816, he succeeded Suvée (q.v.) as director of the French Academy. Lethière exhibited regularly at the Salons from 1793 until 1831. Professor in 1819 at the Ecole des Beaux-Arts, he became in 1825 a member of the Institut de France. His official career was paralleled by a production that changed little and perpetuated Classical formulas well into the Romantic period.

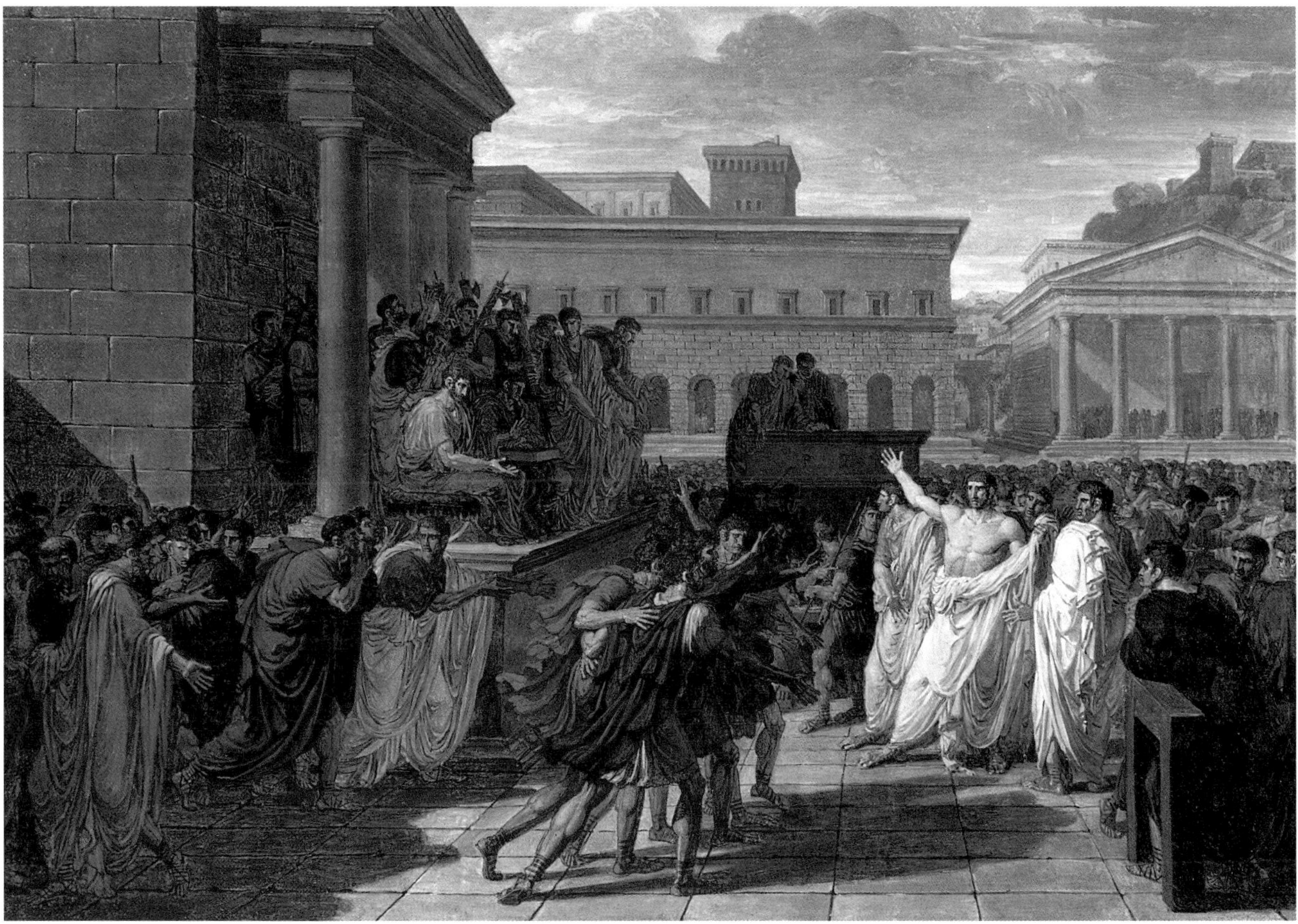

82 Guillaume-Guillon LETHIERE
Brutus Listening to the Ambassadors from the Tarquins, n.d.
Brutus donnant audience aux ambassadeurs des Tarquins
Oil on canvas
19 ¼ × 27 ½" (48.9 × 69.9 cm)

Exhibitions: Albuquerque 1980, no. 41.

The identification of the subject of this painting has been advanced by Robert Herbert (see Albuquerque 1980, no. 41), who recognized in it a lesser-known episode of the life of Lucius Junius Brutus, the founder of the Roman Republic: Brutus listening to the ambassadors of the deposed Tarquins pleading for the return of the royal possessions. Episodes from the life of Brutus, including his oath to avenge Lucretia's death (see cat. no. 28), or condemning his sons to death for conspiring to restore the monarchy, had proved successful for painters in the late eighteenth century. David, in his famous 1789 painting (Paris, Musée du Louvre), had represented the implacable Brutus, as the bodies of his executed sons are brought before him. By choosing the aftermath of that fateful decision, David avoided the facile chill that depictions of their condemnation or death could have provoked. Lethière had first treated the life of Brutus in a sketch executed in Rome in 1788 (a drawing for it is at the Musée Municipal in Château-Gontier; see Paris 1974–75, no. 93). Shown at the 1795 Salon (no. 353), and again in 1801 (no. 229), it was criticized for its bold bloodiness, as it shows on the left the executioner presenting the severed head of one of the sons to the crowd. It was this composition, however, that Lethière chose and altered, for his later version of the subject (1811; Paris, Musée du Louvre).

It can be argued that in 1788, a year before the Revolution, Lethière executed a scene that was too violent for its time and that its implicit moral message was confused with an apology for political murder, and that in 1795, when he showed at the first Salon held under the Thermidorian regime—a new government that had put an end to the bloodbath of the Terror—the image was too emotionally charged and therefore repulsive to many visitors. Indeed, Lethière's early composition may have reminded some visitors of such images as Charles Monnet's widely distributed popular engraving showing Sanson, the French executioner, exhibiting the severed head of Louis XVI to the crowd. Perhaps Lethière displayed more political timeliness in exhibiting the subject of our sketch, a scene that, incidentally, opens Voltaire's often revived play *Brutus*. As early as 1795, the post-Revolutionary government had pardoned most of the émigrés, and many of them began to return to France, where they made timid demands to have their estates restored to them. The question of these compensations remained a burning issue in French politics until the late years of the Bourbon Restoration. It is possible to see in our sketch a thinly disguised illustration of such demands (like so many artists of his generation, Lethière had exchanged his youthful revolutionary fervor for a recognition of the Bourbons' legitimacy). We therefore suggest a date in the first quarter of the nineteenth century, a suggestion reinforced by the style of the sketch, whose composition and many details were used by the artist in his 1812 *Brutus*.

J. P. M.

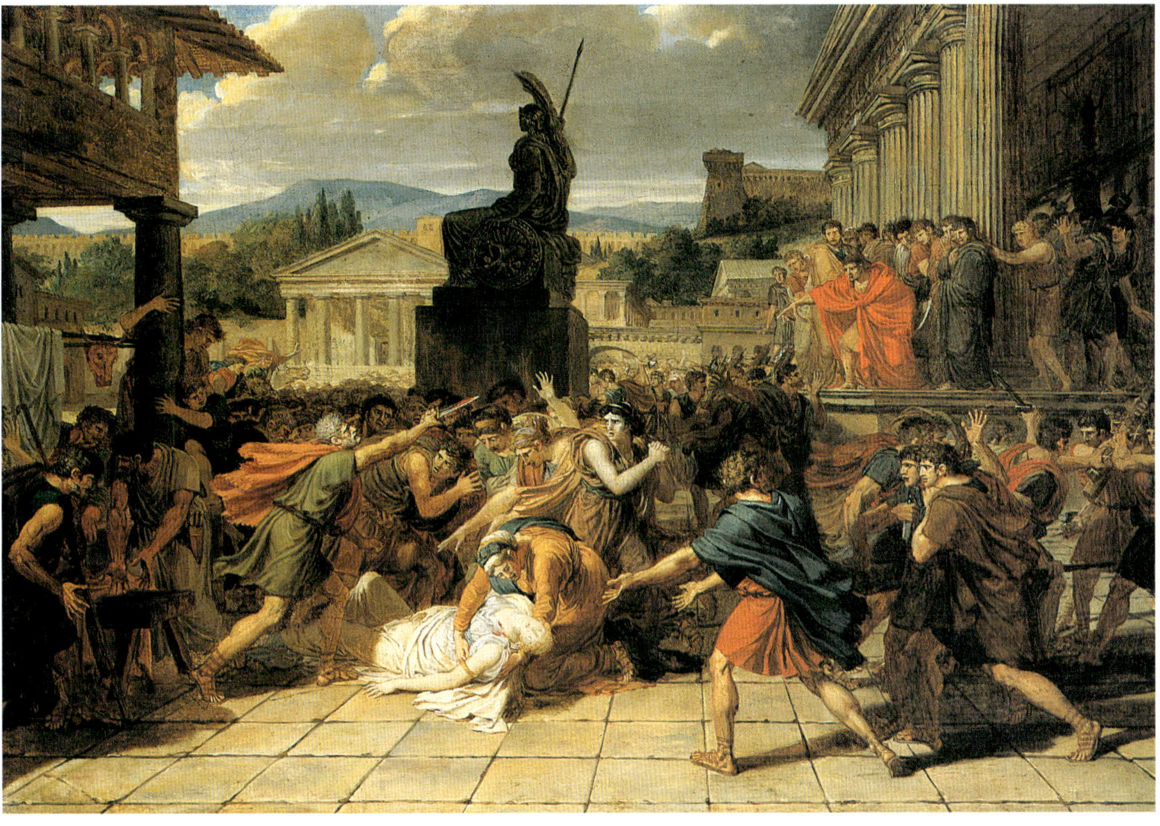

83   Guillaume-Guillon LETHIERE
The Death of Virginia, c. 1800
La Mort de Virginie
Oil on canvas
19 ½ × 30" (49.5 × 76.2 cm)

Exhibitions: Albuquerque 1980, no. 42.

Bibliography: Marandel 1980, pp. 15-16, fig. 11.

The subject of this painting, originally related by Livy (3, 44–58), was retold in the eighteenth century by Aubert de Vertot d'Aubeuf in his *Histoire des révolutions arrivées dans le gouvernement de la République romaine* (1719) and by Charles Rollin in his immensely popular *Histoire romaine* (16 volumes published between 1738 and 1748), a bible for many artists in late eighteenth-century France. Virginia, a young and virtuous Roman woman, demanded to die—and was killed by her own father—rather than yield to the advances of Appius Claudius. This story that extolled moral values and self-sacrifice and exposed the depravity of despots was illustrated by several artists before Lethière (Doyen, Salon of 1759; Parma, Pinacoteca; and Brenet, Salon of 1783; Nantes, Musée des Beaux-Arts). It should also be noted that the frontispiece to Rollin's second English edition of his *Roman History* (1754) was an engraving of *The Death of Virginia* made in 1739 (see Rosenblum 1967, pp. 65–66).

At the Salon of 1795, both Lethière's and Le Barbier's entries—a drawing (no. 354) and a painting (no. 306), respectively—demonstrate the continuing appeal of the subject. Lethière returned to the subject late in life. In 1828, he signed and dated a gigantic painting (4.58 × 7.83 m), which he exhibited at the Salon of 1831 (no. 1384; Paris, Musée du Louvre). It is tempting to relate this sketch to that late work, however, their different compositions prevent us however from doing so. As noted by Walch (Albuquerque 1980, no. 42), several drawings and oil sketches on this subject are listed in Sandoz (1975, pp. 31–32), to which Walch has added a small sketch on the New York art market in 1979 (New York 1979, no. 84).

Lethière's depiction of violent scenes—a practice common to many artists of the period, but particularly so with Lethière—had been noted by his contemporaries: "Toujours du sang, des échaffauds / Lethière, cachez donc vos esquisses," exclaimed one critic (cited in Paris 1974–75, under no. 93). Not surprisingly, Lethière had inaugurated his career with a painting treating a related theme, the Death of Camilla, his entry for the 1785 Prix-de-Rome (Marandel 1980, pp. 12–17).

While the attribution of the sketch to the artist is irrefutable (note, in particular, the way in which Lethière typically sets his scene away from the front of the canvas, thus giving the illusion of a stage set), its date is more problematic. Walch suggested a date around 1800, which is particularly valid if one recognizes in this painting an early thought for the large 1828 composition.

J. P. M.

Baron François-Xavier FABRE

(Montpellier 1766–Montpellier 1837)

upil of David, Fabre obtained the Prix-de-Rome in 1787. His stay in Rome was interrupted in 1793 by the growing acceptance of Republican ideas among the French artists in residence. Preferring neutrality, he sought refuge in Florence, where he earned his living as a portrait painter. His friendship with the great Italian poet Alfieri and the poet's mistress, the Contessa d'Albany, opened for Fabre the doors to a brilliant and cosmopolitan society that offered him patrons. During his lifetime Fabre assembled large collections that he eventually bequeathed to his home city, where they formed the nucleus of the museum that bears his name and which he directed upon his return to France in 1825.

84 Baron François-Xavier FABRE
Oedipus and Antigone, n.d.
Oedipe et Antigone
Oil on paper on canvas
7 × 8 ¾" (17.8 × 22.2 cm)
Inscribed on the stretcher: *Oedipe roi de Thèbes et sa fille Antigone / Esqu. de Fabre 1796* (19th-century handwriting)

Exhibitions: Houston 1973-75, no. 21.

Bibliography: Pellicer, 1982, vol. 3, no. 49a, and under 51d and 87; Spoleto 1988, under no. 28.

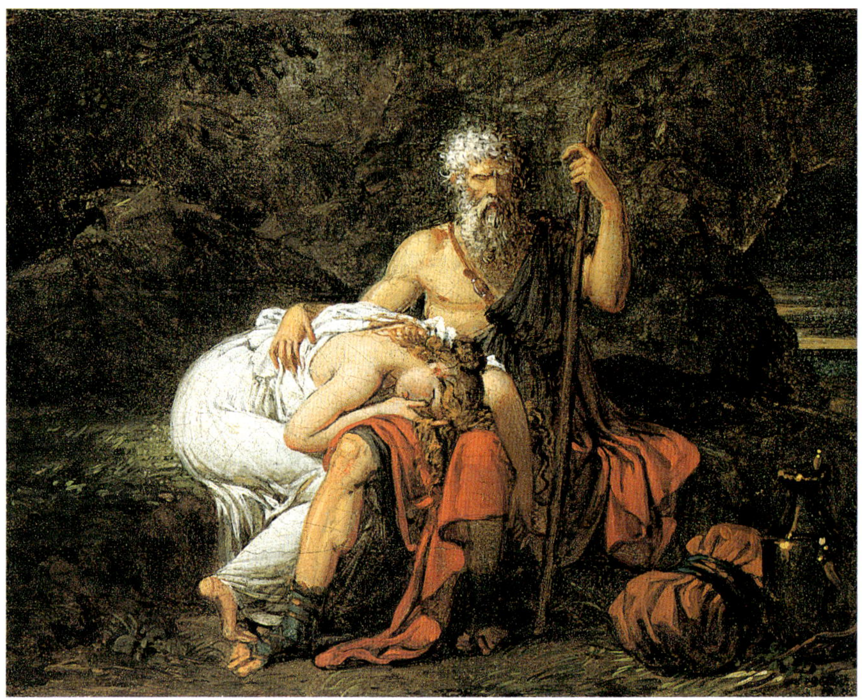

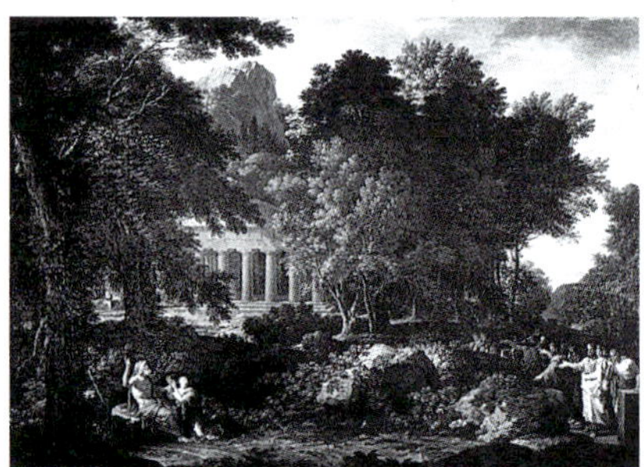

Fig. 11. Baron François-Xavier FABRE. ***Oedipus and Antigone*** (Oedipe et Antigone), 1808. Oil on canvas. Musée Fabre, Montpellier, Cliché Fédéric Jaulmes. Photo: © Claude O'Sughrue.

The date inscribed on the back of this small oil sketch is of particular importance, as it establishes that this composition belongs to the artist's first years in Florence. He had arrived in the Tuscan capital in 1793, after fleeing the Revolutionary atmosphere of Rome. In date and style, this work is close to some of the artist's most important compositions of the time, the history paintings *Marius and the Gaul* (1796) and *Ariadne and Theseus* (1797, collection Lady Agnew), both commissioned by Lord Holland. The antique ewer figures in our sketch as well as in the *Marius*, exemplifying the use by the artist not of studio props, but of drawings carefully done after the antique in the manner of David, Fabre's master. Neither this oil sketch, nor another of the same subject and, according to Laure Pellicer, of the same date (Montpellier, Musée Fabre, 837.1.571; Pellicer 1982, vol. 3, no. 49 b), were fully developed into large compositions, but Fabre returned to this subject in 1808, in one of his first historical landscapes (fig. 11). Pellicer has suggested that the more stylized features of our Antigone—compared, in particular, to the statuesque, Niobide-inspired Antigone of 1808—are possible evidence of a brief influence of Flaxman over Fabre.

J. P. M.

Charles MEYNIER

(Paris 1768–Paris 1832)

Pupil of Vincent (q.v.), Meynier won the Prix-de-Rome in 1789, along with Girodet. Revolutionary events forced Meynier out of Rome, but his return to Paris marked the beginning of a brilliant career. During the Empire, Meynier executed many works illustrating military victories and other events of Napoleon's reign. He also provided designs for the bas-reliefs of the Arc de Triomphe of the Carrousel. During the Bourbon Restoration, he painted decorations and ceilings for the Tuileries and the Louvre.

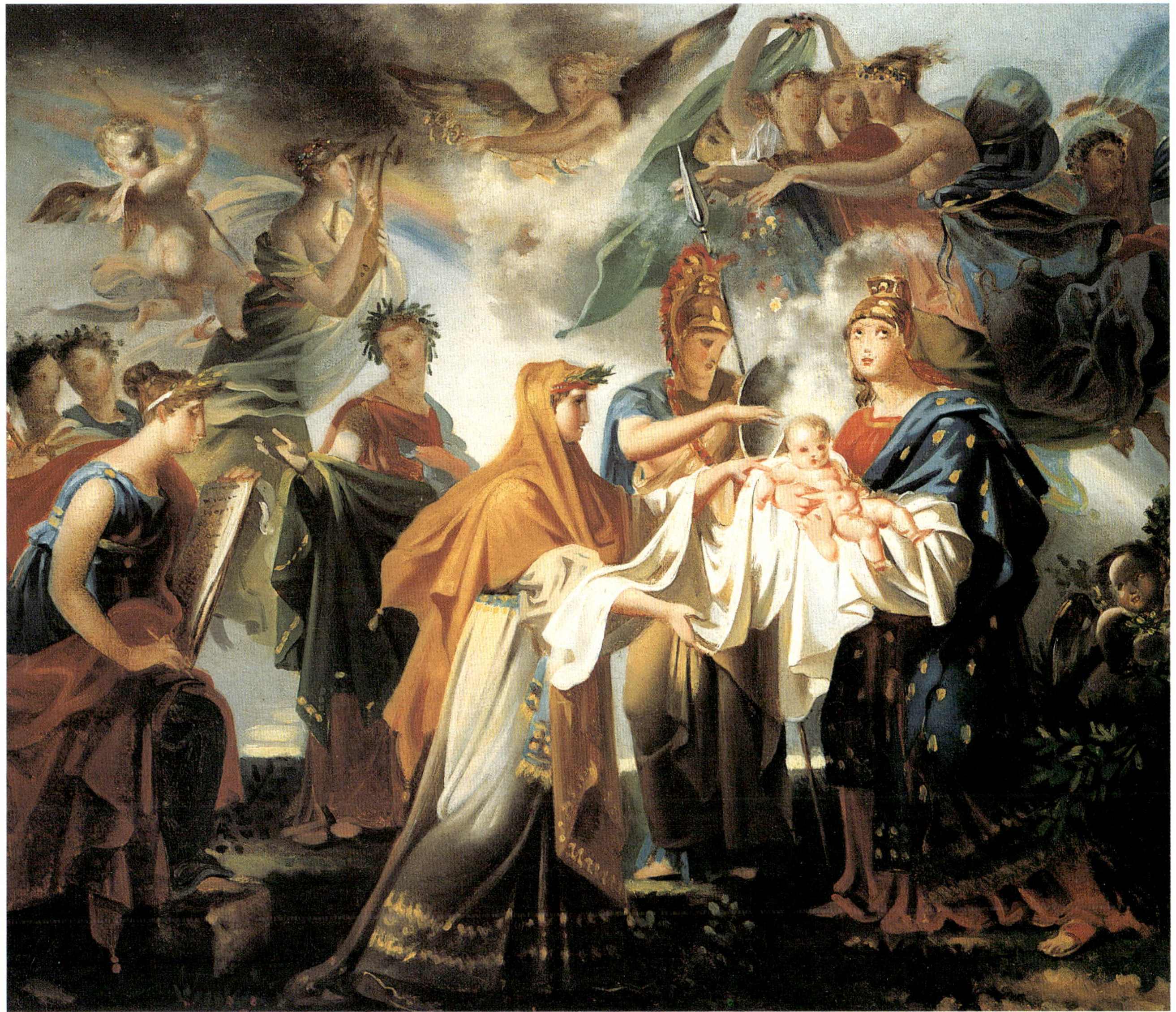

85   Charles MEYNIER
Allegory of the Birth of Louis XIV, c. 1814
Allégorie de la naissance de Louis XIV
Oil on canvas
18 ¼ × 21 ¾" (46.4 × 55.2 cm)

The Salon of 1814, which took place shortly after Napoleon's exile to the Island of Elba, saw a swift return—often on the part of artists who had been the apologists of the Imperial regime—of paintings treating historical or allegorical subjects related to the lives of the past French kings. Portraits of the royal family and such royalist subjects as Menjaud's *Louis XVIII Ordering the Continuation of the Royal Church at Saint-Denis* or the entrance of the same king in Paris, by Vergnaux, offered a glorified image of the current ruler. The return of Napoleon to France and his rapid advance toward Paris during the period known as the Hundred Days delayed the publication of engravings after paintings exhibited at the Salon, their publishers preferring to excise from these collections some of the most politically *engagé* subjects rather than face possible censorship.

One of Charles Meynier's entries (no. 699) in that year's Salon—for which the painting exhibited here is a study—was a composition intended for the Salon of the "Enfants de France" at the Tuileries Palace. It represented, as carefully explained in the Salon's *livret*, "The Birth of Louis XIV. Allegorical subject. After thirty-two years of marriage, the wishes of Louis XIII are fulfilled. Heaven gives him a son. France receives the child from the hands of Juno Lucina, goddess of parturitions. She [France] presses the child against her heart and thanks heaven for its gift. Celestial divinities shower flowers over the beloved child. The Muses celebrate the birth of a prince whose exploits they have celebrated."

Meynier's finished painting escaped the destruction of the Tuileries in 1870 and is now at the City Hall in Amboise. Meynier, who had executed some spirited Napoleonic paintings (*The Soldiers of the 76th Regiment Finding Their Flags in the Arsenal of Innsbruck*, 1808; Versailles, Musée National), has here returned to a more moderate Neoclassicism. Both the composition and the grouping of the figures are particularly close to one of Meynier's earliest known compositions, the sketch *Triumphant France Encouraging the Arts and Sciences in the Midst of War* of around 1793 (Boulogne-Billancourt, Bibliothèque Paul Marmottan), which Cuzin (Paris/Detroit/New York 1974–75, p. 540) found imbued with the spirit of the eighteenth century in spite of its revolutionary subject. There is some irony in Meynier's harking back in his first commission for the Bourbons to a style he had first formulated as an homage to the Revolutionary government. Perhaps this was a result of the artist's genuine desire to find a courtly style different from the one used under Napoleon—and for which only somewhat old-fashioned formulas could provide a model.

J. P. M.

Baron François-Pascal-Simon GERARD

(Rome 1770–Paris 1837)

Covered with honors by the end of his life, Gérard had begun his career under favorable auspices. He studied with Pajou, Brenet (q.v), and more important, with David, who also became his protector. Winning a second Prix-de-Rome in 1789, he went back to Italy—where he had spent the first twelve years of his life—in 1791. In 1793, the protection of David allowed him to pass through the Revolutionary tempest without having to enlist in the army or declare his political allegiance. His immense successes at the Salons of 1795 and 1798 secured his reputation, and from 1800 onward the patronage of Bonaparte. Gérard executed decorations (*Ossian* for Malmaison) for Bonaparte and his court and was the official portrait painter of the new regime. After Waterloo, he served the Bourbon kings with equal enthusiasm, and in 1831, he painted the portrait of Louis-Philippe. Gérard also worked on the decoration of the Panthéon in Paris (1820–36).

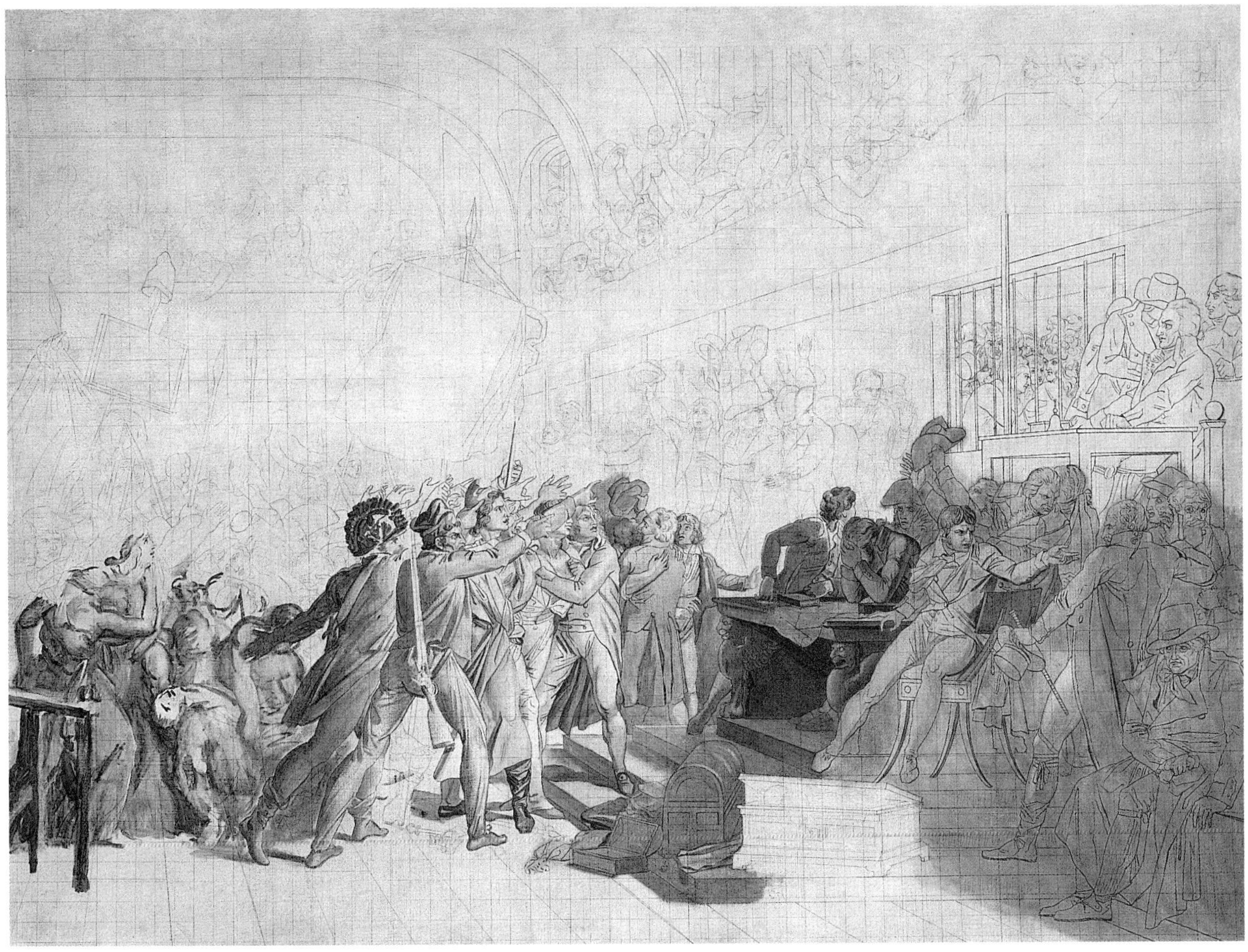

86 Baron François-Pascal-Simon GERARD
The 10th of August, 1792, 1794
Le 10 aôut 1792
Oil on canvas
42 × 56 ¾" (106.7 × 144.1 cm)

Provenance: Family of the artist, by descent.

Exhibitions: Houston 1973–75, no. 26; Chapel Hill 1978, no. 34; New York 1989, no. 31A.

Bibliography: Olander 1983, pp. 317–19, fig. 22; Bordes 1983, pp. 86, 89, 119 (n. 322), fig. 42; Paris 1989, p. 858.

An unfinished sketch for a composition the artist never carried through completely, this painting represents one of the most violent and explosive moments of the French Revolution. It was on this day that the fate of the monarchy was decided. "From the beginning of the day," writes Simon Schama, "it was apparent that blood would flow more freely than at any time since the beginning of the Revolution" (1989, p. 614). What provoked such exasperation among the people was a combination of disastrous economic factors with a fear that a foreign invasion, intended to support the monarchy, was imminent. Delegates from French provinces, in Paris since the celebration of the Fédération on July 14th, declared that they would stay until the abolition of the monarchy. When the populace stormed the Tuileries Palace, where the royal family resided, strong resistance was offered by the National Guards and the Gardes Suisses (the King's personal guard), culminating in violent carnage. The guards were massacred, but not before they killed over fifteen hundred civilians and injured at least as many (the massacre itself was the subject of a painting by a certain P. Berthaud—otherwise unknown—exhibited at the 1793 Salon; Versailles, Musée National du Château, reproduced in Bordes/Michel 1988, p. 41. fig. 34). The King fled with his family and sought refuge at the Legislative Assembly. Physically unharmed, he had nevertheless to listen to the pronouncement of his deposition. His reign was over.

In January 1793, about a year after the execution of Louis XVI, the Committee of Public Safety announced its intention to create a painting competition for subjects dealing with contemporary events. One hundred and forty artists submitted entries, varying from traditional allegories to illustrations of individual deeds. Gérard's entry, a finished drawing (Paris, Musée du Louvre), was arguably one of the most political statements and one of the few entries to deal with a popular event. Gérard, a favorite pupil of David, had certainly been encouraged by his master to enter the competition and select his subject. Furthermore, David's own *Tennis Court Oath* (1790) provided Gérard with a modern example of history painting dealing with a contemporary subject.

With his pen-and-ink sketch Gérard obtained the first prize of 30,000 francs, a studio at the Louvre, and the commission to complete his project on a life-size scale. Gérard carried his project only as far as the sketch presented here. He executed some individual figure studies (New York 1989, pl. 31b), as well as another oil sketch (ibid., p. 223, fig. 2), which—as argued by this author elsewhere (ibid., p. 223)—is contemporary with the drawing from which it differs only by its dramatization of the scene through strong lighting effects. This large monochrome sketch may represent in turn a further step in the artist's creative process. It differs from the submitted drawing principally in the group of figures on the extreme left (its loose and sketchy treatment indicates also a barely formulated idea on the part of the artist), with the introduction of a fallen figure being brought vengefully to the attention of the president of the Legislative Assembly while the King and Queen, represented in the cage of the court recorder, look away.

In spite of its debt to David's *Oath*, Gérard's *The 10th of August* differs greatly from David's stark statement. While it remains heroic in spirit, it is nevertheless more anecdotic, more accurate in its telling of a story than the *Oath*, and prefigures rather the kind of history painting Gérard, Gros, and many other artists would soon execute to extoll Napoleon's glory.

J. P. M.

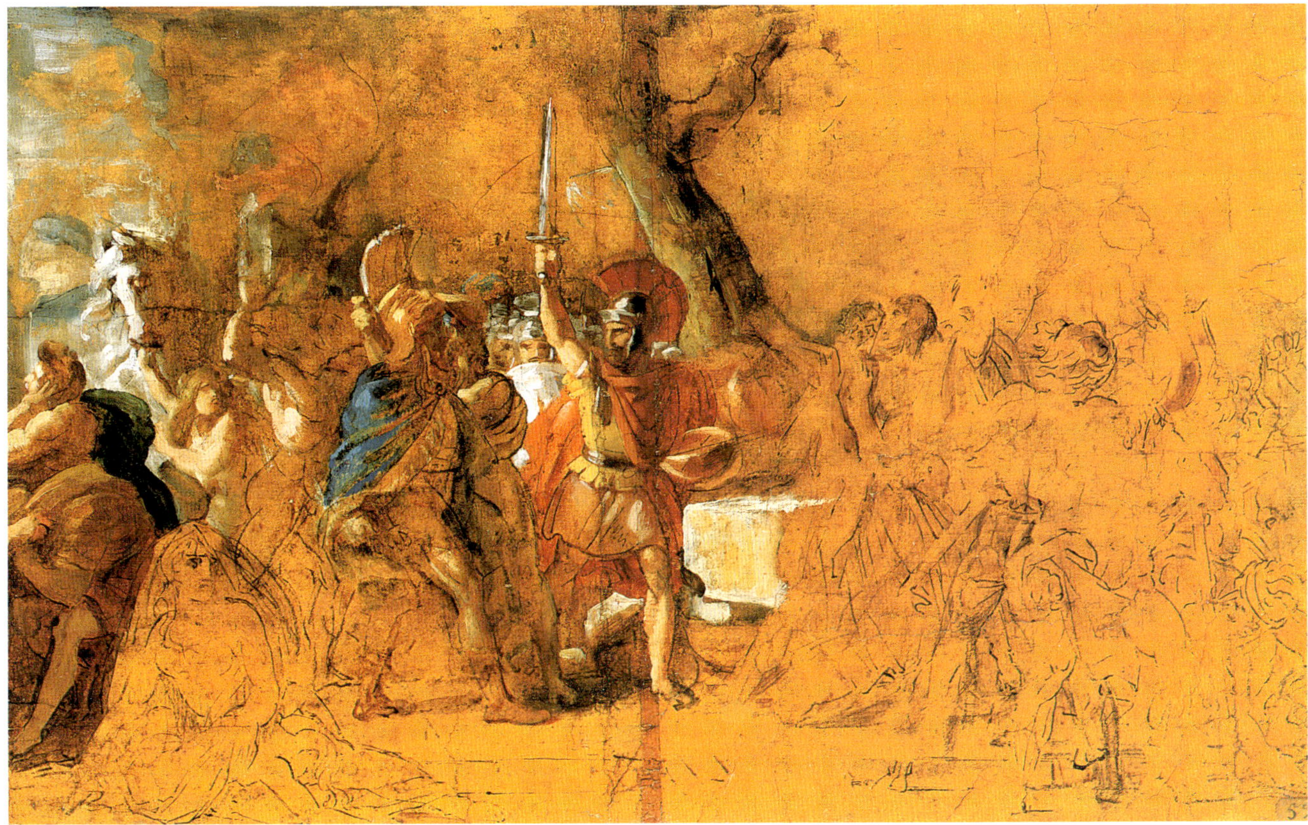

87   Baron François-Pascal-Simon GERARD
Scene from Roman History, n.d.
Scène de l'histoire romaine
Oil on canvas
14 ⅛ × 23" (35.9 × 58.4 cm)

Provenance: Henri Gérard, the artist's nephew; by descent to Comtesse Foy.

Bibliography: New York 1990; New York 1992.

The subject of this composition, evidently drawn from Roman history, has not been identified. It may be one of the two sketches dealing with subjects of antiquity mentioned but not reproduced in Henri Gérard's first catalogue of the oeuvre of the artist (1857, vol. 3). It probably belongs to the early years of the artist, between 1786 and 1791, while he was still in the studio of his teacher, David, which he frequented. Under the influence of his teacher, and caught up in the political events of the French Revolution, Gérard painted several scenes extolling the virtues of heroic Romans. (A recently rediscovered sketch representing Marius returning to Rome, which belongs to that period, was acquired by the Museum of Fine Arts, Houston (see New York 1990, no. 13).

This sketch could, in fact, be a first thought for the Houston object. Gérard often tried several compositions before settling on one. The foreground group of the mother shielding her child seen here recurs in other works by the artist. The same woman, albeit without child, appears in an 1810 composition, *Aeneas Before Burning Troy*, recently exhibited (New York 1992, p. 28).

A. Latreille

88   Baron François-Pascal-Simon GERARD
Landscape near Boulogne, n.d.
Paysage près de Boulogne
Oil on canvas
11 ¾ × 16 ¼" (29.8 × 41.3 cm)

Provenance: Henri Gérard, the artist's
nephew; by descent to Duchesse
d'Harcourt, Paris.

Bibliography: Lenormant 1847; Gérard
1886.

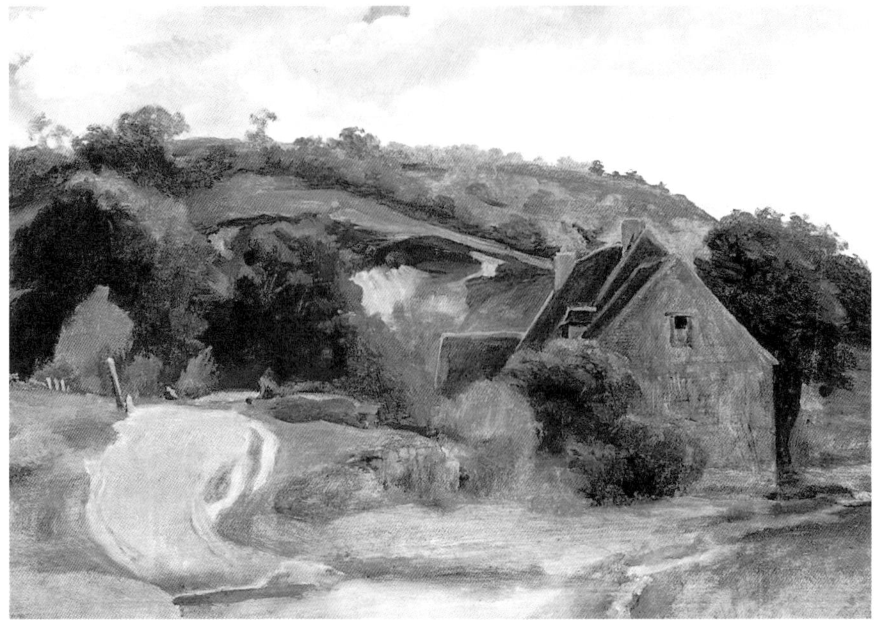

An academic painter by training and vocation, Gérard did not neglect the study of
nature. Even in such formal compositions as his famous *Daphnis and Chloe* (1824; Paris,
Musée du Louvre), the artist was eager to imbue his figures with realistic traits. Commenting on that painting, he declared that he wanted the viewer to realize his mythological figures "had been fed with goat meat" (Lenormant 1847, p. 53, n. 1).

Gérard's attraction to nature also expressed itself in his friendship with the
flower painter Gérard van Spaendonck, in whose company he often visited the forest at Montmorency, near Paris, in search of attractive and rare specimens. Gérard,
in spite of his official duties in Paris, spent the summer months in his house at Auteuil,
then a country village distinct from Paris. After 1825, the artist spent his summers
outside of the Paris region, notably in Normandy near Le Havre and Dieppe. His
stay in Boulogne is confirmed in a letter addressed to the painter by his friend, the
painter and scientist Mérimée (Gérard 1886, vol. 2, pp. 308–10).

Gérard's nephew and biographer (Gérard 1887 p. 401) mentioned several studies after nature executed by his uncle during these trips to Normandy. Although this
sketch is not specifically mentioned among them, it belongs clearly to this period of
the artist's career. Henri Gérard informs us that such sketches were not executed out-
of-doors but rather were reconstructed from memory in the artist's studio. In spite of
this traditional technique, our sketch seems to echo the spontaneous *plein-air* studies
of Paul Huet and to prefigure the direct and unaffected style of Corot.

A. Latreille

Louis LAFITTE

(Paris 1770-Paris 1828)

*P*upil of G. Demarteau and J. B. Regnault (q.v.), Lafitte won the Prix-de-Rome in 1791 and exhibited at the Salon for the first time that year. A regular exhibitor until 1817, Lafitte spent some time in Italy during the 1790s, and was made a member of the Florentine Academy in 1793. He worked at Malmaison, and under the Bourbon Restoration was made Dessinateur du Cabinet du Roi.

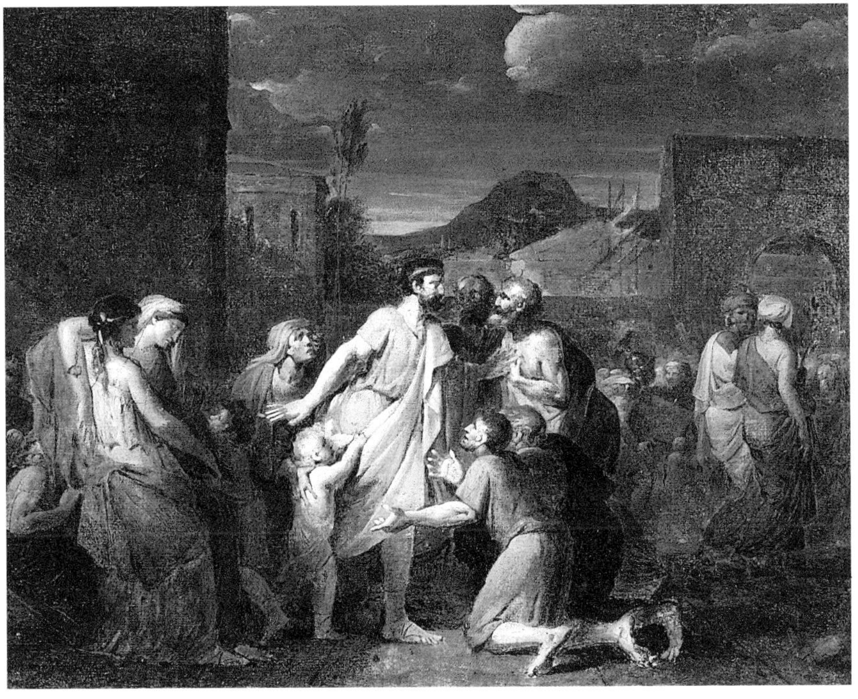

89 Louis LAFITTE
Regulus Returning to Carthage, 1791
Le Retour de Régulus à Carthage
Oil on paper on canvas
13 × 16 ¼" (33.0 × 41.3 cm)

Louis Lafitte shared the Prix-de-Rome in 1791 with Charles Thévenin (1764–1838). The subject imposed on the candidates that year was Regulus Returning to Carthage. Marcus Atilius Regulus, Roman Consul in 256, after initial victories over the Carthaginians, was finally defeated and sent to Rome to negotiate an exchange of prisoners. Notwithstanding the entreaties of his family, he returned to Carthage, as promised to the victors, and died there in captivity. Lafitte's Prix-de-Rome painting is at the Ecole des Beaux-Arts, Paris. Beside this oil sketch, several other preparatory studies are known: a drawing—inscribed "Girodet"—at the Musée des Beaux-Arts, Rouen (Baderou collection, 975-4–1336); another—part of the Leblanc Sale—was presented at the Hôtel Drouot, Paris, December 14, 1990, no. 53 (A partial study of the kneeling supplicants was in London 1975; the same drawing appeared in a Sotheby's, Monte-Carlo, sale of December 8, 1984, no. 67, and was most recently with William Foucault in Paris in 1991.) Lafitte's composition was engraved by Landon and published in his *Annales du Musée* (2nd edition, Ecole Française Moderne, 1833, vol. 2, pl. 1, pp. 5-9). Landon's judgment on Lafitte was severe—"as a history painter, Lafitte occupies only a secondary rank." However, Landon, who with Lafitte was the original co-editor of the *Annales du Musée,* had a great deal of respect for Lafitte's design work. As Landon wrote, "as a designer, be it of book vignettes, or of interior decorations, or of ornaments for gold and silver pieces . . . his name will never be forgotten" (ibid., p. 7). Indeed, Lafitte's best-known works are his designs for wallpapers (*Story of Psyche*).

J.P.M.

Baron Antoine-Jean GROS

(Paris 1771–Meudon 1855)

Gros entered the studio of David in 1785. Although he failed to win the Prix-de-Rome in 1792, Gros traveled through Italy the next year, eventually settling in Genoa. Napoleon appointed him to the commission entrusted with the confiscation of Italian works of art. More important still, his familiarity with the military campaign in Italy led to his appointment as illustrator of Napoleon's other European campaigns. Like Gérard, Gros served the Bourbon monarchy upon the collapse of the Empire and in 1816 replaced David—his former master, who had been exiled to Brussels—as professor at the Ecole des Beaux-Arts. His lack of success, in spite of the admiration of younger artists including Delacroix, led him to commit suicide by drowning in 1835.

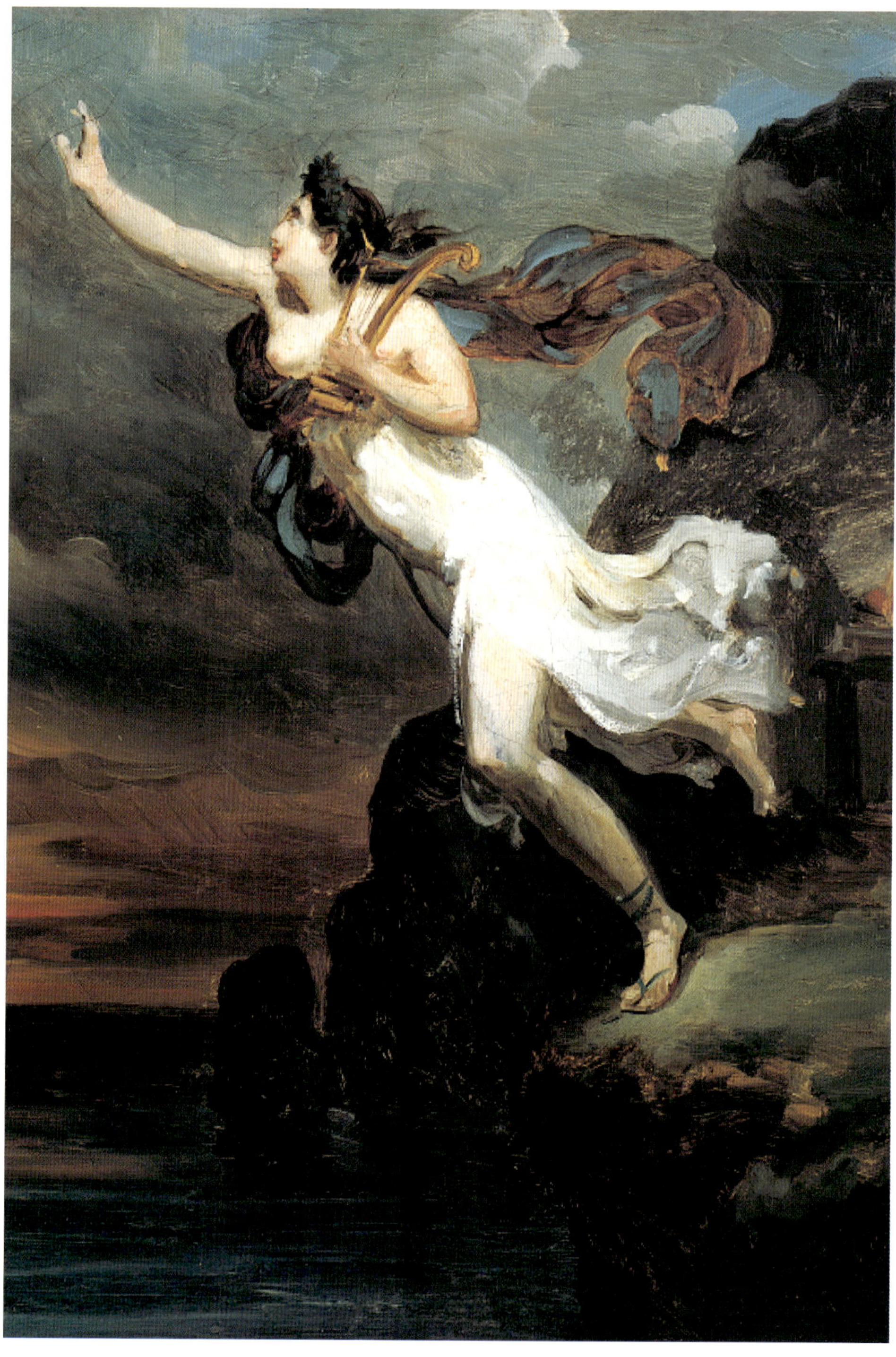

90 Baron Antoine-Jean GROS
Sappho at Leucadia, c. 1800
Sapho à Leucate
Oil on canvas
13 ½ × 10" (34.3 × 25.4 cm)

Provenance: Comte Parfait de Bizemont, Orleans (?).

Exhibitions: Albuquerque 1980, no. 29.

Gros's celebrated painting representing the Greek poetess jumping to her death (Bayeux, Musée des Beaux-Arts) was exhibited at the 1801 Salon, where it received lukewarm reviews at best. Most critics reproached the artist for his lack of realism (see Paris/Detroit/New York 1974–75, pp. 462–63), objecting to details ranging from the physical type of the heroine ("less Greek than Egyptian") to the rendition of night effects in blue-green tones ("Why," said another critic, "does Antoine Gros ignore the fact that the light cast by the moon is not green?"). The subject itself was not new, however, and had been well received when treated by Taillasson (1791 Salon; Brest, Musée des Beaux-Arts).

Gros had painted at least one, and possibly several, preparatory oil sketches for this composition. The catalogue of the 1936 Gros exhibition in Paris affirms the contention of Gros's early biographers, Tripier-LeFranc (1880, p. 673) and Delestre (1867, p. 60), that "the sketch was done in Milan, the painting in the Paris studio" (Paris 1936, p. 53). The sketch was formerly in the collection of a Mme Carbonet. As noted by Peter Walch, it is impossible to say (Albuquerque 1980), whether the Carbonet sketch is identical with the one presented here. Other compositions of the same subject have been recorded, including a painting (not the one in Bayeux) in the sale following Gros's death in 1835.

The oil sketch presented in this exhibition was reputedly at one time in the collection of Comte Parfait de Bizemont, the first director of the museum in Orléans, although it does not figure in the catalogue of that collection (Davoust 1891). There are differences between our sketch and the final painting. In the sketch, Sappho thrusts herself forward with Romantic élan. In the final painting, she holds her lyre close to her ear, her entire posture folded in and hesitating on the verge of death. It is possible that the critics reacted negatively to this non-gestural pathos. Had the rhetorical grandiloquence of the sketch been carried to a larger scale the painting might have garnered some praise.

J. P. M.

Jérôme-Martin LANGLOIS

(Paris 1779–Paris 1858)

One of David's favorite pupils, Langlois helped his master with the execution of such paintings as *Leonidas and Napoleon Crossing the Alps*. He received the Prix-de-Rome in 1809. He made his debut at the Salon in 1806 and continued to exhibit there until 1837. Langlois was a painter of religious and historical subjects. His most famous portrait is of his teacher, David, painted in Brussels in 1824.

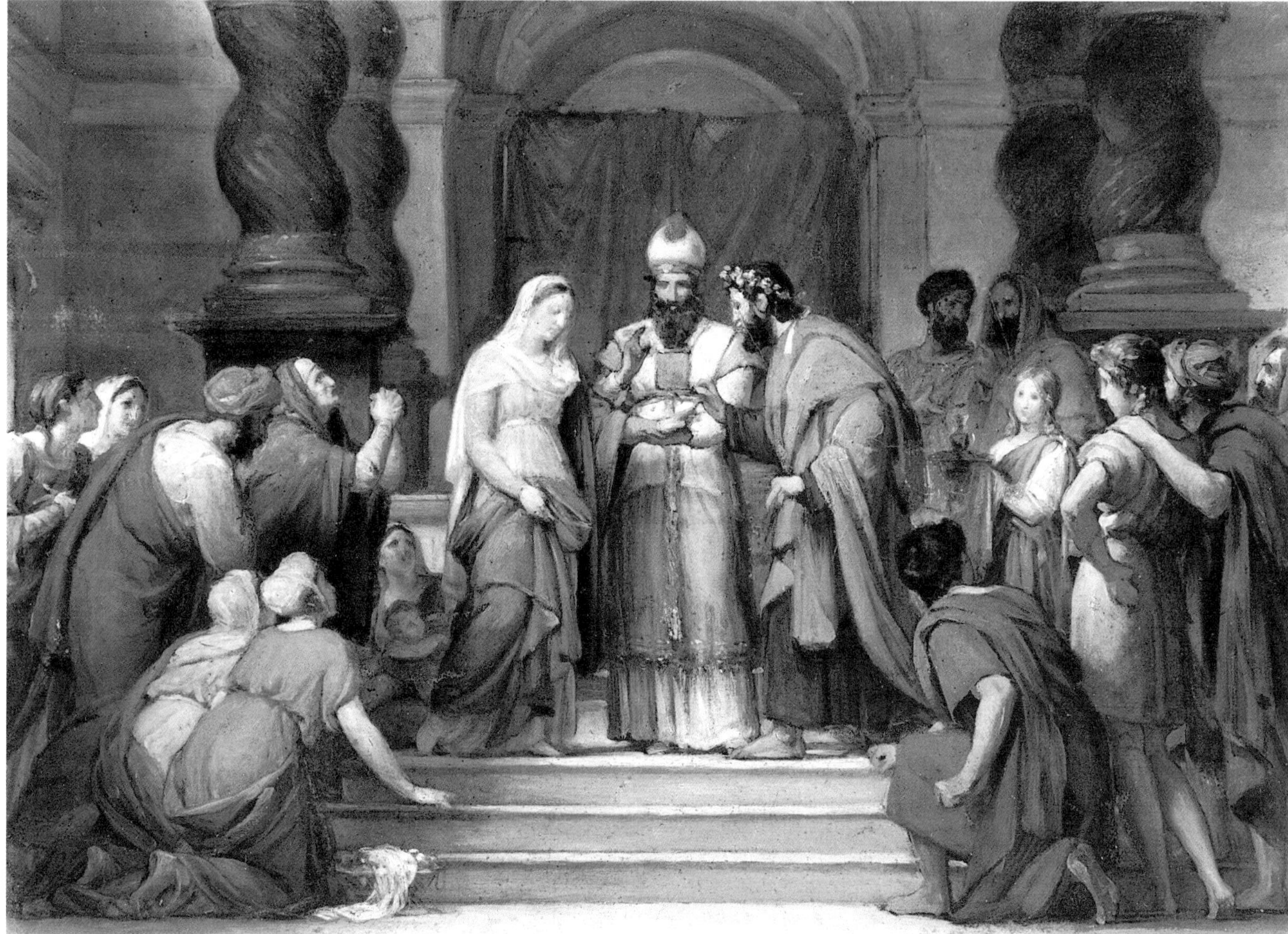

91 Jérôme-Martin LANGLOIS
The Marriage of the Virgin, 1833
Le Mariage de la Vierge
Oil on canvas
13 ¼ × 18 ¼" (33.7 × 46.4 cm)

Exhibitions: Peoria 1980, no. 33; New
York 1980, no. 16.

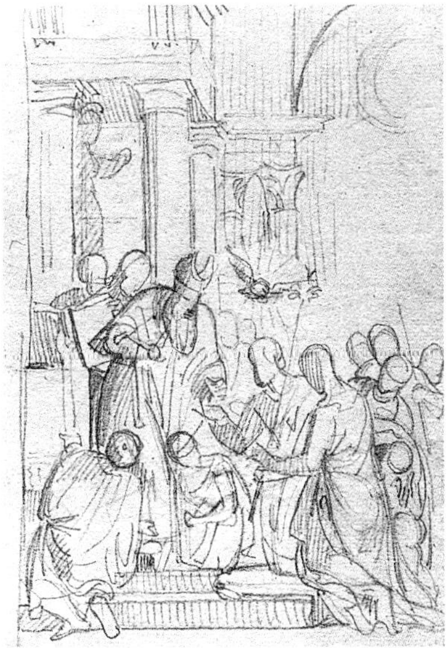

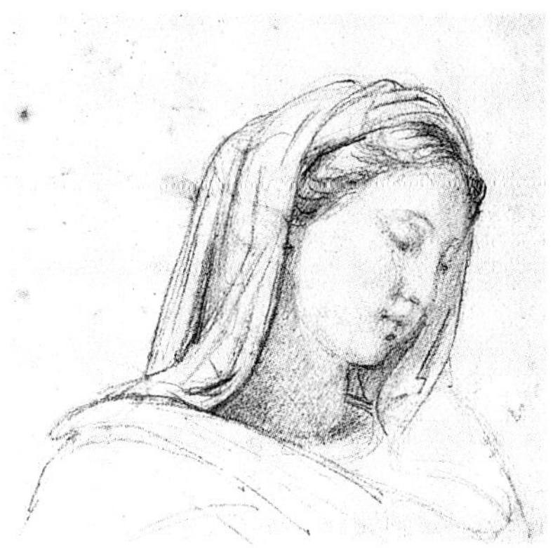

Fig. 12. Jérôme-Martin LANGLOIS.
The Marriage of the Virgin (Le Mariage
de la Vierge), c. 1832–33. Black chalk on
paper. Private collection, Paris

Fig. 13. Jérôme-Martin LANGLOIS.
Study for the Head of a Virgin (Etude
pour une tête de Vierge), c. 1832–33.
Black chalk on paper. Private collection.
Photo: Coll. Photo AGRACI.

Eight different artists each contributed one painting representing a scene from the
life of Mary to decorate the nave of the Church of Notre-Dame-de-Lorette in Paris.
Serving as an anthology of religious painting under the July Monarchy, the church
features the work of Raymond-Auguste Monvoisin (q.v.; *The Birth of the Virgin*, 1833),
François-Louis de Juinne (*The Assumption*, 1835), Jean-Perrin Granger (*The Adoration of
the Magi*, 1835), Nicolas-Auguste Hesse (*The Adoration of the Shepherds*, 1835), Aimable-
Paul Coutan (*The Visitation*, 1833), François Dubois (*The Annunciation*, 1833), Auguste-
Jean-Baptiste Vinchon (*The Presentation of the Virgin*, 1833), and Jean-Marie Langlois,
whose *Marriage of the Virgin* was also executed in 1833.

A simple program based on the chronology of Mary's life seems to have dictated the repartition of the paintings around the perimeter of the church, resulting in the
unfortunate juxtaposition of *The Adoration of the Shepherds* and *The Adoration of the Magi*,
two related compositions that would benefit from being distanced from one another.
Each side of the nave displays two large horizontal paintings flanked by windows and
vertical compositions in the corners. Integrated with the architecture, the paintings
had to fit strictly defined areas and, above all, be legible from below. Most commissioned artists carried out this task within the limits of a conservative style that is somewhat at odds with the often more audacious decoration of other parts of the church.
Langlois, himself an esteemed pupil of David, adopted for the purpose a traditional
composition derived from Renaissance prototypes and a type of Virgin clearly derived
from Sassoferrato.

Langlois may have been asked at first to treat the same subject for one of the
vertical corner paintings: a vertical drawing of the same subject in a French private
collection might relate to the project (fig. 12). A study for the head of the Virgin is in
the same collection (fig. 13).

J. P. M.

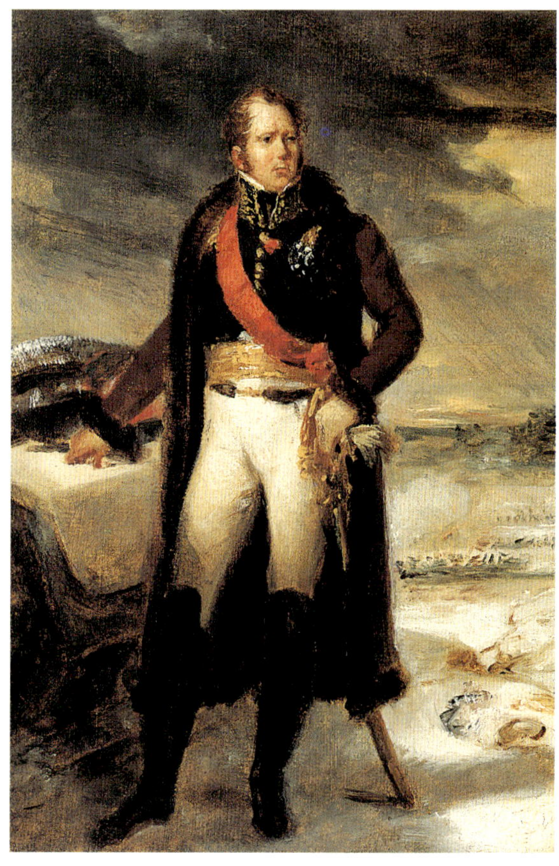

92 Jérôme-Martin LANGLOIS
    Study for a Portrait of Marshal Ney,
    1831–32
    Esquisse pour le portrait du Maréchal
    Ney
    Oil on canvas
    11 ⅜ × 7 ⅞" (28.9 × 20.0 cm)
    Inscribed on the back: *"Esquisse première
    idée pour portrait de Maréchal Ney qui était
    dans la salle des Maréchaux aux Tuileries et
    [qui] fut brûlé pendant la Commune. Par Jer-
    ôme Martin Langlois, Membre de l'Institut"*
    Paul Langlois ("Sketch, first idea for the
    portrait of Marshal Ney which hung in
    the salle des Maréchaux at the Tuileries
    and [which] was burnt during the Com-
    mune. By Jerôme Martin Langlois, Mem-
    ber of the Institute" Paul Langlois [son of
    the artist])

Provenance: Yvonne ffrench collection,
London.

Exhibitions: Peoria 1980, no. 34.

Michel Ney, Duke of Elchingen, Prince of the Moskowa (1769–1815), led a distinguished military career and was created a marshal of the Empire by Napoleon in
1804. After Waterloo, he was court-martialed and executed, but his fame and the
memory of his military prowess survived the collapse of the Empire.

Under Napoleon, a Salle des Maréchaux was created at the Tuileries Palace,
where portraits of the marshals of the Empire were hung. On their deaths, their portraits were to be transferred to the Invalides. Ney's portrait was painted by Charles
Meynier in 1805. It depicts Ney in military dress, booted and spurred, grasping the
pommel of his sheathed sword in one hand and his hat in the other, and standing
against a background of campaign tents and bivouacs. After the fall of the Empire,
the portraits of the marshals remained in the Tuileries, but during the July Monarchy
the principle of displaying living marshals was reinstated. Therefore, after Ney's
execution the Meynier portrait was taken down and in 1819 presented to his widow.
When Louis-Philippe came to power, he hastened to commission a replacement portrait of Ney from Jerôme-Martin Langlois, in the belief that the Meynier portrait
could not be recovered.

The Langlois portrait of Ney was first placed in the Invalides in 1832, but when
the Musée de Versailles, dedicated to "all the glories of France," opened in 1837, it
was transferred there. In 1852, when the Prince-President was installed in the Tuileries, he decided to bring back the portraits of the first marshals created in 1804, and
so the portrait of Ney by Langlois was placed in the Salle des Maréchaux—where in
1871 it was destroyed with all the portraits of the marshals when a fire ravaged the
Tuileries.

The present sketch, which represents the painter's first ideas for his painting of
Ney, is a valuable historical record. The final painting, which depicted Ney during the
Russian retreat, is known only from a very mediocre copy by Eugène Battaille (Musée
de Versailles). The present sketch is totally different from that painting, in which Ney
stands with horses in snow, holding a drawn sword, his arms crossed, and his head
turned the opposite way. Langlois's preliminary sketch in many ways comes closer to
the original pose of the Meynier portrait, but is reversed, perhaps suggesting that he
was working from an engraving of the Meynier. The latter portrait eventually reap-
peared and entered the Musée de Versailles in 1960 (see Zieseniss 1962, p. 28).

J.R.B.

Merry-Joseph BLONDEL

(Paris 1781–Paris 1855)

The son of a contract painter, Blondel began his artistic career by painting in a porcelain factory. He then became a pupil of Jean-Baptiste Regnault, and in 1803 won the Prix-de-Rome with *Aeneas Carrying Anchises*. His departure for Italy was delayed until 1809, however, because of the suspension of scholarships. After returning to Paris in 1812, Blondel exhibited regularly at the Salon. In 1817, he won the gold medal for his *Death of Louis XII* and in 1821 was decorated with the Legion of Honor for his *Saint Elizabeth of Hungary*. He received numerous public commissions, notably for the Galerie de Diane at Fontainebleau (1822); the cupola of the Galerie d'Apollon (1821); the ceiling of the Salle Henri II (1822) in the Louvre; and a series of historical portraits for Versailles. He also worked in several Parisian churches, including Notre-Dame-de-Lorette and Saint-Thomas-d'Aquin. Blondel was appointed professor at the Ecole des Beaux-Arts and elected to the Institut in 1832.

93 Merry-Joseph BLONDEL
Louis XIV, 1827
Oil on canvas
23 × 16 ¼" (58.4 × 41.3 cm)

Exhibitions: Peoria 1980, no. 6.

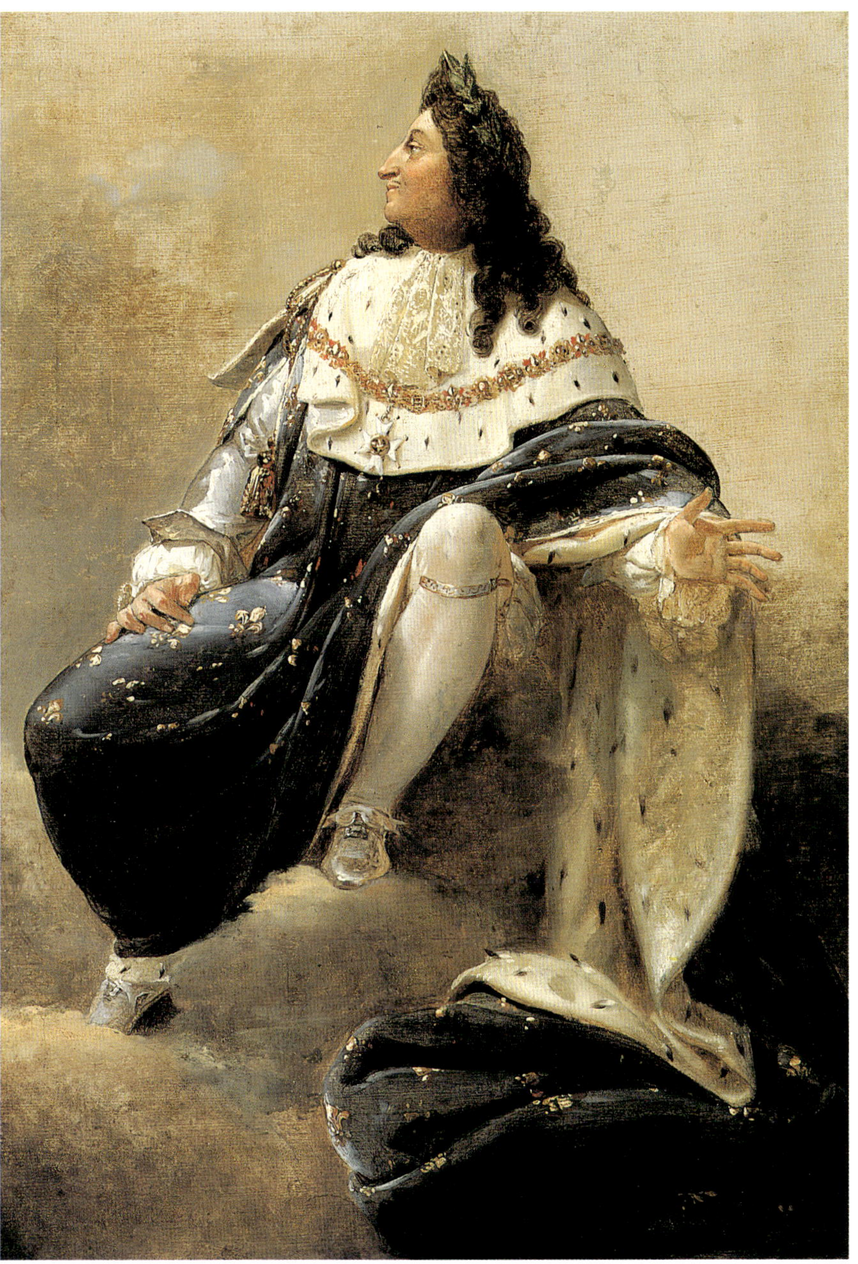

A leading academic history painter, Blondel's accomplished yet rather *retardataire* style reflects the tradition of French decorative painting in the grand manner, combined with the influence of his Neoclassical teacher Jean-Baptiste Regnault..

This sketch of the Sun King, Louis XIV, is a study for one of the main figures in a large ceiling in the Louvre. A black chalk drawing with white highlights on blue paper, which relates to this sketch, is also known (Nouveau Drouot, Paris, April 11, 1981, lot. 27).

The ceiling was commissioned in 1826 and is signed and dated 1827. It is in the "Donation Camondo" room (Département des Objets d'Art), which was formerly the second room of the Conseil d'Etat (State Council). The elaborate central composition includes the allegorical figure of France, surrounded by the French legislator kings and their legal advisers, receiving the Constitutional Charter from Louis XVIII. The vaults contain eight bas-reliefs painted *en camaïeu* of episodes highlighting the "democratic" legislation introduced by French monarchs of the past; for example, the subject of the present sketch, Louis XIV, is shown creating the Conseil d'Etat. Other scenes include the creation of the Parlements by Saint Louis, the Freeing of the Serfs by Louis the Great, and the Creation of the Chambres by Louis XVIII. The episodes are interspersed with the five scenes of the allegorical virtues that inspired the legislators: the Genius of Law showing Charity to Hope and Faith; Charity; Abundance; Piety; and Fidelity. In the corners, the arms of France are borne by Mars and Neptune, Vulcan and Hercules, an allegorical figure of Silence and Apollo, and Mercury and an allegorical figure of Constance.

This vast and complex decorative scheme was designed to promote the monarchy at a time when it was receiving strong criticism by much of the population. The iconography underlines the image of beneficent democracy, which the new government wished to advance, and the choice of the official history painter, Blondel, to execute the work was, through the traditionalism of his style, also an attempt to inspire confidence in the new regime.

J.R.B.

Alexandre-Denis ABEL DE PUJOL

(Valenciennes 1785–Paris 1861)

The illegitimate son of the founder of the Académie de Peinture et Sculpture at Valenciennes, Pujol de Morty, Baron de la Grave, Alexandre-Denis Abel attended this Académie before going to Paris. Unable to afford the fees of David's studio, he was admitted free once David had seen his painting *The Recognition of Philopoemen* and recognized his talent. In 1806, Abel won a first-class medal at the Académie and followed this in 1810 with a medal at the Salon for his *Jacob Blessing Joseph's Offspring*. When Abel won the Prix-de-Rome in 1811, his father recognized him, and he added the surname Pujol to his own. Due to poor health, he remained in Italy only for eight months. After his return to France in 1814, he won a gold medal for his *Death of Britannicus*. He exhibited *The Stoning of Saint Stephen* at the Salon of 1817, and this work, for which he won a medal, firmly established his reputation. He showed regularly at the Salons and received many official honors. Abel de Pujol received numerous public commissions, particularly for murals, including those for the Louvre and for Parisian churches.

94 Alexandre-Denis ABEL DE PUJOL
Portrait of a Magistrate, n.d.
Portrait d'un magistrat
Oil on card on panel
10 × 7 ¾" (25.4 × 19.7 cm)

Exhibitions: Peoria 1980, no. 42.

Bibliography: London 1978, no. 15.

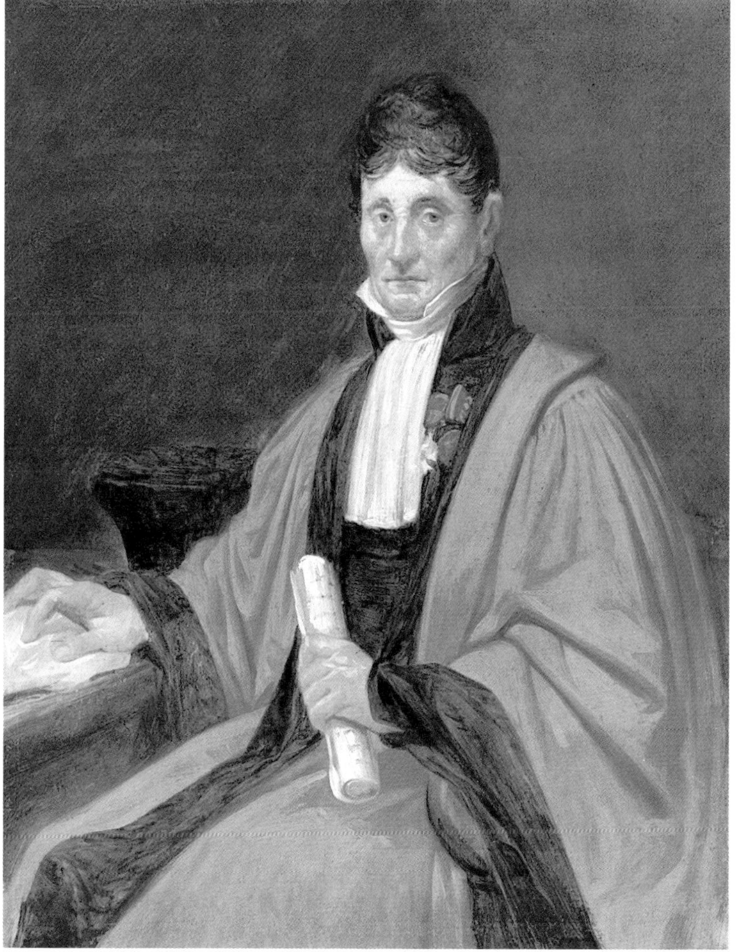

This is a sketch for the highly finished, signed *Portrait of a Magistrate* (100 x 80.5 cm), which was exhibited by the Heim Gallery, London, in 1978 and is now at the Norton Simon Museum in Pasadena, California. There are only very minor differences between this sketch and the final composition.

The identity of the sitter is unknown, and it has not been possible to identify this portrait as any of those that Abel de Pujol exhibited at the Salons. The pose is typical of formal portraits of the period, and the somber color of the background is skillfully juxtaposed with the bright red of the magistrate's gown.

The austerity of the work compares with other Neoclassical portraits, such as the celebrated *Monsieur Bertin* by Ingres of 1832 (Paris, Musée du Louvre). Perhaps

the closest parallel, however, is to be found in another magisterial portrait, that of
François Fedas by Ingres's teacher, Joseph Roques (q.v.), which is in the Musée des
Augustins, Toulouse (see "Actes du colloque international: Ingres et son influence,"
1980, p. 182, fig. 6). This work, which is very close in both the pose and the dignified
mood of the sitter, is datable to about 1833. Abel de Pujol seems to have produced
most of his portraits in his early years, when he most needed the income they provided. However, the final painting of the present composition has an assurance of handling and high degree of finish that indicates it is one of the rarer portraits from the
artist's maturity.

J.R.B.

95 Alexandre-Denis ABEL DE PUJOL
Cleomenes Bidding Farewell to His
Mother, n.d.
Cléomène faisant ses adieux à sa mère
Oil on canvas
15 ⅜ × 11 ⅞" (39.1 × 30.2 cm)

Exhibitions: Peoria 1980, no. 43.

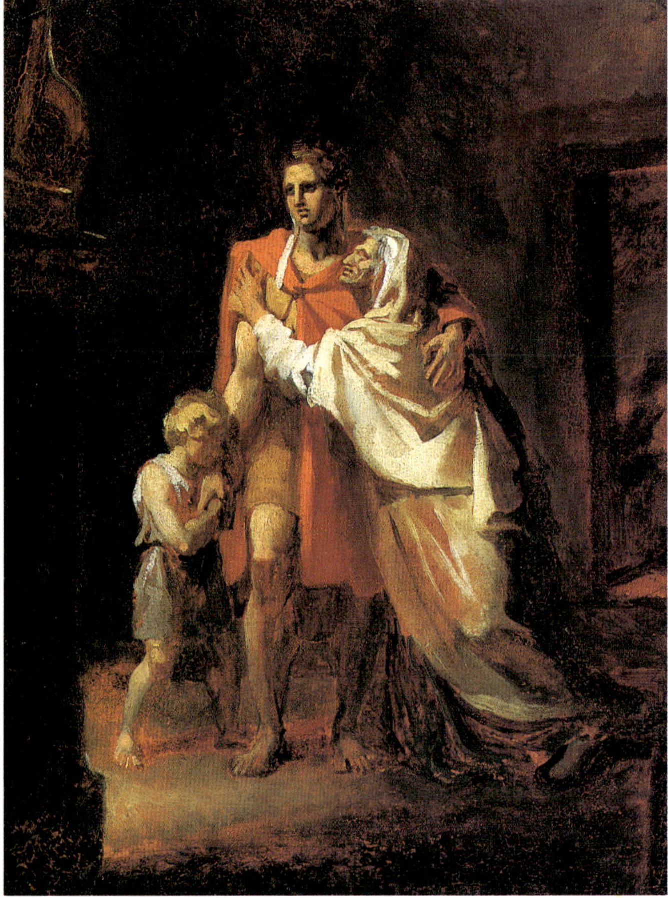

Both the subject and the composition of this Neoclassical sketch reflect the profound
influence of Jacques-Louis David on Pujol's work. The final painting, for which this
is the sketch, is unknown, but must have been an early work in the artist's career. Pujol
produced other Classical history paintings at this time, such as *The Wrath of Achilles* of
1810 and *Lycurgus Presenting the Heir to the Throne to the Spartans*, with which he won
the Prix-de-Rome in 1811.

    The subject of the present sketch, like that of the Prix-de-Rome of 1811, relates
to the history of Sparta. The scene is taken from an episode in Plutarch's life of Cleomenes. Cleomenes was King of Sparta; after his defeat at Sellasia, he looked for support to Ptolemy Euergetes, King of Egypt, who had promised him assistance. The
Egyptian, however, demanded Cleomenes's mother, Cratesidea, and his children as
hostages. Cratesidea readily agreed to act as hostage, and when all was ready for the
voyage to Egypt, they went by land to Taenarus. The present sketch depicts the moment when, Cratesidea, ready for departure, took Cleomenes aside into Neptune's
temple and embraced him. He was "much dejected and extremely discomposed." She
said, "Go to, King of Sparta; when we come forth at the door, let none see us weep,
or show any passion that is unworthy of Sparta" (Clough 1893, p. 488). Then she
boarded the ship, accompanied by her small grandson.

J.R.B.

Alexandre-Charles GUILLEMOT

(Paris 1786–Paris 1831)

The pupil of Jacques-Louis David at the Ecole des Beaux-Arts, Guillemot won the Prix-de-Rome in 1808 for *Erasistratus Discovering the Cause of the Illness of Antiochus*. He exhibited at the Salon from 1814 until his death. Guillemot's most notable Salon works include *Bacchus and Faun*; *Descent from the Cross*, for the Church of Saint-Thomas-d'Aquin, Paris, 1817; *Jesus Raising the Son of the Widow Nain* and *Sappho and Phaon* (Musée de Rennes); and *The Death of Hippolytus* (whereabouts unknown) of 1822. In 1824, Guillemot executed frescoes from the life of Saint Vincent de Paul for the Church of Saint Sulpice. He was also commissioned to paint *The Clemency of Marcus Aurelius Toward the Asian Rebels* for the main room of the Conseil d'Etat in the Louvre. There are drawings by Guillemot in the Louvre and in the museums of Angers and Rochefort.

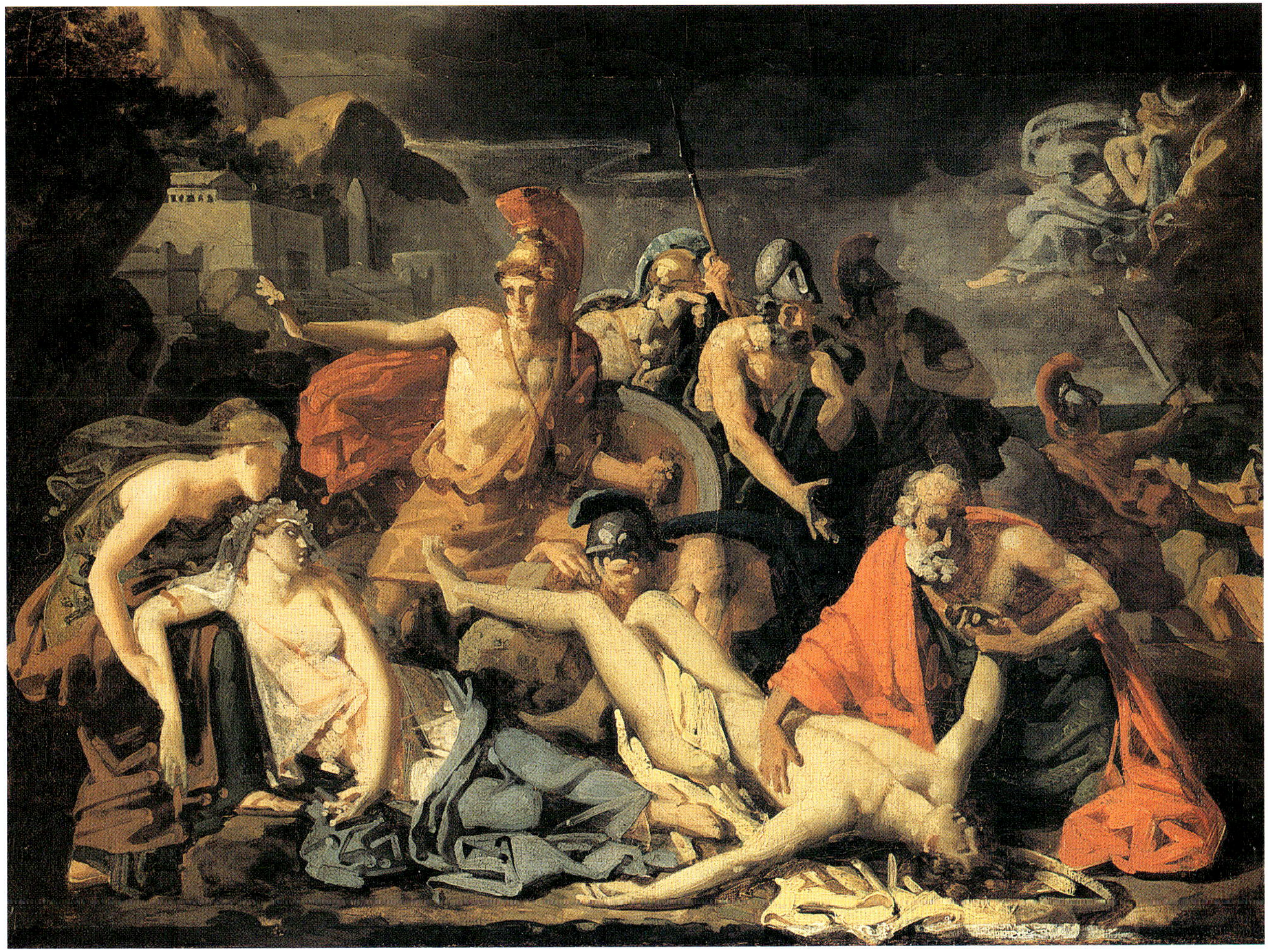

96 Alexandre-Charles GUILLEMOT
The Death of Hippolytus, n.d.
Le Mort d'Hippolyte
Oil on canvas
17 ⅛ × 24" (43.5 × 61.0 cm)

This canvas is a sketch for the large painting of the subject, commissioned by the King, which Guillemot exhibited at the Salon of 1822. The whereabouts of the final composition, last recorded at the Musée de La-Roche-sur-Yon, are today unknown. It is, however, known from an engraving, which is reproduced by Landon (1822, pl. 57).

In Greek mythology, Hippolytus was the son of Theseus by the Amazon Hippolyte. After the death of Hippolyte, Theseus married Phaedra, the daughter of Minos. During Theseus's long absence in the Underworld, Phaedra attempted to seduce Hippolytus, but he was honorable and repulsed her advances. Phaedra then hanged herself and left behind a letter incriminating Hippolytus. On his return, Theseus refused to believe Hippolytus's protests of innocence, and banished him. Theseus then called upon his father Poseidon to avenge him by killing Hippolytus. Poseidon sent a sea monster, which frightened Hippolytus's horses, and he was thrown from his chariot and dragged to death. Theseus learned the truth from Artemis, depicted weeping in the top right of this sketch, but too late.

The Salon version of this painting was much admired for the way Guillemot related the myth, but it was also severely criticized for poor composition (Landon 1822, p. 90). The main criticism of the Salon painting appears to have been that the two principal foreground figures, Hippolytus and Arcia, a young princess, are isolated from the rest of the composition and that the group of background figures is crowded and unrelated. Comparison of this sketch with the engraving reveals that the composition was considerably changed in the final painting. This sketch is therefore particularly significant, since it appears to achieve a more satisfactory solution to the composition. In the final work, the background figures are treated in a more general way: they are not so striking, and there is less interaction with the two central characters.

Guillemot appears to have favored Classical subject matter, although he also executed religious works and portraits. Another Classical subject by Guillemot, *Sappho and Phaon*, was also included in the 1822 Salon.

J.R.B.

(Paris 1786–Paris 1868)

Pupil of Vincent (q.v.) and of David, Picot won the Prix-de-Rome in 1813. He exhibited at the Salon from 1819 until 1838. Decoration for churches (Notre-Dame-de-Lorette, Saint-Thomas-d'Aquin, Saint Vincent-de-Paul) and public buildings constitute a large part of his work. Picot enjoyed sustained patronage from the Orléans family. A member of the Institut in 1836, Picot was also an influential teacher. Bouguereau and Gustave Moreau were among his many students.

97 François-Edouard PICOT
Head of a Woman (Personification of an Antique City), 1831
Tête de femme (Personnification d'une cité antique)
Oil on canvas
25 ¼ × 21" (64.1 × 53.3 cm)

Exhibitions: Peoria 1980, no. 41.

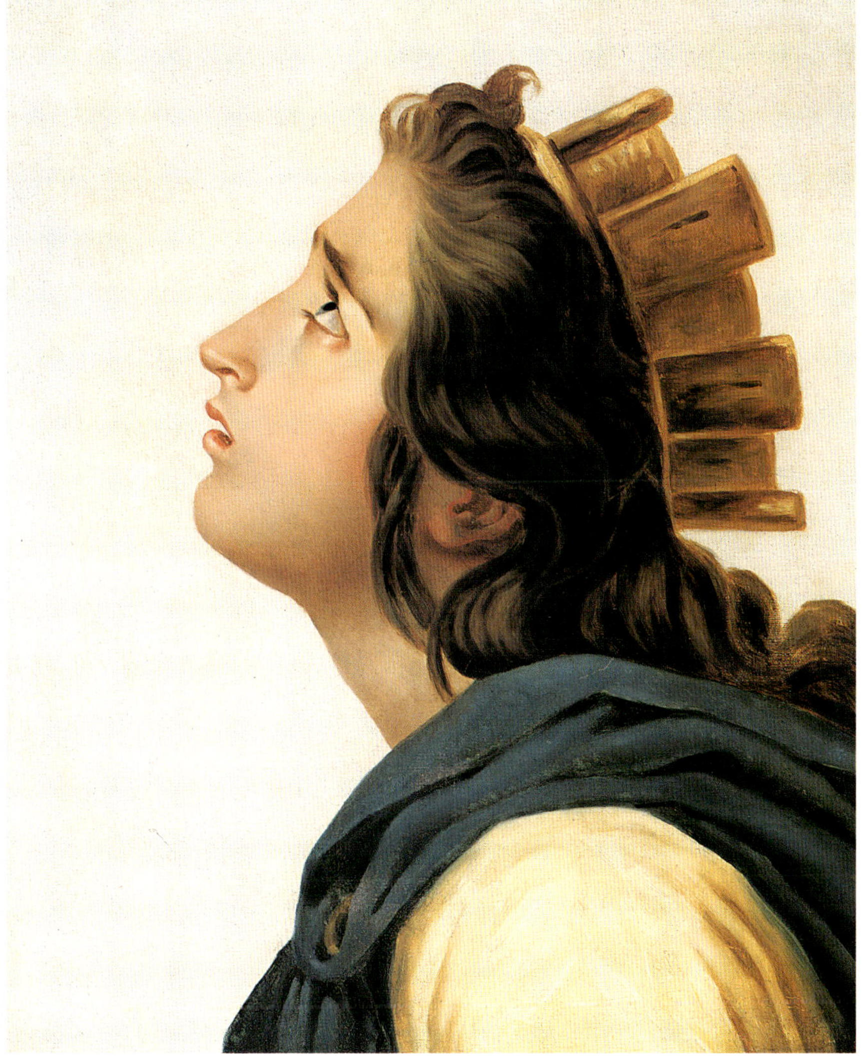

Beginning in 1826, a large renovation project altered the configuration and interior decoration of several rooms intended to become the Musée Charles X within the larger complex of the Louvre (Aulanier 1947–68, vol. 8, pp. 38 ff.). The architect Pierre-François-Léonard Fontaine (1762–1853), who had already distinguished himself under Napoleon, was put in charge of the project. These new galleries were intended for the display of antiquities—in particular the collection of "Etruscan" vases assembled by Edmé-Auguste Durand, which the museum had acquired in 1824—and of Renaissance metalwork. The sumptuous yet practical design of these galleries included specially designed cases (lit with reflecting mirrors) and ambitious ceiling decorations that followed a program illustrating the function of the galleries and the origin of the artifacts displayed within. Chosen by the director of the Administration of

the Fine Arts, Sosthène de la Rochefoucauld, and by the director of the museum,
Count de Forbin, the artists were the finest Academicians of the time: Ingres, Heim,
Meynier, Evariste Fragonard, Picot, Abel de Pujol, Horace Vernet, and Baron Gros.

On the ceiling of a gallery of Egyptian antiquities, Picot painted *Study and
the Genius of the Arts Revealing Ancient Egypt to Greece*. The ceiling was widely admired at
the opening, and preferred by most critics to Ingres's *Apotheosis of Homer*, which decorated a gallery nearby. Such was not the case, however, with Evariste Fragonard's
Francis I Receiving the Paintings and Sculptures Brought from Italy by Primaticcio, a large
troubadour composition (dominating a display of Renaissance enamels) that failed to
win the approval of either the public or connoisseurs. Deemed "too dark," it was transferred to another part of the Louvre a few years later, along with the Renaissance collection. When that gallery became part of an expanded suite of rooms devoted to
antiquities, it was once again appropriate to commission a ceiling illustrating Greco-
Roman history. Perhaps because of his initial success a few years earlier, Picot was
once again awarded the commission. He painted for the room *Cybele Protecting the
Cities of Stabia, Herculanum, Pompeii, and Resina from the Fires of Vesuvius*. The ceiling
was first shown to the public during the Salon of 1831. It was probably installed a
few months later, in 1832, when the ceiling by Evariste Fragonard was itself transferred (Aulanier 1947–68, vol. 8, p. 49).

This head, a study for one of the four personifications of cities in the above-
mentioned ceiling, shows Picot's strict adherence to the Classical and academic principle of the *tête d'expression*. Through simple and set pictorial means, the artist is able to
express fear and the supplicative attitude of his subject with discreet pathos and eloquent emotion.

J. P. M.

Emile-Jean-Horace VERNET

(Paris 1789–Paris 1863)

randson of the marine painter Claude-Joseph Vernet, Horace studied under his father, Carle, and his maternal grandfather, Moreau *le jeune*. At first, he helped his father with his battle paintings, but in 1810 made his own Salon debut with *The Taking of a Fortified Encampment near Glatz*, painted for Napoleon's brother, King Jerome of Westphalia. Vernet was then appointed draftsman to the Dépôt de la Guerre and distinguished himself in action in the defense of the Barrière de Clichy in 1814. Vernet was an ardent Bonapartist and painted a series of works glorifying the military achievements of the Empire, under the patronage of the Duke of Orléans, later Louis-Philippe. These paintings brought Vernet considerable notoriety and culminated in the rejection in 1822 of two of his works from the Salon, because their subjects were associated with the previous regime. As a result, Vernet mounted a one-man exhibition at his studio. Charles X countered the Duke of Orléans's patronage of Vernet by also commissioning works and by appointing him director of the French Academy in Rome in 1828, where he remained until 1834. Vernet returned via Algeria, the first of several trips there. He also visited the Middle East, which resulted in his *Salle de Constantine* in the Musée de Versailles and a series of Old Testament paintings with figures in Arab dress. Vernet was invited to Russia by the Tsar and made several trips there. Vernet's popularity enabled him to adjust to the changes of political regime, and his facility as an artist allowed him to embrace many different subjects, from battle scenes to the Romantic, biblical, historical, and genre.

98 Emile-Jean-Horace VERNET
Equestrian Portrait of the Duke of Orléans, c. 1840
Portrait équestre du Duc d'Orléans
Oil on canvas
10 × 7 ¼" (25.4 × 18.4 cm)

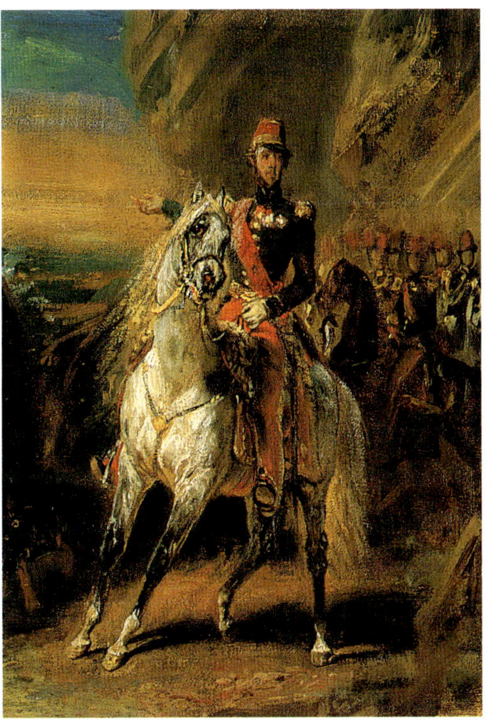

Vernet enjoyed the patronage of the Duke of Orléans, who later became Louis-Philippe, King of the French (1830–48). An intensely ambitious man who wished to bring about his own accession to the throne, the Duke, who commissioned many paintings from Vernet glorifying the military history of the Empire, was frequently portrayed in prominent roles. This was a political move on the Duke's part, designed to incite public discontent by creating Bonapartist and patriotic nostalgia.

The present sketch may have been the study for a large portrait of the Duke. Equally, it may be the study for part of a larger military composition, similar to the series of four paintings, commissioned by the Duke and bought by Lord Hertford from his estate sale in 1851, which are today in the National Gallery, London. These celebrate the heroism of the Duke of Orléans at the battles of Jamappes (1792), Hanau (1813), Montirail (1822), and Valmy (1826).

This study is similar to other sketches by Vernet, such as that for *The Taking of Abd-el-Kader* (Paris, Musée Nationale des Arts Africains et Océaniens) of 1843.

J. R. B.

Léon COGNIET

(Paris 1794–Paris 1880)

ogniet entered the studio of Guérin in 1812 and won the Prix-de-Rome in 1817. His Salon debut took place in 1822 with two paintings sent from Rome, which critics found too sentimental. He fared better in 1824 with his *Massacre of the Innocents*. Cogniet exhibited with some regularity at the Salons until 1855. His career is marked by a series of important commissions for Parisian churches, including Saint-Nicolas-des-Champs and the Church of the Madeleine. He was also a painter of history subjects and of portraits. A respected teacher, he was a drawing instructor at the Lycée Louis-le-Grand and at the Ecole des Beaux-Arts, where he proved to be both popular and successful. The portrait painter Léon Bonnat (q.v.) was one of his most famous pupils.

99   Léon COGNIET
Saint Stephen Carrying Alms to a Poor Family, c. 1827
Saint Etienne portant secours à une famille pauvre
Oil on canvas
13 ¼ × 10" (33.7 × 25.4 cm)

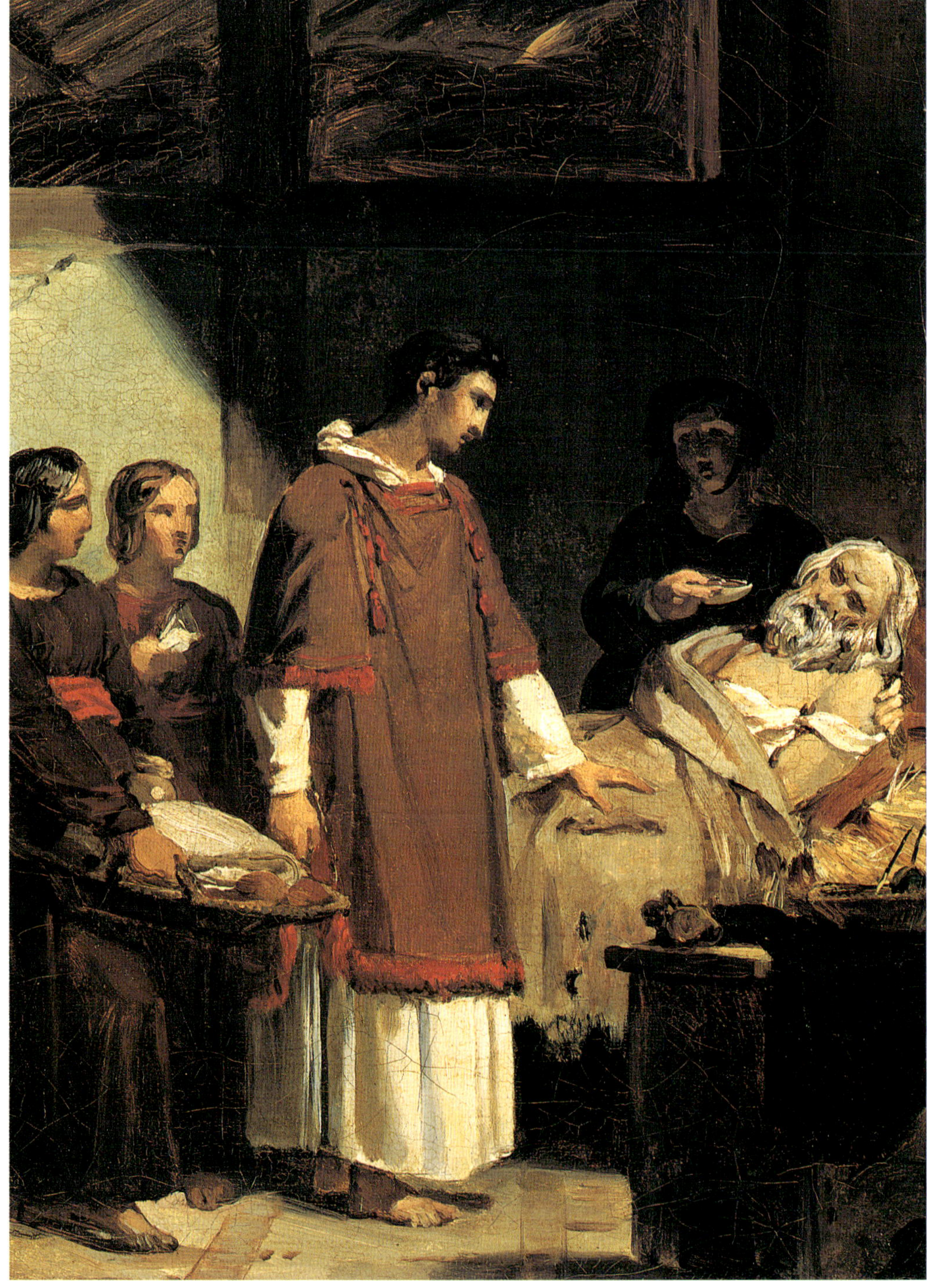

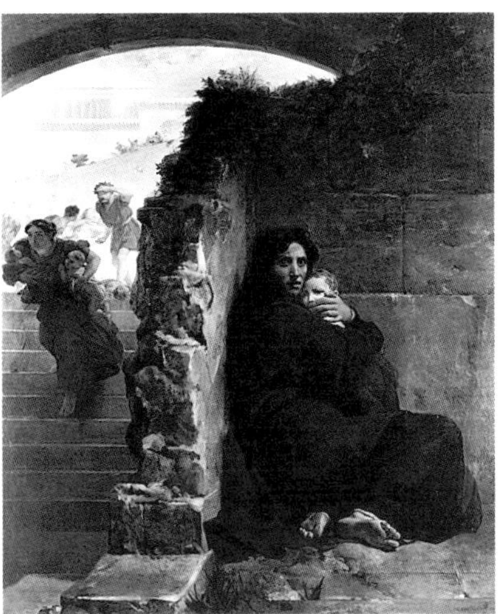 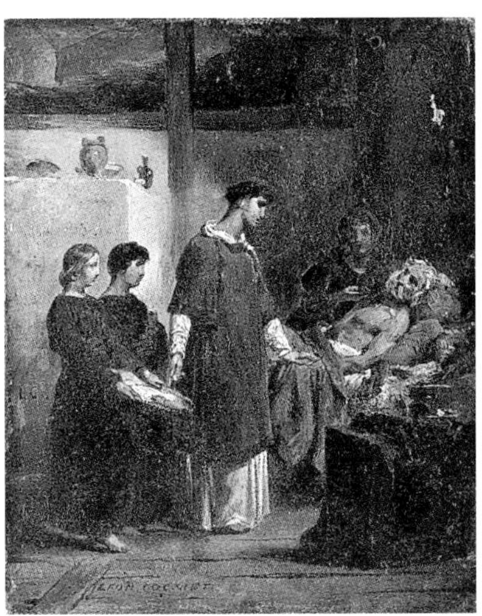

Fig. 14. Léon COGNIET. *Scene from the Massacre of the Innocents* (Le Massacre des innocents), 1824. Oil on canvas. Musée des Beaux-Arts de Rennes

Fig. 15. Léon COGNIET. *Saint Stephen Carrying Alms to a Poor Family* (Saint Etienne portant secours à une famille pauvre), c. 1827. Oil on canvas. Private collection, Los Angeles

Whereas the Salons of the late eighteenth century were dominated by paintings with moral and heroic subjects and those of the Empire with paintings extolling the Napoleonic image, under the Bourbon Restoration, religious painting made an unprecedented comeback (Foucart 1987, pp. 75–105). Landscapes and portraits may have won the approval of the larger public, and of most collectors, but religious painting was the expression of official taste and painters working in that genre were the recipients of important commissions. Younger artists competing for these commissions turned to traditional subjects and moral themes (reflecting the conservative direction of the new regime), but enlivened them with original treatments and individual vigor.

Cogniet's large painting (2.97 × 2.29 m) *Saint Stephen Carrying Alms to a Poor Family* was commissioned by the Comte de Chabrol, Préfet of the Seine Department, to decorate the Church of Saint-Nicolas-des-Champs in Paris (still *in situ*). The political acceptability of the subject—charity, the main social remedy the government envisioned for the neediest classes—and the clarity of Cogniet's style, a prudently revised Classicism, ensured the success of the composition at the 1827 Salon. In 1824, Cogniet had shown himself to be an original artist capable of renewing traditional Christian iconography with his *Scene from the Massacre of the Innocents* (fig. 14), a painting in which the artist traded the conventional description of the massacre for a powerful depiction of a mother fearfully holding her child. His *Saint Stephen* offers a less Romantic, more traditional approach, harking back to the Neoclassical depiction of such figures as the heroic sufferer consoled by the dignified hero.

Baudelaire commented sarcastically on Cogniet in his review of the 1845 Salon, "M. Léon Cogniet est un artiste d'un rang très élevé dans les régions moyennes du goût et de l'esprit" (M. Leon Cogniet is a high-ranking artist in the middle areas of taste and spirit) (Baudelaire 1962, p. 410). This judgment, modified somewhat by Baudelaire in later writings, did not prevent the artist from enjoying a long and successful career. In 1855, his *Saint Stephen* was removed from the church to be shown publicly once again at the Exposition Universelle. By then, however, religious painting no longer appealed to enlightened critics. In their review of that exhibition, the Goncourt brothers exclaimed, "La peinture religieuse n'est plus" (Religious painting is no more) (Goncourt 1893, p. 171).

The Musée des Beaux-Arts, Orléans, owns a preparatory study for the head of Saint Stephen (Orléans 1990, no. 90). A small unpublished sketch (17.5 × 14.4 cm), signed and monogrammed, is in an American private collection (fig. 15).

J. P. M..

Ary SCHEFFER

(Dordrecht, Holland 1795–Argenteuil 1858)

Born in Holland of a German father and a Dutch mother, Ary Scheffer—along with his two brothers, Henry (also a painter) and Arnold—was taken to Paris by his mother. In 1810, he was skilled enough to be in Prud'hon's studio and a year later in Guerin's at the Ecole des Beaux-Arts. Scheffer's career was spent entirely in Paris, where he became one of the leading figures of the Romantic movement. He first exhibited at the Salon in 1812. Throughout his career, he treated not only historical subjects but also genre scenes, portraits, and themes inspired by literature (Goethe, Scott, Shakespeare). Sentimental and Romantic, his work reflects, as much as it had shaped, the sensibility of his era.

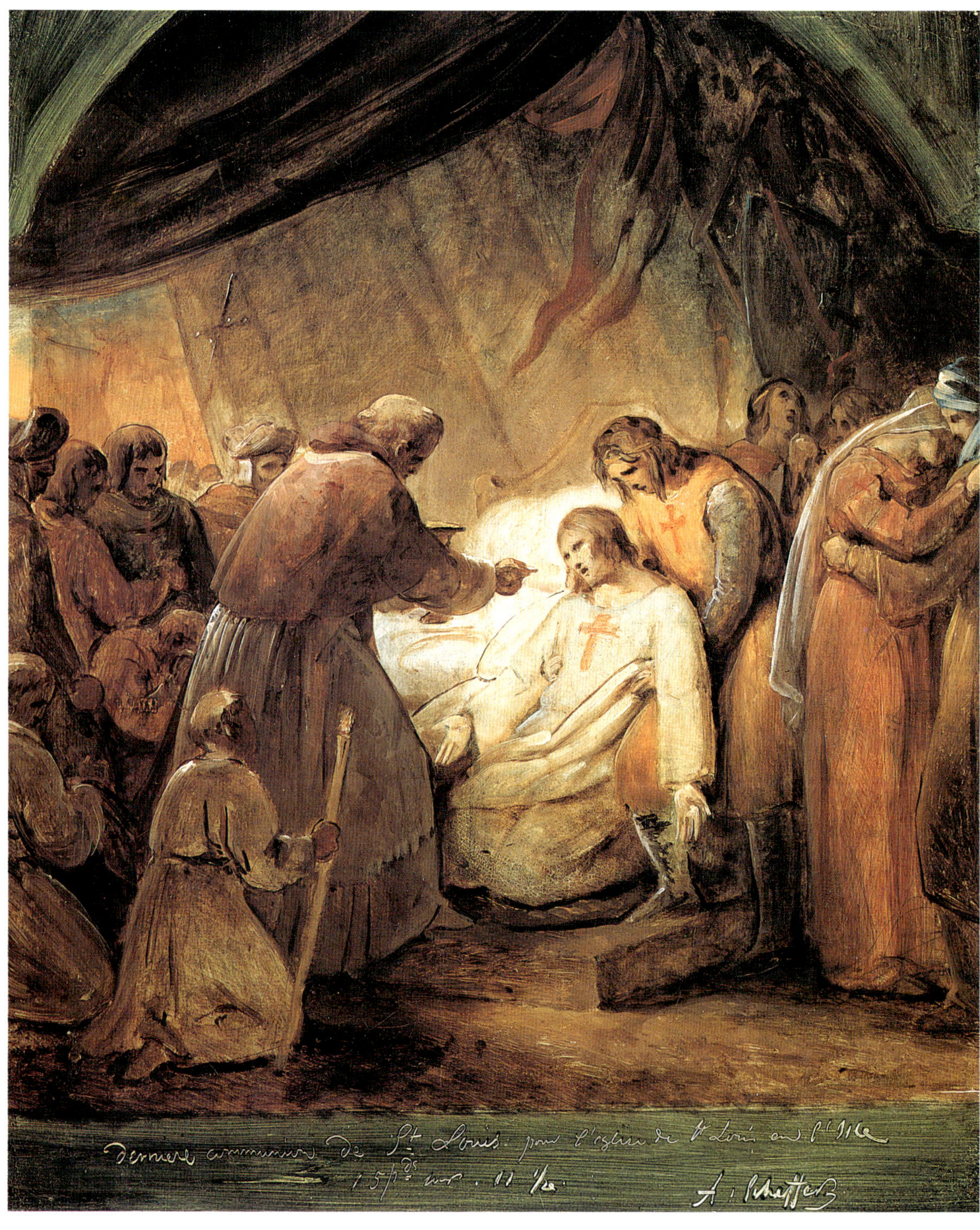

100 Ary SCHEFFER
The Last Communion of Saint Louis, 1823
La Dernière Communion de Saint Louis
Oil on canvas
18 ¼ × 15 ¼" (46.4 × 38.7 cm)
Signed and inscribed at the bottom:
derniere communion de Saint Louis pour
l'eglise de Saint Louis en l'Ile/15 pds sur 11
1/2/A. Scheffer

Provenance: Mme Aubry Vitet; Paris,
Hôtel Drouot, March 6, 1972 (Salles 10-
11), no. 36.

Exhibitions: Peoria 1980, no. 47; New
York 1980, no. 34.

Bibliography: Kolb 1937, pp. 279–80;
Ewals 1986, vol. 2, pp. 227–28.

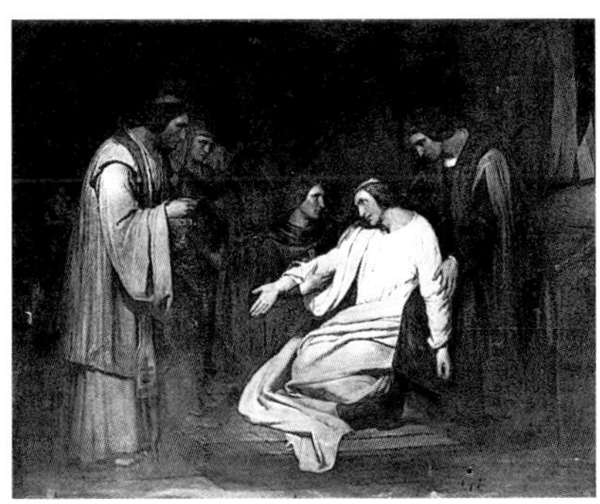

Fig. 16. Ary SCHEFFER. ***The Last
Communion of Saint Louis*** (La Dernière
Communion de Saint Louis), 1823. Oil
on canvas. Photo: Ministère de la
Culture et de la Communication,
Direction du Patrimoine, Archives
Photographiques.

Fully described in Marthe Kolb's monograph on the artist, this sketch for a large
painting in the Chapelle de la Communion in the Church of Saint-Louis-en-l'Ile (fig.
16) is inexplicably misdated 1815 by the author, who also declares that the large painting appeared at the Salon of that year. In fact, Scheffer could not have exhibited at
the 1815 Salon since one was not held that year (see Ewals 1980, p. 9.). The painting
was commissioned in 1823 (Boinet 1964, p. 38), and this sketch must precede the
painting's execution by only a few months. Thus the work does not, as argued by
Kolb, open the series of paintings devoted by Scheffer to the life of Saint Louis, but
rather concludes it, the artist having already shown at the 1817 Salon a *Death of Saint
Louis* (Paris, same church), and at the 1822 Salon *Saint Louis Visiting His Plague-
Stricken Soldiers* (Church of Saint-Jean-Saint-François).

Scheffer's interest in representing heroic scenes from the life of Saint Louis
may have been aroused by an opportunistic intention to glorify the Bourbons, just
reestablished on the French throne at the time of Scheffer's first *envoi* on the subject to
the Salon. It also clearly reflected the desire of a young generation of painters to re-
new history painting by borrowing new themes and motifs from French history, in
particular, from the Middle Ages. In that rejuvenation of French subject matter, Kolb
has underlined the important role played by Ingres, who encouraged his disciples to
study Bernard de Montfaucon's *Monuments de la monarchie française*, a monumental
five-volume work on the Middle Ages published between 1729 and 1733.

This Romantic interest in medieval subject matter explains the innovative appearance of Scheffer's composition. Indeed the sketch for *The Last Communion*, even
more than the finished composition, succeeds in combining the brilliance of paintings
associated with the somewhat facile genre of "costume pieces," with the dignity of
history painting, and the emotion required by religious art. In the final work, Scheffer pared down the elements of his composition, reducing the number of attendants
—and thus the display of exotic costumes—to concentrate on the figure of the saint,
whose image is fully Romantic, while harking back to the Baroque prototype of the
suffering Christ on Mount Olive.

J. P. M.

101 Ary SCHEFFER
Women from Souli, c. 1827
Femmes souliotes
Oil on canvas
13 ⅛ × 16 ⅛" (33.3 × 41.0 cm)

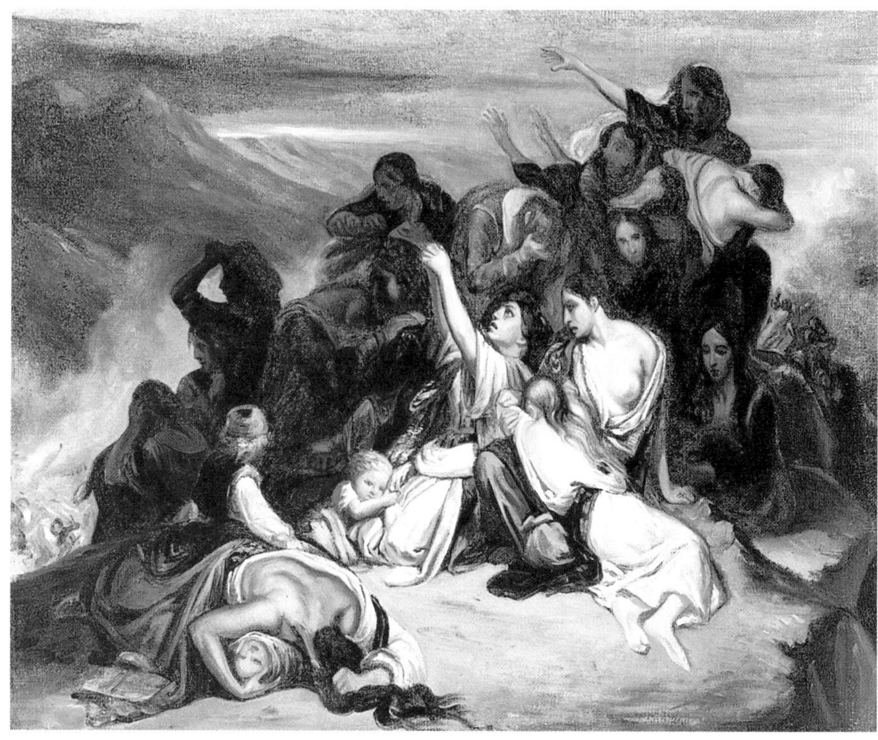

From the early 1820s until about 1832, Ary Scheffer executed several works dealing
with contemporary Greek subjects. The period marked the height of the Philhellenic
movement in Western Europe, and Scheffer, who sympathized with the Greeks' resistance to the Turks, subscribed fully to its ideals. Writers, politicians, and journalists
vehemently defended the cause of the Greek people, while artists illustrated their
plight, as well as the exotic beauty of their costumes. Géricault executed such compositions, but it may have been Delacroix, with whom both Ary and his brother Henry
were associated, who more directly aroused Scheffer's interest in subjects inspired by
the Balkan wars (Delacroix had shown his *Massacres at Scio* at the 1824 Salon). Scheffer's "Orientalist" production—which included *A Young Greek Defending his Father* (1825),
Episode in the Siege of Missolonghi (1826), or *Young Greek Women Imploring the Virgin Mary
During a Battle* (1827)—culminated in his great Romantic statement shown at the 1827
Salon, a representation of *Women from Souli* (Paris, Musée du Louvre). The story of
the heroic women of Souli—a small village in Albania that had been the stronghold of
the resistance against the Turks in 1803—who hurled their children to deaths, then
rejoined them in the abyss rather than be taken prisoner by the Turks, had captivated the imagination of all those sympathetic to the Greek cause. The French Romantic
poet Alphonse de Lamartine told the story in an addendum to his *Dernier Chant du
pélerinage d'Harold*, and C. Fauriel had also related the episode in his *Chants populaires
de la Grèce moderne* (Paris 1824).

Scheffer's *Women from Souli* is indebted both to the Classical tradition and to the
more recent example of Géricault's *The Raft of the Medusa*. Yet in order to represent
this modern Massacre of the Innocents, Scheffer turned also to Reni's celebrated version of the biblical subject (Bologna, Pinacoteca). Scheffer in fact copied faces from
that painting in a contemporary sepia drawing (United States, private collection) that
is stylistically close to our sketch.

Scheffer executed countless studies for his large painting, often varying the position or relationships of the groups with one another (Paris 1980, nos. 47–54). This
sketch, unknown to Ewals, differs from the other versions he lists (1986, vol. 2). It is
more finished than the Dordrecht museum sketch, which is usually considered the
prime study for the Louvre painting. The slight differences between this sketch and
from the Salon painting indicate that this sketch is not a copy after the finished work.
(Such a copy, in the Dordrecht museum, was made by Scheffer's mother and,
because it was so popular, probably by many other artists at the time.)

J. P. M.

138

Raymond-Auguste Quinsas MONVOISIN

(Bordeaux 1796–Paris 1870)

*M*onvoisin was first apprenticed in Bordeaux to the local painters Pierre Lacour and Pierre Lacour *fils*. He later studied with Guérin in Paris and first exhibited at the Salon in 1819. He won the second-place Prix-de-Rome in 1820, and was sent to Rome, where he spent three years. Monvoisin treated historical, mythological, and religious subjects, and painted portraits. In addition, he participated in the decoration of the Church of Notre-Dame-de-Lorette (1833). Differences with the administration of the Fine Arts Department prompted his departure for South America. He settled in Peru, where he founded a local academy, and then in Chile, where he was credited with bringing the latest style from Paris. Monvoisin subsisted there mostly on portrait commissions. He returned to Paris in 1853, and again exhibited at the Salons. In the later years of his life, he received some commissions for religious works (Church of Saint-Leu, Paris).

102 Raymond-Auguste Quinsas MONVOISIN
The Holy Family, 1846
La Sainte Famille
Oil on panel
10 × 6 ½" (25.4 × 16.5 cm)
Inscribed on back of panel: *r.Q./Monvoisin Chile — 1846 — A su amigo Frederico Janes*

Exhibitions: Peoria 1980, no. 38; New York 1980, no. 30.

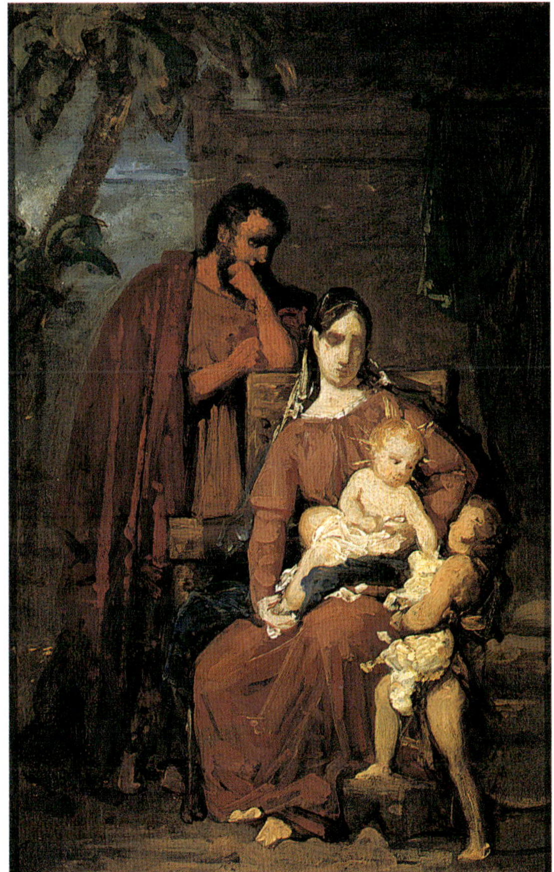

Dedicated to an unidentified Frederico (*sic*) Janes three years after the artist's arrival in Chile, and presumably executed that year, this sketch does not relate to any painting known to have been produced during Monvoisin's lengthy stay in South America (Monvoisin n.d., pp. 77–87). The artist had achieved a respectable career in Santiago as a portrait painter. Given his previous achievements in France as a history painter, it may be surmised that a small study such as this was executed to bring in larger commissions, or at least to give friends and admirers a broader notion of his talent. More suited by training to compositions with figures than to portraits, Monvoisin remained a traditional painter attached to established formulas. The appearance of this Holy Family, harking back to Raphael, exemplifies a common dilemma among nineteenth-century painters of religious subjects: while the iconic composition seems the only one appropriate to the dignity of the subject, the artist attempts to enliven it through spirited brushwork that owes much to the innovations of the more advanced artists of the time.

J.P.M.

Eugène-Louis LAMI

(Paris 1800–Paris 1890)

*S*on of a civil servant, Lami's first drawings were of military and equestrian subjects. In 1813, he entered the studio of Horace Vernet (q.v.) and from 1817 attended the Ecole des Beaux-Arts, where he studied with Gros. During the three years he spent with Gros, he met Paul Delaroche and the English water-colorist Richard Parkes Bonington, who greatly influenced his technique in this medium. Lami obtained his first commission through Vernet (q.v.), for a series of watercolors engraved by Michel-Olivier Le Bas and published by Gide. In 1822, in collaboration with Horace Vernet, he produced twenty-four lithographs for the series *The Uniforms of the French Army from 1791 to 1814*. Around this time, together with Géricault, he also illustrated the poetry of Byron. Lami made his Salon debut in 1824 with *Study of Horses* and *Combat at Puerto de Miravete* and continued to exhibit until 1878. In 1826 and again in 1829, he visited London, where he produced two albums and some sepia drawings. In 1829 Lami also produced a very successful series of colored lithographs of the famous costume balls given by the Duchess of Berry. By 1830, he was giving drawing lessons to the Duke of Orléans and this relationship proved most beneficial to him. He executed a large number of battle scenes for Louis-Philippe and was awarded the Legion of Honor in 1837. Lami then turned his attention to fashionable society, attending salons, balls, and the theater, and constantly sketching scenes; many of the drawings were assembled in an album titled *Histoire de mon temps*, which entered the collection of the Prince Demidoff, who was one of his patrons. In 1848, Lami followed Louis-Philippe to London, but after the latter's death returned to Paris and worked for the Imperial court. In 1862, he was made an Officer of the Legion of Honor.

103 Eugène-Louis LAMI
The Swearing-in of Louis-Philippe, King of the French, 1830
La Proclamation de Louis-Philippe, roi des Français
Oil on canvas
6 ¼ × 8 ¼" (15.9 × 21.0 cm)
Signed lower right: E. L. 30
Inscribed on the reverse: *"Esquisse pour la proclamation de Louis-Philippe, roi des Français."*

Exhibitions: Peoria 1980, no. 32.

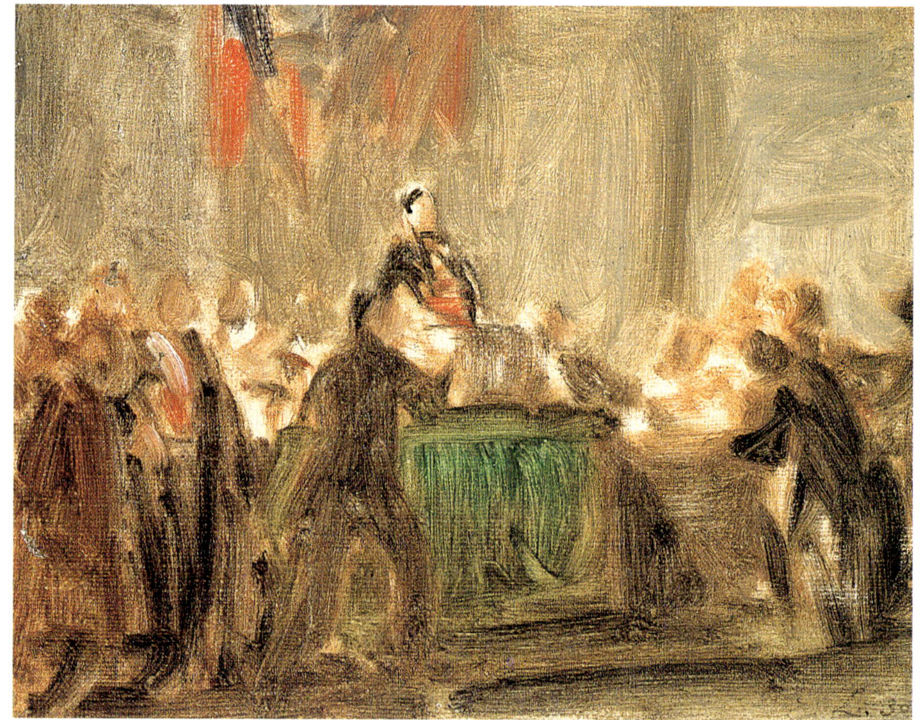

As the inscription records, this work is a sketch for *The Swearing-in of Louis-Philippe*, an event which took place on August 9, 1830. The subject was a particularly important episode in the history of the French monarchy, because for the first time sovereignty was not determined by the "divine right of kings," as exercised by the Bourbons, but rather by a signed legal agreement with France's elected deputies, which involved the official swearing in of the new monarch.

François Guizot, Louis-Philippe's first minister of the interior, decided that the Swearing-in of Louis-Philippe should be one of the five subjects for paintings to be hung in the Chamber of Deputies. This subject, which was a particularly powerful piece of propaganda, was to occupy the place of honor above and behind the speaker's rostrum in the Salle des Séances. The artist was to be decided by competition, which attracted twenty-seven entrants in total. No final painting of the competition by Lami is known, which points towards this sketch being the first idea for a larger painting that was never executed.

Louis-Philippe was an accessible monarch and, in fact, at this time Lami was giving him lessons in drawing and watercolor. Lami, who had trained under Baron Antoine Gros and Horace Vernet, was the son of a civil servant, and from an early age had been encouraged to enjoy the pomp and ceremony of the court. There is another work from this period—*Louis-Philippe on Horseback* (Paris, private collection)—plausibly by Lami, which although a "non-official" painting, represents a precise historical record of an important political event. It depicts Louis-Philippe when still the Duke of Orléans riding from the Palais-Royal to meet Lafayette at the Hôtel de Ville (Marriman 1988, p. 6, fig. 6).

In 1832, Lami was made official painter to Louis-Philippe. He executed thirteen battle scenes for the King at Versailles and turned his attention to painting elegant contemporary scenes of society. After Louis-Philippe's death, Lami continued to work for the new regime. One of the founders of the Société des Aquarellistes Français in 1874, Lami was a particularly gifted amateur watercolorist. This is conveyed in the present work, which, although in oil, is painted thinly and has the luminous appeal of a watercolor.

J.R.B.

Alexandre-Gabriel DECAMPS

(Paris 1803–Fontainebleau 1860)

*D*ecamps spent his youth in the country, in Picardy. When he came to Paris, he first entered the studio of the architectural painter Etienne Bouhot and then became the pupil of Abel de Pujol (q.v.) but left the latter's atelier to work on his own. He exhibited small-scale landscapes and around this time came to the attention of the Baron d'Ivy, who became his patron. In 1827, he made his Salon debut with *Hunting Plovers* and *Soldier of the Guard of the Vizier* (London, Wallace Collection). Decamps had a passion for travel; he had already visited central France and Switzerland, and, at the end of 1827, he left for Asia Minor on a long trip that had a major influence on his style. Back in France, Decamps turned his attention to lithography and published a group of hunting scenes, which appeared in *Croquis par divers artistes* (1829). From 1830 to 1831, he also contributed satirical drawings to *Figaro* and *Caricature*. Decamps achieved his first Salon success in 1831 with *The Turkish Patrol*, for which he received a second-place medal. He then visited Italy and on his return painted the large work *The Defeat of the Cimbri by Marius* (Paris, Musée du Louvre), which was very successful and brought him the first-place medal at the 1834 Salon. He did not exhibit for the next five years, but began to paint a series of works from the Old Testament, which included *Joseph Sold by His Brothers* (1835; London, Wallace Collection) and *Moses* (1837; London, Wallace Collection). Decamps received patronage from the House of Orléans and experienced difficulties after the 1848 Revolution, following which he did not exhibit at the Salon until 1851, when he was made an Officer of the Legion of Honor. He sent sixty works to the Exposition Universelle of 1855 and was awarded three medals. Toward the end of his life, Decamps's health began to fail and he moved to Fontainebleau, where he died.

104 Alexandre-Gabriel DECAMPS
Two Dogs Following the Scent of the Quarry, n.d.
Deux chiens traquant une proie
Oil on canvas
6 ⅜ × 8 ¾" (16.2 × 22.2 cm)

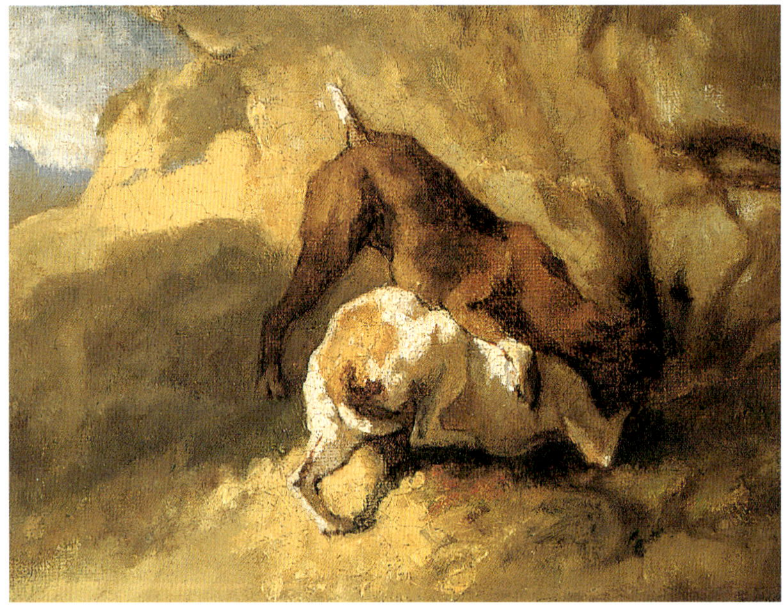

This sketch of two dogs jostling each other to sniff out the quarry may have been a study by Decamps for a small finished canvas of the subject, but it seems far more likely to have been the study for an element in a much larger composition of a hunting subject.

Decamps's art was very much related to the circumstances of his life. His early years, spent in the countryside of Picardy, had left him with a keen interest in country scenes, as witness such works as *Searching for Truffles* (Amsterdam, Rijksmuseum). Hunting was a country pursuit that he particularly enjoyed, and his first Salon exhibit depicted a plover hunt. He painted a series of at least four hunting scenes at the end of 1828 and beginning of 1829, probably inspired by the time he had passed at Arsy. Although the painting for which this is an associated study has not been identified, it is probably datable to this period.

Decamps also painted groups of dogs and kennel scenes and larger, more elaborate compositions such as *The Dog's Valet* of 1842 (Paris, Musée du Louvre). He excelled at these hunting and animal compositions, since he was an innately keen observer of nature. It was these works that first brought Decamps financial success.

J.R.B.

Louis-Gabriel-Eugène ISABEY

(Paris 1803–Montévain 1886)

ugène Isabey was the son and student of miniaturist Jean-Baptiste Isabey. A member of the Romantic movement of 1830 along with his friend the landscape painter Paul Huet (1803–1869), Isabey was acknowledged by Baudelaire, in his *Salon of 1845*, as one of the most important artists among the new painters. Isabey won a first-place medal in 1824 and then traveled to England in 1825, where like Delacroix, he was influenced by Bonington and the English watercolorists. After the July Revolution, he was named official painter of the French Expedition to Africa and traveled to Algiers in 1830 as an illustrator attached to the expedition. At the Salon of 1839, he won a second first-class medal for *The Battle of the Texel, 1694*. He first traveled to Normandy with Jongkind in 1850. After 1851, he spent all of his summers at Varengeville, Normandy, where he found the themes that interested him most—fishing and portside scenes, tempests, and shipwrecks. Isabey continued to exhibit at the Salon until 1878 and participated in both the 1855 and 1878 Exposition Universelle in Paris. A colorist interested in the effects of light and air on color, he devoted much of his time at the end of his life to watercolor. He is often described as a "pre-Impressionist."

D.G.

105 Louis-Gabriel-Eugène ISABEY
A Royal Marriage, n.d.
Un Mariage royal
Oil on canvas
31 ¼ × 23 ¾" (79.4 × 60.3 cm)
Monogrammed *EI*
Stamped: *Vente Isabey*

Provenance: Isabey sale, Galerie Georges Petit, Paris, March 30/31, 1887, no. 138, bought Florenville; March 19, 1975, H. D. Delorme, Paris; Heim Gallery, London 1978.

Exhibition: London 1978, cat. no. 20.

Bibliography: Miquel 1980, vol. 2, p. 217, no. 1232 (as *Mariage princier ou le sacre*) not reprod., and p. 218, no. 1237 (as *Le Sacre*) reprod.

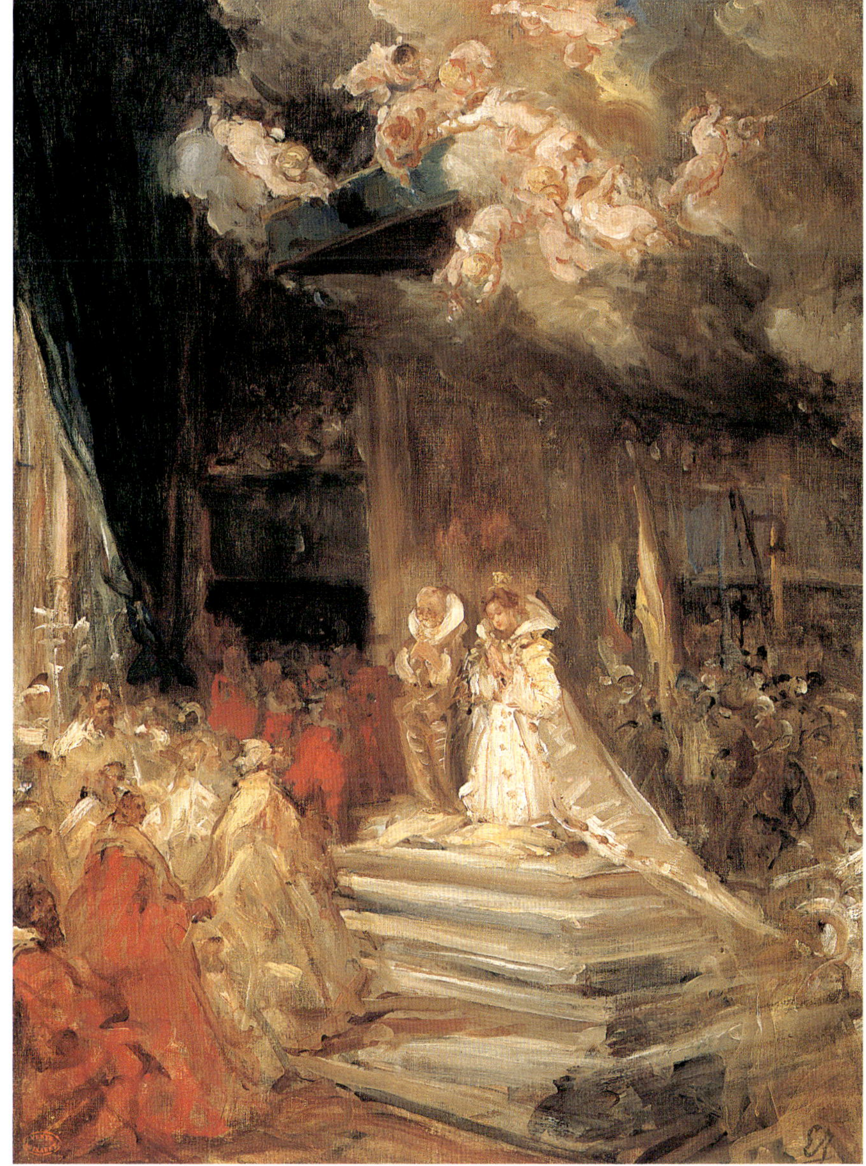

This painting was featured in the Isabey sale held, a year after the artist's death, in 1887 with the title *Un Mariage royal* and a century later passed through the hands of the Parisian auctioneers H. D. Delorme. Since then, it has become the subject of considerable confusion.

Pierre Miquel lists this painting twice in his catalogue of Isabey's work, believing it to be two separate works. First it is listed without illustration as *Mariage princier ou le sacre*, and recorded as being sold in the Isabey sale of 1887 and in the Delorme sale of 1975. Then, under no. 1232, Miquel illustrates the present sketch, this time omitting the Isabey sale provenance, but repeating that it passed through the Delorme sale. Since we know that the present work was included in the Isabey sale, there can be no doubt that this is one and the same work.

Prior to Miquel's publication, when the painting was exhibited in 1978, catalogued as *The Marriage of Henri IV*, it was identified as Isabey's Salon exhibit of 1850 no. 1584. This Salon painting, *Episode du mariage de Henri IV*, (whereabouts unknown; reprod. in Miquel 1980, p. 221, no. 1261), in fact shows a gallery of guests eagerly jostling with each other to gain a better view of the wedding ceremony of Henri IV and Marie de Medici in the far distance. Contemporary descriptions referring to this composition leave little doubt that it is the work illustrated by Miquel (no. 1261) and not the present composition. Geoffroy, for example, declared that "before his *Marriage of Henri IV*, one feels an excitement as great as that created by the tumultuous buzz of an opera ball" (*Revue des deux-mondes*, 1851). The present sketch does not depict such a bustling scene, but rather the tranquillity of the spiritual moment, when the couple take their marriage vows.

The composition reflects Isabey's characteristic skill for creating a *mise en scène* of theatrical quality. He seems to have favored church scenes in the late 1840s. For example, one can compare this sketch with *A Ceremony in the Church of Delft* (Paris, Musée d'Orsay, R.F. 1430), which was exhibited at the Salon of 1847. Isabey was fascinated with the past, and recreated historical dress and detail in scenes full of Romantic atmosphere, as for example, *A Marriage Under Louis XIII* (Miquel 1980, p. 174, fig. 94).

Isabey enjoyed considerable royal favor, and this scene could represent a number of royal weddings or even an imaginary episode. Although the impressionistic quality of the sketch does not allow clear identification of the main protagonists, it is entirely possible that the subject is Henri IV's second marriage to Marie de Medici. Certainly there are elements, particularly in the allegorical inclusion of *putti* and the warmth of the coloring, which suggest the influence of the series of paintings by Rubens in the Louvre depicting the life of Marie de Medici.

J.R.B.

Narcisse-Virgilio DIAZ DE LA PENA

(Bordeaux 1807–Meuton 1876)

Narcisse-Virgilio Diaz de la Peña, born to Thomas Diaz de la Peña and Maria Emanuele Valasco, was raised by a Protestant pastor in Meudon when both parents died before he reached the age of twelve. As an adolescent, he worked in a printer's shop and then, having made the acquaintance of Jules Dupré, was employed as a decorator of porcelain at the Dupré porcelain factory. At this time, probably with the encouragement of Jules Dupré, Diaz began to paint, taking lessons from Gouchon and copying at the Louvre, especially the works of Correggio. Beginning in 1831, he exhibited regularly at the Salon. By 1836, Diaz was in Barbizon, taking advice from the landscape painter Théodore Rousseau, whose work he staunchly supported all his life. At the Salon of 1837, Diaz exhibited the first of his many views of the forest of Fontainebleau; in 1851 he was awarded the Legion of Honor. Diaz was celebrated during his life for his Oriental scenes and Romantic subjects, but is now remembered primarily for his paintings of Fontainebleau. Rousseau, Dupré, Constant Troyon, and Diaz formed the nucleus of the Barbizon School.

D.G.

106 Narcisse-Virgilio DIAZ DE LA PENA
Orientals, n.d.
Orientaux
Oil on panel
18 ¾ × 11" (47.6 × 27.9 cm)
Old collection seal on the back

Exhibitions: Peoria 1980, no. 19.

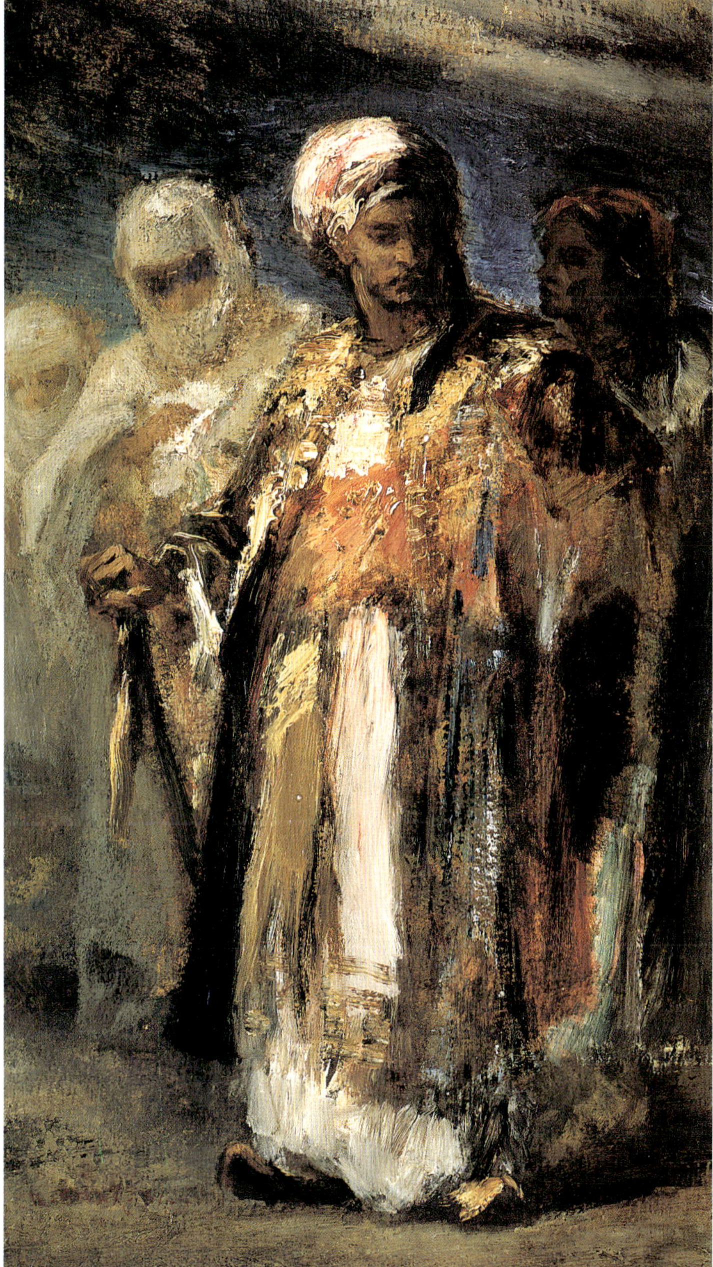

Diaz began his career first as a decorator of porcelain and then as a *peintre de fantasie*. He painted a variety of works in the latter vein, including landscapes, *scènes galantes*, and imaginary Oriental scenes. Diaz first exhibited at the Salon of 1831 as a figure painter, inspired by Correggio and Prud'hon.

This sketch shows Diaz as a figure painter executing imaginary Oriental scenes. Although he never visited the Middle East, it obviously intrigued the artist and provided him with a wealth of subject matter for his work. Like the present sketch, his paintings tended to be small in format and rich in color. His work was well received and found a ready market during his lifetime.

In 1836, Diaz met Théodore Rousseau and following this encounter, the direction of his work changed: he took on the Barbizon aesthetics and painted numerous landscapes. The present sketch, however, is typical of Diaz's imaginary Oriental scenes. It is very colorful and almost impressionistic in style, and in this connection it is interesting to note that his work was admired by the Impressionists. In his Salon critique of 1845, Baudelaire described Diaz's use of color as "kaleidoscopic," and in the present sketch this has enabled the painter to achieve a particularly strong image. The sketch combines a dramatic use of light and shade with a bold impasto technique, which creates an appealing surface texture together with a sense of drama and mystery. Diaz exhibited works entitled *Orientales* at the three Salons over the years from 1845 to 1847; it is likely that this sketch was related to one of these compositions and therefore probably dates from that period.

J.R.B.

E ugène Devéria studied with his brother Achille (1800-1857) and also with Girodet and Lethière (q.v.). His first success was at the Salon of 1827, where his *Birth of Henri IV* (Paris, Musée du Louvre) was hailed as the manifesto of Romanticism, the new painting. By then, Devéria had rejected his Neoclassical training in favor of influences inherited from Rubens and the Venetians. A prolific artist, Devéria painted historical subjects as well as genre scenes and portraits. He was also a highly regarded painter of religious subjects, but abandoned this field after his conversion to Protestantism. A highly cultivated man whose Parisian salon was a meeting place for artists, writers, and musicians, Devéria filled his work with references to literature and poetry.

107 Eugène-François-Marie-Joseph
DEVERIA
***Glorification of the Life of Saint
Genevieve***, 1835
Glorification de la vie de Sainte
Geneviève
Oil on canvas
29 × 17" (73.7 × 43.2 cm)

Exhibitions: Peoria 1980, no. 18; New
York 1980, no. 70.

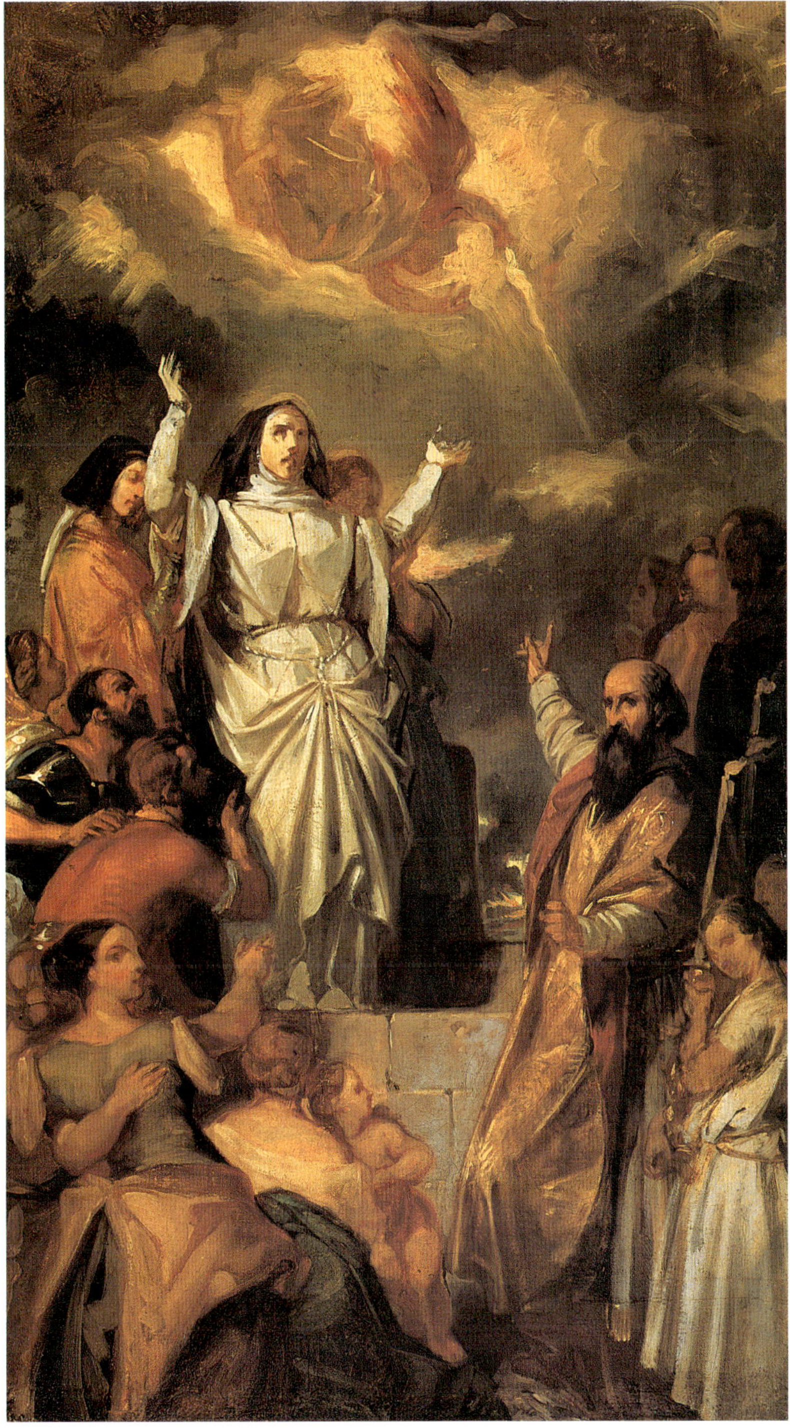

Begun in 1823 by the architect Hippolyte Lebas (1782–1867) in the then newly developed Parisian neighborhood of the Nouvelle-Athènes, the Church of Notre-Dame-de-Lorette was completed in 1832. The decoration of the church—reflecting perhaps the liberalism of the new regime—demonstrated the eclecticism of contemporary French painting. Works by Victor Orsel and Alphonse Perrin, artists who worked within the Classical idiom but revised its traditional boundaries to a pared down and extreme form of Neo-Raphaelism, appear along with the creations of a host of artists (twenty-three in all contributed paintings or frescoes to the new church) who exemplified an accessible *juste milieu* style (see cat. no. 91). At least one Romantic artist, Eugène Devéria, was invited to contribute two paintings.

The two large paintings Devéria executed—*A Miracle of Saint Genevieve Restituting Her Mother's Vision* and *The Glorification of Saint Genevieve*—were installed in the second chapel on the left, on each side of a window, looming somewhat incongruously over a small altarpiece by Madame H. Deherain (see a watercolor by H. Lebas showing the placement of the paintings, in Columbia/Rochester/Santa Barbara 1989–90, p. 64, figs. 2–13). The choice of Devéria for these compositions is enigmatic. Although the artist had previously executed large religious pictures, they were mostly outside Paris (notably at the Church of Saint-Léonard at Fougères, in Britanny [1833; see Gauthier 1925, pp. 108–09]); his reputation was more firmly established as a painter of historical subjects. Furthermore, the artist had failed to attract the attention of the public. In 1834, he did not exhibit at the Salon, preferring to show his paintings for the Church of Saint Leonard at Fougères in his own atelier, an event barely noted by the Parisian press. Devéria did not submit works to the Salon of 1835, where, Delacroix's *Christ on the Cross* and Corot's *Agar in the Wilderness*, to name only two examples, typified new directions in religious painting. In 1836, the year Devéria executed his compositions for Notre-Dame-de-Lorette, his submissions to the Salon were rejected, and in 1837 he again refused to exhibit there. It is thus puzzling to note that this important commission took place at a low point in Devéria's career. The paintings were reportedly admired by Delacroix (Gauthier 1925, p. 116) and may have been one of the reasons for Devéria's next—and last—large religious commission, the decoration of the Chapel of the Virgin at Notre-Dame-des-Doms, in Avignon.

Devéria executed at least one other oil sketch for the same composition. More finished, and showing slight differences from this one, it is nearly the same size (Paris, Musée du Petit-Palais, inv. 2151).

J.P.M.

Jean-Hippolyte FLANDRIN

(Lyon 1809–Rome 1864)

Flandrin began his studies in Paris in 1822 in the studios of the minor painter Magnin and sculptor Héral, but soon returned to Lyon. In 1829, back in Paris, he entered Ingres's studio. Ingres had a lasting influence on Flandrin, who may be considered his best disciple. Winner of the Prix-de-Rome in 1832, he remained six years in Rome. A devout Catholic, Flandrin considered his art to be part of his service to God. He contributed to the decoration of some of the most important Parisian churches. Influenced by the spirit of the Italian Quattrocento, Flandrin's art is not a servile imitation of these models, but instead a radical—and successful—attempt to rejuvenate the language of religious painting in the nineteenth century.

108 Jean-Hippolyte FLANDRIN
The Sacrifice of Isaac, 1860
La Sacrifice d'Isaac
Oil on board
18 ½ × 23 ½" (47.0 × 59.7 cm)
Signed lower left: *Flandrin 1860*

Provenance: The artist; his sale, Paris, Hotel Drouot, May 15–17, 1865, no. 11 (1,600 F.); Paravey collection; Paravey sale, Paris, Hôtel Drouot, April 13, 1878, no. 25, sold to Raynaud; sale, Paris, Hôtel Drouot, December 4, 1973, no. 116.

Exhibitions: Peoria 1980, no. 31; New York 1980, no. 81; Paris/Lyon 1984–85, no. 68.

Bibliography: Lanvin 1967, vol. 2, p. 269; Horaist 1979, nos. 65, 66.

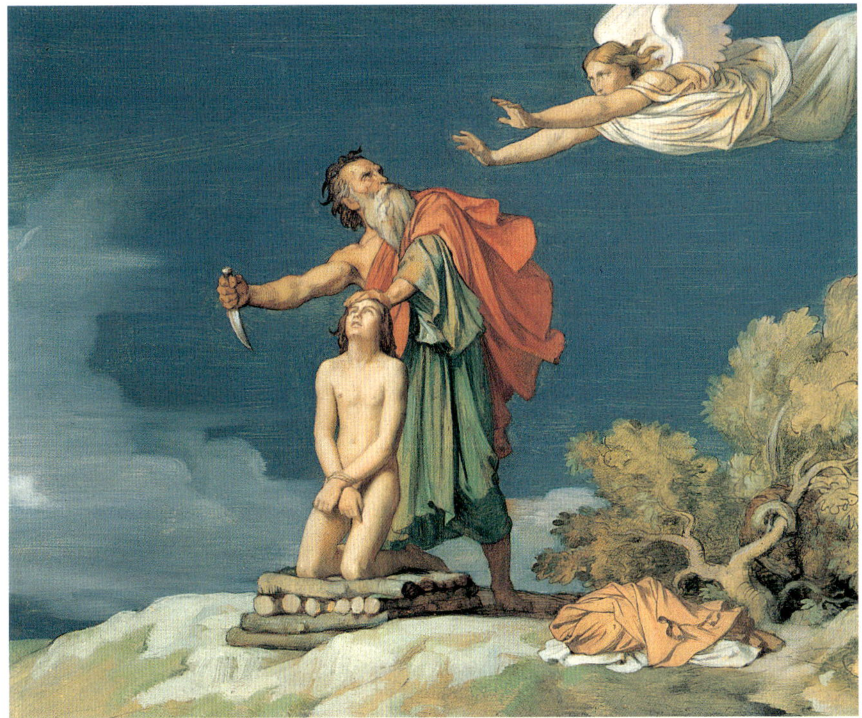

In 1856, shortly after completing the decoration of the Church of Saint-Vincent-de-Paul in Paris (1849–53), Hippolyte Flandrin was invited to work on the decoration of the nave of Saint-Gemain-des-Près. The artist, whose career since 1839 had included the decoration of several sanctuaries (Saint-Severin, 1839-41; Saint-Paul in Nîmes, 1848–49; Saint-Martin d'Ainay in Lyon, 1855), had already provided the paintings of its choir (1842–46) and those of the Chapel of the Apostles (1847) for the former Parisian abbey. The decoration of its nave was to be Flandrin's last major work. In fact, it remained unfinished until completed by his brother Paul and some of Hippolyte's pupils (Flandrin 1902, pp. 226–242).

The architecture of the church gave Flandrin neither an extensive surface to create a long procession of saints, as he had at Saint-Vincent-de-Paul, nor large walls on which to execute single scenes. Flandrin circumvented the problem by dividing in two each section contained between the columns. On the upper tier, on each side of the windows, he painted single figures from the Old Testament. Underneath, rather than painting large scenes, which in each section would have awkwardly had to accommodate an arch, he again divided the space in two, thus limiting the architectural intrusion to a small arc in each composition. This also allowed him to implement an iconographic program that juxtaposed scenes from the Old and New Testaments. A fervent Catholic, Flandrin was no doubt aware of the Church's tradition of reading the Old Testament in the light of the New, and seeing in biblical stories the prefiguration of events in the life of Christ. Such a program, in which Flandrin may have been helped by an ecclesiastic, the R. P. Cahier (1807–1882), was not innovative. The seventeenth-century church of the Jesuits in Antwerp decorated by Rubens was one famous precedent the decorative scheme of which, although lost, was well known through engravings.

Both *The Sacrifice of Isaac* and its pendant, the *Crucifixion*, are treated in simplified terms. The *Crucifixion* features only the four essential protagonists—Christ, Mary, Saint John, and Mary Magdalene—while the figures of Isaac, Abraham, and the Angel, set against the even background of the sky, are rendered in a stylized manner. Flandrin's typical rejection of anecdotal details is almost complete in this composition, whose strength relies solely upon the power of graphic elements.

It was Flandrin's general practice to prepare his large decorations with many drawings and painted sketches. Other sketches for the series are kept at the Musée du Petit-Palais, Paris, and the museums in Quimper, Poitiers, Lille, and Lyon, among others. Our sketch is one of the few that does not include the depiction of the architectural arch, an element Flandrin had to take into consideration in his final composition. At least twelve drawings have been identified for this *Sacrifice* (Paris/Lyon 1984–85, p. 146).

J.P.M.

Thomas COUTURE

(Senlis 1815–Villiers-le-Bel 1879)

homas Couture moved to Paris with his family when he was eleven and began to study drawing at the Ecole des Arts et Métiers in about 1829. In 1830, he entered the atelier of Gros and in 1831 became a student at the Ecole des Beaux-Arts. After the death of Gros, Couture worked in the atelier of Paul Delaroche. As a student, Couture competed six times for the Prix-de-Rome between 1834 and 1839, winning the second Grand Prix in 1837, even though he had been awarded the first prize in a preliminary judgment. After competing for two more years, Couture left the Ecole. Couture harbored a bitterness against the Académie for the rest of his life, and after winning universal acclaim at the Salon of 1847 for *Romans of Decadence*, he opened his own school of art on the rue de Laval in Montmartre. Couture was especially important for American painting students, and in 1867 when he published his theories of teaching in a book entitled *Méthode et entretiens d'atelier*, he dedicated it to America in recognition of his American friends, students, and patrons. After 1863, when he closed his atelier to students, he continued to teach privately until his death. With the exception perhaps of Edouard Manet, Couture's most famous pupil, his students—the Americans among them included Eastman Johnson, William Morris Hunt, and John LaFarge—greatly admired his talent and his personality.

D.G.

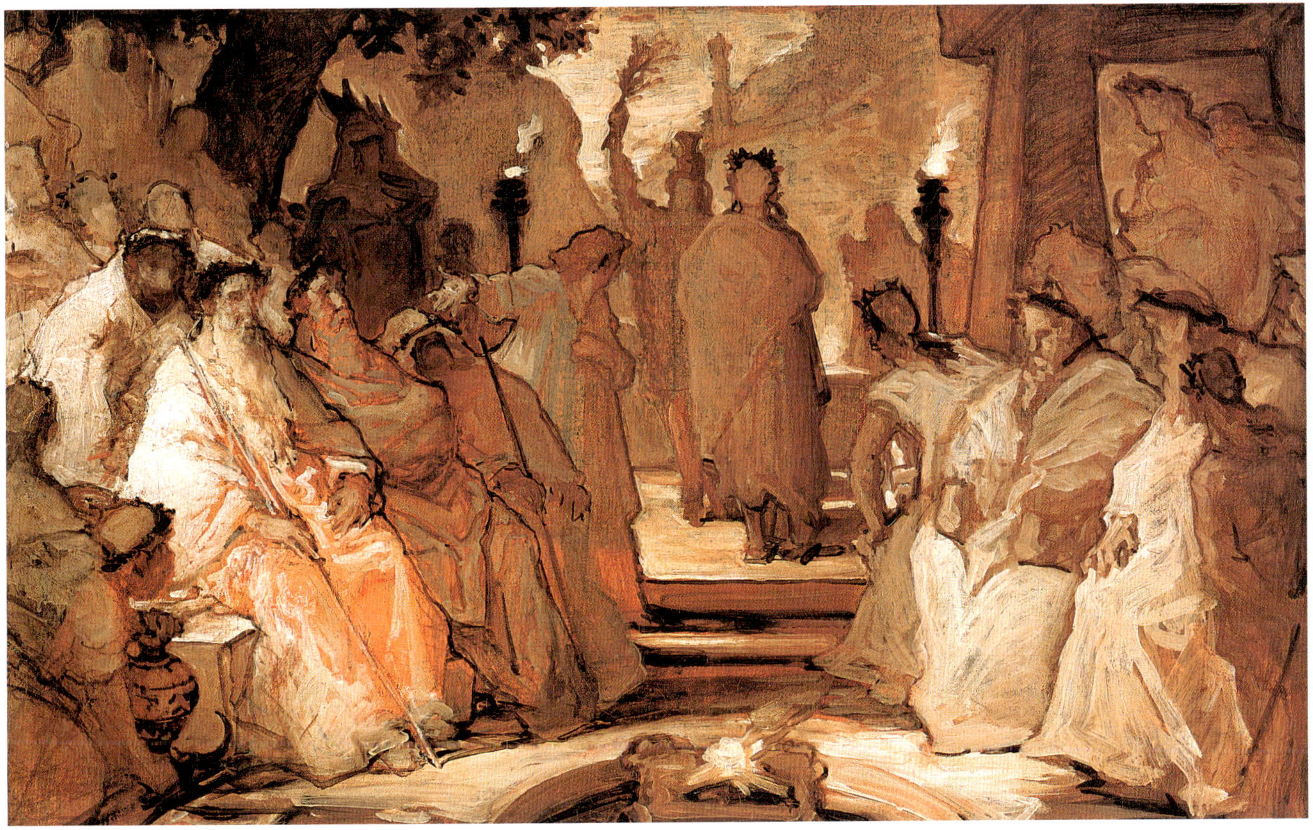

109 Attributed to Thomas COUTURE
A Greek or Roman Entering an Assembly,
n.d.
Un Grec ou un Romain entrant au sein
d'une assemblée
Oil on canvas
21 × 34" (53.3 × 86.4 cm)

It is difficult to determine whether the present sketch is intended to represent an actual episode from Classical history or literature, or is merely an imaginary scene. It is also unclear whether it is set in Greece or Rome; the soldier behind the central figure, who is being ushered into the assembly, wears what appears to be a Roman helmet, yet the elders in the foreground have beards, which is more suggestive of a Greek setting. The scene may be an imaginative rendering of a celebrated man, possibly even an Emperor, triumphantly entering an important assembly, perhaps the Senate. Equally, since all the protagonists wear laurel crowns—the emblem of orators, poets, and philosophers—the scene may represent a *recitatio*, or literary gathering. At such assemblies, literary works were read from a platform by the author himself, in which case the central figure here could represent an eminent poet or writer, such as Virgil or Cicero. Laurel crowns were worn by the spectators at certain other gatherings, as for example, the *Ludi Apollinares*, a Roman cultural event associated with literature, music, and dance.

The work must date from the second half of the nineteenth century and is in many ways reminiscent of the *tableaux vivants*, depicting Romans, which became particularly popular toward the end of the century. The sketch is thinly painted with strong use of outline, and it is probably this technique above all that has suggested the traditional attribution to Thomas Couture, since it is typical of his working practice.

The study may be compared with Couture's celebrated Salon painting of 1847, *Romans of Decadence* (Paris, Musée du Louvre) and perhaps most tellingly with his sketch (c. 1845) for that composition (formerly in the collection of Mrs. Henry Potts Russel, Carmel, California; Boime 1980, p. 141, VI. 7). The scenes share a frieze-like composition and a sense of Classical grandeur. In all of these works one can also detect a debt to Raphael's *Stanze* in the Vatican, and indeed Couture deeply admired that artist's work. There is, however, a complete absence in the present sketch of any sense of decadence or licentiousness, which is apparent in Couture's known Classical subjects, as, for example, his earliest composition in this vein, *Horace and Lydia* (London, Wallace Collection), or indeed in *Romans of Decadence*. By contrast, the subject here is treated in a staid and sober manner. While an attribution to Couture seems tenable in terms of both composition and technique, it is also possible that this study could be by one of his more accomplished followers, such as Thomas Satterwhite Noble.

J.R.B.

Jean-Louis Ernest MEISSONIER

(Lyons 1815–Paris 1891)

Meissonier's family moved to Paris when he was three years old, but in 1825, when his mother died, he was sent to Grenoble to live with family friends. After his return to Paris, he was apprenticed to a druggist, but at the same time received initial artistic training from Julien Potier. In 1833, he entered the atelier of Léon Cogniet and made his Salon debut a year later with *Dutch Burghers* (London, Wallace Collection). From 1836 to 1839, Meissonier became active as a book illustrator for the publishers Curmer and Hetzel. A major influence on Meissonier during this period was Paul-Marc-Joseph Chenavard, and around this time he began to paint genre scenes. In 1843, Meissonier won a first-class medal for *A Painter in His Studio*, and seven years later he executed one of his most celebrated and powerful works, *A Memory of Civil War* (Paris, Musée du Louvre). His greatest success came at the 1855 Exposition Universelle, where he won a gold medal for *The Brawl*, a painting that was purchased by Napoleon III. In 1859, the Emperor invited Meissonier to go to Italy to record the war with Austria. Several works resulted, including *Napoleon III at Solferino* and *The Emperor Surrounded by His General Staff*, both of which were purchased by the Imperial family. In 1865, Meissonier's son and pupil, Jean-Charles, made his Salon debut. A member of the Institut, in 1889 Meissonier was elected president of the jury for the Exposition Universelle. Meissonier also contributed to the founding of the Société Nationale des Beaux-Arts and was its first president.

110 Jean-Louis Ernest MEISSONIER
The Return of Napoleon from Elba (?),
n.d.
Le Retour de Napoléon de l'île d'Elbe (?)
Oil on canvas
10 ¾ × 12 ¼" (27.3 × 31.1 cm)
Signed at lower right with monogram: M

Exhibitions: Peoria 1980, no. 37.

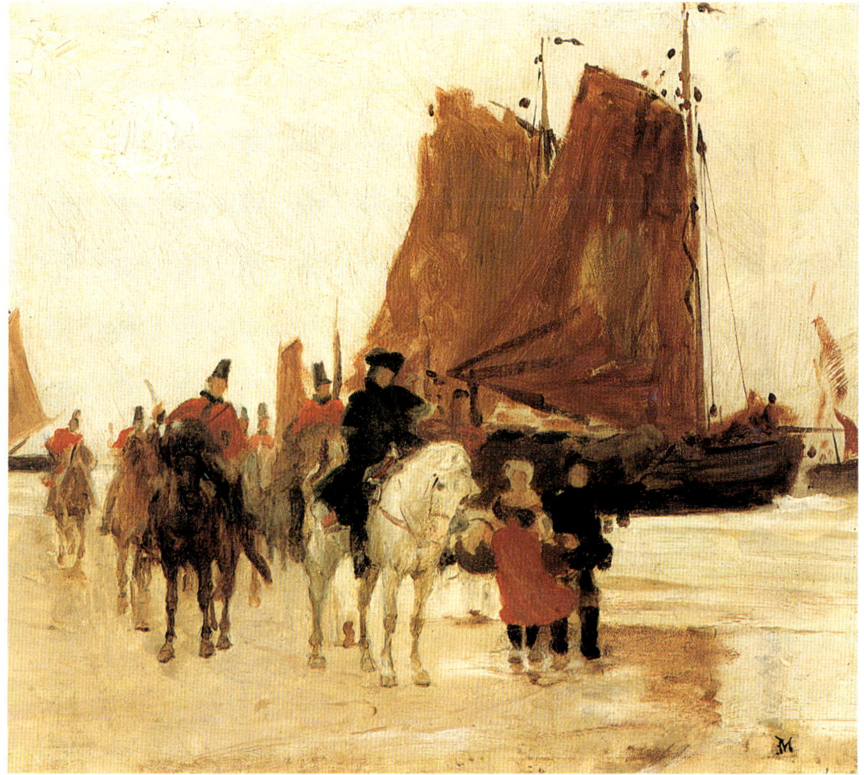

This sketch is not recorded in Gréard's catalogue of Meissonier's work (Gréard 1897), nor is a final painting of the subject known. It does, however, bear Meissonier's distinctive monogram and is typical of his Napoleonic scenes.

Until the Salon of 1864, Meissonier's reputation had been based on his work as a genre painter. At this Salon he embarked upon a new stage in his artistic career, as a painter of military subjects, primarily from the Napoleonic period. His first work in this vein, *The Emperor Napoleon III at the Battle of Solferino* (Compiègne, Musée National du Château), reflected his patronage by Napoleon III. It was in his patron's honor and in accordance with his wishes that Meissonier chose episodes from Napoleonic history. He followed his initial military painting with *1814 The Campaign of France* (Paris, Musée du Louvre), a work begun in 1860 but completed only in 1863. It shows Napoleon I in 1814, mounted on his white horse, at the head of his troops, in a manner similar to the present sketch. Meissonier was a great admirer of Napoleon and seems to have regarded him as an icon of patriotism.

The scene in this sketch has not been firmly identified, but J. Patrice Marandel (see Peoria 1980, no. 37) has very plausibly suggested that it represents Napoleon's return from the Island of Elba. Certainly the sailing ships lined up along the shore make this a distinct possibility. Meissonier himself had traveled to Italy in 1859, and a sketchbook has been discovered that contains notes (about his itinerary) and sketches, including a head of Napoleon I (Lyon 1993, p. 200, n. 1). This visit to Italy could have inspired the present sketch.

Stylistically this oil-on-canvas sketch may be compared with other military subjects executed by Meissonier. Most frequently these works, like much of the painter's oeuvre, were executed on panel. Meissonier frequently sketched single figures from his compositions. A single unfinished sketch of a horse, in the Musée des Augustines, Toulouse (inv. 67.39.2; exh. cat. 1993, cat. no. 116), for example, is particularly close to Napoleon's horse in the present work. In *The Return of Napoleon from Elba*, Meissonier has evoked a somewhat somber and subdued atmosphere. The group of soldiers is relatively static, and Napoleon's horse stands at a halt. The sketch makes a strong contrast with a later work by Meissonier, also a coastal scene, *General Championnet on the Beach* (Lyons, Musée des Beaux-Arts), which, while displaying a similar treatment of both the seashore and the sky, shows riders galloping across the sands at a furious pace, reflecting the angry mood of the protagonists.

J. R. B.

Louis-Edouard DUBUFE

(Paris 1820–Versailles 1885)

The son of the painter Edouard-Marie Dubufe, Louis-Edouard emulated and eventually surpassed his father as the most sought-after society portraitist of his day. Pupil of his father and Paul Delaroche, Dubufe began his career as a painter of religious and historical scenes. These works, such as *The Annunciation* and *A Huntress*, with which he made his Salon debut in 1839, were competent and well received, but would not have earned him a reputation of particular merit. During the following decade he exhibited a number of works with religious or literary subjects, and only the occasional portrait. From 1848 onward, however, he turned almost exclusively to portraiture. He spent the years from 1849 to 1851 in England, and the works he exhibited at the Royal Academy in London included *Portrait of Rachel* (1851; Paris, Théâtre-Français), the celebrated tragedienne. The following decades marked the peak of Dubufe's career, and he was in much demand as a portrait painter of society ladies and the leading figures of the Second Empire. He continued to exhibit until 1879, mostly portraits, but also the great triptych *The Prodigal Son*, a work in the style of Veronese, which he showed at the 1866 Salon. Dubufe regularly received medals and the acclaim of the public, although the critics were often hostile to his work.

111 Louis-Edouard DUBUFE
Principessa Brancaccio-Massimo, n.d.
La Princesse Brancaccio-Massimo
Oil on canvas
16 ½ × 11 ½" (41.9 × 29.2 cm)

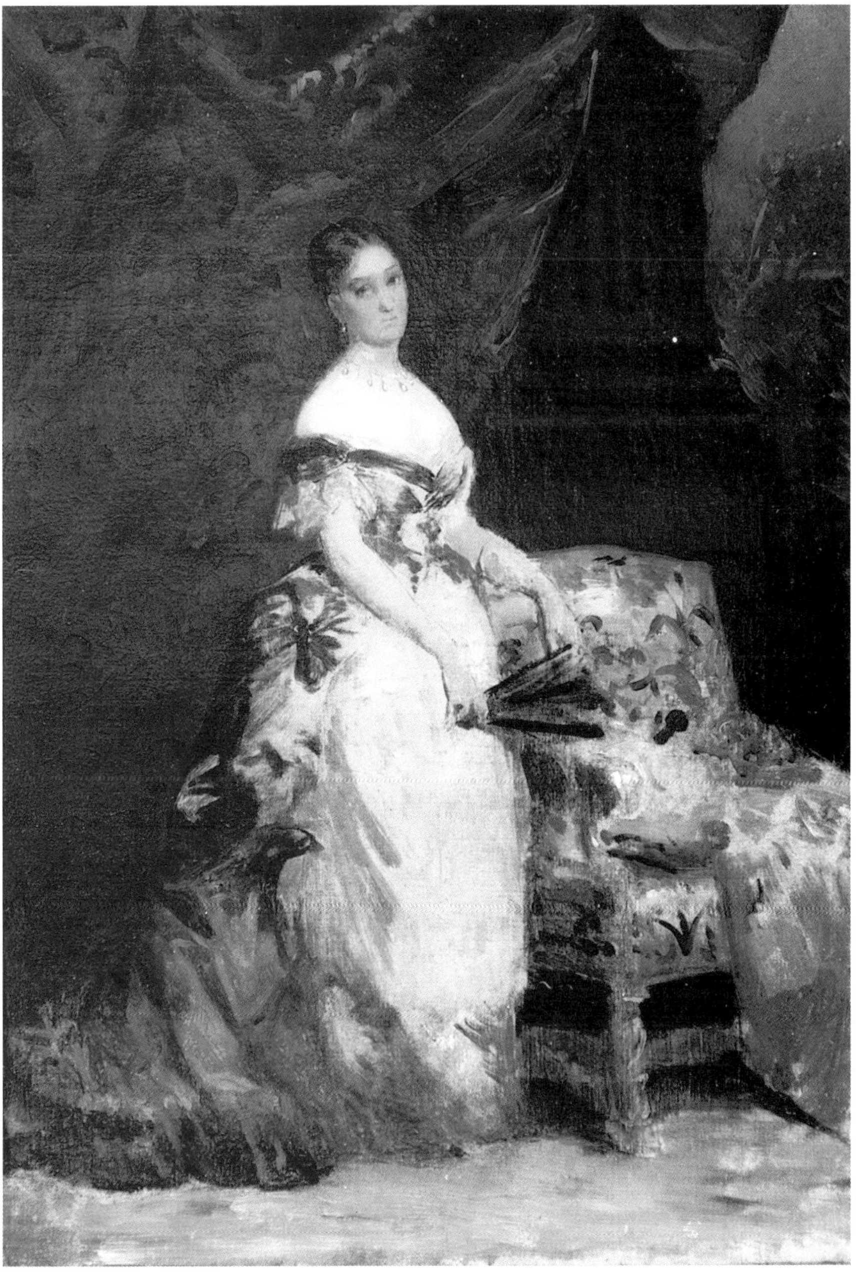

By the late 1840s, Dubufe, like his father, had turned to portraiture. Dubufe had an ability to beautify faces and add a sparkle to eyes, which together with his mastery of the complexities of female fashion, made him much sought after by society ladies. His portrait entries for the Paris Salons read like the guest list for some splendid *grand bal*. In 1853, he exhibited portraits of the Empress Eugénie, the Comtesse de Montebello, and Baron Gaston d'Hauteserve; in 1857 those of Mme Rouher and the artist Rosa Bonheur; and in 1861 Princess Mathilde, the Marquise de Galiffet, and the Duchess of Medina-Coeli. Dubufe's more celebrated male portraits include such notable figures as the Comte de Nieuwerkerke, Alexandre Dumas *fils*, and Prince Demidoff.

This attractive painting is the study for a full-length portrait of Principessa Elisabetta Brancaccio, *née* Elisabeth Hickson-Field (1846–1909). The sitter was an American by birth from Philadelphia, who married into the patrician Neapolitan family of the Brancacci. Her husband was Salvatore Brancaccio (1842–1924), and by him she had one son, Don Marcantonio Gerardo Giulio Marino Maria, born in Rome in 1879. He in turn married Fernanda Ceccarelli in 1939, but died in 1961 without issue. The name did not die out, however, since in 1968, by special decree, Don Filippo Massimo added the family name of Brancaccio to that of his branch of the Roman Massimo family, in accordance with the wishes of the last of the Brancacci. This study, therefore, in recent years has simply become known as "Principessa Massimo."

The sketch is probably datable to the late 1860s or 1870s, prior to the birth of the sitter's son. It is not only typical of society portraits of the period, fulfilling the Second Empire ideal of fashionable portraiture, but also in the use of the heavy background curtain, the Classical pillar, and the fine armchair, it is very much in the tradition of grand Italian portraiture. In the freeness of its handling and the elegance of the pose, this sketch may be compared with a finished composition by Claude Monet of approximately the same date, *Mme Louis Joachim Gaudibert* (1868; Paris, Musée d'Orsay).

J.R.B.

Charles-François EUSTACHE

(Paris 1820–Cherbourg 1870)

The son of an engineer, Eustache displayed artistic talent from an early age and by the time he was thirty was well-established as both a painter and a lithographer. He married young, but was widowed after only a few years and from that time on devoted himself entirely to art. A pupil of Prosper Marilhat and friend of Eugène Fromentin, Eustache developed a taste for Oriental subject matter, but always maintained a personal vision of it. He traveled continually in Egypt, Switzerland, Provence, and Italy, and the works he submitted to the Salon in 1849, 1850, and 1852 greatly enhanced his reputation. Poor health eventually prevented him from traveling, and by 1857 he had retired to Cherbourg, where he continued to work, mainly in charcoal and pastel, both from where memory and from the inspiration provided by the surrounding countryside.

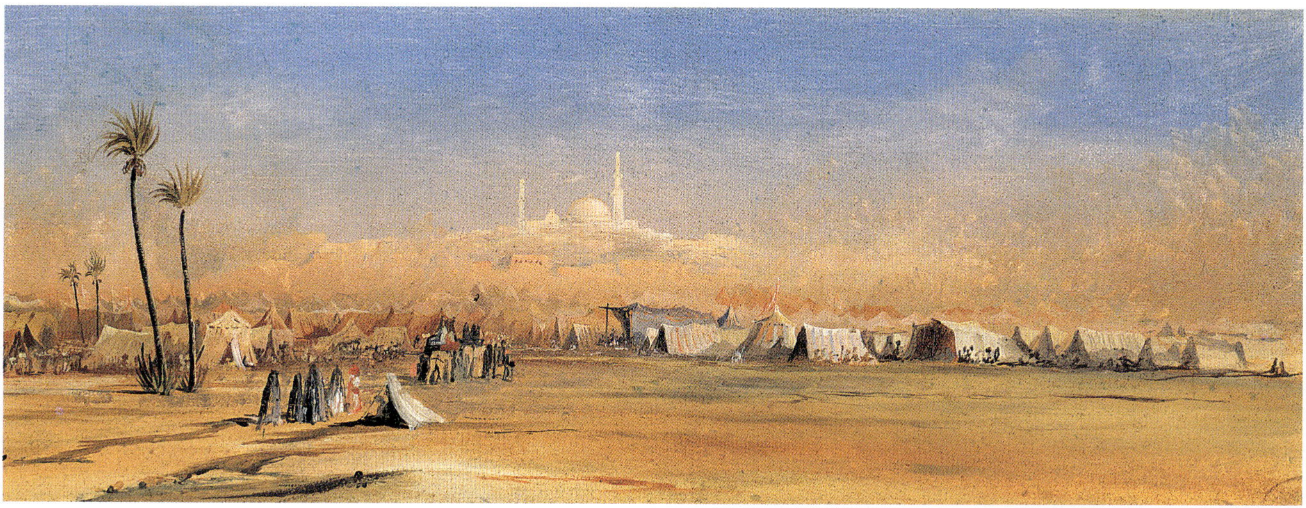

112 Charles-François EUSTACHE
View of Cairo, n.d.
Vue du Caire
Crayon and gouache on paper on canvas
6 ½ × 16 ¾" (16.5 × 42.5 cm)
Lower right: Estate stamp

Provenance: Descendants of the artist.

Exhibitions: Peoria 1980, no. 27.

Bibliography: Marandel 1977, p. 28, fig. 1.

With its contrasts of light and shade, flat expanse, broad sky, and mirage-like view of Cairo, this sketch captures the atmosphere of the desert, and is typical of Eustache's individual talent. It bears witness to a fascination with the Orient that Eustache maintained throughout his life. At that time, the so-called Orient included the lands of North Africa and the Middle East. Egypt in particular, as a result of Napoleon's Egyptian campaign of 1798, had become a fertile source of artistic inspiration for a group of painters called "the Orientalists."

Eustache had first visited the Middle East with his teacher, the landscape painter Prosper-Georges-Antoine Marilhat. Following the death of his wife, he decided to devote himself to topographical art. He returned to Egypt in 1842 and 1847.

Although Eustache's interest in the Orient is attested by his correspondence with his friend the painter and writer Eugène Fromentin, his diaries are untraced and, as a consequence, little is known about the chronology of his work. The present sketch may have been one of the numerous small-format studies he brought back from his travels. Eustache's working methods are largely unknown, but it is probable that his most finished pastels and charcoals date from his second visit to Egypt. It is also possible that this sketch was executed after 1857, when, due to poor health, he traveled far less and stayed mainly in his atelier in Cherbourg, where he continued to work, drawing inspiration from his earlier *plein-air* studies.

According to his granddaughter, Denise le Mallier, Eustache's private income allowed him to paint purely for his own pleasure, and although he gave paintings away to his friends, he sold nothing during his lifetime. As a result, although he exhibited at the Salons of 1849, 1850, and 1852, his work remained virtually unknown and forgotten until his family decided to disperse his atelier nearly twenty years ago.

J.R.B.

113 Unknown artist
Arcadian Scene, n.d.
Scène en arcadie
Oil on canvas
14 × 10 ¾" (35.6 × 27.3 cm)
Inscribed on stretcher: *Bénouville 8*

Exhibitions: Peoria 1980, no. 4 (attributed to François-Léon Bénouville).

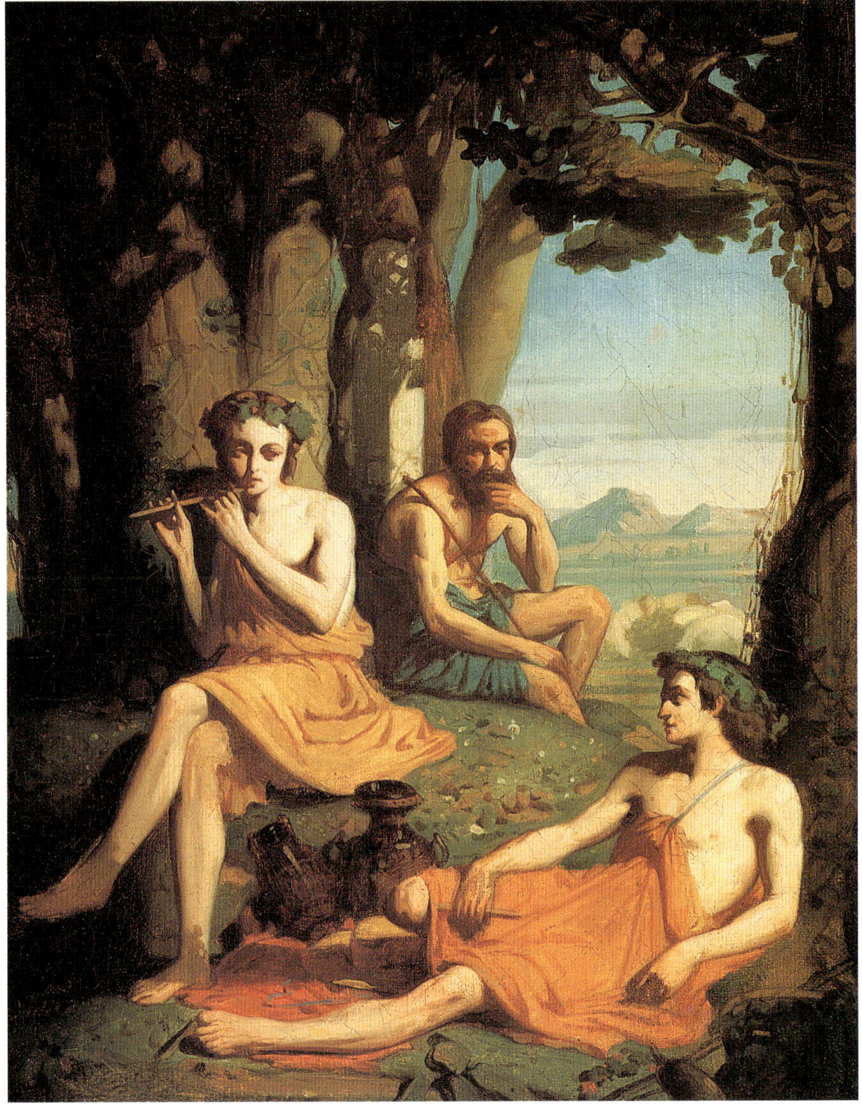

The traditional attribution of this sketch to François-Léon Bénouville may have arisen from the inscription on the back of the stretcher, which is a comparatively recent addition. This attribution seems unlikely, however, on grounds of stylistic comparison with Bénouville's known works.

J. Patrice Marandel has pointed out that stylistically this sketch is closer to the work of Dominique-Louis-Féréal Papety, who was much inspired by the utopian writings of François Fourier. Papety's work certainly displays stylistic similarity; one can note, for example, the foliage in *An Italian Peasant Girl* (London, Wallace Collection) and the facial types in *A Neapolitan Fisherman* (formerly London, Wallace Collection), which have parallels in our sketch.

Another possible candidate for the authorship is Victor-François-Eloi Biennoury, whose painting *Mercury and Argus*, his *concours* submission to the Ecole des Beaux-Arts in 1842, recreates the style of an earlier period in a very similar way.

J. R. B.

Charles LANDELLE

(Laval 1821–Chennevières-sur-Marne 1908)

Son of a calligrapher in the French civil service, Landelle was inspired to become a painter by being a model for Ary Scheffer when he was eleven. In 1837, he became the pupil of Paul Delaroche at the Ecole des Beaux-Arts and made his Salon debut four years later with *Self-Portrait* (Musée de Laval). He continued to exhibit regularly at the Salons until his death. In 1842, he exhibited his first religious composition, *Beato Angelico Seeking Inspiration from God*. Landelle refused to compete for the Prix-de-Rome, but made the first of several visits to Italy in 1845. He won a medal at the Salon of that year with his painting *The Three Marys Going to the Holy Sepulchre*, which greatly enhanced his reputation. At the Salon of 1850, Landelle exhibited *La Mauresque*, which was the first in a series of women of North Africa and the Middle East that were to become the specialty of his later career. Landelle's public commissions in Paris included work for the Conseil d'Etat in 1850 and the Hôtel de Ville in 1852, both of which were destroyed under the Commune. He also worked in the Elysée Palace (1859) and several Parisian churches, including Saint-Roch (1850), Saint-Germain-l'Auxerrois (1856), and Saint-Sulpice (1875). Landelle was made a Chevalier of the Legion of Honor in 1855.

114 Charles LANDELLE
The Three Marys Going to the Sepulchre,
1845
Les Saintes Femmes se rendant au
Tombeau du Christ
Oil on panel
8 ½ × 6 ¼" (21.6 × 15.9 cm)

Provenance: Private collection, Paris.

Exhibitions: Peoria 1980, no. 17
(attributed to Paul Delaroche); New
York 1980, no. 45 (attributed to Paul
Delaroche).

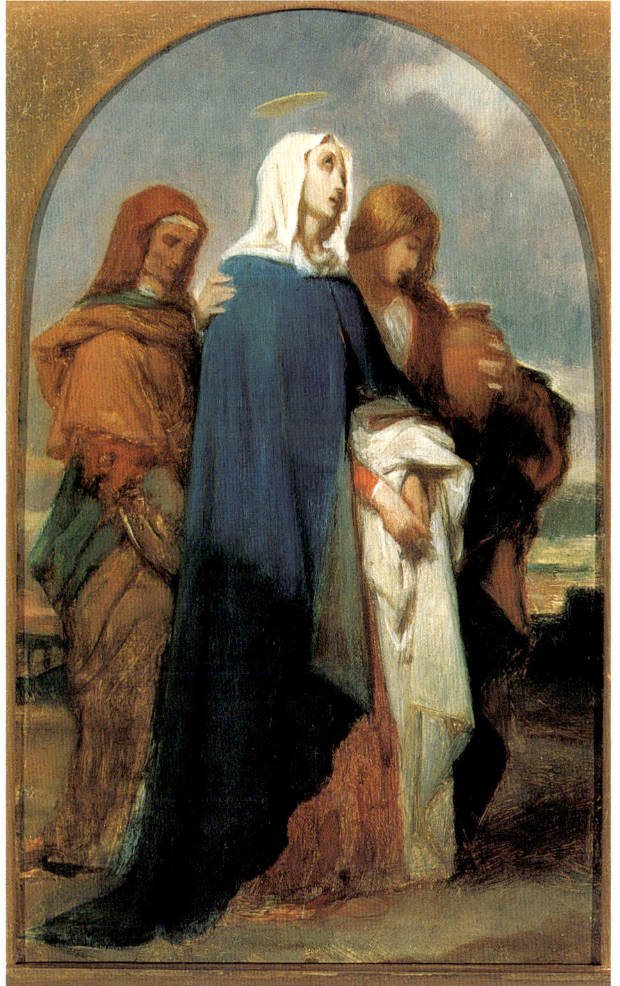

Exhibited at Lakeview and New York in 1980, this sketch was attributed to Delaroche. However, Alastair Laing has since identified it as the study for the painting *The Three Marys Going to the Sepulchre* by Charles Landelle. Landelle was the pupil of Delaroche, and their stylistic similarities explain the misattribution. Indeed, it is known that Delaroche also treated the subject, because the sale following his death contained a work entitled *The Virgin with the Three Marys*.

Landelle was commissioned to paint this composition by the French government for the Church of Saints-Lieux, Lavaur (Tarn), and it was exhibited at the Salon of 1845. It is significant that it was in this year that the artist visited Italy for the first time, since Bruno Foucart has remarked that Landelle derived inspiration from the Italian Renaissance painter Fra Angelico. To support this assertion Foucart cites Landelle's painting *Beato Angelico Seeking Inspiration from God*, which was exhibited at the Salon of 1842 (Foucart 1987, pp. 257–58). However, it is quite clear that the present composition has a Raphaelesque quality, which derives from the influence of Ingres. There can be little doubt that Ingres was a major influence on Landelle's style. According to the latter's biographer and nephew, Stryienski, when visiting Ingres and confronted with that artist's works, Landelle declared, "This is the style I strive for" (Stryienski 1911, p. 13).

Landelle's style emulated that of Ingres in many ways. It was suave and careful, but with a soft gentleness that made his religious work particularly accessible. Delaroche was also preoccupied with creating religious painting that would excite the public. The style that he and Landelle developed had a contemporary parallel in the religious works of Ary Scheffer and his follower Hippolyte Lazerges, who also came under the influence of Ingres.

Religious subjects constituted a large part of Landelle's oeuvre. The heads and poses of the models used in this sketch appear in other works, for example, in *The Death of St. Joseph* (Paris, Saint Sulpice) and in the *Beatitudes* (Musée de Laval). There is also a masculine equivalent of the present composition in his *Christ with Saints Peter and John*, which was exhibited at the Salon of 1850.

J.R.B.

Ziem studied at the Ecole d'Architecture de Dijon, where he was acknowledged a gifted student. Employed as Chef de Chantier (site manager) at Marseilles, he began to paint in watercolor. His successes as an amateur painter encouraged him to pursue a career in art. Ziem traveled to Italy in 1841, to Russia in 1841–43, and to Holland and England in 1845. His visits to Egypt in 1856, Algeria in 1858, and Tunisia in 1859 excited a lifelong passion for the Orient. His two favorite subjects were Venice, where after 1845 he spent part of each year, and Constantinople, which he first visited in 1856. Ziem first exhibited at the Salon of 1849 and in 1852 won a first-class medal. During this time he came under the influence of Corot and began painting with Théodore Rousseau in Barbizon, where he lived between 1866 and 1868. The greater part of his life was divided between his Montmartre studio, equipped with orientalizing architectural motifs, including a minaret and cupola, and his studio in Venice. Highly honored and hugely successful, Ziem was a friend to young artists, giving them encouragement and financial support. He died on November 10, 1911, at the age of ninety.

D.G.

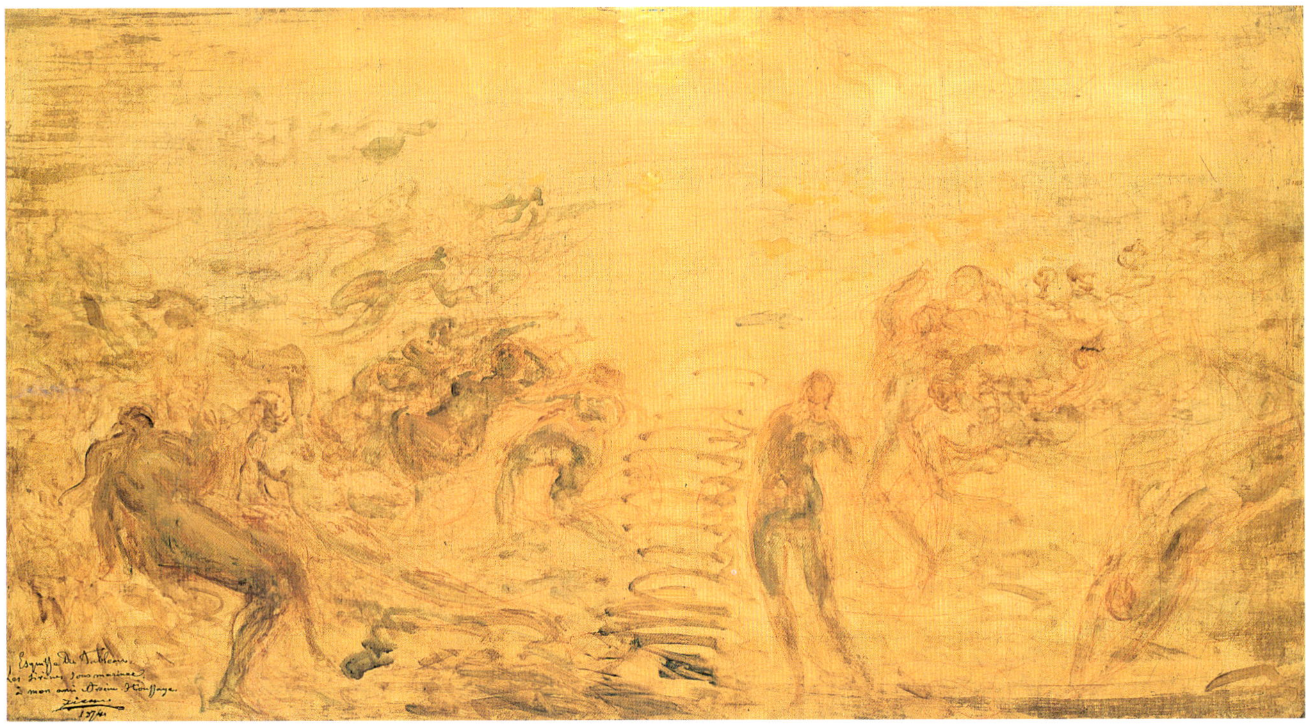

115 Félix ZIEM
Mermaids Under Water, 1874
Les Sirènes sous-marine
Oil on canvas
14 ¼ × 26" (36.2 × 66.0 cm)
Inscribed lower left: *Esquisse du tableau Les Sirenes sous-marines/à mon ami Arsène/Ziem/1874.* Inscribed on back: *Projet de décoration pour maison d'Arsène Houssaye aujourd'hui démolie (emplacement de la maison Durand-Ruel)*

Provenance: Arsène Houssaye collection (?).

Exhibitions: Peoria 1980, no. 50.

Bibliography: Miquel 1978, vol. 2, p. 23.

This sketch is identifiable as the one recorded in the catalogue of paintings from his atelier that Ziem himself drew up. Listed under the year 1874, the date on the present work, it is described as "no. 482. Arsène Houssaye–Aquarium, Sirenes, offert" (see Miquel 1978, vol. 2, p. 23). The sketch is dedicated to the writer and critic François-Arsène (1815–1896), who was a close friend of Ziem's. They had met in 1849, the same year in which Houssaye became director of the Théâtre-Français, and they moved in similar artistic and literary circles, in particular, sharing a mutual friendship with Théophile Gautier. In his biographical notes, Ziem wrote of Houssaye that he had never ceased to be amiable, gracious, and full of praise, ever since their first meeting (Miquel 1978, vol. 1, p. 65).

The imaginative subject matter of this sketch is a departure from Ziem's more literal seascape views. It was probably executed by Ziem as a souvenir for Houssaye of the decorative scheme that he had painted in the writer's house in rue Lafayette. Since this house has now been demolished, it is not known whether the decorative scheme was painted in fresco or oils. An oil painting on panel entitled *Sirènes* was sold by Sotheby Parke Bernet, New York, on March 5, 1942 (lot 80), and although not illustrated in the auction catalogue may either have been an associated composition or may even have formed part of the actual decorative scheme. The art dealer Durand-Ruel had moved into the house by 1870, and since it appears that the signature, date, and inscription were added to the present sketch at a later date, it seems likely that Ziem decided to present one of his original sketches for the decorative scheme to Houssaye some time after the writer had left his residence in the rue Lafayette.

The work is characteristic of Ziem's fresh palette and lively style of painting, which gives the impression of rapid execution. Comparison may be drawn with several of his other sketches, for example, the very freely painted *Sur l'Aire (Cau Cado)*, the *Assumption at Venice*, and *The Grand Canal*, all of which are in the Musée du Vieux-Martigues, Martigues. There are also close stylistic parallels in works such as his watercolor *Bridge of Sighs* (Paris, Petit Palais), in which he has used similar vertical wavy lines as a shorthand to suggest the effect of rippling water.

Houssaye owned other works by the painter, for example, Ziem's catalogue also records him giving his friend a "grisaille magnifique" representing the Church of San Simone in Venice (Miquel 1978, vol. 2, p. 18, no. 233).

J.R.B.

Jean-Léon GEROME

(Vesoul 1824–Paris 1904)

érôme, whose father was a watchmaker, was born on May 11, 1824, in the town of Vesoul near Besançon. As a student at the lycée in Vesoul he displayed a precocious talent for drawing, and at age sixteen he entered the atelier of Paul Delaroche in Paris. After Delaroche closed his atelier in 1844, Gérôme traveled with Delaroche to Italy and upon his advice entered the atelier of Gleyre, but left soon after. At the Salon of 1847, the scene of his first success, he won a third-class medal and extravagant praise from the influential art critic Théophile Gautier for *The Cock Fight* (Paris, Musée du Louvre). Gautier named him the leader of a new school, the "Néo-Grecs," including the artists Toulemouche, Picou, Jobbe-Duval, and J. L. Hamon. The Néo-Grecs specialized in historical genre paintings; Gérôme's works in particular were admired for their technical finish, as well as their scientific and ethnographical detail. In 1855–56, Gérôme spent eight months in Egypt sketching all that he saw. Like Delacroix, he was drawn to North Africa and the Middle East and believed he had found the living remnants of Classical civilization. This was the first of many visits. In later years, Gérôme turned to sculpture, marking his debut in sculpture at the Exposition Universelle of 1878 and frequently exhibiting sculpture at the Salons. Highly successful financially and admired as a teacher, Gérôme lived in Paris with his wife, Marie Goupil (daughter of the dealer and publisher), surrounded by a large collection of Oriental art.

D.G.

116 Jean-Léon GEROME
Arabian Woman in a Doorway, n.d.
Une Femme arabe dans un passage
Oil on canvas
13 ¼ × 10 ¼" (33.7 × 26.0 cm)
Stamped lower left: *ATELIER J.L. GEROME*

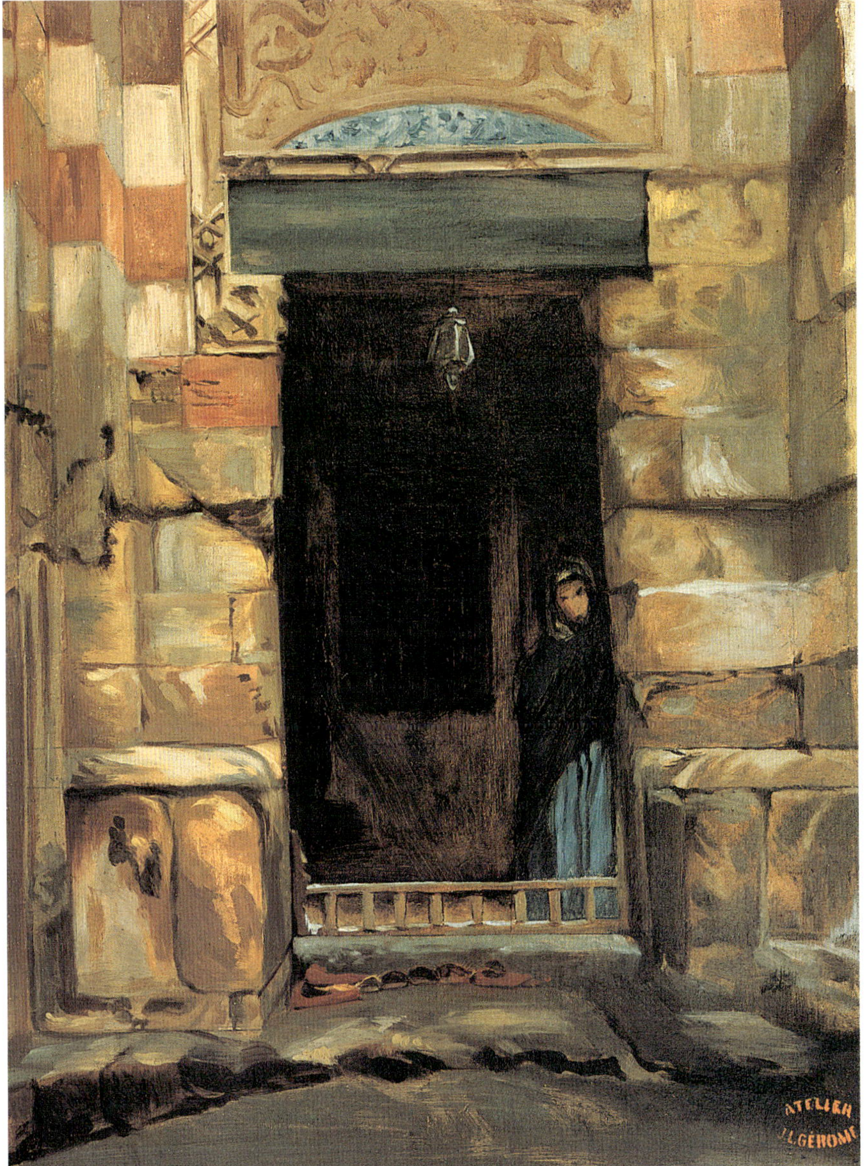

This attractive "Orientalist" genre scene is not included in Ackerman's recent catalogue of Gérôme's oeuvre (1990), since it does not relate to any known finished work. Ackerman includes sketches for unknown final works only when they are highly finished. Gérôme made numerous sketches on his various trips to the Middle East; not only are some of these unrelated to finished works, but they are also difficult to date with precision, because of their similarity.

The present freely painted study is nonetheless typical of Gérôme's work, and the motif of the woman standing in a door or alleyway is one that recurs regularly in his oeuvre. This sketch is probably datable to the 1870s and relates to series of similar compositions such as *Cairene Women* of 1872 (whereabouts unknown; Ackerman 1990, cat. no. 227, [reprod.]) and *Arab Girl in a Doorway* of 1873 (private collection; Ackerman 1990, cat. no. 229 [reprod.]). In later years, Gérôme returned to this theme, as, for example, in *The Woman of Cairo at Her Door* of 1897 (Syracuse, New York, Syracuse University Art Collection; Ackerman 1990, cat. no. 442 [reprod.]), where he used the same model as in the earlier scenes. A figure in the doorway is also to be found in Gérôme's other genre scenes, such as *The Carpet Merchant* of 1887 (Minneapolis Institute of Art; Ackerman 1990, cat. no. 349, [reprod.]).

Gérôme visited Egypt for the first time in 1856 and made subsequent trips to the Middle East in 1862, 1868, 1871, 1872, and 1874, and visits to Constantinople and Asia Minor in 1871 and 1875. He produced a variety of Oriental images, which he exhibited regularly at the Salon. His genre scenes combine veracity of detail with close observation of people and a fascination with Arabian architecture. The latter feature is evident in the simple but effective suggestion of the brickwork in the present sketch.

Oriental women were a subject that fascinated the West, and Gérôme satisfied this curiosity with his compositions. In the present sketch, the way the veiled woman emerges from the doorway is handled with mystery, intrigue, and exoticism. The scene in this sketch is quite subtle compared with his blatantly erotic Néo-Grec scenes of women bathing. It was very much in this vein that Gautier wrote ironically, "Nothing decorates better a voyage to the East than an old woman who, at the turning of a deserted alleyway, makes a sign for you to follow her and leads you by a secret door into an apartment decked with all the most sought-after objects of Asian luxury" (*Constantinople*, 1853, p. 88).

This sketch bears an atelier stamp, probably added when the work left the studio. There was no sale after Gérôme's death, but the works were divided up and gradually sold through various dealers such as Boussod; Goupil & Co.; Valadon & Cie in Paris; and Knoedler in New York.

J.R.B.

Carpeaux was the son of a stonemason from Valenciennes, and he briefly followed courses at the Académie des Beaux-Arts in that city before attending the Petite Ecole in Paris. In 1844, he entered the Ecole des Beaux-Arts, where he studied first with the painter Abel de Pujol (q.v.) and then with the sculptor François Rude. In 1850, he left Rude to join the studio of the academic sculptor Francisque Duret, in order to prepare himself for the Prix-de-Rome. After making his Salon debut in 1853 with a plaster relief, *The Submission of Abd-el-Kader*, he succeeded in persuading Napoleon III to order its execution in marble (Musée de Valenciennes). Carpeaux finally won the Prix-de-Rome in 1854 with *Hector and His Son, Astyanax*. In 1856, he went to Italy where he was based until 1862, and from there he dispatched two of his most celebrated works, the *Fisherboy with Shell* and *Ugolino*. Carpeaux obtained patronage from the Imperial family, notably Princess Mathilde, and from governmental circles. In 1864, he received a commission to execute an elaborate decorative scheme for the Pavillon de Flore at the Louvre, and the following year undertook the commission *The Spirit of the Dance* (1866–69) for Charles Garnier's new Opera House in Paris. After fleeing to London in 1871 during the Commune, Carpeaux returned to complete his last major commission, *The Fountain of the Four Continents* for the Paris Observatory (1867–74). Weakened by stomach cancer, and feeling persecuted by his wife, he spent his last years under the protection of the Romanian Prince Stirbey.

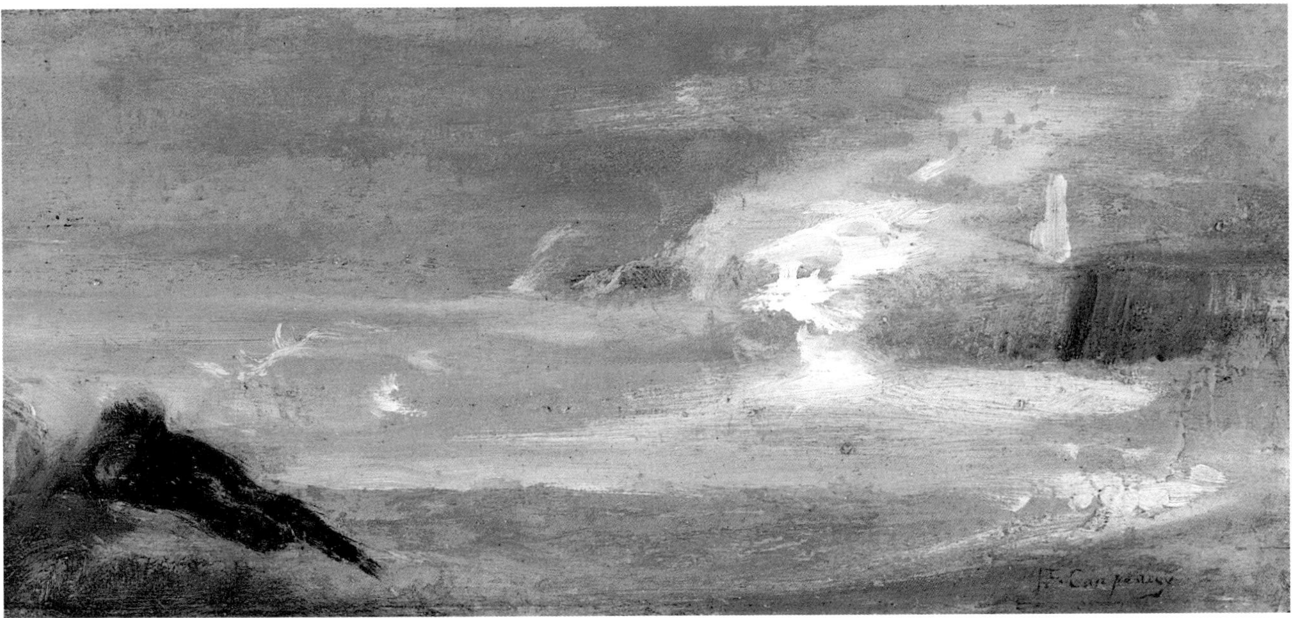

117 Jean-Baptiste CARPEAUX
  Seascape, n.d.
  Marine
  Oil on canvas
  6 × 12 ¼" (15.2 × 31.1 cm)
  Signed: *J. Bt. Carpeaux*

Bibliography: Peoria 1980, illus.

Carpeaux was the leading figure and influence in French sculpture in the mid-nineteenth century. Although he worked in both oils and watercolor throughout his life, he is not well known for his painted oeuvre, and least of all for his landscapes.

Victor Liet, a painter, sculptor, and writer from Carpeaux's native town of Valenciennes, was the first to encourage him as an artist, and it is significant that at the beginning of his career, Carpeaux worked in the atelier of the painter Abel de Pujol. In 1854, Carpeaux won the Prix-de-Rome for sculpture and the next six years were spent in Italy, where he painted several landscapes. For the most part, these comprised views of the countryside surrounding Rome, some with ruins. *A View of the River Tiber*, which has an obvious debt to the landscapes of Jean-Baptiste Camille Corot, has been seen as one of his most notable compositions from this period (Jamot 1908, vol. 40, p. 194). The spontaneous and impressionistic quality of the present sketch suggests a slightly later date in Carpeaux's oeuvre. It displays the artist's ability to achieve the effect of light by use of color and may be compared with other views, such as *Sunrise* (private collection; Peoria 1980, no. 10). Similar use of color and very free technique may be seen in Carpeaux's figurative work, such as *Ball at the Tuileries* (Paris, Musée d'Orsay). His artistic training and his friendship with several painters, such as Bruno Chérier, must have encouraged his activities in this medium.

J. R. B.

118 Jean-Baptiste CARPEAUX
Scene of Devilry, n.d.
Scène de diablerie
Oil on canvas
11 ¾ × 14 ½" (29.8 × 36.8 cm)
Signed lower right: *JBC*

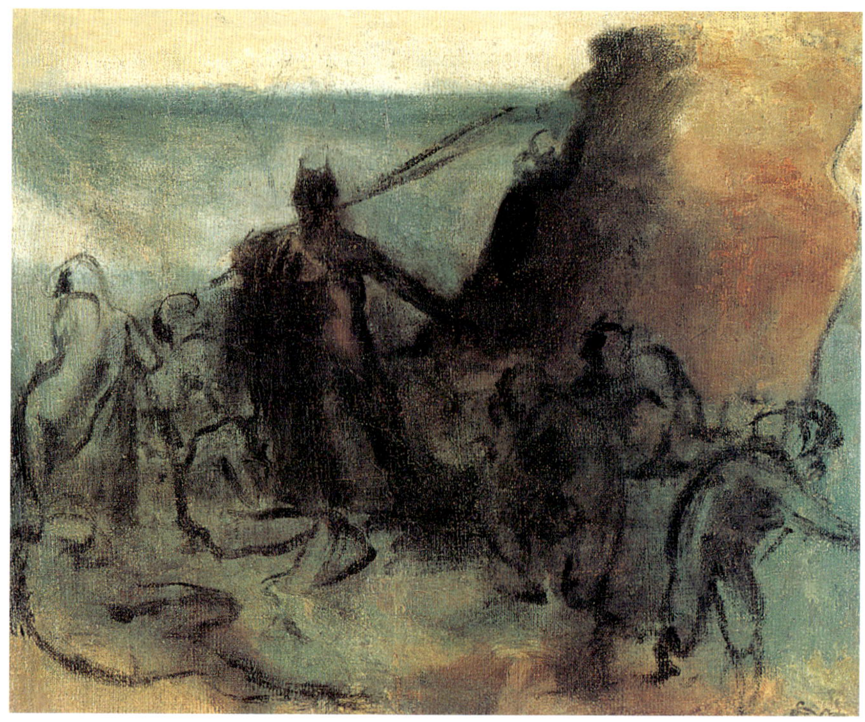

This oil sketch, with its strong linearity, is very similar in treatment to many of Carpeaux's drawings. Sketching was a vital part of the sculptor's creative process, which
enabled him to explore the different possibilities of composition. Many of his major
sculptures were preceded by preparatory drawings, but not all his drawings and
sketches are related to known works. A series of *carnets*, recording everyday scenes
and detailed studies, were given by Carpeaux to his patron, Prince Stirbey, and are
today in the Musée des Beaux-Arts in Valenciennes. These display a similar use of
line and shading to achieve drama and movement.

The composition of this sketch, with its suggestion of lively movement, may
have been inspired by a scene from the ballet or opera. The central figure of the devil
surrounded by frolicking figures has compositional equivalents in several of Carpeaux's sculptural works, for example, *The Spirit of the Dance*, which he executed over
the years 1866 to 1869 for Charles Garnier's new Opera House in Paris. It would
seem likely that this sketch was produced while Carpeaux was working on this project. Stylistically, it is very close to his painting *The People's Uprising* of around 1870
(Museum of Bremen; Bremen 1973, ill. 568). The composition as a whole has similarities with his designs for bas-reliefs; the little *putto* in the right foreground, for
example, is reminiscent of several figures in Carpeaux's sculptures.

J. R. B.

Jean-Alexandre-Joseph FALGUIERE

(Toulouse 1851–Paris 1900)

Son of a mason, Falguière first studied in his native town and was then given a scholarship by the city of Toulouse to study at the Ecole des Beaux-Arts in Paris, where he entered the studio of the sculptor François Jouffroy. In 1857, he made his debut at the Salon with a statuette, *Theseus as a Child*, and won the Prix-de-Rome in 1859. At the Salon of 1864 he received a medal for his bronze *The Winner of the Cockfight*, and at the Salon of 1868 his marble *Tarcisius, Christian Martyr* was awarded the Medal of Honor. During the Siege of Paris, he served in the National Guard, and modeled a celebrated statue, *Resistance*, in snow. Under the Second Republic, he received numerous honors and was commissioned to execute many public monuments, as for example, *Switzerland Welcoming the French Army in 1870*, for Toulouse in 1875, *The Triumph of the Revolution* on the Arc de Triomphe, and several statues, such as *Gambetta* (1884, Cahors) and *Armand Barbe* (1886, Carcasonne). In 1882, he became professor at the Ecole des Beaux-Arts and was elected to membership in the Académie des Beaux-Arts. Falguière was extremely productive; he exhibited at the Salon every year from 1863 until 1899, and his female figures in particular attracted public attention. He sent works to the Exposition Universelle of 1867 and 1878 and the Exposition Centennale of 1900. From 1871 until 1892, he also sent paintings to the Salons; among the most notable of these were *The Wrestlers* and *Cain and Abel*.

119 Jean-Alexandre-Joseph FALGUIERE
Figures Seated Around a Lamp, n.d.
Figures assises autour d'une lampe
Oil on canvas
9 ¼ × 13" (23.5 × 33.0 cm)
Signed: *A.Fg*

Exhibitions: Peoria, no. 30.

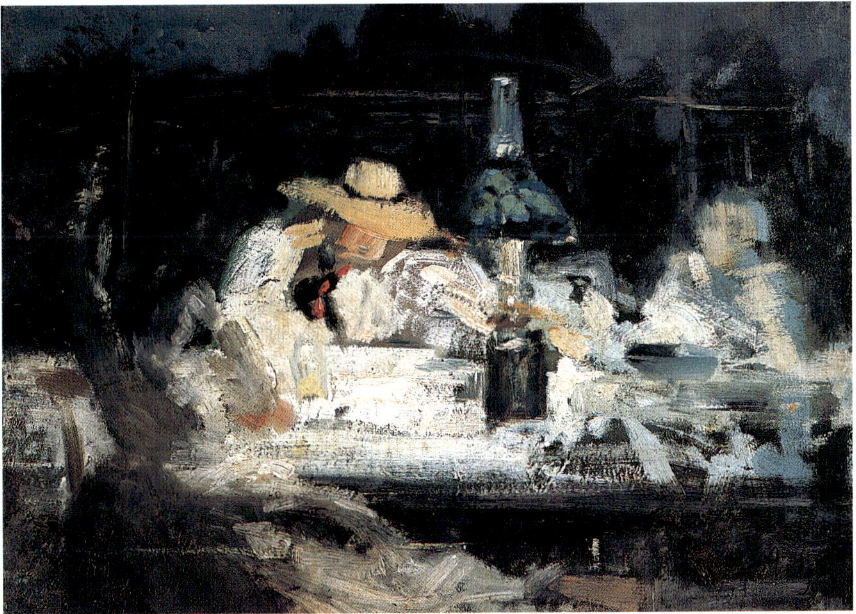

This atmospheric sketch was almost certainly not intended as a study for a larger painting. Falguière has used broad, freely painted brushstrokes to create blocks of light and shade, which give the effect of mass. While this technique undoubtedly reflects the artist's training and sculptural practice, it also displays an assurance and confidence of handling that indicate experience and a certain level of accomplishment. This sketch is therefore likely to be a fairly late work in Falguière's oeuvre, probably dating from the late 1880s or 1890s. *Figures Seated Around a Lamp* differs considerably in concept from cat. no. 120 and even more so from the formal treatment of Falguière's Salon exhibits, such as *The Wrestlers*. Breaking totally with academic convention, it is an impressionistic sketch that has qualities prefiguring the early Intimist works of Edouard Vuillard, such as *Still Life with Salad Bowl* (c. 1887-88; Paris, Musée d'Orsay), *Under the Lamp* (1892; Saint-Tropez, Musée de L'Annonciade), and *At the Ransons* (c. 1895, private collection).

Falguière regarded his painting as a pleasing diversion from sculpture, and this sketch forms part of a small group of works that were never developed into finished compositions, but were executed purely for his own pleasure. These sketches show considerable talent, and although Falguière became famous for his sculpture, his paintings were also appreciated, as an anecdote recounted by Stanislas Lami illustrates.

He tells how Falguière was visited in his studio by his friend the painter Jean-Jacques Henner, who frequently gave him advice. Henner, looking through Falguière's paintings, declared, "That's very good and that's very good," and then turning round suddenly, he saw a group of marble busts and cried out to the sculptor's amusement, "Ah! those are all right too" (Lami 1916, p. 326).

J.R.B.

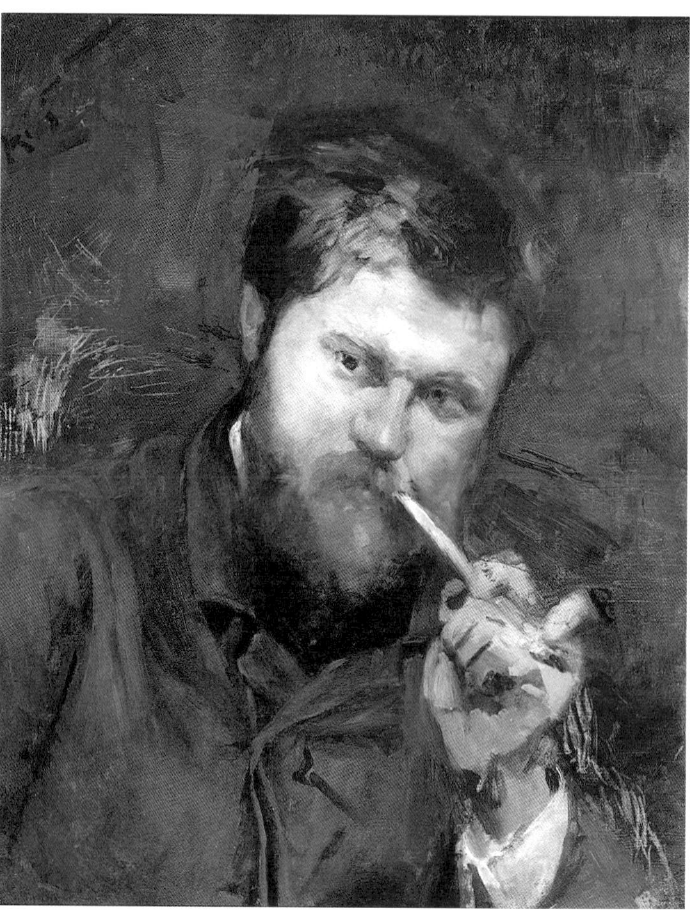

120 Jean-Alexandre-Joseph FALGUIERE
Man Smoking a Pipe, n.d.
Homme fumant une pipe
Oil on canvas
22 × 17 ¾" (55.9 × 45.1 cm)

Exhibitions: Peoria 1980, no. 29.

Although this very free sketch has a bravura and immediacy that create a complete mood of its own, it is in fact the study for the head and shoulders of one of the onlookers in Falguière's first large canvas, *The Wrestlers* (Paris, private collection). The latter, which depicts a group of men watching a wrestling match, was exhibited at the Salon of 1875.

It has been suggested that the sketch may be a self-portrait (see Peoria 1980, no. 29). Certainly there is an intense realism in the work. Not only can it be compared with the early portraits of several of the Impressionists, but also, and perhaps more tellingly, with a chalk drawing by Gustave Courbet titled *Self-Portrait (The Man with the Pipe)* (Hartford, Wadsworth Atheneum), similarly a preparatory study for a painting, which has a parallel realism in handling and concept.

Falguière's reputation was built primarily on his sculptural oeuvre, and, indeed, it is interesting to note that he sculpted the monument to Courbet after the latter's death in 1877. Falguière came to painting only in 1873 and was successful in the directness of his approach, unhampered by academic inhibitions. There is a quality of direct realism in this sketch that one finds also in his modeling. It is particularly intriguing to compare his painted composition of *The Wrestlers* and its slightly stiff and contrived foreground group, with the very free and brutally realistic life-sized tinted plaster group of *The Combat of the Bacchantes* of 1886 (Calais, Musée des Beaux-Arts et de la Dentelle; inv. D. 7722). This plaster group exemplifies the realism that Falguière is credited with having introduced to French sculpture.

J.R.B.

168

Léon-Joseph-Florentine BONNAT

(Bayonne 1833–Monchy-Saint-Eloy 1922)

At the age of fourteen Bonnat moved with his family from Bayonne to Madrid. Here he entered the Accademia Bellas Artes de San Fernando in the atelier of Federico Madrazo and was greatly influenced by the Spanish paintings he saw in the Prado. After his father's death, Bonnat returned to his native town before going to Paris in 1854, where he attended the Ecole des Beaux-Arts and became a pupil of Léon Cogniet (q.v.). In 1857, he competed for the Prix-de-Rome, submitting *The Resurrection of Lazarus*, for which he obtained the second-place prize. Bonnat then went to the French Academy in Rome for three years on a grant from his native Bayonne. He returned to Paris in 1861, and his Salon entries brought him to public attention; members of both Imperial and governmental circles purchased his works. In 1868, Bonnat accompanied Gérôme (q.v.) on a trip to the Orient, and on his return he adopted Oriental subjects, but these did not find as much favor with the public as his previous compositions, particularly his portraits. Bonnat was a talented portraitist and received many commissions from wealthy Europeans and Americans. His portrait of the politician Thiers was one of the principal attractions at the 1877 Salon; his other notable sitters include Victor Hugo, Gambetta, Pasteur, and Puvis de Chavannes. Bonnat was awarded many honors and became a member of the Salon jury in 1869, a member of the Institut in 1881, a professor at the Ecole des Beaux-Arts in 1888 and then director in 1905. A discriminating collector, he bequeathed a fine group of Old Master drawings to the Musée Bonnat at Bayonne.

121 Léon-Joseph-Florentine BONNAT
Study for a Ceiling, n.d.
Esquisse pour un plafond
Oil on canvas mounted on board
9 ¾ × 11 ⅞" (24.8 × 30.2 cm)

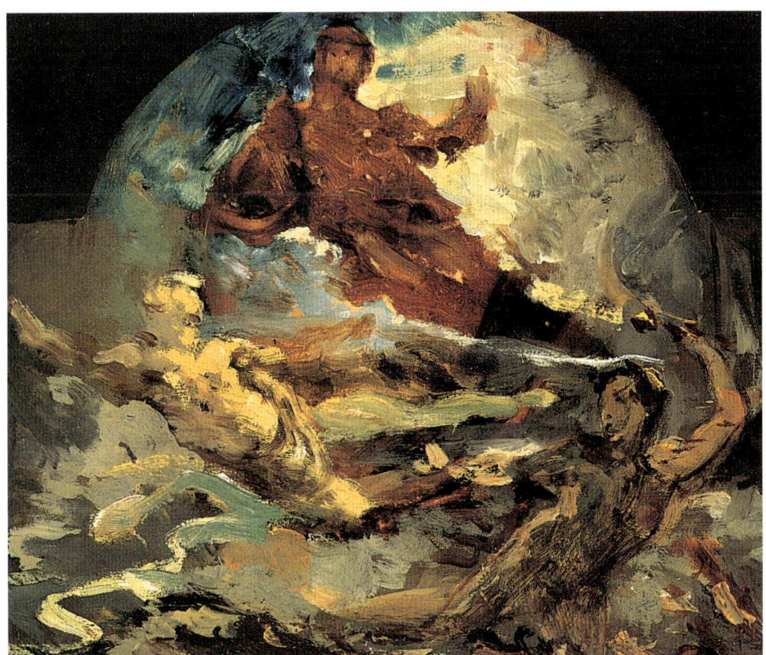

This spirited study appears to be the preparatory design for an unidentified ceiling, probably a large-scale commissioned composition. The impressionistic quality of the work rather obscures the iconography. The central figure, however, appears to represent Justice, since she holds scales in one hand and brandishes a sword with the other. This subject suggests that the composition was destined for a secular public building where the law was administered, perhaps a Palais de Justice.

The sketch is very freely painted, with a strong sense of movement and dramatic use of light and shade. There is evidence not only of the influence of Spanish painting on Bonnat's style, but also, particularly in the vigorous poses of the figures and their treatment, of a debt to Michelangelo, for whom Bonnat had developed an admiration while in Italy. This sketch has certain similarities with another work by Bonnat, *The Assumption*, executed in 1869 for the Chapel of the Virgin in the Church of Saint-André, Bayonne.

Bonnat is known to have made many sketches, particularly of landscapes. Achille Fouquier (1879), for example, states that Bonnat brought back seventy-two sketches from a trip to Egypt, the Sinai, Palestine, Turkey, and Greece, although few of these are known today.

J.R.B.

Henri FANTIN-LATOUR

(Grenoble 1836–Buré 1904)

Henri Fantin-Latour is best known for his paintings of flowers. In 1853, he began to copy at the Louvre; in 1854, he spent three months as a probationary student at the Ecole des Beaux-Arts. Failing to gain admission into the Ecole, Fantin-Latour continued to study at the Louvre for the next twelve years making copies of the work of Delacroix, Veronese, Titian, Giorgione, Tintoretto, Rubens, Rembrandt, Hals, de Hooch, Vermeer, Chardin, and Watteau. He admired Courbet and studied with him at his School of Realism for several months. A friend of Whistler, Degas, Manet, and Monet in the 1860s, Fantin-Latour frequented the Café Guerbois, the gathering place of the Impressionists, but never accepted their radical methods and refused to exhibit with them. After his marriage in 1876 to Victoria Dubourg, a painter of some renown, he socialized very little, preferring to spend his time in his studio or at home with his wife. In 1889, he contributed with many others to a fund-raising campaign initiated by Monet to purchase Manet's *Olympia* for the Louvre. He died at his country home in Buré, Normandy, on August 25, 1904.

D.G.

122 Henri FANTIN-LATOUR
Venus, n.d.
Vénus
Oil on canvas
14 × 9" (35.6 × 22.9 cm)

Provenance: Nigel Foxell, London.

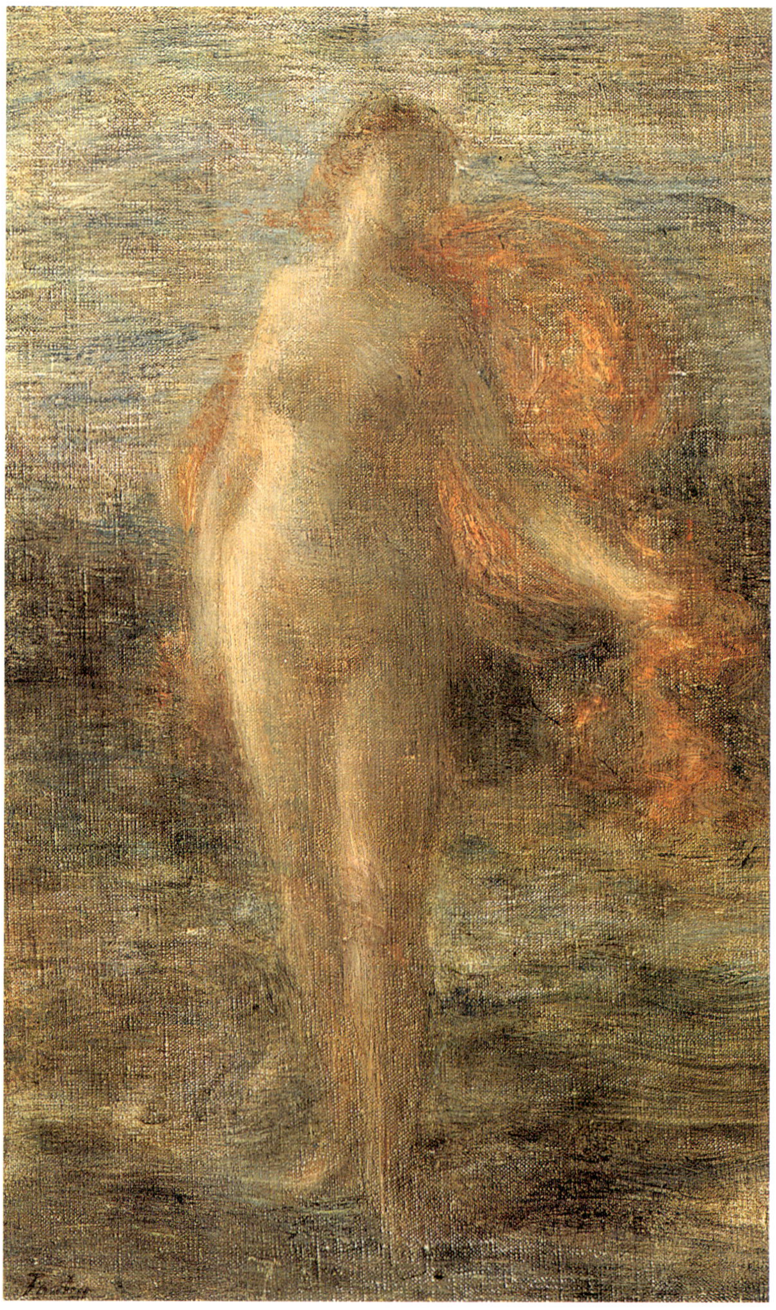

This sketch reflects Fantin-Latour's interest in fantasy. It is almost certainly related to a series of his works that were inspired by the music of Richard Wagner. The composer's ideology was close to Fantin-Latour's, his concept of "music of the future" was echoed by the painter, when, in 1859, he formed the "Société des Vrais Bons," whose stated intention was to inaugurate "the painting of the future."

Venus probably dates from the time of Fantin-Latour's work on his *Tannhäuser: Venusberg* compositions. *Tannhäuser* was the only Wagnerian opera to have been produced in Paris. It was performed in 1861, but Fantin-Latour did not see it because the performance for which he had tickets was cancelled. He would have known it, however, from the French libretto of the Paris production and from *Quatre poèmes d'opéras*, the prose translations of four of Wagner's operas published in 1861.

Fantin-Latour began to execute compositions of Venus and Tannhäuser in 1862. The first lithograph version of the composition is in the Boston Public Library's Print Department. He chose to depict an idyllic scene early in the opera when Tannhäuser is surrounded by Venus and her attendants. He repeated this theme on several occasions, but by the time of his oil painting of the subject, which he exhibited at the Salon of 1864, he had abandoned the grotto specified in the Tannhäuser libretto in favor of an open landscape. Fantin-Latour favored depicting the nude in landscape settings, which reflected both his love of the earlier Venetian masters such as Giorgione and Titian, and the more contemporary influence of Edouard Manet. The present sketch has such a landscape background, and although it does not relate in precise terms to any known finished composition, it is probable that it was inspired by the Venus in Wagner's opera. The sketch may well depict the scene in which, toward the close of the final act, Tannhäuser is looking for the way back to the Venusberg, and Venus appears out of a rosy mist to the magical sounds of the Venusberg music.

Fantin-Latour later returned to the theme of Tannhäuser. In 1876, he attended the first Wagnerian festival at Bayreuth, and this had a powerful impact upon him. As a result, he executed compositions of *Das Rheingold* and a second version of the *Tannhäuser: Venusberg* lithograph (Ottowa, National Gallery; 23362). The present depiction of Venus has certain similarities with his treatment of the Rheinmaiden in *Das Rheingold Final Scenes* (lithograph; Ottowa, National Gallery, 23363), but it is impossible to say whether the sketch should be associated in terms of date with his first or second Tannhäuser period.

In style, the sketch—with its typically small, feathery brushstrokes—is similar to Fantin-Latour's work in pastel. The coloring, with its warm reds and cool blues, are reminiscent of the work of Delacroix, whom he much admired. In fact, it was at the same Salon of 1864, when the *Tannhäuser: Venusberg* was first shown, that he exhibited his painting *Homage to Delacroix*.

J.R.B..

Jean-Paul LAURENS

(Fourquevaux, near Toulouse 1858–Paris 1921)

Laurens began his artistic career by joining a group of itinerant Italian painters. He then entered the Ecole des Beaux-Arts in Toulouse, where he studied under Jean-Blaise Villemsens, who quickly recognized his talent. After winning a scholarship, in 1860 Laurens was able to go to Paris. Here, he entered the atelier of Léon Cogniet (q.v.) and later studied with Alexandre Bida. Laurens made his Salon debut in 1863 with *The Death of Cato of Utica*. He had his first Salon success in 1872 with *Death of the Duke of Enghien* and *The Exhumation of Pope Formosus*, for which he gained a first-class medal. From this time on, his success was assured, and he achieved an international reputation as one of the last exponents of paintings of *grande histoire*. His works were frequently based on rather macabre themes of death and execution, often taken from obscure literary sources. His major Parisian commissions include *The Death of Saint Genevieve* for the Panthéon and decorative schemes in the Hôtel de Ville and the Palais of the Legion of Honor. Laurens became a member of the Institut in 1892 and received the Grand Cross of the Legion of Honor in 1900.

123 Jean-Paul LAURENS
Head of a Woman, n.d.
Tête de femme
Oil on canvas
18 ¼ × 15" (46.4 × 38.1 cm)
Signed upper right with monogram:

Exhibitions: Peoria 1980, no. 35.

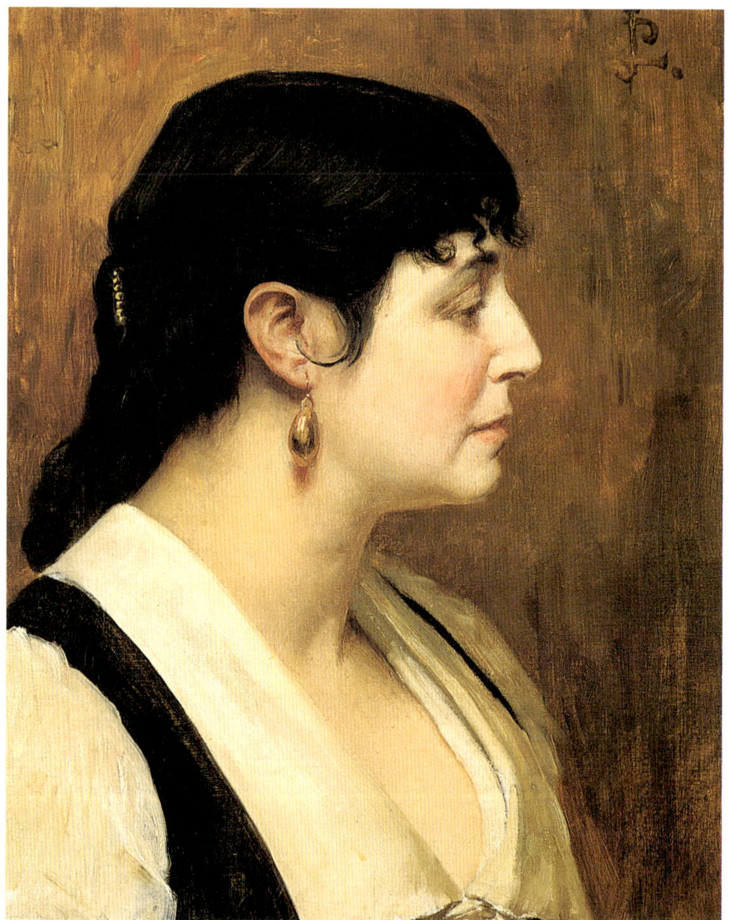

Although Laurens was more famous for his large historical genre scenes, he also painted numerous single-figure studies. This head, with the sparse detail of the comb and earring, is typical of Laurens's more intimate subjects. The heavy drop earring is a motif that recurs regularly in his paintings of women, even in his elaborate historical compositions. The sensitivity of the brushwork and the harmony of the colors compare with other small-scale portraits by the artist, such as that of the marine painter and lithographer Emile Vernier, in the Louvre (R.F. 2799).

    This sketch may have been painted during a quiet period in Laurens's life, perhaps on a return visit to Toulouse. A portrait in its own right, it was probably not intended to be worked up into a finished canvas. It has a charming simplicity that is not found in his more complicated biblical and historical compositions.

J.R.B.

(Nancy 1840–Paris 1904)

In 1856, Lévy went to Paris and entered the Ecole des Beaux-Arts, where he studied with François-Edouard Picot (q.v.) and Alexandre Cabanel. After failing on three occasions to win the Prix-de-Rome, Lévy was discouraged and joined the atelier of Eugène Fromentin. He made his Salon debut in 1865 with *Hecuba Finding the Body of Polydorus on the Seashore*, for which he received a medal. Lévy won further medals at the Salons of 1867 and 1869 with *Joash Saved from the Massacre of Athaliah's Grandsons* and *A Captive Hebrew Weeping over the Ruins of Jerusalem*, respectively. His contribution to the 1872 Salon, *Herodias*, gained Lévy membership of the Legion of Honor and his *Christ in the Tomb*, exhibited at the Salon of 1873, was considered by one critic to be the best history painting exhibited that year. Lévy was a skilled decorative artist and worked on many private residences and public monuments. He executed decorative work for the Panthéon, the Hôtel de Ville, Paris, and the Conseil d'Etat. Around 1894, Lévy became a victim of the anti-Semitism that broke out after the Dreyfus affair. As a result, until his death, Lévy had to rely on selling his works to Paris dealers. He resolutely refused to work under a pseudonym.

124 Henri-Lépold LEVY
Scene After a Slaying, n.d.
Scène de meurtre
Oil on canvas
15 ¼ × 12 ¼" (38.7 × 31.1 cm)
Signed lower left: *Henry Levy*

Exhibitions: Peoria 1980, no. 36.

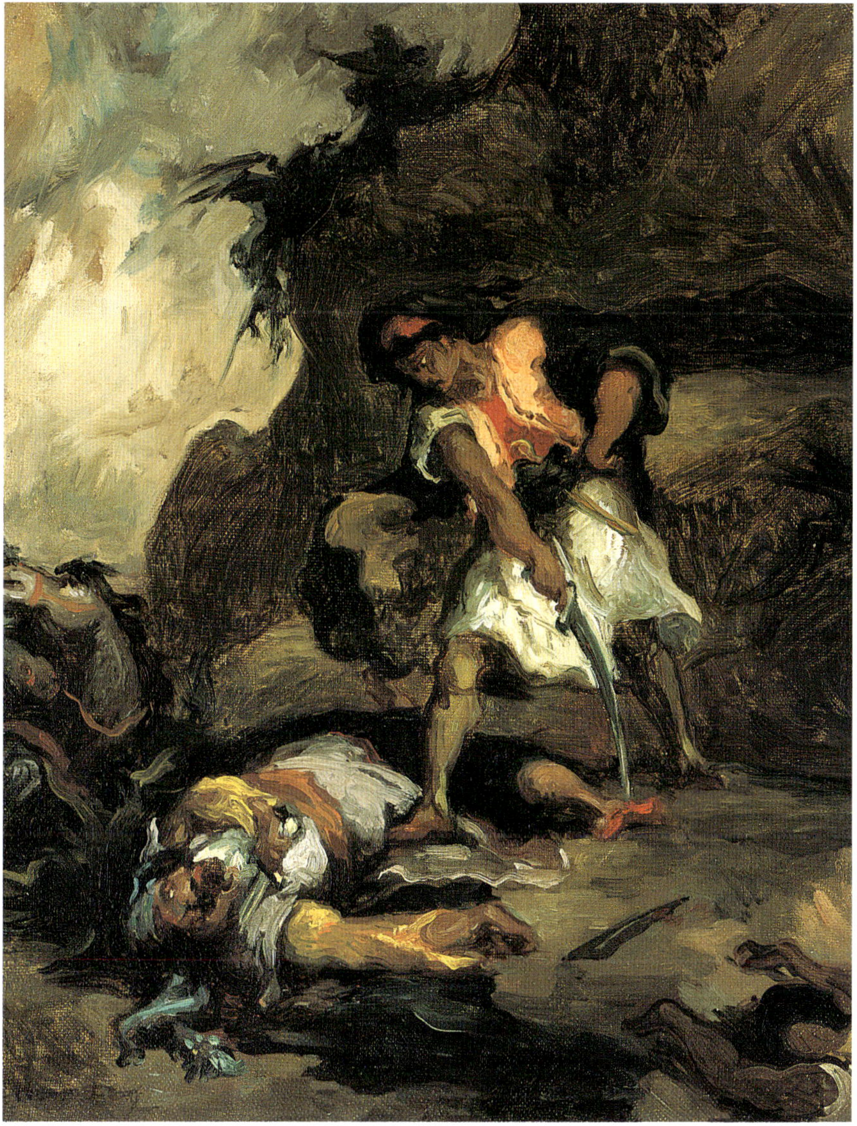

Lévy decided to pursue an artistic career as a history painter and, as a consequence, many of his works were conceived on a grand scale. The size and subject matter of his paintings caused Lévy to become heavily dependent on State patronage, particularly at the beginning of his career. In May 1865, he submitted a request to the government stating that he wished to paint historical subjects and return to literary sources. In the historical and biblical subjects that he chose, Lévy displayed a distinctive originality of conception. The subject matter of the present sketch has not been identified, but may well derive from an obscure historical or religious source.

The vivid coloring of this sketch, which recalls the work of Eugène Delacroix, is characteristic of Lévy's oeuvre and is a particularly striking feature of his preparatory sketches. Lévy's flair for color was remarked upon by his contemporaries. When commenting on *Joash Saved from the Massacre of Athaliah's Grandsons*, which was exhibited at the 1867 Salon and subsequently purchased by the State for the Musée d'Arras, the critic Paul Mantz stated that Lévy possessed "a true feeling of color," and noted that "probably what is appealing to us in his talent is the fact he shows his debt to Delacroix, quite a feat indeed on the part of a student of M. Picot" (Mantz 1867, p. 519).

In terms of both coloring and composition, the present sketch has parallels with other studies by Lévy. In the preparatory sketch *A Captive Hebrew Weeping over the Ruins of Jerusalem* (Nancy, Musée des Beaux-Arts; inv. 87.3.1), for example, the figures are blocked out simply in a similar way and are very freely painted, with lively use of dark reds and blues. There is an even closer parallel in Lévy's sketch of *Herodias* (Nancy, Musée des Beaux-Arts; inv. no. 71.1.1), which is displayed in its original, colorfully painted frame. This sketch has a similar drama and Eastern exoticism in the treatment of the subject. One of Lévy's most successful Salon exhibits of 1872, *Herodias* was praised for its brilliant color and was instrumental in establishing his reputation. The present sketch, with its drama, vigor of handling, and coloring, probably also dates to this period in Lévy's life, or shortly afterward, when he executed private commissions and decorative work with greater frequency.

J. R. B.

Jean-Joseph-Benjamin CONSTANT

(Toulouse 1845–Paris 1902)

Constant spent his childhood in Toulouse and studied at the Ecole des Beaux-Arts in his native town. In 1867 he was awarded an art scholarship and went to Paris, where he entered the atelier of Alexandre Cabanel. He made his Salon debut in 1869 with *Hamlet and the King*, then exhibited *Too Late* in 1870 and *Samson and Delilah* in 1872. A passionate admirer of Eugène Delacroix, Constant became interested in visiting the Orient, and in 1872 he went to Morocco. This had a decisive influence on his career, and he began to exhibit with great success Orientalist paintings such as *The Moroccan Prisoners* (Musée de Bordeaux) and *The Entrance of Mahomet II into Constantinople* (Musée de Toulouse). Constant then turned to decorative work, painting allegories of the Sciences and the Arts for the Sorbonne, which he exhibited at the Salon of 1888, and a ceiling in the Salle des Fêtes in the Hôtel de Ville, Paris, depicting *Paris Inviting the World to Her Fêtes* (Salon, 1892). Constant also painted the great ceiling of the Opéra-Comique in Paris and decorated the Capitole in Toulouse. He was a portraitist of some repute and worked a great deal in this genre after 1890. His portraits were particularly appreciated in England, where he often stayed, and Queen Victoria commissioned him to paint her portrait. Constant was a member of the Institut from 1893 and exhibited at the Royal Academy in London from 1896.

125 Jean-Joseph-Benjamin CONSTANT
The Death of Seneca, 1869
La Mort de Sénèque
Oil on canvas
12 ¾ × 16" (32.4 × 40.6 cm)
Inscribed on the back: *Esquisse de concours de Benjamin Constant à l'Ecole des Beaux-Arts en 1869*

Exhibitions: Peoria 1980, no. 11.

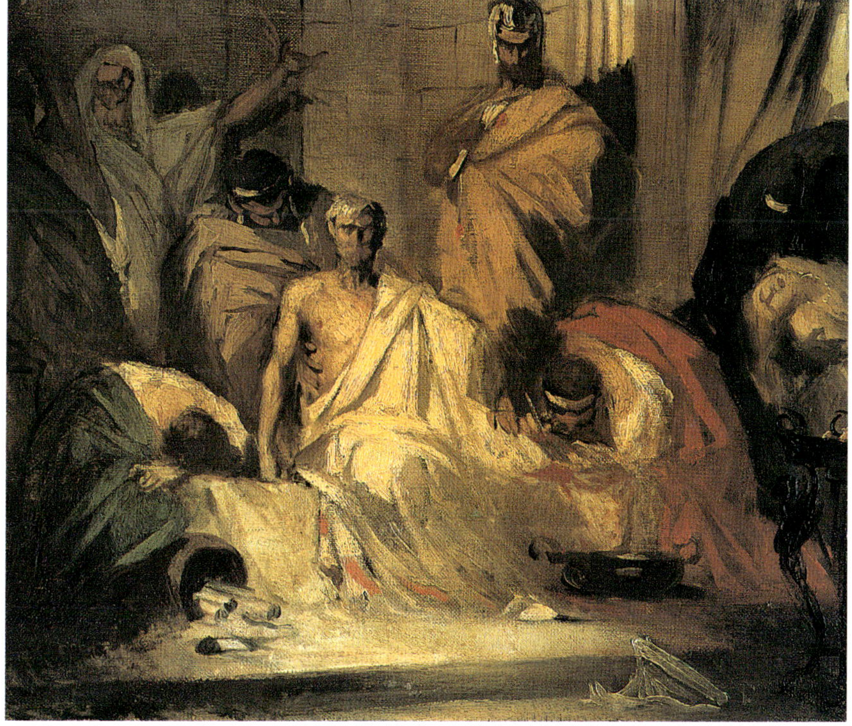

This study for *The Death of Seneca* was Constant's concours entry at the Ecole des Beaux-Arts in 1869. It is a very early work, still completely in the tradition of academic history painting. J. Murray Templeton, a former student in Constant's atelier, has commented that "during this time he scarcely attempted to produce any works of art, but those demanded by the Academy. To this most thorough training he attributes much of his later success." He groups Constant together with his friend Fernand Cormon and Pascal Dagnan-Bouveret as being outstanding artists of the period, because their academic training had given them a level of technical excellence that was a major influence on the following generation of artists (Templeton 1891, pp. 181–82).

The subject of the Death of Seneca had been frequently employed by history painters for over a century, because it had the elements required to create a "noble" composition. The death of the stoic philosopher, forced to commit suicide for allegedly participating in a conspiracy against the government, is sympathetically recounted in the *Annals* (15.64) of the Roman historian Tacitus. In the paintings of the subject, such as the present sketch, drama is created by Seneca, the epitome of calmness in the face of death, being used as a foil for the hysterical grieving of his wife, Pompeia Paulina.

The year in which this sketch was painted, 1869, marks the point at which Constant's career began to develop. He made his Salon debut in this year, with *Hamlet and the King* (Paris, Musée d'Orsay), which is recognized as the first composition to display his true artistic potential.

J.R.B.

Fernand-Anne-Piestre CORMON

(Paris 1845–Paris 1924)

$\mathcal{P}$upil of Alexandre Cabanel at the Ecole des Beaux-Arts from 1863 to 66, Cormon then attended the atelier of Portaels in Brussels and finally completed his studies in Paris with Eugène Fromentin. He made his Salon debut with *The Death of Mahomet* in 1863 and seven years later obtained a medal for a scene taken from the *Nibelungenlied*. Cormon then exhibited every year until his death and was one of the most successful painters of his generation. Among the most famous of the works he exhibited are *Cain* of 1880, *The Age of Stone* of 1884, and *The Conquerors of Salamis* of 1887, for which he received the Medal of Honor. In 1906, he exhibited the cartoon for a tapestry for the town of Bourges, which represented Duc Jean de Berry buying works of art. Cormon executed a great many decorative paintings, including a ceiling and wall panels for the Museum d'Histoire Naturelle in Paris, six murals for the Hôtel de Ville in the IVe *arrondissement* of Paris, and in 1902 the Salle des Mariages of the Hôtel de Ville in Tours. Cormon also painted six murals of the Châteaux of France for the French Embassy in Berlin, and the history of Paris was his inspiration for the three ceilings and ten murals executed for the Petit Palais. In addition, Cormon was a respected portraitist; the painters Lehoux and Gérôme and the sculptor Ernest Carrier-Belleuse were among his sitters. He was a member of the Institut and a professor at the Ecole des Beaux-Arts. His most famous pupil was Henri de Toulouse-Lautrec.

126 Fernand-Anne-Piestre CORMON
Two Figures from the Tribe of Cain, 1880
Deux Figures de la tribu de Caïn
Oil on canvas
31 ¼ × 14 ¼" (79.4 × 36.2 cm)
Signed lower left: *FC*

Provenance: Family of the artist.

Exhibitions: Peoria 1980, no. 12.

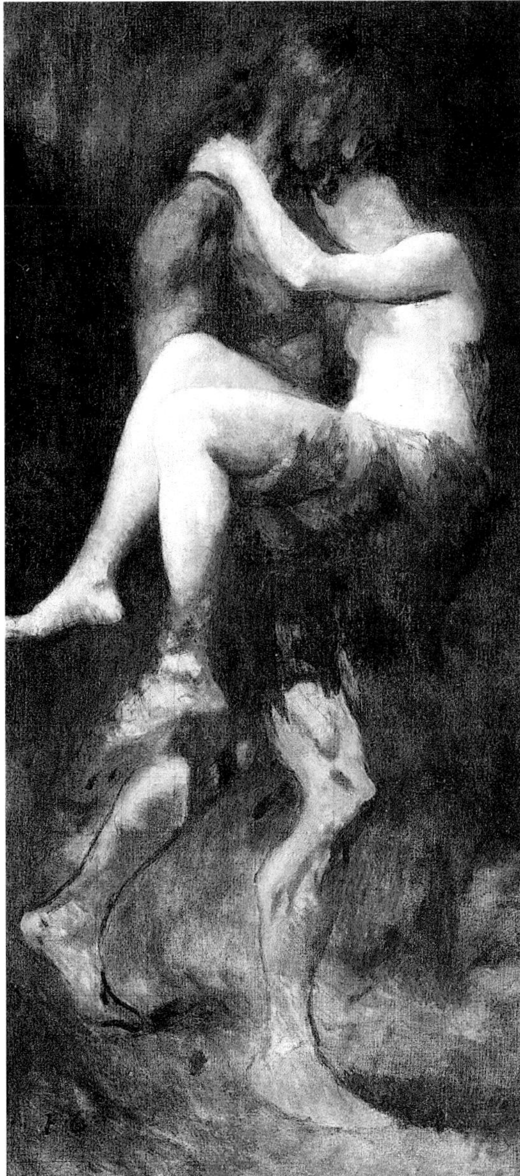

This is a preparatory sketch for two figures from one of Cormon's most important works, *Cain*, which is now in the Musée d'Orsay, Paris (R.F.280). The final painting illustrates an imaginary biblical episode developed from Genesis 4:16 in which the murderer Cain, who had been cast out with his tribe, wandered through the desert, before finally settling in the land of Nod, east of Eden. The desert setting, and indeed the composition as a whole, reflect the work of Cormon's most influential teacher, Eugène Fromentin. In the 1880 Salon *livret*, Cormon quoted three lines from Victor Hugo's *La Légende des siècles* (1859), which elaborates upon the biblical story and the first awakening of human conscience. The massive canvas of *Cain*, which is over one meter wide, dominated the 1880 Salon and, with *The Age of Stone* (1880–84, Château de Saint-Germain-en-Laye), was to establish Cormon's reputation as a history painter.

In this sketch, a swarthy tribesman roughly clad in animal skins carries an exhausted woman. In the final painting these two figures, which are on the left-hand side of the main retinue, are slightly obscured by the figure of a male hunter. The decision to treat this episode with "willful crudeness" and to place it in a prehistoric context is likely to have been influenced by Darwin and contemporary scientific investigation. Robert Rosenblum has further pointed out that Cormon's inspiration may derive from the discovery of the Paleolithic cave paintings of Altamira in Spain in 1879 (1989, p. 388). Cormon was noted for his interest in the prehistoric age, and his work in this area culminated in the decorative scheme, based on the evolution of mankind, which he executed for the Museum d'Histoire Naturelle in Paris in 1898.

The earth colors and fluent, yet rough brushwork apparent in this sketch are retained in the final painting. Cormon was criticized at the time for the coarseness of his style, which was a departure from the traditional highly finished technique, but nonetheless adds to the primeval ruggedness of the painting.

J.R.B.

Jacques-Emile BLANCHE

(Paris 1861–Offranville 1942)

The son of a doctor of psychiatry, Blanche spent most of the holidays in Dieppe. He first studied art with the history painter Mélicourt, president of the Société des Amis des Arts, and then entered the atelier of Gervex, whom he helped to paint the Hôtel de Ville at La Villette. Following this he worked with Humbert on the Panthéon and also studied with Edouard Manet. Around 1882, he went to London with Whistler and developed a lasting friendship with the latter's pupil, Walter Sickert. Blanche turned to portraiture early in his life: Doctor Blanche (1885), the writer Francis Poictevin (1887), and Marcel Proust (1889) were among the first of his eminent sitters. Rejected from the Salon des Artistes Français, Blanche was a member of the Salon de la Société National des Beaux-Arts from its foundation. He also organized a Salon at the Galerie Georges-Petit in Paris, where he exhibited with his friends. In 1896, Blanche had his first great public success with *The Painter Fritz Thaulow and His Family* (Musée d'Art Moderne de la Ville de Paris). From 1904, Blanche spent part of the year in London. He painted *Queen Alexandra* and portraits of members of the English aristocracy, as well as landscapes, and his series of views of London is particularly noteworthy. He had a great interest in music and the Russian ballet, and his studio at Auteuil was a gathering place for artists, musicians, and writers. His portraits of these visitors include James Joyce (1902), Claude Debussy (1902), Auguste Rodin (1904), Igor Stravinsky (1915), and Paul Valéry (1922). Blanche was one of the founders of the Salon des Tuileries, in which he participated from 1933 until 1939. He was also a prolific author, whose works include *Cahiers d'un artiste, 1915-19*, *Propos de peintres, 1919-28*, and *Mes Modèles: Souvenirs littéraires* of 1928. Blanche's abundant oeuvre is comprised of portraits, English and French landscapes, and still lifes. He is represented in many European and American collections, but the largest number of his works is in the Musée de Rouen.

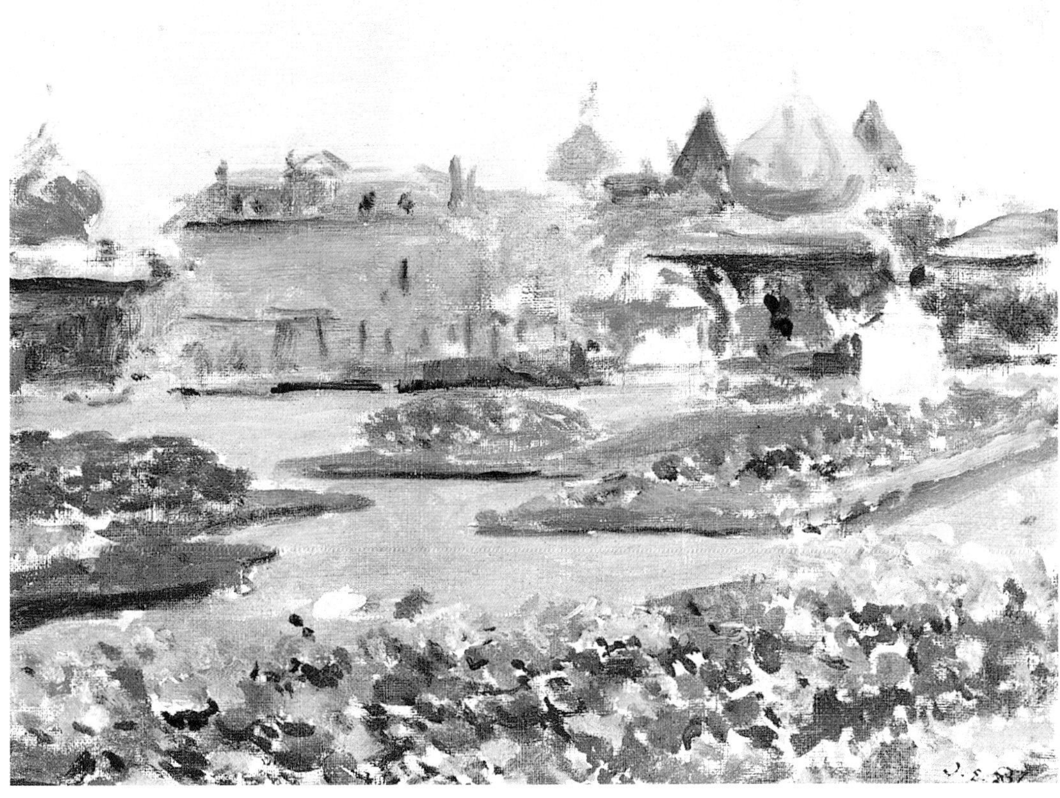

127 Jacques-Emile BLANCHE
View of Brighton (?), n.d.
Vue de Brighton (?)
Oil on canvas
10 ⅜ × 13 ¾" (27.0 × 34.9 cm)
Signed with monogram lower left: *J.E.BL*

Considered one of the society painters par excellence of the late nineteenth and early twentieth centuries, Jacques-Emile Blanche had almost a dual nationality, dividing his time between Dieppe and London, where he had a studio in Knightsbridge. He moved in influential intellectual and cultural circles. He not only worked in London, but also in other towns such as Peterborough, Epsom, and particularly Brighton, which he found stimulating as the English equivalent of Dieppe.

Blanche was a close friend of the British impressionist Walter Sickert and was himself a disciple of Edouard Manet. This colorful impressionistic sketch is typical of his scenes of the fashionable Victorian and Edwardian seaside resort. His other Brightonian views include the beach, the promenade, and the fish market.

This attractive sketch may be based on a view of Brighton with the domes of the Royal Pavilion in the background and is almost certainly executed from memory. Painting scenes from memory, and not on the spot, was a practice that Blanche shared with Sickert.

Blanche sometimes signed his work fully, but often with his very sketchy compositions such as this, he would just add a monogram. The form of signature on this canvas was one that Blanche appears to have used most frequently between 1933 and 1935.

J.R.B.

Bibliography

ACKERMAN, G. *The Life and Work of Jean-Léon Gérôme.* London and New York, 1990.

"Actes du colloque international: Ingres et son influence." *Bulletin spécial des amis du Musée Ingres.* Montauban, 1980.

ADHEMAR, H. "Autour de quelques oeuvres inédites de Delobel." *Gazette des beaux-arts*, vol. 49 (March 1957), pp. 175–77.

ANANOFF, A. *François Boucher.* 2 vols. Lausanne and Paris, 1976.

ANTAL, F. "Reflections on Classicism and Romanticism." *The Burlington Magazine*, vol. 66 (1935).

AULANIER, C. *Histoire du Palais et du Musée du Louvre.* 10 vols. Paris, 1947–68.

AXELETTE, J. A. "François Casanova." Unpublished thesis, Paris, Ecole du Louvre, 1929.

BACHAUMONT, L. PETIT DE. "Jugement de Bachaumont sur l'exposition de 1763." Manuscript, Paris, Bibliothèque Nationale, Fonds Deloynes, vol. 8, no. 104.

BATOWSKI, Z. *Podroze artystyczne Jana Christjana Kamsetzera, 1776–1782.* Cracow, 1935.

BATOWSKI, N. and Z.; KWIATWOWSKI, M.; KAMSETZER, J. C.; *Architekt Stanislawa Augusta.* Warsaw, 1978.

BAUDELAIRE, C. *Curiosites esthétiques: L'Art romantique et autres oeuvres critiques.* Paris, [Garnier ed.], 1962.

BAUDICOUR, P. DE. *Le Peintre-graveur français continué.* 2 vols. Paris, 1859–1861.

BEAN, J., with the assistance of L. Turcic. *15th–18th Century French Drawings in The Metropolitan Museum of Art.* New York, 1986.

BELLIER DE LA CHAVIGNERIE, E., and AUVRAY, L. *Dictionnaire général des artistes de l'école française.* 5 vols. Paris, 1882-1887.

BOIME, A. *Thomas Couture and the Eclectic Vision.* New Haven and London, 1980.

BOINET, A. *Les Eglises parisiennes*, vol. 3. Paris, 1964.

BOPPE, A. *Les Peintres du Bosphore au XVIIIe siècle.* New ed., Paris, 1989.

BORDES, P. *Le Serment du Jeu de Paume de Jacques-Louis David.* Paris, 1983.

BORDES, P., and MICHEL, R., eds. *Aux armes et aux arts! Les arts de la Révolution, 1789–1799.* Paris, 1988.

BROOKNER, A. *Jacques-Louis David.* New York, 1980.

BUROLLET, T. *Musée Cognacq-Jay: Peintures et dessins.* Paris, 1980.

CARACCIOLO, M. T. "La malinconia settecentesca." *Antologia di belle arti*, nos. 39–42 (1991–92), pp. 5–16.

CHENNEVIERES, H. DE. "Histoire d'un tableau de Carle Vanloo, les grâces enchaînes par l'Amour (1761–1762)." *Nouvelles Archives de l'Art Français*, 3rd series, vol. 2, 1886, pp. 101–05, 122–25.

CHOMER, G. "Le peintre Pierre-Charles Le Mettay (1726–1759)." *Bulletin de la Société de l'Histoire de l'Art Français*, 1981, pp. 81–102.

CLOUGH, A. H. *Plutarch's "Lives," the Translation Called Dryden's.* London, 1893.

CUZIN, J. P. *Fragonard: Life and Work.* New York, 1988.

———. "Vincent reconstitué." *Connaissance des arts*, no. 409 (March 1986), pp. 38–47.

———. "Esquisses de Vincent dans les musées français." *Revue du Louvre et des Musées de France*, vol. 30, no. 2 (1980), pp. 80–87.

DACIER, E. *Catalogue des ventes et livrets de Salons illustrés par Gabriel de Saint-Aubin*, vols. 1, 2. Paris, 1909.

DAUD-BOVY, D., and BOISSONAS, F. *Peintres genevois, 1702–1817, Première série.* Geneva, 1903.

DAVOUST, E. *Le Comte de Bizemont, artiste-amateur orleanais: Son Oeuvre et ses collections.* Orléans, 1891.

DELESTRE, J. B. *Gros et ses ouvrages.* 2nd ed., Paris, 1867.

DEZALLIER D'ARGENVILLE, A. N., *Explication et critique impartiale . . . de toutes les peintures . . . exposées au Louvre.* Paris, 1791.

DUPONT de NEMOURS, P. S. "Lettres sur les Salons de 1773, 1777 et 1779 adressées par Du Pont de Nemours à la Margave Caroline-Louise de Bade." *Archives de l'Art Français*, nouvelle période, vol. 2 (1908), pp. 1–123.

DUSSIEUX, L.; SOULIE, E.; CHENNEVIERES, PH. DE; MANTZ, P.; and MONTAIGLON, A. DE. *Mémoires inédits sur la vie et les ouvrages des membres de l'Académie Royale de peinture et de sculpture publiés d'après les manuscrits conservés à l'Ecole Imperiale des Beaux-Arts.* 2 vols. Paris, 1854, 1856.

ENGERAND, F. *Inventaire des tableaux commandés et achetés par la Direction des Bâtiments du Roi, 1709–1792.* Paris, 1901.

EWALS, L. "Ary Scheffer: Sa Vie et son oeuvre." Unpublished thesis, University of Nijmegen, 1986.

———. "La carrière d'Ary Scheffer, ses envois aux Salons parisiens." See Paris 1980; pp. 6–31.

FARMER, D. H. *The Oxford Dictionary of Saints.* Oxford, 1978.

FLANDRIN, L. *Hippolyte Flandrin: Sa Vie et son oeuvre.* Paris, 1902.

FLORISOONE, M. *La Peinture française: Le Dix-huitième siècle.* Paris, 1948.

FOUCART, B. *Le renouveau de la peinture religieuse en France, 1800–1860.* Paris, 1987.

FOUQUIER, A. *L. Bonnat: Première partie de sa vie et ses oeuvres.* Paris, 1879.

GAETHGENS, T., and LUGAND, J. *Joseph-Marie Vien, peintre du Roi (1716–1809).* Paris, 1988.

GASTON, J., "Les Images de confréries parisiennes avant la Révolution," Paris, 1910. *Société d'Iconographie Parisienne*, vol. 2. Paris, 1910.

GASTON-DREYFUS, P. "Catalogue raisonné de l'oeuvre de Nicolas-Bernard Lépicié." *Bulletin de la Société de l'Histoire de l'Art Français*, 1922 (1923), pp. 134–283.

GAUTHIER, M. *Achille et Eugène Devéria.* Paris, 1925.

GERARD, H. *Lettres adressées au baron François Gérard, peintre d'histoire, par les artistes et les personnages célèbres de son temps.* Paris, 1886.

———. *L'Oeuvre du Baron Gérard.* Paris, 1857.

GONCOURT, E. and J. DE. "Le Salon de 1852, la peinture à l'exposition de 1855." In *Etudes d'art.* Paris, 1893.

GREARD, M. O. *Meissonier.* Paris, 1897.

HORAIST, B. "Hippolyte Flandrin à Saint-Germain-des-Prés." *Bulletin de la Société de l'Histoire de l'Art Français.* Paris, 1979.

JAMOT, P. "Carpeaux peintre et graveur." *Gazette des beaux-arts*, 40 (1908), p. 194.

KOLB, M. *Ary Scheffer et son temps (1795–1858).* Paris, 1937.

LAMI, S. *Dictionnaire des sculptures de l'ecole française.* Paris, 1916.

LANDON, C. P. *Annales du Musée et de l'Ecole Moderne Beaux-Arts.* Paris, 1822

LANVIN, C. "Hippolyte Flandrin." 3 vols. Unpublished thesis, Paris, Ecole du Louvre, 1967.

LASTIC, G. DE. "Les 'Grâces' de Carle Vanloo." *Bulletin de la Société de l'Histoire de l'Art Français*, 1973, pub. 1974, pp. 193–98.

LEE, V. "Jacques-Louis David: The Versailles Sketchbook, II." *The Burlington Magazine*, vol. 3 (June 1969) pp. 360 ff.

LENOIR, A. "Cabinet du feu Regnault." *Journal des artistes et des amateurs*, January 10, 1830.

LENORMANT, C. *François Gérard, peintre d'histoire.* Paris, 1847.

LOSSKY, B. "Leonardo da Vinci mourant dans les bras de François Ier." *Bulletin de l'Association Léonardo da Vinci*, 55 (1967).

MACLER, F. *Histoire d'Heraclius par l'évêque Sebeos.* Paris, 1904.

MANTZ, P. "Salon de 1867," *Gazette des Beaux-Arts*, vol. 22, pp. 513–58.

MARANDEL, J. P. "The Death of Camille: Guillaume Guillon-Lethière and the 1785 Prix de Rome." *Antologia di belle arti*, vol. 4, nos. 13–14 (1980), pp. 12–17.

———. "Pour Charles-François Eustache (1820–1870)." *L'Oeil*, no. 267 (October 1977), pp. 28–33.

MARCEL, P. "Une 'Vie de saint Benoit' de Louis de Silvestre et Louis Galloche." *La Chronique des arts et de la curiosité*, March 19, 1904, pp. 95–97.

MARIETTE, P. J. *Abecedario de P. J. Mariette et autres notes inédités de cet amateur sur les arts et les artistes.* Published by Ph. de Chennevieres and A. de Montaiglon. 6 vols. Paris, 1853–54.

MARMOTTAN, P. *Le Peintre Louis Boilly (1761–1845).* Paris, 1913.

MARRIMAN, M. *Painting Politics for Louis-Philippe: Art and Ideology in Orléanist France, 1830–1840.* New Haven, 1987.

McCORMICK, T. J. *Charles-Louis Clerisseau and the Genesis of Neo-Classicism.* New York, 1990.

MIQUEL, P. *Eugène Isabey (1803–1886): La Marine au XIX siecle.* Paris, 1980.

———. *Félix Ziem (1821–1911).* 2 vols. Maurs-la-Jolie, 1978.

MONTAIGLON, A. DE. *Procès-verbaux de l'Académie Royale de peinture et de sculpture, 1648–1793, d'après les registres originaux conservés à l'Ecole des Beaux-Arts.* Paris, 1875–1892.

MONTGOLFIER, B. DE. "Deux suites de peintures sur la vie de Saint Benoit: Essai de regroupement." *Bulletin des Musées Royaux des Beaux-Arts* (Brussels), nos. 3–4 (July–December 1962), pp. 285–304.

Monvoisin. Essays by Guillermo Feliu Cruz, Waldo Vila Silva, Eugenio Pereira Salas, Antonio R. Romera. Santiago: Universidad de Chile, Instituto de Extension de Artes Plasticas, n.d.

NAGLER, G. K. *Neues allgemeines Künstler Lexikon.* Munich, 1845.

NICLAUSSE, J. *Tapisseries et tapis de la Ville de Paris.* Paris, 1948.

OLANDER, W. "Pour transmettre à la postérité: French Painting and Revolution, 1774–1795." Unpublished Ph.D. dissertation, New York, Institute of Fine Arts, 1983.

OURSEL, H. *Musée des Beaux-Arts de Lille: Acquisitions nouvelles.* Lille, 1971.

OVID. *Metamorphoses.* Translated by Frank Justus Miller. 2 vols. London, 1925.

PAILLET, A. *Catalogue des tableaux, dessins sous verre et en feuilles etc., composant le Cabinet et les Etudes de feu Joseph-Marie Vien.* Paris, 1809.

PASSEZ, A. M. *Adelaïde Labille-Guiard: Biographie et catalogue raisonné de son oeuvre.* Paris, 1973.

Peintures: Ecole francaise XIX siècle. Paris, 1961.

PELLICER, M. L. "Le Peintre Francis-Xavier Fabre (1766–1837)." Unpublished thesis, Paris, Université de Paris IV, 1982.

PEREZ, M. F. "Tableaux de N.-G. Brenet (1728–1792) conservés dans la région lyonnaise." *Bulletin de la Société de l'Histoire de l'Art Français*, 1973, pp. 199–212.

PIGLER, A., *Barockthemen.* 3 vols. New ed., Budapest, 1974.

PLUTARCH, *The Lives of the Noble Grecians and Romans.* Translated by John Dryden. New York, n.d.

PORTALIS, Baron R. *Henry-Pierre Danloux, peintre de portraits et son journal* durant l'Emigration (1755–1809). Paris, 1910.

PRAZ, M. Conversation Pieces. University Park, Md., and London, 1971.

REAU, L. "Carle Vanloo (1705–1765)." Archives de l'Art Français, nouvelle période, vol. 19 (1938), pp. 7–96.

———. "La Décoration de l'Hôtel Grimod de la Reynière d'après les dessins de l'architecte polonais Kamsetzer." Bulletin de la Société de l'Histoire de l'Art Français, Fascicule I, 1937, pp. 7–17.

REIMERS, H. C. VON. L'Académie Impériale des Beaux-Arts à St. Petersbourg depuis son origine jusqu'au règue d'Alexandre I en 1807. St. Petersburg, 1807.

ROLLE, F., and MONTAIGLON, A. DE. Procès verbaux de l'Académie. 10 vols. Paris, 1875–92.

ROSENBERG, P. "Le XVIIIe siècle français à la Royal Academy," Revue de l'Art, no. 3 (1969), pp. 98–100.

ROSENBERG, P., and SCHNAPPER, A. "Beaufort's Brutus." The Burlington Magazine, vol. 112 (November 1970), p. 760.

ROSENBLUM, R. Paintings in the Musée d'Orsay. New York, 1989.

———. "A Source for David's 'Horatii.'" The Burlington Magazine, vol. 112 (May 1970), pp. 269–75.

———. Transformations in Late Eighteenth-Century Art. Princeton, 1967.

———. "Gavin Hamilton's 'Brutus' and Its Aftermath." The Burlington Magazine, vol. 113 (January 1961), pp. 8–16.

RUCH, J. E. "An Album of Early Drawings by François Boucher." The Burlington Magazine, vol. 106 (November 1964).

RUIZ, J. C. Le Grand Siècle en pays de Meaux. Meaux, 1982.

———. "Quatre scènes de la vie de Saint Martin par Jean Senelle." Bulletin de la Société des Amis de Bossuet. Meaux, 1980, pp. 5–13.

SANDOZ, M. Jean-Baptiste Deshays (1729–1765). Paris, 1979.

———. Nicolas-Guy Brenet, 1728–1792, Paris, 1979.

———. Gabriel-François Doyen (1726–1806). Paris, 1975.

———. "The Drawings of Gabriel-François Doyen (1726–1806)." The Art Quarterly, vol. 34, no. 2 (1971), pp. 149–80.

———. "Précisions sur les peintures éxécutées en Russie par Gabriel-François Doyen." In Actes du Congrès International d'Histoire de l'Art. Budapest, 1969, pp. 84–99.

———. "Etudes et esquisses peintes ou dessinées de Jean-Baptiste Deshays (1721–1765)." Gazette des beaux-arts, April–June 1951 [published 1960], pp. 129–46.

SCHAMA, S. Citizens: A Chronicle of the French Revolution. New York, 1989.

SCHIAVO, A. The Altieri Palace. Rome, 1962.

SCHLEIER, E. "Two New Modelli for Vouet's St. Peter Altarpiece." The Burlington Magazine, vol. 114, no. 827 (February 1972), pp. 91–92.

———. "Vouet's Destroyed St. Peter Altarpiece: Further Evidence." The Burlington Magazine, vol. 110, no. 787 (October 1968), pp. 573–74.

———. "A Bozzetto by Vouet, Not by Lanfranco." The Burlington Magazine, vol. 109, no. 770 (May 1967), pp. 272–75.

SCHNAPPER, A. "A New Parrocel at the Picker Art Gallery." Colgate University, Picker Art Gallery, Annual Report and Bulletin, 1985–86, pp. 8–17.

———. Jean Jouvenet (1644–1717) et la peinture d'histoire à Paris. Paris, 1974.

———. "Deux tableaux de Joseph Parrocel au Musée de Rouen." Revue du Louvre et des Musées de France. vol. 20, no. 2 (1970), pp. 78–82.

———. "Quelques oeuvres de Joseph Parrocel." Revue des arts, nos. 4–5 (1959), pp. 163–76.

SEELIG, L. "Tableaux des néo-classicismes français et belge de la Résidence de Coblence." Revue de l'art, no. 87 (1990), pp. 52–58.

SELLS, C. "Esquisses de J.-B. Regnault." Revue du Louvre et des Musées de France. vol. 24, no. 6 (1974), pp. 405–10.

SEZNEC, J., ed. Diderot: Salons, Volume 4, 1769, 1771, 1775, 1781. Oxford, 1967.

———. Diderot: Salons de 1759, 1761, 1765. Paris, 1967.

———. Diderot: Salons, Volume 3, 1767. Oxford, 1963.

SUSLOV, A. V. Zimnĭ dvoretz . . . [The Winter Palace (1754–1927), a historical sketch]. Leningrad, 1928.

STRYIENSKI, C. Une Carrière d'artiste au XIXe siècle, Charles Landelle. Paris, 1911.

TEMPLETON, J. M. The Magazine of Art. New York, 1891, pp. 181–82.

TRIPIER-LE-FRANC, J. Histoire de la vie et de la mort du baron Gros. Paris 1880.

VILAIN, J. "Une Esquisse de Jean-François de Troy au Musée de Lille." La Revue du Louvre, no. 6 (1971), pp. 353–56.

WARK, R. R. French Decorative Art in the Huntington Collection. San Marino, 1962.

WEIGERT, R.-A. "Documents inédits sur Louis de Silvestre (1675–1760) suivis du catalogue de son oeuvre in L'Art français dans les pays du Nord et de l'Est de l'Europe (XVIIIe-XIXe siècles)." Archives de l'art français, nouvelle période, vol. 17 (1932), pp. 361–488.

WILLK-BROCARD, N. François-Guillaume Ménageot (1744–1816), peintre d'histoire. Paris, 1978.

ZIESENISS, O. "Un Portrait du Maréchal Ney au Musée de Versailles." La Revue du Louvre, vol. 12, no. 1 (1962), p. 28.

Exhibitions

ALBUQUERQUE 1980 *French Eighteenth-Century Oil Sketches from an English Collection*. Albuquerque, New Mexico Art Museum, March 2–April 20, 1980. Catalogue by Peter Walch, published in *New Mexico Studies in the Fine Arts*, 5, 1980.

BREMEN 1973 *Catalogue of Nineteenth and Twentieth Century Paintings*. Bremen, 1973.

CHAPEL HILL 1978 *French Nineteenth-Century Oil Sketches: David to Degas*. Chapel Hill, Ackland Art Museum, University of North Carolina, March 5–April 16, 1978. Catalogue by John Minor Wisdom.

COLUMBIA/ROCHESTER/SANTA BARBARA 1989–90 *The Art of the July Monarchy: France, 1830–1848*. Columbia, Museum of Art and Archaeology, University of Missouri, October 21–December 3, 1989; Rochester, Memorial Art Gallery of the University of Rochester, January 21–March 12, 1990; The Santa Barbara Museum of Art, March 31–May 20, 1990. Catalogue by Robert J. Bezucha, Michael Paul Driskel, Patricia Condon, Gabriel P. Weisberg, and Petra Ten-Doesschate Chu.

DUNKERQUE/VALENCIENNES/LILLE 1980 *Trésors des Musées du Nord de la France, IV: La Peinture française aux XVIIe et XVIIIe siècles*.

GRENOBLE/RENNES/BORDEAUX, 1989–90 *Laurent de La Hyre (1606–1656)*. Grenoble, Musée des Beaux-Arts, January 14–April 30, 1989; Rennes, Musée des Beaux-Arts, May 9–August 31, 1989; Bordeaux, Musée des Beaux-Arts, October 6, 1989–January 6, 1990. Catalogue by Pierre Rosenberg and Jacques Thuillier.

HOUSTON 1973–75 *French Oil Sketches from an English Collection: Seventeenth, Eighteenth, and Ninenteenth Centuries*. Houston, The Museum of Fine Arts. Also shown at the Indianapolis Museum of Art; Louisville, J. B. Speed Art Museum; Providence, Museum of Art, Rhode Island School of Design; Madison, Elvejhem Art Center; University Art Gallery, State University of New York at Binghamton; Jacksonville, Cummer Gallery of Art; and Minneapolis Institute of Arts. Catalogue by J. Patrice Marandel.

LILLE 1988–89 *Boilly 1761–1845: Un Grand Peintre français de la révolution à la restauration*. Lille, Musée des Beaux Arts, 1988–89.

LONDON 1993 *Tradition and Revolution in French Art, 1700–1800*. London, National Gallery.

LONDON 1981 *Painting from Nature*. London, Arts Council, Royal Academy of Arts.

LONDON 1979 *A Selection of French Paintings and Drawings*. London, Adrian Ward-Jackson, Summer 1979.

LONDON 1978 *Forgotten French Art from the First to the Second Empire*. London, Heim Gallery, November 23–December 22, 1978.

LONDON 1977 *Aspects of French Academic Art, 1680–1780*. London, Heim Gallery, Summer Exhibition, 1977.

LONDON 1975 *French Drawings: Neo-Classicism*. London, Heim Gallery, February 20–March 27, 1975.

LONDON 1972 *The Age of Neo-Classicism: Fourteenth Exhibition of the Council of Europe*. London, The Royal Academy and the Victoria and Albert Museum, September 9–November 19, 1972.

LONDON 1968 *France in the Eighteenth Century*. London, The Royal Academy, 1968. Catalogue by Denys Sutton.

LYON 1993 *Ernest Meissonier Retrospective*. Lyon, Musée des Beaux-Arts de Lyon, March 25–June 27, 1993.

MEAUX 1989 *De Nicolo dell'Abate à Nicolas Poussin: Aux sources du classicisme, 1550–1650*. Meaux, Musée Bossuet, November 19, 1988–February 28, 1989.

MONTARGIS 1989 *Un Peintre sous la Révolution: Charles-Nicaise Perrin (1754–1831)*. Montargis, Musée Girodet, June 25–September 15, 1989. Catalogue by Sylvain Bellenger and Régis Michel.

NANTES/LAUSANNE/ROME 1985 *Les Frères Sablet: dipinti, disegni, incisioni, 1775–1815*. Nantes, Musées Départementaux de la Loire-Atlantique, January 4–March 10, 1985; Lausanne, Musée Cantonal des Beaux-Arts, March 29–May 12 1985; Rome, Museo di Roma, Palazzo Braschi, May 21–June 30, 1985. Catalogue by Jean-Pierre Cuzin, Erika Billeter, Maria Elisa Tittoni Monti, and Anne Van de Sandt.

NEW YORK 1992 *Baron François Gérard*. Galerie Arnoldi-Livie-Jill Newhouse, New York, April 1992.

NEW YORK 1990 *Master Drawings, 1760–1880*. New York, W. M. Brady & Co., Inc., 1990.

NEW YORK 1989 *1789: French Art During the Revolution*. New York, Colnaghi's, October 10–November 22, 1989. Catalogue edited by Alan Wintermute.

NEW YORK/DETROIT/PARIS 1986–87 *François Boucher 1703–1770*. New York, The Metropolitan Museum of Art, February 17–May 4, 1986; The Detroit Institute of Arts, May 27–August 17, 1986; Paris, Réunion des Musées Nationaux, Grand Palais, September 19, 1986–January 5, 1987. Catalogue by A. Laing, with contributions by Pierre Rosenberg, J. Patrice Marandel, Edith A. Standen, and Antoinette Faÿ-Hallé.

NEW YORK/NEW ORLEANS/COLUMBUS 1985–86 *The First Painters of the King: French Royal Taste from Louis XIV to the Revolution*. New York, Stair Sainty Matthiesen, October 16–November 22, 1985; New Orleans Museum of Art, December 10, 1985–January 19, 1986; Columbus Museum of Art, February 8–March 26, 1986. Catalogue by Colin B. Bailey.

NEW YORK 1980 *Christian Imagery in French Nineteenth Century Art, 1789–1906*. New York, Shepherd Gallery, Spring 1980. Catalogue edited by Martin H. Reymert and Robert J. F. Kashey.

NEW YORK 1979 *Nineteenth-Century French and Other Continental Drawings, Watercolors and Oil Sketches*. New York, Shepherd Gallery, 1979.

NICE/CLERMONT/FERRAND/NANCY 1977 *Carle Vanloo, premier peintre du Roi (Nice, 1705–Paris, 1765)*. Nice, Musée

Cheret, January 21–March 13, 1977; Clermont-Ferrand, Musée Bargoin, April 1–May 30, 1977; Nancy, Musée des Beaux-Arts, June 18–August 15, 1977. Catalogue by M.-C. Sahut.

ORLEANS 1990 *Léon Cogniet (1794–1880)*. Orléans, Musée des Beaux-Arts, June 14–September 10, 1990. Catalogue by David Ojalvo and Françoise Demange.

PARIS 1991–92 *Images de confrèries parisiennes*. Paris, Bibliothèque Historique de la Ville de Paris, Hôtel d'Angoulême-Lamoignon, December 18, 1991–March 7, 1992. Catalogue by Jose Lothe and Agnes Virole.

PARIS 1991 *Maîtres anciens et du XIXe siècle*. Presented by Bruno Dijol at Galerie William Foucault, Paris, March 20–April 20, 1991.

PARIS 1990–91 *Vouet*. Paris, Galeries Nationales du Grand-Palais, November 6, 1990–February 11, 1991. Catalogue by Jacques Thuillier, Barbara Brejon de Lavergnée, and Denis Lavalle.

PARIS 1990 *Acquisitions, 1984–1989: 96e Exposition du Cabinet des dessins*. Paris, Musée du Louvre, May 31–August 27, 1990.

PARIS 1989–90 *Jacques-Louis David (1748–1825)*. Paris, Musée du Louvre and Musée National du Château, Versailles, October 26, 1989–February 12, 1990. Catalogue by Antoine Schnapper, Arlette Serullaz, Lina Propeck, and Elisabeth Agius-d'Yvoire.

PARIS/ROME 1987 *Subleyras 1699–1749*. Paris, Musée du Luxembourg, February 20–April 26, 1987; Rome, Académie de France, Villa Medicis, May 18–July 19, 1987. Catalogue by Olivier Michel and Pierre Rosenberg.

PARIS 1984–85 *Diderot et l'art de Boucher à David: Les Salons, 1759–1781*. Paris, Hôtel de la Monnaie, October 5, 1984–January 6, 1985. Catalogue by Marie-Catherine Sahut and Nathalie Volle.

PARIS/LYON 1984–85 *Hippolyte, Auguste et Paul Flandrin: Une Fraternité picturale au XIXe siècle*. Paris, Musée du Luxembourg, November 16, 1984–February 10, 1985;

Lyon, Musée des Beaux-Arts, March 5–May 19, 1985. Catalogue by Jacques Foucart, Bruno Foucart, and others.

PARIS 1980 *Ary Scheffer (1795–1858): Dessins, aquarelles, esquisses à l'huile*. Paris, Institut Neerlandais, October 16–November 30, 1980. Catalogue by Jan Jaap Heij, Leo Ewals, and J. M. de Groot.

PARIS 1979 *Jacques Gamelin (1738–1803)*. Paris, Galerie Joseph Hahn, May 16–June 30, 1979. Catalogue by O. Michel and G. Sarraute.

PARIS/CLEVELAND/BOSTON 1979, *Chardin (1699–1779)*. Paris, Grand Palais, January 29–April, 30, 1979; Cleveland Museum of Art, June 6–August 12, 1979; Museum of Fine Arts Boston, September 18–November 19, 1979. Catalogue by Pierre Rosenberg.

PARIS/DETROIT/NEW YORK 1974–75 *De David à Delacroix, La Peinture française de 1774 à 1830*. Paris, Grand Palais, November 16, 1974–February 3, 1975; The Detroit Institute of Arts, March 10–September 7, 1975; New York, The Metropolitan Museum of Art, June 12–September 7, 1975. Catalogue by Frederick J. Cummings, Robert Rosenblum and Antoine Schnapper.

PARIS 1974–1975 *Le Néo-Classicisme français: Dessins des Musées de Province*. Paris, Grand Palais, December 6, 1974–February 10, 1975. Catalogue by Arlette Sérullaz, Jean Lacambre, and Jacques Vilain.

PARIS 1973–74 *P.-H. de Valenciennes*. Paris, Galerie de Bayser.

PARIS 1972 *La Peinture narrative en France, 1500–1800*. Paris, Galerie Joseph Hahn, March 3–31, 1972.

PARIS 1936 *Gros, ses amis, ses élèves*. Paris, Petit-Palais, 1936.

PEORIA 1980 *The Changing Image: Aspects of Nineteenth Century French Art*. Peoria, Lakeview Museum of Arts and Sciences, 1980. Catalogue by J. Patrice Marandel, published in *Lakeview Museum Bulletin*, vol. 2, no. 2. 1980.

ROCHESTER/NEW BRUNSWICK/ATLANTA 1987–88 *La Grande Manière:*

Historical and Religious Painting in France, 1700–1800. Rochester, Memorial Art Gallery, University of Rochester, May 2–July 26, 1987; New Brunswick, N.J., Jane Voorhees Zimmerli Art Museum, Rutgers University, September 6–November 8, 1987; Atlanta, High Museum of Art, December 7, 1987–January 22, 1988. Catalogue by Donald A. Rosenthal.

ROME/DIJON 1983 *Bénigne Gagneraux (1756–1795), un pittore francese nella Roma di Pio VI*. Rome, Galleria Borghese, April–June 1983; Dijon, Musée des Beaux-Arts. Catalogue by Sylvain Laveissiére, Paola Hoffmann, Birgitta Sandström, and Sara Staccioli.

ROUEN 1970 *Jean Restout (1692–1768)*. Rouen, Musée des Beaux-Arts, June 17–September 15, 1970. Catalogue by Pierre Rosenberg and Antoine Schnapper.

SPOLETO 1988 *François-Xavier Fabre*. Spoleto, XXI Festival dei due Mondi, Palazzo Racani-Arroni, June 27–August 28, 1988. Catalogue by Laure Pellicer, Bruno Mantura, Pierre Rosenberg, Thierry Bajou, and Luigi Mascilli-Migliorini.

TOKYO/OSAKA/HOKKAIDO/YOKOHAMA 1990 *Three Masters of French Rococo: Boucher, Fragonard, Lancret*. Tokyo, Odakuy Grand Gallery, April 4–22, 1990; Umeda-Odaka, Daimaru Museum, May 9–21, 1990; Hokkaido Hakodate Museum of Art, May 26–June 24, 1990; Yokohama, Sogo Museum of Art, July 4–August 12, 1990. Catalogue by J. Patrice Marandel.

TOKYO 1988 *An Exhibition of French Paintings, 1600–1800*. Tokyo, Iida Gallery.

TOLEDO/CHICAGO/OTTOWA 1975–76 *The Age of Louis XV: French Painting, 1710–1774*. The Toledo Museum of Art, October 26–December 7, 1975; The Art Institute of Chicago, January 10–February 11, 1976; Ottawa, National Gallery of Canada, March 19–May 2, 1976. Catalogue by Pierre Rosenberg.

TOULOUSE 1989–90 *Toulouse et le Néo-classicisme: Les Artistes toulousains de 1775 à 1850*. Toulouse, Musée des Augustins, October 11, 1989–January 7, 1990. Catalogue by Jean Penent and Jean-Pierre Suzzoni.

The American Federation of Arts
Benefactors Circle

Mrs. Brooke Blake

Ruth Bowman

Mr. and Mrs. Peter M. Butler

Constance Caplan

Mrs. Gardner Cowles

Mr. and Mrs. Donald M. Cox

David L. Davies and John D. Weeden

Mr. and Mrs. Kenneth N. Dayton

Ambassador and Mrs. Edward E. Elson

Madeleine Feher

Mr. and Mrs. John A. Friede

Mrs. Melville W. Hall

Mr. and Mrs. Lee Hills

Mr. and Mrs. Theodore S. Hochstim

Harry Kahn

Mr. and Mrs. Peter Kimmelman

Mr. and Mrs. Gilbert H. Kinney

Mr. and Mrs. Richard S. Lane

Irvin L. Levy

Mr. and Mrs. Robert E. Linton

Mr. and Mrs. Henry Luce, III

Mr. and Mrs. Frederick R. Mayer

Mrs. C. Blake McDowell, Jr.

Mr. and Mrs. Robert M. Meltzer

Barbara Babcock Millhouse

Mr. and Mrs. Roy R. Neuberger

Mrs. P. Roussel Norman

Mr. and Mrs. Peter O'Donnell, Jr.

Elizabeth Petrie

Mr. and Mrs. Leon B. Polsky

Mr. and Mrs. Rudi H. Scheidt

Mr. and Mrs. Rudolph B. Schulhof

Barbara Slifka

Mr. and Mrs. John W. Straus

Mr. and Mrs. David J. Supino

Mr. and Mrs. Martin S. Weinberg

Nancy Wellin

Mr. and Mrs. Dave H. Williams

Enid Silver Winslow
   and Dr. Arthur Gillman